THINKING ABOUT
SOCIAL
PROBLEMS

THINKING ABOUT
SOCIAL
PROBLEMS

RICHARD L. HENSHEL
UNIVERSITY OF WESTERN ONTARIO

With a Foreword by
JAMES A. GESCHWENDER

Under the general editorship of
ROBERT K. MERTON
Columbia University

HBJ

HARCOURT BRACE JOVANOVICH, PUBLISHERS

SAN DIEGO   NEW YORK   CHICAGO   AUSTIN   WASHINGTON, D.C.

LONDON   SYDNEY   TOKYO   TORONTO

Requests for permission to make copies of any part of the work should be
mailed to: Permissions Department, Harcourt Brace Jovanovich, Inc., 8th
Floor, Orlando, Florida 32887.

ISBN: 0-15-591488-X

Library of Congress Catalog Card Number: 89-82383

Printed in the United States of America

FOREWORD

Richard Henshel has taken an interesting and exciting approach in *Thinking about Social Problems*. This textbook is one of the very few that carefully considers the process of creating and resolving social problems rather than examining a series of conditions whose status as social problems is accepted as self-evident. This feature makes this book more valuable than traditional textbooks.

Some characteristics of this book stimulate extended commentary, and in the next few pages I will respond to Part One with some thoughts on the relationship between social problems and social movements. In viewing social problems from the perspective of social policy, Henshel has recognized the essence of all social problems. He emphasizes the fact that not all stressful conditions automatically constitute social problems. Social problems are social in nature—a prescription most eloquently stated by C. Wright Mills:

> *Troubles* occur within the character of the individual and within the range of his immediate relations with others; they have to do with his self and with those limited areas of his social life of which he is directly and personally aware . . . An *issue* is a public matter: some value cherished by publics is felt to be threatened . . . In these terms, consider unemployment. When, in a city of 100,000, only one man is unemployed, that is his personal trouble, and for its relief we properly look to the character of the man, his skills, and his immediate opportunity. But when in a nation of 50 million employees, 15 million [people] are unemployed, that is an issue, and we may not hope to find its solution within the range of opportunities open to any one individual. The very structure of opportunities has collapsed.[1]

---

[1]C. Wright Mills, *The Sociological Imagination* (New York: Oxford University Press, 1959).

It was Mills who first made this all-important distinction between what he called "the personal troubles of milieu" and "the public issues of social structure." The distinction is now almost universally accepted in principle if less consistently observed in practice. Henshel makes a strong effort to deal with the question of just why some of these "public issues of social structure" become social problems while others do not. In so doing, Henshel tries to walk the tightrope between those advocating a "subjectivist" position (the social construction of social problems) and those advocating a more objectivist position (one that sees social problems as existing even if they are not recognized as such).

Henshel acknowledges that objective conditions, no matter how seemingly undesirable in their consequences, do not constitute social problems until, and unless, they are socially defined as such. Historically, abortion and infanticide have been fairly common practices in times of economic scarcity. The Innuit (Eskimo) also allowed their elderly to die under similar circumstances. Regardless of what one's moral position may be with regard to these practices, they did not constitute social problems since they were not socially defined as such. They were not social issues around which conflict and struggle might develop. Nor were they latent problems waiting to be recognized. Rather, they were viewed as necessary, and practical, survival techniques; they maximized the chances for the community's survival even at the cost of some of its members.

Some might question whether the customs were necessary, but no one can doubt that they were practical. In these cases, the sacrificed community members were those who could best be spared because they would have continued to consume scarce resources while contributing the least to the community. The values that underlie these actions were widely shared. The aged Innuit "wandered off" to die while others made no effort to keep them with the group or to find and save them. Infants were simply too young to have values or participate in rational debate. Fetuses were aborted before they became human. Consequently, the situation had no value conflicts and was not defined as an issue needing resolution.

In contemporary times, conditions have changed and, as a consequence, so have social definitions. Child abuse, abuse of the elderly, and both abortion and the use of direct-action tactics in the attempt to prevent women from exercising their legal right to an abortion have all come to be socially constructed as social problems. Important value conflicts over objective conditions exist in these areas. No one justifies child abuse but considerable disagreement occurs over just what it is. Many parents believe that they have the right and the obligation to discipline their offspring. They, and others, believe that many of society's ills result from the fact that parents do not impose sufficient discipline on their children. But where does legitimate discipline end and child abuse begin? Where does protecting the elderly from self-harm, and protecting property from accidental damage, end and abuse of the elderly begin? I could continue with other examples, but the point has been made. These are the questions that compose the issues around which debate and struggle take place. These issues are social issues and the conditions constitute social problems precisely because of value differences in society and because these areas of disagreement are socially defined as important and worth struggling over. But the important thing to remember is that times have changed. It is the social changes taking place over time that lead to altered situational priorities and, in so doing, allow for the emergence of value conflicts that simply could not have become salient under earlier circumstances.

This is the approach that appears to underlie the majority of Henshel's analysis, but at times, for purposes of simplification to be sure, he refers to problem situations as if they were objective conditions waiting to be recognized as social problems. This is not a formulation that I could accept in the absence of clearly specified criteria regarding the nature of the objective conditions. Rather, I would insist that certain sets of objective circumstances may or may not come to be defined as problem situations. If they are, they will become social problems. If they are not, they are neither social problems nor problem situations.

I recognize that my approach does not produce unambiguous indicators of social problems. Rarely does a complete consensus occur in society as to whether a given condition does or does not constitute a social problem. Slavery existed in America for approximately two centuries. Throughout that time period, it was legal and considered to be moral and just by a large segment of the population. Thus, at first glance it would appear that slavery was not a social problem. And slavery would not, in fact, have constituted a social problem had the entire population felt that way. However, considerable evidence exists that the slave population never considered it to be moral and just. They resisted it in numerous ways ranging from running away to engaging in armed rebellion. A number of free Afro-Americans and Euro-Americans also considered the slave system immoral and struggled to end it. Others opposed it because of the competitive advantage it gave to slaveowners. It is precisely the fact that disagreement over the issue occurred that made slavery into a social problem.

It is not possible to precisely define just how much disagreement is necessary to make a condition into a social problem. The best we can do is to say that it has to be a significant amount—more than a handful of people have to be involved. Anything less may constitute more individual troubles rather than social problems. However, I am not comfortable with this. I would like a bit more clarity. I do not have the requisite formula. On the other hand, I do not think that Henshel goes far enough in stressing the fact that social problems are socially constructed. They are neither given by nature nor are they the simple collective recognition that preexisting objective conditions constitute a problem for society. At the same time, I recognize that we cannot take the extreme subjectivist position that everything is whatever we choose to define it to be. We need more guidelines.

The 1986 Presidential Address that Rodolfo Alvarez presented to the Society for the Study of Social Problems focused, in part, on this question. This was a very important address, in which he developed a sound rationale for proposing the existence of seven more or less universal values. Alvarez argued that, by and large, most people tend to prefer life over death, health over sickness, knowing over not knowing, cooperation over conflict, freedom of movement over physical restraint, self-determination over direction by others, and freedom of expression over communication restraint. Alvarez carried his analysis on to consider the question of the emergence of social problems. He stated:

> Given these universal values, we can ask the question *WHAT IS A SOCIAL PROBLEM?* Elsewhere, Armand Mauss has argued, and I am in substantial agreement with him, that a social problem is a special type of social movement. That is not to say however, that it is easy to create a social movement. Plenty of would-be leaders have tried, not many succeeded. How are participants drawn into the movement, that is to say how do people become persuaded that a social problem exists, that they can do something to alleviate it and that they should cast their loyalties and energies on one side or another of a controversy? I seriously doubt that any call to action would attract a diverse or numerous or committed following unless an argument could be made that some combination of universal human values were at issue . . . *Within* the normative boundaries of a given population a social movement might make considerable progress, even if based on values other than those I here hypothesize to be universal, so long as it was based on values subscribed to by that population. The *critical test* would come when an appeal was made for additional participants from beyond those normative confines, to populations guided by very different values. At that point the appeal would have to be shaped in the form of common values or, more coarsely put, self-interests that can be universally understood. To draw participants *across* the normative boundaries by which group membership is defined requires an assumption of a universal criterion by which people with one social construction of reality can understand the appeal made to them by people with a different social construction of reality.[2]

_____

[2]Rodolfo Alvarez, "Personal Initiative in an Interdependent World," Presidential Address presented before the 1986 meetings of the Society for the Study of Social Problems, New York.

Many scholars would be reluctant to accept the existence of universal values. Others may agree that universal values exist, but disagree as to which ones they are. However, regardless of whether Alvarez is correct in postulating his particular list of near-universal values, he certainly has presented us with a list of values around which social issues can and will emerge. What is more, he has firmly located his analysis within a theoretical perspective that recognizes social problems as a special form of social movement—the need for those most negatively affected by existing conditions to attract allies who are not themselves similarly situated—and he provides an analysis of how those alliances may be formed.

Henshel's social issue approach to social problems is quite compatible with social movement analysis, as may be illustrated by the example of gender oppression. Anthropologists disagree considerably about the degree to which gender oppression may be assumed to have existed throughout history. Nevertheless, it is safe to say that women have occupied subordinate positions in society more often than not, but the extent to which gender oppression has constituted a social issue—has been recognized as a social problem—varies considerably. A number of social developments have helped to thrust this issue into the forefront of societal consciousness since the end of World War II. These include the ideological spillover from the civil rights movement in the United States, improved means of contraception, rising cost of living, and the shift from manufacturing to service industry. The latter has meant decreasing numbers of jobs for males and increasing numbers of jobs for females. All of this has brought about a high degree of consciousness on the status of women. Society has been divided into advocates for change, defenders of the old order, and those simply not involved.

Inasmuch as Henshel is quite concerned with the manner in which public policy on the best way to attack social problems is formed —for example, how social issues get resolved—it would behoove us to pay close attention to the portion of social movement theory that examines the formulation of strategy and tactics within movements.

Three basic types of strategies exist: persuasion, bargaining, and coercion.[3] Persuasion, the attempt to elicit the desired response from the target group through symbolic manipulation, is the most desired strategy from the movement's perspective because its use does not cost anything. It is also the least effective strategy because the only incentive for the target group to act in the desired manner is the possibility of a sense of moral well-being. Consequently, persuasion tends to be used only when a movement lacks access to resources needed for either bargaining

[3]Ralph H. Turner, "Determinants of Social Movement Strategies," in *Human Nature and Collective Behavior: Papers in Honor of Herbert Blumer*, ed. Tamotsu Shibutani (Englewood Cliffs, N.J.: Prentice-Hall, 1970), pp. 147–49.

or coercion. Bargaining is the attempt to exchange some resource possessed by the movement but wanted by the target group for the desired action by the target group. For this to be a viable strategy, the movement has to have, and be willing to give, something the target group wants. Coercion is the threat to inflict costs on the target group if it fails to act in the desired manner. This requires that the movement have the capability, and willingness, to inflict such costs. Social movements often develop among segments of the population excluded from existing decision-making apparatus and for whom the existing balance of power is arrayed to their detriment. The selection of a coercive strategy lays a movement open to severe retribution and will normally be chosen only in the absence of viable alternatives.

Lauer notes that strategies simultaneously bear a relation to the achievement or failure of movement objectives; have an impact on the recruitment, retention, and commitment of members; and present the movement's face to the public.[4] Turner and Killian say the same thing using different language.[5] Each acknowledges an element of rationality in the selection of strategies and an expressive element oriented toward the values and attitudes of movement adherents. Members must also consider the potential impact of strategies in gaining or losing support among the various publics. The ideal strategy would (1) be consistent with the values possessed by movement adherents, (2) be rationally effective in influencing target-group actions, (3) attract the support of cooperative publics, (4) not activate any potential oppositional groups, and (5) not involve bystander publics.

This ideal strategy is virtually impossible to achieve. Social movements are not simple, unidimensional phenomena. They tend to have a varied membership and multiple objectives.[6] Gerlach and Hine suggest that movements normally have two levels of objectives.[7] There may be a relative consensus among participants about general goals and a great deal of dissension on specific ones. Thus it is difficult to find strategies that will achieve heterogeneous and often contradictory objectives and that also satisfy hetereogeneous and often contradictory participant values. This selection is complicated by the fact that the degree to which the movement constituency and the various publics will ac-

---

[4]Robert H. Lauer, *Social Movements and Social Change* (Carbondale: Southern Illinois University Press, 1976), pp. xix–xxii.

[5]Ralph H. Turner and Lewis M. Killian, *Collective Behavior*, 2nd ed. (Englewood Cliffs, N.J.: Prentice-Hall, 1972), pp. 292–97.

[6]Lauer, *Social Movements*, pp. xx–xxi; Lewis M. Killian, "Social Movements," in Robert E. L. Faris, ed., *Handbook of Modern Sociology* (Chicago: Rand McNally, 1964), pp. 426–55.

[7]Luther P. Gerlach and Virginia H. Hine, *People, Power and Change: Movements of Social Transformation* (Indianapolis: Bobbs-Merrill, 1970), p. 165.

cept a given strategy as plausible (i.e., as both potentially effective and morally acceptable) is a function of a changing social context.[8]

Readers should realize that I have responded to one prominent portion of Henshel's book, and have done so by setting out my own "agenda" thereto. But that is what a good book is supposed to do: stir the mental connections in creative directions.

James A. Geschwender
Binghamton, New York

---

[8]J. Kenneth Benson, "Militant Ideologies and Organizational Contexts: The War on Poverty and the Ideology of Black Power," reprinted in Lauer, *Social Movements*, pp. 107–25.

PREFACE

In setting out to write *Thinking about Social Problems* I had three audiences in mind: students in social problems courses, students of public/social policy or applied sociology, and intelligent readers who want to independently develop their understanding of what might, with trepidation, be called social problems theory. This book is therefore designed both for students having only a brief acquaintance with sociology and as a means of integrating otherwise scattered material for the concerned individual reader.

As one can see immediately by examining the table of contents, this is not a typical textbook on social problems or even on the resolution of social problems. Most textbooks of the latter sort provide illustrations of specific remedies for specific problems. The reader will find few such detailed discussions in this book. This text is instead oriented around ideas of social problems *policy*.

In this book I treat the broader issues that nag at both students and practitioners when dealing with social problems. What are the basic strategies of intervention? What are the possible alternatives? How did we get where we are today in terms of society's means of coping with social problems? Are we becoming more or less effective in dealing with problem conditions, and why? What are some of the effects of increased expertise? of the increased use of social science? Why did people of earlier eras not intervene in certain problems? How did today's intervention institutions come into existence in the form we now see? What are some of the hidden pitfalls, the unanticipated consequences of intervention? How can we be sure we are producing any results, and how can we choose between competing remedies?

These are basic, essential questions. Obviously, some of the answers proposed here are subject to controversy, and whenever it seemed important I mentioned this in the text.

ORIENTATION

This book examines a set of topics involving social action taken to cope with recognized social problems. The reader is directed to the opening chapters for discussion of the nature of social problems, for brief histories of the conceptualization of selected problems in earlier periods, and for analysis of the role of moral entrepreneurs, victims, intellectuals, and the mass media in the selecting and defining of social problems. Whereas the earlier chapters focus on the definition and recognition of social problems, Part Two considers issues surrounding their treatment and resolution. "Intervention" in this context refers to all of the ways human beings have collectively reacted to recognized social ills.

I frequently adopt a historical perspective, focusing on how institutions, ideas, and modes of intervention emerged and developed, instead of treating them at a single point in time. This treatment is seen most clearly in Chapters 1, 2, 6, 7, and 11. The historical emphasis was initially not a conscious strategy, but it was adopted as a seemingly natural outgrowth of the topics presented. The reader can thus begin to acquire both the historical and theoretical understanding so essential to insight into social problems, especially into the prevailing treatment of social problems by a society. What this book does not provide is equally clear: discussions of specific problems (except as illustrations), their apparent causes, and recommended methods of treatment. It might therefore be used in conjunction with some traditionally oriented readings.

The *sociology of knowledge* as a perspective has also seemed congenial for the subjects discussed in this book. I disagree with those who feel that this orientation is too difficult for readers who lack extensive experience in sociology—using my own classes as guides. It is true, however, that I have not found standard works in the sociology of knowledge very helpful in preparing this book, and the sociology of knowledge is not treated as a separate topic; rather, it seeps through in numerous discussions of other subjects.

One theme of this book, the principal focus of Part One, is the definitional aspects of social problems. Although I do not fully subscribe to the implications of Herbert Blumer's thesis, I have taken as my point of departure his statement that "social problems are fundamentally products of a process of *collective definition* instead of existing independently as a set of objective social arrangements with an intrinsic make up."[1] It has become increasingly clear that the definitional processes are crucial.[2]

---

[1] Herbert Blumer, "Social Problems as Collective Behavior," *Social Problems* 18 (1971), p. 298, italics mine.

[2] See *The Collective Definition of Deviance*, ed. F. James Davis and Richard Stivers (New York: Free Press, 1975).

A second theme running through this book is that worldview and ideology are the chief determinants of societal reaction to social problems, and that this is the case whether the worldview of the local law-enforcement official is being analyzed or that of the sociologist. It follows that a study is needed that treats the stereotypes of both the police on the beat and the sociologist in the classroom in a common frame of reference, or at least that considers their positions as perceptual matters deserving similar treatment. Such is the point of view of this book. What happens before and after X breaks into the neighborhood bank is a result of the worldviews of legislators (perhaps long dead), intellectuals, experts on neighborhood bank robberies, the police officers who capture X, and the newspeople who report it, as well as X's own viewpoint. This is not to say that I treat all perspectives with equal sympathy, but I treat them all as perspectives.

Central to my personal views and therefore recurrent in the text are questions of objectivity and of values. While I present as many viewpoints as possible on any topic covered, I also raise questions, many of which have no clear-cut answers. And each answer begets more questions. Social problems do not lend themselves to study as unambiguously as mechanical or biological situations. The very nature of the problems—that is, their social and human aspects, combined with the social and human nature of the reader—renders the entire process very difficult, and entanglements with perceptions, values, and ideologies are unavoidable. It is one purpose of sociology as a discipline to provide a framework within which such extra-scientific factors can be recognized, analyzed, and placed in perspective.

COMPOSITION AND DIDACTIC DEVICES

Many of the ideas expressed here (the dialectic, for example, or functionalism) are in truth enormously complex. I have had to steer a narrow course between the rock of oversimplification to the point of error and the hostile shore of excessive difficulty, and I hope I have succeeded. Fortunately, the two examples just given, along with many others, need only be examined in a limited context to be conceptually useful in thinking about social problems, and thus many of their complexities and ambiguities can be avoided in this book. As a compromise, I have periodically introduced references to more elaborate treatments and have hinted at the complexities.

Readers will notice that in addition to current citations the text often references older works. This is a deliberate policy. Citing only the most recent reworkings of old ideas can lead to a form of "presentism" in which it seems that all good ideas are quite recent. Or when recent references are mixed with a few from the nineteenth-century sociological classics readers perhaps wonder what all those well-intentioned sociologists of, say, the 1920s through the 1960s, were doing. For these reasons I have frequently resorted to a mixed strategy of giving some recent references, so that readers who wish to do further reading can be brought up to date on the matter, and some of the best "dated" materials as well.

The text incorporates devices to heighten interest and understanding. The usual aids for students and researchers are included in the name and subject indexes. In addition to this traditional back matter an *extended table of contents* goes beyond the usual chapter and subchapter headings to include phrases describing specific subjects covered. This is a deliberate adaptation from nineteenth-century books whose tables of contents incorporated virtually every subject discussed. This type of table of contents is a didactic aid that I have found helps students grasp the connection of material, have some idea of what is coming up next, and see overall patterns. Finally, as even the casual reader will quickly discover, scattered throughout the work are *highlighted epigrams.* These statements are designed to stimulate interest and anticipation.

ACKNOWLEDGMENTS

Great thanks are due, first, to Anne-Marie Ambert. Her editorial comments on early versions were most helpful, and her contributions to the first two chapters in particular were very great indeed. Furthermore, the original impetus for the book came from her.

I am particularly grateful to those of my colleagues and associates, past and present, who read and commented on the manuscript. For the early version I thank Orrin Klapp, John Kunkel, Craig McKie, Allan MacDougall, Raymond Morris, Alice Propper, Anthony Richmond, James Rinehart, Ian Rockett, Vince Sacco, Robert Silverman, Jay Turner, and Mark Wexler. More recently I have been assisted by the suggestions of Samuel Clark, George Comninel, David MacLennan, Paul Maxim, and Kevin McQuillan, and by the research assistance of Judith Aldridge.

With respect to publishing, I have benefited from the gracious support of Robert K. Merton, who has set a standard at Harcourt Brace Jovanovich for social problems textbooks that I have worked hard to emulate. Keith Thompson, now publisher for Wall and Thompson and formerly of HBJ Canada, got the ball rolling; were it not for his encouragement I might have postponed this project yet again. Marc Boggs, executive editor at Harcourt Brace Jovanovich, put up with my many idiosyncrasies and with my on-again-off-again schedule of work.

I also thank the manuscript editor, Kay Kaylor; production editor, Michael Kleist; production manager, Mandy Van Dusen; and designer, Suzanne Montazer.

Finally, I acknowledge my debt to the students in my social problems course, who have offered suggestions of the greatest practical value. Graduate students Mary Dionysakopoulous and Oliver Stoetzer went through the manuscript with great care. Veronica D'Souza and Denise Statham contributed their ever-efficient secretarial services.

To all of these people I express my sincere thanks. They are responsible for whatever errors remain; I alone must take responsibility for the good parts.

Richard L. Henshel

CONTENTS

LIST OF EPIGRAMS

P A R T   O N E

1

WHAT IS A SOCIAL PROBLEM? CONFLICTING VIEWS AND THEIR IMPORTANCE

One of the main themes throughout this book is the existence of a wide divergence of opinion concerning most aspects of social problems. Subject to disagreement are such questions as, Which situations constitute social problems? Who should decide what a social problem is? How should social problems be treated? Who should pay for the treatment and who should dispense it? Dissension on these and related questions cannot be merely attributed to confused terminology or ignorance; it reflects ideological differences in the population at large, as well as among social scientists. Answers to these questions reflect one's view of the world and how the world should be changed. Although substantial agreement exists in principle about the definition of a social problem, we will see that matters become more involved when we confront theory with reality. This chapter is, therefore, much more than a simple definitional exercise: it is an examination of the consequences of stressing one aspect of a definition over another. Difficult choices have to be made both in the definition and then in its application. To start with, I present a definition accepted by most sociologists, but from then on I will follow a path that will take us some distance from this comfortable state of consensus.

A *social problem* has been defined as "a collective object of concern, a condition felt to pertain to society as a whole or to important parts of it, and believed to be both undesirable and changeable."[1] The

---

[1] John P. Hewitt, *Self and Society*, 4th ed. (Boston: Allyn & Bacon, 1988), p. 200. A definition first written in 1923 illustrates the extent of agreement across the decades: "A social problem is a problem which actually or potentially affects a large number of people in a common way so that it may best be solved by some measure or measures applied to the problem as a whole rather than by dealing with each individual as an isolated case, or which requires concerted or organized human action." Quoted in James H. S. Bossard, *Social Change and Social Problems*, rev. ed. (New York: Harper and Brothers, 1938), p. 2.

key word to define for my purposes will be *social* because, when sociologists attempt to differentiate social problems from other categories of deleterious conditions, they often use three criteria: social problems must be social in origin, social in definition, and social in treatment.[2] But, depending on the sociologists' orientation, there are important variations in the relative significance accorded these points. How various public conditions fit into sociological conceptions of social problems will be explored as the three criteria are discussed.

SOCIAL IN ORIGIN

Social problems, as considered in this book, are social factors that adversely affect significant numbers of individuals in a similar way. Such a definition implies that the origins of a problem—its causes or certain aspects thereof—have been *diagnosed* as social. Social problems, such as property crime or family breakup, are thereby distinguished from other unpleasant conditions that affect large segments of the population in a way not perceived as social. Thus the emphasis for the first criterion is on *perception*. For instance, polio used to be a serious problem before the Salk vaccine. But its origin is perceived to be purely biological. It is a physical disease that is, insofar as we know, unrelated to social factors. Does this mean that even when it affected thousands of persons it was not a social problem? From one perspective, it was a social problem because it adversely affected large numbers of individuals. People were, in addition, aware of the gravity of the situation and urgently wanted a solution; therefore, it was also social in definition (the second criterion). And Dentler maintains that the matter of collective social responsibility gives a problem its social aspect, rather than its origin.[3] Merton adopts a similar perspective and prefers to abandon the distinction stressing origins.[4] Thus, an undesirable condition such as polio can be viewed as a social problem if we eliminate the criterion of social origins.

However, with such a widening of the definition, virtually every public problem could become a social problem. We have to narrow it

[2] Paul B. Horton and Gerald R. Leslie, *The Sociology of Social Problems*, 4th ed. (New York: Appleton–Century–Crofts, 1970), p. 6.

[3] Robert A. Dentler, *Major Social Problems*, 2nd ed. (Chicago: Rand McNally, 1972), p. 6.

[4] Robert K. Merton, "Social Problems and Sociological Theory," in *Contemporary Social Problems*, 3rd ed., edited by Robert K. Merton and Robert Nisbet (New York: Harcourt Brace Jovanovich, 1971), p. 802. Merton also retains what we call "disasters" within the nomenclature of social problems, whereas I prefer to view social problems as phenomena that are lasting in their origins or causes, or that are recurrent. While a flood may have lasting consequences that will affect people psychologically and socially, it is, in terms of origins, a one-time "act of God." But were floodings recurrent, as in some areas, they could be included in my classification.

down for the purpose of sociology. To return to the example of polio, it is improbable that a sociologist could become involved in such a problem as a direct subject of study because, outside of the fact that it affects human beings and that society may define it as a problem, it does not lie within the social realm in terms of biological causes. But the social organization of medical research and treatment is a topic for sociology, as is the social organization for research on any subject.[5] And the attitude of the population vis-à-vis medical problems is also a topic of concern for sociologists, as well as the quality of life of the individuals affected by any medical problem.

In terms of definition, cancer presents a related but different dilemma. It is a major human problem and is recognized as such by everyone. For sociologists, cancer is not intrinsically a social problem because of its biological nature. But cigarette smoking is causally related to lung cancer[6] and is a cultural phenomenon (exacerbated by advertising, socialization, and peer groups); hence, lung cancer is a social problem by virtue of its relationship to a cultural act—smoking cigarettes.[7] The same arguments can be advanced for the correlations between some forms of cancer and the exposure to certain substances, such as asbestos, in the workplace. Workplace exposure is closely related to social class, and so, too, the incidence of some forms of cancer is closely linked to social class. It is therefore accurate to posit that, because of the social aspects of the origins of cancer, this problem is of some concern to sociologists.[8]

Pollution, a key component in the rising concern with the environment, is another problem of interest here. Like lung cancer, pollution as a social problem is a borderline case. Pollution is certainly a human problem because it adversely affects entire populations. It is also "social in definition" because a segment of public opinion is aroused against it and wants the situation brought under control. Yet, from the perspective of origins, pollution is not social because it is produced by chemical components that are not social per se, just as polio is produced by a virus and is therefore biological. However, inasmuch as carbon monoxide as a pollutant is produced by machinery that is, in turn, produced by human beings, we have a cultural component in the origin of this problem. In addition, people have now become aware of the noxious consequences

---

[5]Here is an example, related to my next topic: *The Cancer Mission: Social Contexts of Biomedical Research*, by Kenneth E. Studer and Daryl E. Chubin (Beverly Hills: Sage Publications, 1980).

[6]The first commission to clearly and unequivocally state this causal relationship reported it in *Smoking and Health*, Report of the Advisory Committee to the Surgeon General (Washington, D.C.: U.S. Government Printing Office, 1964).

[7]The terms "social" and "cultural" are used interchangeably here for purposes of simplification.

[8]See the discussion in Chapters 13 and 14 of *Smoking and Health*.

of the release of carbon monoxide into the air, and their refusal to cope with this problem, or with conflicts over the cost of its control, is definitely a social phenomenon. From that point of view, it can be said that even in origin a social component exists with respect to pollution.

In contrast to defining the difficult cases above, consider now the case of several hundred poor, black victims of syphilis in the American South who, in an organized experiment started in the 1930s, went for decades without treatment in order to furnish a medical baseline for what untreated syphilis does to the brain and other organs. The problem in this case is discrimination based on race. Although race is a biological category, sociologists can certainly study and contribute to the redress of this and similar phenomena, and certainly such discrimination is a social problem. Likewise, although leprosy is obviously of biological origin, some experts regard it as more of a social problem than a tropical disease. The victims of leprosy are treated as pariahs by many societies, even though they pose virtually no health threat to others. Here, again, the problem is largely social in nature.

The most recent situation of this kind is, of course, the AIDS epidemic. AIDS is a purely biological disorder, and its cure, when it comes, will be purely biological as well, but the social component here is of overwhelming importance.[9] AIDS victims are subjected to ostracism, vile abuse, and a paranoid level of fear and loathing. It falls to sociologists to study the causes of such reactions and to propose remedies. A tempting resolution to our definitional difficulties would be that AIDS itself is not a social problem, while the unreasonable public reaction to AIDS is, but alas, there is another social (or cultural) component to AIDS. Its spread, its pattern of contagion, is clearly a function of patterns of sexual activity that are culturally structured and conditioned.

In contrast to the examples of polio, cancer, pollution, AIDS, and leprosy, which are difficult to classify if we insist on faithfully applying the criterion of social origin, there are problems that spring directly from social forces and their interrelations and, especially, those on which there is consensus on the preeminence of their social origin (although not necessarily so on the specific causes).[10] Let us consider the example of crimes against property. Everything in a criminal act of this type is

---

[9]Excellent discussions are found in Susan Sontag, *AIDS and Its Metaphors* (New York: Farrar, Straus, & Giroux, 1988); Dennis Altman, *AIDS in the Mind of America* (New York: Doubleday, 1987).

[10]It should be noted that, in spite of the best definitions, the traditional demarcations of sociological interest in specific social problems are at least partly arbitrary. Thus the extremes of economic cycles (producing severe depressions and inflationary periods) are social problems by any logical definition, but are treated only by economists, not by sociologists. For a partial exception, see Julian Le Grand, *The Economics of Social Problems*, 2nd ed. (London: Macmillan & Co., 1984).

social in origin. Under one interpretation, individuals are driven to committing property crimes by personal concerns that spring largely from their situations and the alternatives society offers, or that they perceive society to be offering. As many observers have noted, our society places a high emphasis on economic gain and material rewards. In addition, this society's values are such that individuals are expected to achieve in the material realm and, in principle, the system is supposed to provide individuals with institutionally acceptable means of reaching this goal. Equality of opportunity is the motto, although considerable evidence points to strong limitations on it. On the one hand, therefore, we have a cultural ethos emphasizing material achievement, frequently attainable only through formal education channels. On the other hand, the society is so structured that some cannot reach this goal even if highly qualified.[11] Legitimate opportunities are not always within reach, be it because of poverty, behavioral patterns learned through socialization, or other sociocultural factors. Some individuals who cannot achieve through the regular channels or who want to climb more rapidly may turn to illegal means, which are also provided by our society.[12]

In the above analysis, I have presented two factors that are typically considered sociocultural: cultural goals and social structure. Other theories of crime causation also emphasize various social factors, such as family influences, peer group associations, deviant role models, assimilation of deviant codes of conduct, cultural conflict, awareness of legal loopholes, and so on.[13]

On the whole, the criterion of social origin is useful in delineating the range of social problems for the purpose of sociological analysis; however, as we have seen, the various social ramifications of certain human problems (such as pollution or AIDS) diminish the conclusiveness of this criterion.

---

[11] Several studies have indicated that, for instance, parental socioeconomic status is an important factor in the probability that a person will be able to pursue higher education. See Natalie Rogoff Ramsoy, "On the Flow of Talent in Society," *Acta Sociologica*, 9 (1965), pp. 152–74.

[12] Students of deviance will recognize that this discussion is directly borrowed from Robert K. Merton, *Social Theory and Social Structure*, rev. and enl. ed. (Glencoe, Ill.: Free Press, 1957), pp. 132ff. See also Robin M. Williams, Jr., "Relative Deprivation," in *The Idea of Social Structure*, ed. Lewis A. Coser (New York: Harcourt Brace Jovanovich, 1975), p. 355.

[13] I have deliberately restricted the subject here to economic (property) crime, and can therefore disregard biological theories, such as that chromosomal abnormalities pertain to violent crime. The general view in criminology today is that even if such biological theories are established for certain criminals, they would account for only a small part of total crime, and even then cultural and social factors are apparently involved in virtually all cases. See Jack P. Gibbs, "Review Essay of *Crime and Human Nature*," *Criminology* 23 (1985), pp. 381–88. For a contrary view, see biological advocates James Q. Wilson and Richard J. Herrnstein, *Crime and Human Nature* (New York: Simon and Schuster, 1985).

SOCIAL IN DEFINITION

According to Tallman and McGee, "a social problem exists if a sizable group of individuals share the view that a given event or process is problematic."[14] The implication is that a situation is a problem *only when so perceived*. Kavolis, among others, referred to this as the "public awareness conception" of social problems.[15] Blum adopted a similar perspective and maintained that it is not the event itself but the way the event is regarded that defines the problem.[16] And Blumer has made this emphasis on *subjective* (as opposed to *objective* or de facto) factors the central thesis of an article: "Social problems are fundamentally products of a process of collective definition instead of existing independently as a set of objective social arrangements."[17]

Blumer's position is provocative and controversial, for if we define a social problem subjectively, as existing only when a condition is *perceived* as undesirable, it means that a social problem is first and above all the theoretical construct of certain people.[18] From the objective perspective, on the other hand, a social problem exists as soon as a significant number of individuals are adversely affected by a phenomenon related to social factors, *even if no one recognizes it*. In contrast, Horton and Leslie state that "no condition, no matter how dramatic or shocking to someone else, is a social problem unless and until the values of a considerable number of people within the society define it as a problem."[19] This point of view requires further attention as it pertains to the critical questions of just who the definers of a social problem are and just how a situation becomes labeled as a problem—topics that will be the focus of Chapters 3 through 5. Horton and Leslie go further and add that "when a condition affects enough people so that many of them take notice and begin to talk and write about it, a social problem exists. . . . When numerous articles appear, it is clear that the condition has attracted widespread concern and has become a social problem."[20]

---

[14] Irving Tallman and Reese McGee, "Definition of a Social Problem," in *Handbook on the Study of Social Problems*, ed. Erwin O. Smigel (Chicago: Rand McNally, 1971), p. 40.

[15] Vytautas Kavolis, *Comparative Perspectives on Social Problems* (Boston: Little, Brown, and Co., 1969).

[16] Alan F. Blum, "Methods for Recognizing, Formulating, and Describing Social Problems," in *Handbook on the Study of Social Problems*, ed. Erwin O. Smigel (Chicago: Rand McNally, 1971), p. 180.

[17] Herbert Blumer, "Social Problems as Collective Behavior," *Social Problems*, 18 (1971), p. 298. See also Malcolm Spector and John I. Kitsuse, *Constructing Social Problems* (Menlo Park, Calif.: Cummings, 1977).

[18] Sociologists such as Coser, Dentler, and Merton have recognized and discussed this situation. See Lewis A. Coser, "Sociology of Poverty," *Social Problems*, 13 (1965), pp. 140–48; Dentler, Merton, *Major Social Problems/Contemporary Social Problems*.

[19] Horton and Leslie, *Social Problems*, p. 5 (italics in the original text eliminated).

[20] *Ibid.*, p. 4. Surveys of what people think are the major social problems thus become significant.

In other words, these writers are saying a condition is defined as a social problem only if it is noticed or if concern arises, especially—and here is an additional element—by people who control societal resources, in this case the mass media. While such a definition appears biased from the point of view of the sufferers, it may, nevertheless, correspond to reality in terms of obtaining treatment or a solution to a problem.

This controversy between the subjective and objective interpretation of a social problem continues to vex sociological analysts.[21] It has some very important ramifications I will address now that the basic contrast is clear.[22]

Let us look at some of the implications of choosing one or the other conception. Initially we tend to think, objectively speaking, that a social problem exists as soon as significant numbers of people are adversely affected by some condition. For instance, if many American Indians are indigent, suffer from ill health, and are chronically unemployed, this is a social problem whether others notice it or not. It need not wait for our culture's goodwill, nor for changes in our value orientations. The situation may not have been conceptualized as a problem for many decades—perhaps because our culture believed in the supremacy of Western civilization, or because most American Indians are geographically too distant to concern our daily lives.[23] But during all those silent decades, the problem was nevertheless real. More recently, our culture has become enlightened enough to make the diagnosis. The new attitude merely reinforces the existence of the problem in terms of social visibility and attention, but does not create it. Merton invokes a helpful terminological distinction here by speaking of *manifest* social problems—those that are recognized—and *latent* social problems—those that are real but unnoticed.[24]

The subjective or interactionist conception, on the other hand, is grounded in two challenges to the straightforward objective conception.

Challenge One   It is difficult if not impossible to arrive at an objective, entirely uncontaminated view of what is going on in society. Instead, various parties *claim* to know what is going on. Some claims are

---

[21] A similar difficulty occurs with respect to the important concept of deviance. Is an act automatically deviant if it violates a major norm, or is it deviant only if people notice and react negatively? For a sophisticated analysis of the latter perspective, see Jack P. Gibbs, "The Sociology of Deviance and Social Control," in Morris Rosenberg and Ralph H. Turner, eds., *Social Psychology: Sociological Perspectives* (New York: Basic Books, 1981), pp. 483–522.

[22] I have been using some rather dated sources here because these are how I first became interested in the problem. For excellent recent treatments of this question from the subjectivist standpoint, see the materials in Joseph W. Schneider and John I. Kitsuse, eds., *Studies in the Sociology of Social Problems* (Norwood, N. J.: Ablex Publishing, 1984).

[23] For a similar opinion on the effect of social (and physical) distance, see Merton, *Contemporary Social Problems*, p. 812.

[24] *Ibid.*, pp. 806–10.

accorded more legitimacy by a given society than other claims, but that in itself is very suspect. And people have vested interests in advancing certain social problem claims. Just to mention one other factor, we all have had certain experiences, and these experiences tend to support some of the claims we encounter over others. So the upshot is that any judgment that some things constitute social problems is entirely subjective.

Challenge Two   Even if all could agree on what is taking place, and its importance, they still would have difficulty deciding what to do—if anything—because values are relative. So any judgment that something is a social problem is based on subjective ethical evaluation.

Several of the following chapters are devoted to exploring the first challenge in great detail, although I will take the liberty of exploring in those chapters some other important topics, too. That being the case, we will consider Challenge Two, the matter of ethical relativism, in this chapter.

ETHICAL RELATIVITY AND ITS PROBLEMS

I cannot refute the learned arguments for the relativity of ethical values, but I refuse to believe that the only thing wrong about wanton cruelty is that I don't like it.

Bertrand Russell

The discussion to this point leads us to consider whether those who suffer from a condition should be the only ones to define the nature of their situation. This is a very difficult question to settle. In Chapters 3 and 9, for instance, I will ask whether anything should be done to help individuals with mental and emotional problems if they do not perceive a need to improve their own situation. The same question could be asked of members of any geographically marginal minority group. If they do not perceive their situation as problematic, is it? In other words, by others' standards, they could be poor, unemployed, in ill health, and chronically subject to alcoholism. Yet, if they do not see anything abnormal in their condition, nor feel deprived, do others have the right (or perhaps the obligation) to diagnose their situation as a social problem and, consequently, to initiate programs to improve it?[25]

---

[25]This question is important from yet another perspective. Remedial programs frequently carry the germs of unanticipated harms (unanticipated consequences) that only magnify the problem they were originally set to alleviate. Intervention can therefore worsen a situation. For an extended discussion of this difficulty, see Merton, *Social Theory*, and Chapter 6 of this book.

Minority groups have a culture of their own, with a distinct set of values.[26] Saying that by all objective standards they are poor and that poverty in general is a problem may mean denying the validity of non-material values, such as asceticism. Negating these values places majority groups in the elitist position of saying that they know what is good for a people even though those in question may not want it. This was a problem common to most justifications of imperialism in the nineteenth century: it was supposedly the "white man's burden" to lead "inferior" peoples into the "light of civilization," but how could the presumed superiority of European values be a certainty? In point of fact, it was superior military technology and transportation that established and perpetuated the colonial system. *Cultural relativism* recognizes the validity and equality of all cultures and, therefore, the right to cultural self-determination.

The principle of noninterference in the affairs of other cultural groups (at times called isolationism in world politics) is not in itself an absolute answer, however; it leaves the door open to frightening moral dilemmas. What of the Holocaust before and during World War II? Following a policy of noninterference, France and Great Britain abstained from intervention in the German situation during the greater part of the 1930s. This abstention—motivated by politics rather than by values—ultimately cost millions of lives and permitted unprecedented suffering. Indeed the Nazi Holocaust led anthropologist Melville Herskovits, a prominent adherent of cultural relativism, into the depths of an ethical as well as a philosophical dilemma. We are comforted by the thought that the Nazi era was an exceptional period; perhaps the *principle* of noninterference is intact. Yet there is no certainty that similar events will not be repeated. For instance, mass slaughters have taken place in recent years in Asia and between certain African peoples. Therefore, we are still left with the dilemma, since unquestionable "exceptions" to ethical and cultural relativism, such as genocide of entire populations, recur again and again. The resolution of these ethical questions has proven elusive.[27]

With regard to North American Indians or similar geographically cohesive groups, the political concept of pluralism allows, at least in principle, for cultural (if not economic) autonomy. But, in situations where this pluralism cannot apply because the minority members are

---

[26] As Barton Meyers has pointed out, the very term "minority group" is misleading and carries considerable ideological baggage. See his "Minority Group: An Ideological Formulation," *Social Problems* 32 (1984), pp. 1–15. This article has more than passing relevance to the present discussion.

[27] Bell and Mau suggest that the possibility of common and universal values should be investigated. See Wendell Bell and James A. Mau, "Images of the Future: Theory and Research Strategies," in *The Sociology of the Future*, ed. Wendell Bell and James A. Mau (New York: Russell Sage Foundation, 1971), p. 38.

too closely interwoven with the rest of the society, what is to be done? Closely related to this question is the dilemma posed by the case of emotionally disturbed individuals. The latter are usually situated within the majority culture, making this no longer a question of cultural relativism or pluralism but one of intra-cultural deviance. The psychological state of certain individuals may be viewed, from the vantage point of the rest of society, as harmful to those afflicted, and even to the society as a whole. Since this is not a question of imposing one's standard on another cultural group, interference (in this case, psychiatric treatment) could be said to be more appropriate within this context than in the cross-cultural example. But here other complications arise because of the difficulty of diagnosis and the potential for serious abuse in the labeling and treatment processes. I will discuss these in Chapter 9.

Returning to the question of elitism, of imposing one's own views of social problems, consider a concept known as "false consciousness," originally a Marxian notion now generally understood throughout sociology. A member of a downtrodden sector of society who sympathizes with, and especially who adopts, the doctrinal standpoint of the dominant sector of that society, is said to suffer from false consciousness. On closer inspection, this turns out to have elitist connotations, in the sense that the user of the term is saying indirectly that he or she is better qualified to say what a person's true interests are than is that very person.

But maybe that is so! One of the chief complaints concerning the mass media is that it tends to adopt a standpoint that presents the views of the dominant sector, a condition known as hegemony.[28] Under such a condition, it is all too easy for members of a lower class to follow a line of thinking opposed to their own interests—assuming those interests are identifiable. So maybe the astute independent observer who recognizes the media hegemony *is in fact* in a better position to prescribe for oppressed classes than they are themselves. But we had best be sure we see the implications involved in accepting this argument!

This point highlights the fact that value differences exist not only between cultures but within a single culture. Viewing our ethical difficulty only between cultures ignores or minimizes the fact that typically not all members of a culture *agree* on whether something is problematic.[29]

---

[28] See Joseph V. Femia, *Gramsci's Political Thought: Hegemony, Consciousness, and the Revolutionary Press* (New York: Oxford University Press, 1981). See also David Altheide, "Media Hegemony: A Failure of Perspective," *Public Opinion Quarterly*, Vol. 48, 1984, pp. 476–90.

[29] Another difficulty that deserves brief mention is that, even when sociologists subscribe in theory to the collective definition approach, they do not always follow this rule in practice. Lauer surveyed textbooks on social problems and found a considerable disparity between the problems they treated and the concerns of the public as evidenced by some forty years of Gallup polls. See Robert H. Lauer, "Defining Social Problems: Public and Professional Perspectives," *Social Problems*, 22 (October 1976), pp. 122–34.

Cultural relativity, or the relativistic perspective on social problems, places one in a "hands-off" dilemma: if no standards are sound, then sociologists have nothing to say about objective criteria, and in effect the strongest social advocates succeed in defining social problems. (They might do so at any rate, but the relativistic position abdicates any responsibility of sociologists.) Thus if Nazis in Germany define the existence of Jews in Germany as a social problem, they have a perfect right to do so, and to proceed to exterminate them. Of course the Jews also have a right to disagree with this definition, and to fight back, but if the Nazis are stronger (and more numerous) than the Jews, and enforce their definition of the situation, who can say they are wrong? All values are relative, leaving no objective criteria for social problems.

The advocates of the public-awareness conception of social problems are among the most humanitarian of scholars; they would be the first to disagree with such a perversion. But such is the logical implication of their argument, in spite of its initial appeal and humanitarianism with respect to letting weak cultures define their own problems. On the other hand, if there *are* objective ethical criteria for defining and determining social problems, *what are they*? We do not know, except by intuitive feelings, which are admittedly inadequate. Bertrand Russell captured the dilemma nicely in the humane lament given as the epigraph for this section. He admitted that he could not refute the learned arguments for the relativity of ethical values, but stated, "I refuse to believe that the only thing wrong about wanton cruelty is that I don't like it." This quote captures why I cannot completely accept a subjective interpretation of social problems.

Numerous efforts to resolve this problem have been forthcoming, all revolving around some form of "psychological ethics"—the attempt to ground ethical principles in studies of human psychology (or sociology). I will mention a few of the most insightful.[30] Kavolis has attempted to derive a common set of social problems by a comparative study of different cultures, locating "universals" defined as problems everywhere.[31] Barrington Moore maintains that, although happiness is achieved in exceedingly diverse ways that are fluid and subjective, a substantial degree of unity or commonality exists among the ways people define extreme misery or suffering. To use an example of my own, we can all readily conjure up images of Hell (torment), but we have trouble visualizing Heaven (with harps?) because your heaven is not my heaven.

---

[30]Older efforts are summarized in C. Kluckhohn, "Cultural Relativity," in *A Dictionary of the Social Sciences*, ed. J. Gould and W. Kolb (New York: Free Press, 1964), pp. 160–62.

[31]Kavolis, *Comparative Perspectives*. As Kavolis notes, universally held norms are very few and far between; practically speaking, the difficulties of such an approach are monumental. See also Graeme Newman, *Comparative Deviance: Perception and Law in Six Cultures* (New York: Amer. Elsevier, 1976).

Moore suggests that we can move beyond cultural relativism in some cases by concentrating on conditions of extreme misery, conditions on which there is substantial agreement.[32] Horowitz suggests defining a social problem in terms of the disparity between the existing situation and people's norms or values (for instance, equality of opportunity). The nice feature of this approach is that both the situation and the values can be matters of observable fact.[33] These and other contributions can make valuable inroads on the difficulty, but none are entirely successful in resolving it.[34]

INTRODUCTION TO THE DEFINING PROCESS

Even if one rejects the subjective conception of social problems as a means to determine what is problematic, one can see its value in determining whether or not remedial action occurs. The act of defining a phenomenon as a social problem implies that the situation is undesirable *and* that something should be done to remedy it. Or, as the definition quoted at the outset of this chapter implies, collective action is necessary—even if by collective we only mean the action of a society's leaders. A latent social problem may exist for decades but never be diagnosed as such; therefore, society will not be moved to act collectively to solve it. Before a label is bestowed on a problem, there is little hope any relief will be forthcoming. Consequently, the subjective or public-awareness conception of social problems has considerable utility in estimating the likelihood of treatment.

A condition becomes defined as problematic when a substantial number of people, be they sufferers or observers, notice the situation and define it as undesirable and, therefore, as in need of public action. But in one sense the situation will become an officially recognized social problem only when people who are *strategically located* in a society's power structure deign to acknowledge its existence. Others could have spoken about it previously but with so little persuasive power to

---

[32]Barrington Moore, Jr., *Reflections on the Causes of Human Misery* (Boston: Beacon Press, 1970). See the chapter titled "On the Unity of Misery and the Diversity of Happiness."

[33]Irving Louis Horowitz, *Professing Sociology* (Chicago: Aldine, 1968), pp. 80–100. One problem with such an approach is that it would not exclude Nazis defining the presence of Jews in otherwise "clean" German cities as a social problem. (See earlier discussion.) For an overview of attempts to create a science of ethics that would give absolute standards for social problems, see Chapter 5 of Robert Friedrichs, *A Sociology of Sociology* (New York: Free Press, 1970).

[34]The classical works on the subject of cultural relativity were done by Melville Herskovits. His scattered writings have been collected in M. J. Herskovits, *Cultural Relativism: Perspectives in Cultural Pluralism,* ed. Frances Herskovits (New York: Random House, 1972).

their credit that not even their peers would accept their definition. As soon as a relatively important segment of the population makes the diagnosis, a "new" social problem is seen. The segment may be important numerically and have access to the political power structure. In such a case, it may exert pressure on those in power.[35] Or a population segment may be important not because of its numbers but because of its strategic "location." We could include in this category members of the government, the intelligentsia, the press, executives, organized labor, students, and even some minority groups who are the victims of social problems. A social problem with public attention is one that has been read about, seen and heard on television, discussed at cocktail parties, and lectured about in classrooms.

Certain social conditions facilitate the transformation of an objective deleterious situation into a manifest social problem.[36] Sociological investigations of social influence allow us to enumerate some of the major factors involved: the number of people believed to be affected; the perceived gravity of their affliction; the perceived injustice of their condition; whether those who cause their misfortune do so deliberately; the type of group(s) that first diagnoses the inequity; the type of group(s) disseminating knowledge on the problem; the means the group(s) adopts to publicize the situation; the groups' degree of public access; their degree of access to those in positions of power; the ideological and cultural readiness of the society; the strength of the groups whose vested interest would be hurt by a redress of the situation; and the degree of potential harm to such groups.

Because so many factors are involved before a condition is publicly defined as problematic, restricting "social problem" to a condition perceived by a public may violate the term's conventional meaning. Tallman and McGee, among others, relate the urgency of a problem to its "magnitude," substantiated by (a) the number of people affected and (b) the intensity of feeling the problem generates.[37] I feel that the first factor, along with intensity of suffering, is perhaps the only reliable indicator of a social problem; passion or feelings by groups attempting to solve a situation is a less objective criterion, and a more volatile one. It is volatile because the intensity of people's feelings is subject to manipulation

---

[35] But a segment of the population can be numerous and yet be excluded from the political system. The situation of the black population in the Republic of South Africa—far and away the most numerous sector of the population, yet denied even a minuscule say in the government—is a case in point.

[36] For an excellent review of the research on this subject from the subjective or interactionist perspective, see Joseph W. Schneider, "Social Problems: The Constructionist View," *Annual Review of Sociology* 11 (1985), pp. 209–29. On the notion of natural "stages" in the attention to a social problem, see Lawrence E. Hazelrigg, "Were It Not for Words," *Social Problems* 32 (1985), pp. 232–37.

[37] Tallman and McGee, *Handbook*, p. 42.

for various reasons and from various quarters. A group with easy access to the media or to official communication channels can "educate" the public in such a way as to bring about passionate feelings and ill-founded responses. To the Nazis, for instance, the existence of Jews in the Fatherland was a social problem, and they systematically set about heightening anti-Semitic feelings through the mass media. The long-run bureaucratization of the "final solution" to the Jewish question, and its resemblance to an attack on a traditional social problem, should serve as an object lesson on the unreliability of passion as a convincing criterion for the worthiness of a movement against "problems."[38] The criterion of passion cannot be used in the definition of a social problem, even though it is essential for coming to grips with treatment.

This section is only an introduction to the major issue of just how a social condition comes to be defined as a social problem. So vital is it to understand just why and how a given condition does or does not come to be regarded by the public as a social problem that I devote the better part of Chapters 3 through 5 to this issue.

SOCIAL IN TREATMENT

The third common criterion for a candidate for social problem status is that it be social in treatment. Clearly, a condition need not be erased or effectively treated to be a real social problem. Indeed, it could be stated that many social problems, even some that are socially recognized, are never treated. Perhaps powerful groups or persons block the treatment for personal reasons. Perhaps resolving one social problem would create others.[39] Perhaps its resolution would do away with other highly valued aspects of a society.[40] Perhaps the cause(s) is unknown and the society must depend on the tedious process of trial and error in order to remedy a situation. We can therefore conclude by saying that one part of the definition of a social problem is that it has to have at least the *potential* to be socially remedied.

---

[38]See Raul Hilberg, "The Destruction of the European Jews," in *Mass Society in Crisis*, ed. Bernard Rosenberg *et al.* (New York: Macmillan & Co., 1964). Probably the most pronounced advocacy of the subjective definition of social problems is in Malcolm Spector and John Kitsuse, *Constructing Social Problems* (Menlo Park, Calif.: Benjamin-Cummings Publishing, 1977). This is an excellent treatment of this viewpoint.

[39]Some economists, for example, have maintained that a "trade-off" between unemployment and inflation exists: as one of these problems is reduced below a certain level it automatically brings about an increase in the other. I do not wish to take sides on this question, but if the theory is correct we have an unsolvable set of social problems. See an extensive discussion of such "trade-offs" in Chapter 7 of this book.

[40]See, for instance, the suggested causes of crime in Daniel Bell, "Crime as an American Way of Life," *Antioch Review* 13 (1953), pp. 131–54.

If the origins of a problem are perceived to be social, the remedy also will be social in most cases. Returning once more to the example of polio, its treatment is related to its biological causes and, even though money and social activities are required to apply it, the remedy will consist largely of vaccination and hospitalization for those already afflicted. Unless discrimination against a group or social class exists in the polio treatment, it will be of no concern to the student of social problems.[41] Therefore, polio does not fulfill the third defining criterion of a social problem: it is not social in treatment, not even potentially so. (We also have seen that it is not social in origin.)

However, if we deal with pollution as an example, although the treatment measures will be largely physical (design of different power sources, building of new treatment plants), other measures also will be involved. These include convincing the public of the gravity of the problem, educating people to accept the required life-style changes, and redirecting the lives of so many whose livelihoods depend on pollution and depletion of the environment.[42] Factors such as social power and the pursuit of profit minimize the effectiveness of educational efforts. So, although pollution's immediate cause is physicochemical, and although its ultimate treatment also will be physical and material, the decisional aspects take on unusual importance, making this a marginally social type of problem.

Another example discussed in the section on origins was crimes against property. In order to alleviate this problem, the solutions will probably have to be social in nature.[43] Assuming that sociologists have some understanding of the genesis of crime, and that their diagnosis points to cultural goals, what remedy could be prescribed? As one example, the society could de-emphasize material rewards and offer new goals to its members—although these new goals may themselves become a springboard for other types of problems later on. Or, in terms of the society's structure, true equality of opportunity in all spheres might be sought, whereas there is now only theoretical equality. Other approaches might also be attempted, depending on assumptions about the causes of crime.[44] Some of these approaches might be so costly in

[41]Medical sociologists study various aspects of medical treatment (patient-doctor relationships, hospital and ward structure) but do so outside of the social problem framework, unless discrimination exists.

[42]See Kimon Valaskakis et al., *The Conserver Society* (Don Mills, Ont.: Fitzhenry and Whiteside, 1979).

[43]For a different view, see Amitai Etzioni and Richard Remp, *Technological Shortcuts in the Treatment of Social Problems* (New York: Russell Sage Foundation, 1972).

[44]One need not have knowledge of all, or even most, of the factors behind a social problem to begin work on its removal. If the demand for a "war against double-parkers" was sufficiently strong, double-parking probably could be eliminated by mandatory $1,000 fines and two policemen on every block—even with minimal knowledge of why people double-park.

relation to desirable features of the culture or social structure that the cure becomes worse than the disease.[45] In virtually all approaches to the problem, the dominant features would be sociocultural; property crime is clearly a social problem.

SUMMARY

The question I have raised is, What constitutes a social problem? What criteria can we legitimately use to determine that one condition affecting large numbers of individuals is a social problem, whereas another condition is not? Three commonly used criteria were discussed: social problems, it is said, are harmful conditions that are social in origin, social in definition, and social in treatment.

However, we saw that when we try to apply these criteria to specific examples of deleterious conditions, matters become more difficult. It is true that most social problems, as currently defined in our society, do fit into these definitional requisites. Thus, conditions such as unemployment, poverty, crime, drug abuse and addiction, alcoholism, and mental illness are social in origin (until proven otherwise), in definition (we do recognize these conditions as problems), and in treatment (various social programs are initiated to alleviate them). But when we turn to conditions such as cancer, we hesitate. It is of biological origin, we say, and therefore so is the treatment. But what of the sociocultural component of cigarette smoking? In addition, even problems that are purely physical or biological in origin have social dimensions if people are stigmatized by them or receive differential levels of attention, treatment, or aid for them. And cases such as pollution have a social component in the need to mobilize society to combat the problem.

But the issue lying at the heart of the matter is whether social problems have an independent, objective reality apart from whether people view them as problematic. Blumer and others have maintained that defining what is problematic is purely a matter of perspective—members of society can collectively define virtually anything as a problem, and, contrarily, can ignore virtually anything. If the members of a society like something, can outsiders define it as a social problem? Obviously not, and the Blumer perspective also fits well with the modern notions of cultural and ethical relativity in anthropology and ethics.

---

[45] For instance, it could be objected that the "solution" proposed in the footnote above would be exceedingly irrational, and indeed one aim of the study of social problems is not only to determine what would "work" but what would be effective at the least cost to what we hold dear.

Certainly the question of social or collective definition—how, why, and when a society selects some social problems for attention and action—is critical. Public awareness is ordinarily essential for treatment to be initiated, except when treatment becomes unnecessary in the rare cases of what might be called "natural remission" of a problem. Seemingly paradoxically then, since I feel we must reject the extreme implications of the perceptual or public-awareness conception of social problems, several of the following chapters are oriented around the processes by which society actually constructs its conceptions of social problems.

2

BRIEF HISTORIES OF SOCIAL PROBLEM IDEAS

The very concept of a social problem, as currently envisaged, is a relatively recent development in the history of Western societies. Such conditions as mental disorder, crime, and poverty have always existed and are frequently documented in historical records. And a deleterious quality about such conditions has been recognized in some manner in diverse cultures. But these undesirable conditions were generally perceived within a fatalistic, religious, or military perspective. They were *not* generally seen as problems of well-being or of welfare that could be treated socially. Social problems in the past were defined instead as problems against order, against nature, against God, or perhaps, as God's will. And it is only toward the end of the eighteenth century that many of the problems we now consider as social emerged in the public consciousness as such. This change in perception of problems was related to other developments in modern Western thought and social structure that will be discussed later in the chapter. First it is instructive to briefly examine how some specific undesirable conditions were perceived and treated in earlier centuries. By way of illustration, we will retrace historically the ideologies and approaches people have adopted toward mental disorder and poverty.

CASE I: MENTAL DISORDER

Because of religious beliefs and ideologically related concepts of human nature, personal abnormalities were frequently perceived as divine punishment for sins, as just manifestations of divine wrath, as part of the consequences of Original Sin (the Fall), or even as indications of the subhumanity of those so affected. The mentally ill were an obvious example of this philosophy. The records from the later Middle Ages indicate that the agitated insane were kept confined in special "hospitals,"[1] usually in chains, thus underlining their commonality with the animal realm.[2] The emphasis was on protecting society against these "monsters" and on providing a means of social control within the confines of the religious doctrine of the day. "The scandal of madness showed men how close to animality their Fall could bring them; and at the same time how far divine mercy could extend when it consented to save man."[3] And in many countries for which such historical information exists, we find that the madmen—to use the language of the time—were exhibited to the public on certain days, especially Sundays, as a form of distraction, curiosity, and, especially, as a moral lesson.[4] It is said that in England the admission price for these spectacles was a penny, and "the annual revenue . . . amounted to 400 pounds; which suggests the astonishingly high number of 96,000 visits per year."[5] It has been speculated that the madmen replaced the lepers as scapegoats in the public consciousness, and their forced isolation and the fears they evoked served to reinforce this state of affairs.[6] In addition, the insane were commonly incarcerated with criminals, as the distinction between them was blurred and they evoked similar attitudes of apprehension in the public.

In 1656, by royal decree, the Hôpital Général opened in Paris, and a few years later it had six thousand inmates. In 1676, another royal decree ordered every city in France to have an Hôpital Général. In North America, the first institutions for the insane were under Catholic supervision in Quebec in the seventeenth century. However, their role in the care of the insane was very limited, mainly because of their small size and because their clientele consisted predominantly of upper-class females.[7]

---

[1]The term "hospitals" was already old. In 1526, Juan Luis Vives defined them as places where the sick are cared for and fed, "where a certain number of paupers is supported, where boys and girls are reared . . . where the insane are confined." This quote is from *Regulating the Poor: The Functions of Public Welfare*, by Frances Fox Piven and Richard A. Cloward (New York: Random House, 1971), p. 11.

[2]Others, presumably more sedate, were placed aboard ships of fools, old harbor—bound hulks in which both people and ships rotted for decades.

[3]Michael Foucault, *Madness and Civilization: A History of Insanity in the Age of Reason*, trans. Richard Howard (New York: Random House, 1965), p. 81. See also George Rosen, *Madness in Society: Chapters in the Historical Sociology of Mental Illness* (New York: Harper & Row, 1968).

[4]Foucault, *Madness and Civilization*, p. 68.

[5]*Ibid.*

[6]France had more than two thousand registered lepers in 1226. Leper colonies existed throughout Europe until the seventeenth century, at which time only a few known lepers were left and were centralized in two or three institutions.

[7]J. Ivan Williams et al., "Mental Health and Illness in Canada," in *Deviant Behaviour and Societal Reaction*, ed. Craig L. Boydell et al. (Toronto: Holt, Rinehart & Winston, 1972), p. 400.

After the French Revolution, as a consequence of new democratic and liberal attitudes and of scientific development in other spheres, the treatment accorded the insane became relatively humane; the disorders were for the first time seen as subject to cure. The field of medicine became directly involved.[8] Phillippe Pinel unchained the inmates at major French institutions in 1793 and contributed to the development of a new form of therapy, "moral treatment," along with Vincenzo Chiarugi in Italy, William Tuke in England, and Benjamin Rush in the United States.[9]

Several developments led to new neurological and moral approaches to mental illness. Discoveries in the physical sciences as well as those in physiology and medicine were important contributing factors, as were the general trends toward experimentation and scientific optimism.[10] Insanity gradually came to be linked to brain damage rather than to sin or divine will and, as such, was believed to be a readily curable disease.[11] But of even greater relevance in light of current trends was the emphasis moral treatment placed on the effects of a person's environment—although the environment was defined somewhat differently than in present-day conceptions. Various emotions, such as bereavement, guilt, febrile intellectual concentration, romantic disappointment, and pressure caused by poverty and family stress, were seen as impacting on the highly malleable brain. This susceptibility to environmental stimuli meant that parallel factors could be applied in order to erase or modify pathological conditions. The environment of the afflicted was therefore manipulated—by removing the persons from it and placing them in a planned environment.[12]

In the United States, asylums were created that embodied carefully planned regimes. Directed by medical superintendents, they were

---

[8]However, the definition of "medicine" has to be placed within the context of these earlier centuries. For instance, in the United States in the late 1700s and early 1800s, only approximately ten percent of all practitioners had a medical degree. The others were self-made men, many of them charlatans. Norman Dain, *Concepts of Insanity in the United States 1759–1865* (New Brunswick, N. J.: Rutgers University Press, 1964), p. 25.

[9]Ruth B. Caplan, *Psychiatry and the Community in Nineteenth-Century America* (New York: Basic Books, 1969).

[10]Dain, *Concepts of Insanity*, p. 12. Writings about the history of psychiatry have increased enormously since the advent of Foucault's work, *Madness and Civilization*. For detailed analyses, consult W. F. Bynum et al., ed., *The Anatomy of Madness: Essays in the History of Psychiatry*, 2 vols. (London: Tavistock Publications, 1985).

[11]Caplan, *Psychiatry*, p. 4.

[12]This approach bears an interestingly close relation to present emphases on changing the environmental stimuli around the mentally disturbed. Considerable historical controversy exists over the humanity of the "moral treatment." While Foucault, in *Madness and Civilization*, considers a key institution of this persuasion to have been a "gigantic moral imprisonment," Digby, in Bynum, *The Anatomy of Madness*, concludes that this verdict is partially justified but greatly exaggerated.

in theory ruled along humanitarian principles; gone were the restraints, the physical chastisements, and the general filth and bedlam of previous institutions.[13] "Many current therapeutic techniques—open hospitals, nonrestraint, and individual care in small institutions—are in effect a reintroduction of the moral treatment of the mid-nineteenth century."[14] Discipline, work, and a regular routine of daily activities were essential elements of this approach. This regimentation within institutions could be found not only in asylums, but also in penitentiaries and in workhouses for the poor.[15]

Although there was enthusiasm for the new approach to mental illness, it is probably accurate to say that this enthusiasm was predominantly among the educated. Unless affected by the illness of a friend or relative, most people probably gave little thought to the matter and remained influenced by biblical concepts of insanity as "demoniacal possession"—to be treated accordingly.[16]

Subsequent phases of treatment for the insane did not always unfold within a progressive framework. Indeed, much regression occurred in subsequent decades (the late 1800s and early 1900s).[17] The conception of insanity as primarily hereditary and therefore incurable returned, as well as mere custodial care. The quality of the care dispensed to the emotionally disturbed deteriorated, so much so that in the 1880s public concern arose about the brutal treatment received by inmates—a phenomenon that has recurred up to the present.[18] Nevertheless, in spite of regressions, the nineteenth-century approach to mental disorder had definitely entered the modern era and was linked to other ideologies of social problems in general.[19]

This discussion is a drastic simplification of a complex historical process. The only justification for so great a simplification is that it nonetheless imparts a sense of the dramatic differences in the conceptualization of this social problem over time. Let me urge readers to

---

[13]The Association of Medical Superintendents of American Institutions for the Insane became later the American Medico-Psychological Association and, finally, the American Psychiatric Association.

[14]Dain, *Concepts of Insanity*, p. xiii.

[15]David J. Rothman, *The Discovery of the Asylum* (Boston: Little, Brown, and Co., 1971).

[16]Dain, *Concepts of Insanity*, p. 43.

[17]It is fair to say that, prior to Foucault's, histories displayed a "presentism" bias, showing how treatment had emerged from darkness to the enlightenment of psychiatric expertise. One obtains a very different picture from, for example, Andrew Scull, ed., *Madhouses, Mad-Doctors, and Madmen: The Social History of Psychiatry in the Victorian Era* (Philadelphia: University of Pennsylvania Press, 1981).

[18]Caplan, *Nineteenth-Century America*. For an insightful account of regression in treatment at one institution, see Joseph P. Morrissey et al., *The Enduring Asylum: Cycles of Reform at Worcester State Hospital* (New York: Grune & Stratton, 1980).

[19]The turmoil in approaches to mental disorder continues today, as will be seen in subsequent chapters.

consult one or more of the excellent references cited here for a deeper appreciation of the historical evolution of thinking about madness/mental illness.[20]

CASE II: POVERTY

The Law, in its majestic impartiality, forbids the rich and the poor alike to sleep under bridges, to beg in the streets, and to steal bread.

André Malreaux

A historical parallel to the developments in Case I can be drawn with regard to the poor. Not only do interesting similarities exist between the treatment of the mad and the impoverished, but also the cyclical nature of ideologies and approaches to social problems is apparent and revealing. As will be seen, our current system of welfare (and certain related ideologies) can be traced back to Elizabethan *Poor Law*.[21] Although, according to medieval law, the destitute had a right to assistance, and the better-off a duty to provide it, the main emphasis for the cause of poverty was placed on individual sins or faults rather than on social factors.[22] (The same, of course, was true for mental disorder.) In 1388, English beggars who were adjudged able to work were subject to punishment, and the first Law of Settlement allowed those unable to work to beg only within their parishes of residence or of origin, thereby making paupers subject to banishment from parishes to which they migrated. Since charity was dispensed locally, and this law was variously interpreted, the requirement had far-reaching consequences.

In the 1500s, following a period of widespread looting, vagrancy, and criminality, including spectacular food riots, public and official opinion in England shifted regarding the treatment of the poor. Slowly, relying on charity came to be regarded as a form of crime for those who were considered able to work.[23] Beggars, therefore, were frequently

---

[20] Also take note of Gerald Grob's *Mental Illness and American Society, 1875–1940* (Princeton: Princeton University Press, 1983), which is primarily a study of the growth of the psychiatric profession in this period.

[21] Lawrence M. Friedman, *Government and Slum Housing: A Century of Frustration* (Chicago: Rand McNally, 1968).

[22] Blanche D. Coll, *Perspectives in Public Welfare: A History* (Washington, D.C.: United States Department of Health, Education, and Welfare, 1969), p. 2.

[23] *Ibid.*, p. 4.

treated as criminals; in 1532, the Parliament of Paris decided to arrest beggars and force them to work in the sewers of the city, chained in pairs.[24] A very similar law was created by the German emperor in the same period.[25] Yet the economic situation was exacerbated by wars, and when Henry IV began the siege of Paris, there were more than thirty thousand beggars in a population of approximately one hundred thousand.[26] During those decades, beggars were routinely corralled by archers and forced into various institutions, where they were isolated from the rest of the population and at times conscripted to work. In England, a severe economic depression began in 1594, and in certain counties bread riots erupted as famine threatened.

By the middle of the sixteenth century, many of the monasteries and abbeys that used to offer some relief to the poor had been destroyed by Henry VIII in his struggle with the Catholic Church. This background led to Elizabeth's Poor Law of 1597–1601, the first completely secular and comprehensive legislative action on the problem. The Poor Law was progressive for its time, but because of the population's fear of insurrections, it was frequently confused with the Vagrancy Acts in its application, and led to harsh treatment of the pauper. And, once again, the subsequent Settlement Acts of 1662 specified that the poor could be helped only within their own parish, in effect nullifying much of the potential benefits of the Poor Law.

The problem of poverty was not the lot of the Old World countries only. Boston already had an almshouse in 1664 and New York established one in 1700 for cases that could not be helped within their families. Similarly, Catholic charities and related small institutions also existed in Quebec under the French in the seventeenth century. The Poor Law served as a model for the English colonies in the New World, including Canada, and later in the United States after independence. The restrictive effects of the English Settlement Acts appeared only later in the colonies, when the problem of pauperism became more acute, both numerically and economically. Just as the asylums had spread across the United States in the 1820s and 1830s under the reform of "moral treatment," so, too, almhouses spread. They were armed with the same treatment ideology of removal of the poor from the community while providing them with surroundings fostering discipline, work, and moral uplifting in the hope of rehabilitation.

The poor were divided into the "worthy" or "deserving" (for instance, orphans, or the handicapped without family) and the

---

[24]Foucault, *Madness and Civilization*, p. 47.

[25]Sidney and Beatrice Webb, *English Poor Law History, Part I: The Old Poor Law* (Hamden, Conn.: Anchor Books, 1963), p. 32.

[26]*Ibid.*

"unworthy" or "undeserving."[27] With respect to healthy adults who were reduced to beggary, although the effects of certain social circumstances on the lives of the poor were recognized by an enlightened minority (the Society for the Prevention of Pauperism already existed), the tendency to blame the poor themselves for their condition was still strong. Vices such as drinking were stressed as the source of all their misfortunes. What we call "unemployment" today and regard as a systemic problem of the economy was for a long time regarded as the problem of "idleness." As an example, Henry Mayhew entitled one volume of a study of the poor *Those That Will Not Work* (London, 1861).

The treatment of the poor was related to some extent to the economic situation of the society as a whole. For instance, although the Poor Law was profusely debated in the United States in the years of scarcity beginning in 1795, the debate lost some of its urgency between the end of this scarcity period and 1815.[28] In England, a continued increase in expenses incurred from the care of the poor as well as dangers of rural insurrection certainly acted as spurs to legislative rethinking.[29]

The treatment of the poor was also related to ideology. Around the beginning of the nineteenth century a new doctrine emerged that related poor relief to the threat of over-population. Thomas Malthus attacked the English Poor Law, and for a time was successful in having it revoked. He proceeded from the position that people were "inert, sluggish, and averse from labour unless compelled by necessity," and noted that the then extant Poor Law provided for family allowances based on number of children. In the Malthusian view, this practically encouraged the poor to be prolific.[30] In addition, the scientific "laws" of classical economics (about which I will have more to say in Chapter 7) were emerging, and these uniformly pointed to the negative consequences of "encouraging sloth" by aiding the poor.

All of this came to a head in Britain in 1834; the Poor Law was amended to become the New Poor Law, which established the *workhouse* as the principal means of assisting the poor. The workhouse was deliberately designed to be as unpleasant as possible, so as to remove any possibility that people would be encouraged by charity to abandon

---

[27] See Chapter 1 of Michael Morris and John B. Williamson, *Poverty and Public Policy* (Westport, Conn.: Greenwood Press, 1986). For the first recognition of unemployment as a systemic problem of the economy instead of due to individual faults, see Alexander Keyssar, *Out of Work: The First Century of Unemployment in Massachusetts* (New York: Cambridge University Press, 1986).

[28] J. R. Pynter, *Society and Pauperism: English Ideas on Poor Relief, 1795–1834* (Toronto: University of Toronto Press, 1969), p. 186.

[29] Sidney and Beatrice Webb, *English Local Government: English Poor Law History, Part I* (New York: Longmans, Green, 1927), p. 417.

[30] J. Dupaquier, ed., *Malthus Past and Present* (London: Academic Press, 1983).

their work. Those on public assistance were stigmatized severely by, as a contemporary put it,

> imprisoning [them] in workhouses, compelling them to wear special garb, separating them from their families, cutting them off from communication with the poor outside, and, when they died, permitting their bodies to be disposed of for dissection.[31]

Although it is impossible to pinpoint precisely the time when the issue of "poverty amid plenty" moved onto center stage, the publication of Robert Hunter's *Poverty* in 1904 is considered a convenient point of departure.[32] The issue had already been debated for several years; in 1900, conservative sociologist William Graham Sumner pronounced judgment in sentences that remind us in strange ways of discussions on welfare that took place in the 1980s:

> The humanitarians, philanthropists, and reformers . . . in their eagerness to recommend the less fortunate classes to pity and consideration forget all about the rights of other classes . . . When I have read certain of these discussions I have thought that it must be quite disreputable to be respectable, quite dishonest to own property, quite unjust to go one's way and earn one's own living, and that the only admirable person was the good-for-nothing. The man who by his own effort raises himself above poverty appears, in these discussions, to be of no account. The man who has done nothing to raise himself above poverty finds that the social doctors flock about him, bringing the capital which they have collected from other classes.[33]

In the United States and Canada the terrible trauma of the Great Depression of the 1930s acted as a stimulus for dramatic action by federal governments, laying the foundation for the modern welfare state. Piven and Cloward have pointed out the cyclical nature of poor relief in modern societies. They advance considerable evidence for the thesis that only when times are economically harsh—and large numbers of vocal, articulate persons are unemployed—does relief even begin to approach adequacy.[34] In prosperous times, conditions of welfare are

---

[31] As quoted in Albert O. Hirschman, "Reactionary Rhetoric," *Atlantic Monthly* 263 (1989), pp. 63–70. The quote is from p. 69.

[32] Coll, *Public Welfare*, p. 64.

[33] This quote from William Graham Sumner's *What Social Classes Owe to Each Other* (New York: Harper & Row, 1900) can be found in *Poverty in the Affluent Society*, ed. Hanna Messner (New York: Harper & Row, 1966), p. 12.

[34] Piven and Cloward, *Regulating the Poor*.

tightened and provisions are made even less generous. Their assertions thus dispute the common liberal assumption that welfare has steadily improved in the twentieth century.

CULTURAL AND SOCIAL DEVELOPMENTS AND THE RECONCEPTUALIZATION OF SOCIAL PROBLEMS

Everything of importance has been said once before by someone who didn't discover it.

Alfred North Whitehead

The two case studies on the development of modern thinking about mental disorder and poverty spur us to examine the cultural and social structural trends in the unfolding of modern attitudes toward social problems in general. "Social problems"—as a new conceptualization, not a new phenomenon—emerged during the eighteenth and nineteenth centuries as a result of several mutually reinforcing developments. We need to briefly trace these developments. At the social structural level, as we will see momentarily, were severe stresses created by industrialization and urbanization, culminating in abject misery and at times spilling over into unrest and upheaval. Accompanying these social structural transformations were marked changes in social thought on the cultural level: on the one hand, a growing humanitarianism, the rise of middle-class reformers, and democratic trends, and on the other hand, a new scientific ideology, secular rationality, and faith in progress.[35] As we will see, these eventually come together in the scientific study of social problems.

The nineteenth century witnessed an overpowering industrialization and urbanization of society. To take but a single index, in 1840 the United States had only one person in twelve living in cities of eight thousand or more. By 1860, this proportion had grown to one in six. By 1900 it was one in three. The new order created by industrialization was drastically at variance with existing social arrangements, requiring a completely different life-style for which people were not prepared. It was a pervasive change, touching not some isolated aspects in people's lives but their complete social condition. And because the new system

---

[35]Jessie Bernard, *Social Problems at Midcentury* (New York: Dryden, 1957), pp. 90–91.

was everywhere triumphant, the only viable solution was submission and a degree of adaptation. But everything in industrialization was alien: the stresses involved in trying to adapt to this situation without precedent were incalculable.

In addition, industrialization and its accompanying urbanization in no way alleviated old problems that had plagued the masses for centuries. The proletariat was now burdened with long working hours, deficient nutrition, poor health, suffocating housing, and unbearable poverty. Émile Zola, a French novelist of the experimental school in literature, has given us memorable depictions of the misery of the newly industrialized populace and of their dysfunctional coping mechanisms: alcoholism, mental derangement, promiscuity, and brutality, even within the family. In some strange ways, although with obvious differences of detail, his descriptions fit pictures we occasionally see of the most wretched slum dwellers of today. Never before in history had so many people, ostensibly free, toiled under such miserable conditions and within so small and cramped a space.[36] The miseries became too blatant for hiding:

> Commission after commission in Britain documented the inhuman conditions under which people lived in factory towns and city slums. The culture of these new industrial slums was as alien to outsiders as the culture of a distant African tribe. Indeed, after half a century of reform legislation, one passionate observer . . . wrote a book describing "darkest England," comparing it with the "darkest Africa" on which Stanley had just reported.[37]

Alongside this widespread misery, political revolutions took place in Europe—first in France, then a half-century later throughout the entire continent of Europe—in which the masses not only played a major role but also called attention to themselves as human beings rather than as members of a "lower species." The suffering of the masses became socially visible and, for some people in the elite structure, worth paying attention to. A new ideology of humanitarianism arose in the eighteenth century that encouraged condemnation of the situation. In contrast to earlier ideas of the *inevitability* of poverty for the lowly masses, the proletariat's suffering became bona fide human suffering, unnecessary and in urgent need of a solution.

---

[36] See Michael Cross, *The Workingman in the Nineteenth Century*, Readings in Canadian Social History Series (Toronto: Oxford University Press, 1974).

[37] Bernard, *Midcentury*, p. 91, is referring to the founder of the Salvation Army, General William Booth, who wrote *In Darkest England*, published in 1890.

Another element in the emergence of the notion of social problems was the development of middle-class reformers who did not themselves suffer from the conditions they defined as problematic:

> The newly enriched middle classes largely determined the intellectual climate of the eighteenth century, although their accession to power came somewhat later. The middle classes unlike the nobles were trained for peace and not for wars; they were not even accustomed to the blood of the hunting field.[38]

Middle-class reformers were guided by a humanitarian rationalist viewpoint, and were themselves a distinct social category—at once the very creation of this new industrial order and its greatest beneficiaries—in between the afflicted classes and the upper classes responsible for the situation through exploitation and legislation. Members of the middle class, not being completely involved with either of the two extreme class positions, could grasp the situation from a relatively detached perspective. The reformers arising from their ranks were able to achieve a view of the bottom as well as the top. Democracy was also a new product of these ages, thereby making all fellow citizens equal, at least in legalistic theory.[39] As we saw earlier, this meant that the suffering of the "low" classes could at last be recognized as a problem and not as the inevitable affliction of those "born to suffer."

Along with the new drive toward humanitarian reform, a scientific value system and a new conception of progress emerged from the successes of the physical sciences. Secular rationalism, or the secularization of formerly sacred thought, was a development that paralleled or preceded the development of the scientific orientation. One effect of this development was that people no longer viewed the social order as dictated by divine will and therefore unchangeable. This new perception allowed for the rise of reformers and of social movements, a phenomenon previously incompatible with the vision of an unalterable status quo.[40] The successes of the natural sciences and the secularization of thought led intellectuals to consider applying the principles of science to the human realm as well. In the seventeenth and eighteenth centuries, scientific developments inspired a more optimistic and active view of humanity, with the possibility of applying scientific rules for universal betterment.

---

[38]Crane Brinton, "Humanitarianism," in *Encyclopedia of the Social Sciences*, vol. 7 (New York: Macmillan, 1932), pp. 544–48.

[39]For a sense of how hotly debatable the emerging doctrines of legal equality and universal suffrage were in the 1800s, see Christopher Kent, *Brains and Numbers: Elitism, Comtism, and Democracy in Mid-Victorian England* (Toronto: University of Toronto Press, 1978).

[40]Rudolph Heberle, "Social Movements," in *International Encyclopedia of the Social Sciences*, vol. 14 (New York: Crowell–Collier & Macmillan, 1968), p. 440.

This period, particularly the late 1700s, saw the development of a phenomenal faith in human progress.[41] Surrounded by human misery, the writers of the period were nonetheless in virtual awe of the recent intellectual accomplishments in the sciences and humanities. Extrapolating into the future they foresaw endless improvement. Historians of social thought have sometimes termed this period the "Age of Reason," not because the age was so reasonable in the conduct of human affairs but because the elite had such a great *faith* in the powers of reason. (The unreasoning side of the human psyche was yet to be unveiled by Sigmund Freud and others.[42]) This idea of progress prompted such proponents as the Marquis de Condorcet to write these characteristic lines in 1793: "nature has assigned no limit to the perfecting of the human faculties, that the perfectibility of man is truly infinite."[43] Humanitarianism and democratic philosophies are evident in Condorcet's discussion of the three types of inequality he perceived to exist within a nation: the inequality of wealth, that of a man of assured income as opposed to a man whose income depends on his ability to work, and that of the differential education given to children. Saint-Simon was an equally fervent advocate of progress. "He held that the rapid transformation of social and economic conditions which was being brought about by the scientific and industrial revolutions necessitated the creation of a real science of social progress, based upon thoroughly positive [scientific] grounds."[44] While for him this was *la science politique*, it fell to his disciple, Auguste Comte, to call it *sociologie*.[45]

SOCIAL SCIENCE AND SOCIAL PROBLEMS

We thus have the timely beginning of the social sciences.[46] Social science associations, bridging the transition from the amateur to the professional, were created in England (1857), in France (1862), and in the

---

[41] I have more to say about faith in progress in Chapter 7.

[42] See Michael Creal, *The Idea of Progress* (Agincourt, Ont.: Macmillan, 1970).

[43] As quoted in Howard Becker and Harry Elmer Barnes, *Social Thought from Lore to Science*, 3rd ed. (New York: Dover, 1961), p. 474. For an overview of the extreme optimism of the period, see Robert Nisbet, *History of the Idea of Progress* (New York: Basic Books, 1980).

[44] Becker and Barnes, *Social Thought*, p. 501.

[45] For a more detailed discussion of the intellectual ferment in the French capital in this era (Condorcet, Saint-Simon, Comte, and others) see Frank Manuel, *The Prophets of Paris* (Cambridge, Mass.: Harvard University Press, 1962).

[46] One development of the period—which, however, did not immediately become connected with the social sciences—was the emergence in the nineteenth century of statistical data of some reliability. For a discussion of its importance, see Chapter 2 of Burkhart Holzner and John H. Marx, *Knowledge Application: The Knowledge System in Society* (Boston: Allyn & Bacon, 1979).

United States (1865). One purpose of these early associations was to find scientific means to alleviate the recognized social injustices of the time. Conversely, any situation middle-class reformers felt needed remedying became a social problem. And we have here the beginning of what I discussed in Chapter 1 as the social definition of social problems, as well as all the attendant obscurities surrounding this process.

In spite of its early ameliorative emphasis under Saint-Simon and Comte, European sociology developed with considerably less attention to social problems than its American counterpart.[47] However, in 1897, the great French sociologist Emile Durkheim attacked the problem of suicide from this new scientific perspective. His work is now a classic in sociology and greatly encouraged the first, slow beginnings of the scientific study of social problems.[48] In the meantime, social problems had already become a matter of academic interest in the United States, although several years were to elapse before a work of great empirical importance was produced. Nevertheless, under the impetus of the now defunct American Association of Social Sciences, courses on social problems were offered in universities and colleges beginning in 1865, reaching an early peak between 1885 and 1895.[49]

I do not intend to convey the erroneous impression that the social sciences in their formative years were unequivocally in favor of active amelioration of social problems. The concept of laissez-faire had developed at the hands of the classical British economists Adam Smith, Thomas Malthus, and David Ricardo. Ricardo had also formulated the "iron law of wages" which proved, supposedly, that wages of workers could not remain far above the subsistence level. Robert Michels formulated a similar "iron law of oligarchy" to show that all organizations eventually became oligarchical. Even the founder of sociology, Auguste Comte, was by no means an unequivocal advocate of reform, and two of

---

[47] J. Graham Morgan, "Contextual Factors in the Rise of Academic Sociology in the United States," *Canadian Review of Sociology and Anthropology* 7 (1970), pp. 159–71. Early criminology developed independently of sociology, and European contributions to the former were considerable. For an excellent treatment of the development of theories of deviance in the nineteenth century, see Lynn McDonald, *The Sociology of Law and Order* (Montreal: Book Centre, 1976).

[48] Emile Durkheim, *Suicide*, 1897 (Glencoe, Ill.: Free Press, 1951). W. E. B. DuBois's study of the Negro in Philadelphia, published in 1899, and Thomas and Znaniecki's study of the Polish peasant in Europe and America in 1918 are considered the best of the early American studies on social problems.

[49] Edwin M. Lemert, "Social Problems," in *International Encyclopedia of the Social Sciences* (1968), vol. 14, p. 452. For an outstanding overview of the development of professionalism in nineteenth-century social science in the United States, see Thomas L. Haskell, *The Emergence of Professional Social Science* (Urbana: University of Illinois Press, 1977).

the most prominent early sociologists, Sumner (quoted earlier in the chapter) and Spencer, were reactionary. These and other writers will be examined in a separate chapter on obstacles to intervention. In spite of such countertrends, the principal thrust of early social science fields, apart from economics, was clearly reformative or ameliorationist in character.[50]

Between 1920 and 1950, North American sociologists increasingly abandoned the arena of social problems (except criminology) and left it to social workers. A major rift developed between the two disciplines, with sociologists viewing social workers as mere "do-gooders" with little sense of academic objectivity, and the latter retaliating in kind by considering sociologists "pseudo-scientists" in ivory towers.[51] The sociologists' disaffection with social problems during this period resulted from a heightened ideological commitment to social neutrality, accompanying an emphasis on scientific and objective study (positivism).[52] The Hinkles, in their history of sociology, explicitly called this period "the drive to make sociology scientific." The period emphasized studying social phenomena with detachment in order to detect social laws or regularities.[53]

But sociologists' concern with social problems never entirely disappeared, and in 1952 the Society for the Study of Social Problems was founded by sociologists who believed in the possibility of studying social problems objectively and wished to return to their earlier emphasis. After a slow beginning, this trend gained momentum in the 1960s. However, this resurgence took place within the framework of new concerns, such as the need for a social problems theory.[54] The issue of value commitment versus neutrality is still debated and, once again, factions have been created in the field of social problems.[55] In the 1960s value neutrality was questioned as never before and social commitment reentered

---

[50] For historical accounts of the development of sociology, see Becker and Barnes, *Social Thought*; Roscoe C. Hinkle and Gisela Hinkle, *The Development of Modern Sociology* (New York: Random House, 1962).

[51] Arnold M. Rose, "History and Sociology of the Study of Social Problems," in *Handbook on the Study of Social Problems*, ed. Erwin O. Smigel (Chicago: Rand McNally, 1971). See also Hinkle and Hinkle, *Modern Sociology*.

[52] Lemert, "Social Problems," p. 453. Rose, in "History," suggests the shift also arose from sociologists' chagrin over their discipline's low academic status.

[53] For this period, see also Robert C. Bannister, *Sociology and Scientism: The American Quest for Objectivity, 1880–1940* (Chapel Hill: University of North Carolina Press, 1987).

[54] It should not be supposed that the interlude of excessive concern with scientific purity was of no lasting value, even to those sociologists today exclusively preoccupied with social problems. When the discipline returned to its earlier concerns, it did so with far greater sophistication in employment of statistics and other research tools.

[55] James B. McKee, "Some Observations on the Self-Consciousness of Sociologists," in *The Sociology of Sociology*, ed. Larry T. Reynolds and Janice M. Reynolds (New York: David McKay, 1970), p. 102.

the scene—one more example of the cyclical nature of ideologies, even in scientific endeavors.[56] And related to these new trends was the emergence of the labeling school, as discussed in Chapter 8.

SUMMARY

A review of the history of social concerns reveals unmistakably that the conditions we regard today as social problems have not always been regarded as such. In fact, modern conceptions of problematic conditions are just that: modern points of view. The central thrust of this chapter was to provide an overview of the historical development of certain key ideas and, perhaps of even greater importance, to impart a historical perspective on social problem issues.

Two cases demonstrating the slow evolution of social outlook were examined in somewhat greater depth. Mental disorder was regarded at one time as a manifestation of divine wrath, and treatment was bestial because persons so afflicted were in fact regarded as beasts. Conditions improved during the Enlightenment period and very gradually a notion of possible curing began—however naive the treatment seems today. One important notion to be gained here is the cyclical process of reform alternating with regression to harsh treatment over an extended period of several centuries. Views toward poverty display the same cyclical alternation between charitable periods and periods in which poverty is construed as individual sloth and begging as a crime. The course of poverty legislation can be traced from the Elizabethan Poor Law to the origins of the welfare state in the Great Depression.

Turning to the more general trends in viewpoint, the major transformations in culture and social structure in what historians call the modern and early modern periods have shaped contemporary thinking about social problems. In terms of social structure, the uprooting of millions of farmers and peasants by land-enclosure acts, their settlement into squalid, teeming city slums, their sixty-hour work week in impersonal sooty factories—in short, the chaos of early industrialization and urbanization—lent to suffering a quality and visibility not previously encountered. Early urban revolts, even when unsuccessful, heightened this visibility. The rise of a large middle class between the traditional elite and peasant-laborers paralleled major cultural developments—in

---

[56] Very descriptive of new trends in the 1960s was this title: "... Who Shall Prepare Himself to the Battle?" by Thomas Ford Hoult, *American Sociologist* 3 (1968), pp. 3–7. But most importantly, see Alvin W. Gouldner, "Anti-Minotaur: The Myth of a Value-Free Sociology," *Social Problems* 9 (1962), pp. 199–213.

particular, belief in democracy and legal equality. The unrivaled faith in progress throughout much of this period, faith in the power of human rationality and technical achievements, combined with growing democratization produced a demand for and belief in the possibility of improvement in the life of the common citizen. No longer did mass suffering appear inevitable and unavoidable.

The factors that finally led to the perception of deleterious conditions as social problems and to the questioning of the prevailing order are finely and intricately interwoven. These factors—secular rationalism, scientific ideology, and humanitarianism on the ideological level and, on the structural level, industrialization, urbanization, and the rise of a strategically situated middle class—were all in dynamic interrelationship and were perhaps essential prerequisites to the conceptualization of social problems and, especially, the rational study of such problems.

Finally, material abundance, or the possibility of such, in the twentieth century contributes to the social consciousness of new problems. As George and Wilding note, when no possibility of a solution exists, a condition is just a fact, not a problem. Thus "poverty only becomes a problem when there are resources available which *could* be used to reduce it. A society has to attain a certain degree of prosperity before it has any sense of a problem of poverty."[57] So, too, with the inclusion among social problems of conditions related to "malfunctions of roles and status."[58] Problems of sheer survival and physical pain are now complemented by psychological pains. "Modern industrial man is probably the most problem-blessed in all history. For, encouraged by a sense of control over nature, he has joined the survival problems of the past to the style of life problems of the present."[59]

---

[57] V. George and P. Wilding, *Motherless Families* (London: Routledge & Kegan Paul, 1972), p. 175.

[58] Bernard, *Midcentury*, p. viii.

[59] William R. Burch, Jr., "Images of Future Leisure: Continuities in Changing Expectations," in *The Sociology of the Future*, ed. Wendell Bell and James A. Mau (New York: Russell Sage Foundation, 1971), p. 161.

3

DEFINING SOCIAL PROBLEMS: MORAL ENTREPRENEURSHIP

"**M**oral entrepreneurs" are groups or individuals who promote legislation creating new social problem definitions. With this chapter, we begin our discussion of ideology (and vested interest) as a basis for the definition of social problems. The topic will be further developed in subsequent chapters.

CRIME AND THE ORIGINS OF CRIMINAL LAWS

Crime is generally considered one of the most severe of social problems. But what *is* crime, generally speaking? One searches through various possibilities (crime as sin, crime as wickedness), but invariably arrives at either a *legal* or a *social interpretation* (or definition) of crime.[1] These interpretations of crime compete with one another, each having its own special advantages.

The legal interpretation of crime is essentially quite simple: crime is a violation of whatever appears on the statutes at a particular time and place—it is whatever the law says it is. This interpretation has the advantage of simplicity and is also relatively precise.[2] But, as we

---

[1] See Elmer H. Johnson, *Crime, Correction and Society*, rev. ed. (Homewood, Ill.: Dorsey Press, 1968), pp. 13–15. A good discussion is contained in Robert A. Silverman and James J. Teevan, Jr., eds., *Crime in Canadian Society*, 2nd ed. (Toronto: Butterworths Canada, 1980), pp. 3–5.

[2] This still allows considerable latitude for discretion and for abuse, as I note in Chapter 9 on differential treatment.

will see momentarily, it lacks any logical or theoretical cohesion. The social interpretation, on the other hand, is relatively sophisticated theoretically but lacking in precision. According to the social perspective, a crime is a contra-normative act regarded as so unpleasant by the community that it reserves its severest sanctions for these actions.

Unfortunately for those who assume a perfect match between the legal and social interpretations, this match does not exist. There are too many illegal acts that no one regards as "bad" and too many "bad" acts that are not criminal. For example, if some unscrupulous people persuade your aged invalid grandmother to sign over every penny of her savings for something of extremely low value, and then brag about it, they are looked down on as cads—but this is not illegal. Examples abound of the mismatch between the two definitions of crime.[3]

The social interpretation assumes that most community members will agree about the severity of acts, yet this assumption of consensus is not always borne out in fact. The totally different attitudes of conservatives and liberals on the relative harm caused by pollution and homosexuality might be illustrative of the difficulties involved in the social interpretation. Even for crimes in which there does appear to be a consensus on a hierarchy of severity, the hierarchy found by public surveys does not always correspond to the severity of the official sanctions.[4] What is more, some extremely contra-normative acts, such as cannibalism, are not found in the statutes as distinct offenses.

Yet, for all of its weaknesses, the social interpretation at least provides a certain theoretical unity for acts classified as criminal. In contrast, although the legal interpretation is more precise, it amounts to the idea that *crime is whatever legislators say it is*.[5] But we find absolutely absurd crimes on record. In Louisiana a theater manager is guilty of a misdemeanor if he allows people to be seated after a performance has started. In the state of Arkansas, one may not erect a lunch counter on Decoration Day within a half-mile of a Confederate cemetery. The city

---

[3] Many excellent examples of this point are given in Chapter 2 of Edmund Vaz's *Aspects of Deviance* (Toronto: Prentice–Hall Canada, 1976). As will be discussed, the action of making something illegal can by itself make the deed seem nasty or dirty to many people. So the fact that there is a certain degree of "fit" between the two interpretations should not be surprising.

[4] See the Sellin-Wolfgang scale of severity of offenses, in Thorsten Sellin and Marvin Wolfgang, *The Measurement of Delinquency* (New York: Wiley, 1964). For a theory relating law and practice in terms of seriousness in specific social contexts, see D. Black, *The Behavior of Law* (New York: Academic Press, 1976). A largely favorable test of Black's theory has been reported by Larry A. Hembroff, "The Seriousness of Acts and Social Contexts," *American Journal of Sociology* 93 (1987), pp. 322–47.

[5] Furthermore, the insistence on legal precision can itself result in absurd arbitrariness. See an illustration of this point in James C. Hackler, *The Prevention of Youthful Crime: The Great Stumble Forward* (Toronto: Methuen, 1978), p. 5.

council of Moose Jaw, Saskatchewan, passed a bylaw in 1971 making walking on the left side of sidewalks illegal and punishable by a possible $100 fine or thirty days in jail (maximum sentence). Numerous other absurdities could be provided.

Technically, anyone who does these things performs a criminal act, just as if had murdered his wife, sold heroin, incited others to riot, embezzled funds, falsified his income tax, vandalized a school building, or lied under oath. The only thing the above acts have in common, outside of their illegal character, is that someone did not like them. Obviously, if *no one* liked them they would not be illegal—cannibalism, for example, is rarely included in criminal law. Clearly some people do like to embezzle funds or damage school buildings. Why not take their judgment instead of someone else's?

It should be obvious from the above discussion why, if we utilize the legal interpretation, we have no adequate theory (or even theories) about the causes of criminal behavior. Under this perspective, criminal acts have neither logical nor psychosocial unity. We can, of course, have theories about the causes of *specific* crimes, just as for any other human behavior. But *"crime" as it appears in the statutes is not a meaningful collection of actions from a social or psychological standpoint*. As Quinney notes, "crime is not inherent in behavior, but is a judgment made by some about the actions and characteristics of others."[6]

Since persons are prosecuted under the legal interpretation (that is, under a government's criminal code), it is worthwhile to determine precisely how criminal interpretations come into being. Just who decides what should be against the law? The answer varies, of course, with different societies and different times, but one clear conclusion is that laws are universally made by a very limited number of persons, although the laws subsequently become binding for others. In Western democratic societies the criminal law is formulated by representatives in legislatures.[7]

Under democratic theory legislators represent the wishes of their constituents with respect to the laws they promulgate. Without being overly critical of the representative principle, I must nevertheless note that, with criminal law, the legislators cannot avoid—virtually by definition—favoring some of their constituents over others. What guides them in their decisions on which persons to listen to?

---

[6]Richard Quinney, *The Social Reality of Crime* (Boston: Little, Brown, 1970), p. 16. Unfortunately, because of factors of cost and manpower, social researchers are often required to use official statistics collected under less meaningful social categories. This is frequently the case in the study of crime.

[7]For brevity I exclude "judge-made law," that is, judicial decisions that have the effect of radically altering statutory law. See Chapter 9 on differential treatment for a related discussion.

In some cases the legislative decision is easy. Murder has been an offense as long as law has been recorded, and it is almost meaningless to speak of a decision to discriminate against the murderer, or to say that murderers deserve the same consideration as a group with legitimate interests.[8] Many people think of all criminal law in this fashion, while in reality criminal law in most cases does involve a discrimination against what some persons regard as legitimate activities. The rapidity with which formerly legal acts have been criminalized in North America in the twentieth century has been called a *law explosion*. Observers frequently note that Americans in particular have an excessive faith in the efficacy of the law to solve social problems. We will later reconsider some aspects of this extensive criminalization, but at this juncture the point is that each of these additional laws has been added at the expense of certain persons or interests and for the benefit of others. The obviousness that surrounds such traditionally forbidden acts as murder and robbery is not a sufficient explanation for the birth of these new prohibitions.

What answers there are can be derived from an examination of two aspects of the lawmaking process: the backgrounds of the legislators, and the advice they receive from what have been pejoratively called "moral entrepreneurs" and positively termed "social reformers." Legislators in various countries tend to be nonrepresentative of the population in terms of social class and occupation, however much they may be representative in other respects. In the Soviet Union, engineers are in the majority in decision-making bodies; in China, one's family background must be free of bourgeois affiliations. In North America, lawyers are vastly overrepresented in legislative bodies; in virtually all Western, industrialized societies, the upper middle class and upper class form the bulk of the elected leadership.[9] In all cases the vast majority of legislators are older males. These characteristics enter into the nature of the laws passed by such persons, not only because of the vested interests possible (and there are transparent instances of such), but also because the common backgrounds of the legislators mean that they share certain life experiences and outlooks. It may also mean that, as a body, they are blind to certain experiences and correspondingly cannot appreciate certain points of view.[10] This similarity of background is one ingredient in understanding the types of criminal legislation passed, and the types of persons and acts deemed to be "outside the pale" of decency.

---

[8]It is not, however, so meaningless to speak of decisions on matters such as justifiable homicide.

[9]For a recent account of Canada's case, see Neil Guppy et al., "Economic Background and Political Representation," in J. Curtis et al., eds., *Social Inequality in Canada: Patterns, Problems, Policies* (Toronto: Prentice–Hall Canada, 1988), pp. 394–404.

[10]See Gwynn Nettler's discerning article, "Good Men, Bad Men, and the Perception of Reality," *Sociometry* 24 (1961), pp. 279–94.

MORAL ENTREPRENEURS

The term "moral entrepreneur" generally refers to groups and individuals who develop legislation protecting what they see as threatened morality. In effect they try to legislate morality and, contrary to conventional wisdom, they sometimes succeed. Moral entrepreneurs are found today demanding, in various places, antipornography legislation, laws to control gambling or prostitution, or laws mandating religious prayers in the schools. In earlier periods they have tried to control the teaching of evolution—a drive that has reappeared via the efforts of the Moral Majority organization in the United States. To go back still further, they can be seen in the 1400s urging the prosecution of witches in the community.[11] In the most famous twentieth-century instance, moral entrepreneurs succeeded for a time in prohibiting the sale of intoxicating beverages in the United States. Prohibition is a fine example not only of moral enterprising but also of the lack of public consensus on many laws carrying criminal penalties.[12]

The term "moral entrepreneur" was coined by Howard Becker in what has become a classic study of the development of antimarijuana legislation.[13] In his review of this development, Becker found that no marijuana users were consulted (although it was not illegal in many states to use marijuana at that time), that the claims of dire effects from the substance were accepted without expert testimony, and that the driving force behind the legislation was federal narcotics agents who wished to expand the scope of their operations. The same casual quality is found when one investigates the legislation in the same period outlawing heroin and other drugs. Given the overwhelming significance of this legislation today (it created the drug problem at least to the extent of outlawing drugs, and probably in many other ways as well), it is startling to realize how lightly and superficially it was examined at the time. Quinney presents an equally cogent analysis of "blue law" legislation (Sunday closing of businesses) in terms of how business interests that could be hurt by competition on Sunday suddenly became intensely interested in morality.[14]

---

[11] Nachman Ben-Yehuda, "The European Witch Craze of the 14th to 17th Centuries: A Sociologist's Perspective," *American Journal of Sociology* 86 (1980), pp. 1–31. See p. 15. The fact that true witches do not exist did not prevent these moral entrepreneurs from creating new legislation.

[12] Resistance to prohibition was strongest in the large cities of the United States. At that time, due to unequal districting, American legislatures were dominated by representatives of rural areas.

[13] Howard S. Becker, "The Marijuana Tax Act," in *Outsiders: Studies in the Sociology of Deviance* (New York: Free Press, 1963).

[14] Quinney, *Reality of Crime*, pp. 65–70.

The feasibility of moral entrepreneurship "legislating morality" is aided by a curious circular process in which what is made against the law becomes *immoral by this fact* for many people. Although legislation can backlash—as happened with Prohibition and may eventually occur with marijuana—more frequently morality legislation not only alters outward actions but even the attitudes of persons toward the deed.[15]

The law explosion referred to earlier has several dimensions, including an increase in civil adjudication that is not of particular interest here. One of its most striking aspects is a broad expansion of criminal legislation beyond what might be considered the traditional business of the criminal code. In part this has been mandated by the increasing complexity and interdependence of modern society. In part it results from a gradual shift in American society from formations of close personal ties to a predominance of weak secondary relationships.[16] Finally, a part is due to expansion of the purposes of criminal law to include such humanitarian additions as pure food and drug legislation. One cannot explain the law explosion as simply a consequence of the successes of moral entrepreneurs because they are concerned not only with adding new legal prohibitions but also with removing some now in existence.

An increasingly burdensome aspect of criminal law has been its employment in what some refer to as *crimes without victims*—the use of the criminal sanction to forbid acts in which no one is injured. These crimes include many of the most controversial—and frequently unenforceable—laws.[17] Actions in which all those concerned are satisfied are difficult to justify as crimes merely because someone else who *thinks* about the acts does not like them. Such conditions apply to most criminal cases involving pornography, prostitution, homosexuality, and numerous other prohibited or restricted activities. A slowly changing public opinion has challenged the conventional legal wisdom on victimless

---

[15] See Joel F. Handler, *Social Movements and the Legal System* (New York: Academic Press, 1978). For a somewhat different view, see Nigel Walker and Michael Argyle, "Does the Law Affect Moral Judgments?" *British Journal of Criminology* 4 (1964), pp. 570–81. An intriguing companion finding is that laws that are on the books but never strongly enforced despite blatant, well-known violations gradually become *re-legitimized* in the public's attitudes. See A. E. McCormick, Jr., "Rule Enforcement and Moral Indignation," *Social Problems* 25 (1977), pp. 30–39.

[16] See more on the law explosion in Lawrence M. Friedman, *Total Justice* (New York: Russell Sage Foundation, 1985).

[17] See Herbert L. Packer, *The Limits of the Criminal Sanction* (Stanford, Calif.: Stanford University Press, 1968); Edwin Schur, *Crimes Without Victims* (Englewood Cliffs, N. J.: Prentice-Hall, 1965); Sanford H. Kadish, "The Crisis of Overcriminalization," *The Annals* 374 (1967), pp. 157–70; and Gilbert Geis, *Not the Law's Business* (New York: Schocken Books, 1979).

crimes, thus providing an excellent illustration of the power dimension in legislation.[18]

Paralleling the notion of victimless crimes is the older distinction in legal philosophy between crimes that are *mala in se* and other crimes that are *mala prohibita*. Roughly, this can be translated as crimes that are "bad in themselves" and crimes that are "bad because prohibited." Crimes mala in se are what one ordinarily thinks of when considering crime: offenses such as homicide or rape. Even if a jurisdiction somewhere were to legalize such activities, virtually all cultures would continue to regard them as evil in themselves. By contrast, crimes mala prohibita include offenses created for bureaucratic convenience, such as failure to file an income tax return by a given date, or offenses necessary to keep order, such as driving down the wrong side of the street.[19] One reason the distinction is valuable is it helps us to recognize that much of the law explosion is a vast expansion of crimes mala prohibita. The essential question still debated is whether or not "victimless crimes" are merely crimes mala prohibita.[20]

THE ROLE OF RELIGION IN MORAL ENTREPRENEURSHIP

In many societies, religion has power approaching that of lawmakers in social problem definition. The relative powers of religion and state in this crucial arena create an interesting interplay that fluctuates interminably. It is anything but simple or uniform. After the Mexican Revolution of 1911, for instance, because the Catholic church had supported the old regime clerics were shorn of much of their power. More recently, however, they have gradually regained much of their lost authority in Mexico. The states of Israel and Iran—differing in so many other respects—are both avowedly religion based, on the Jewish and Moslem faiths respectively, and experience constant intrusion of religious principles and definitions into what we would consider secular affairs. In such situations, religion and state interpenetrate the defining of social

---

[18] Supporters of decriminalization have made major inroads in the past decade in northern Europe and Canada (for example, Canada's Omnibus Bill legalized homosexual acts under specified conditions). In the United States, penalties for marijuana possession have been reduced in several states, but it is safe to say that decriminalization per se is relatively weak in North America. See Chapter 6 on the strategies of intervention.

[19] For some good examples of the distinction, see Chapter 2 of Vaz, *Deviance*, especially pp. 21–22.

[20] For an excellent exposition of the issues of *mala in se* versus legal interpretations of crime, and of victimless crime, see Edward Sagarin, *Deviants and Deviance* (New York: Praeger, 1975).

problems, forbidding certain activities through criminal law. During the Middle Ages in Europe the Church was in fact the state in most senses of the word, with its own ecclesiastical courts, laws, prisons, and taxes. Even for those apparently secular states with a single dominant religion (e.g., Italy, the Republic of Ireland), the interpenetration can be quite powerful (e.g., in divorce legislation).[21] On the other hand, in Poland, an officially atheist country, the Catholic church wields immense power in secular affairs, but does so outside of the official criminal law that is, as I write, controlled by the Communist Party. A comparative cross-cultural study of such matters, apart from the hints of complexity just given, is beyond the scope of this book, and we will henceforth concentrate on the situation closer to home.[22]

In our own society, the influence of religion on social problem definition can be seen most clearly in ongoing controversies, such as those concerning divorce, contraception, abortion, and homosexuality. However, religion's influence is far more pervasive than it appears: many cultural features that are taken for granted can suddenly become religiously defined social problems when challenged, as the nineteenth-century Mormons discovered when they attempted to set up a regime of polygamous marriages. Not even the great isolation of the Salt Lake area of Utah—at that time a thinly populated territory—precluded a wrathful United States government from threatening to send in the U.S. Army.

The traditional opposition of the Catholic church and evangelical sects to divorce, homosexuality, and legal abortion has meant, from the standpoint of the secular humanist, the persistence of unmanaged social problems of unhappy couples, discrimination based on sexual orientation, and unwanted (and sometimes battered) children. And although overpopulation is not a problem in the United States, it becomes a critical social problem whenever global concerns are addressed. From a clerical point of view, on the other hand, the situation is exactly the opposite: divorce, homosexuality, contraception, and abortion are seen as the critical problems. Insofar as these have been staved off, "moral problems" have been averted; insofar as they have been allowed, society has regressed morally. This is not to say that all Catholics or Evangelicals, or even all clerics of these persuasions, agree with such positions, nor that

---

[21]The history of the intrusion of English Protestantism into Catholic Ireland, taking root only in the north (Ulster), is itself a striking display of church combining with the power of state. It reminds us that England at one time had an official religion, as did most European countries. See Desmond Bowen, *The Protestant Crusade in Ireland, 1800–1870* (Montreal: McGill-Queen's University Press, 1978).

[22]For studies of several cultures on the nature of the linkage between the criminal law and popular views about deviance (not necessarily religion-based views), see Graeme Newman, *Comparative Deviance: Perception and Law in Six Cultures* (New York: Amer. Elsevier, 1976).

such social problems as overpopulation, unhappy homes, or unwanted children are unrecognized. Indeed many Catholic sociologists and clerics work vigorously toward the amelioration of these problems. Rather, a claim is made based on religious belief that there is a right way (e.g., the rhythm method) and a wrong way (e.g., abortion, divorce) to handle these problems, so that if the wrong way is used it becomes a problem in itself.

Although particular issue evaluations originate in the religious sector, they often come to be accepted by other problem-solving agencies in the community. In this way the increasing frequency of divorce is widely conceptualized as a social problem, not only by religious persons to whom it is intolerable but also by nonreligious persons and, ultimately, by welfare agencies. In societies where a single religion is preeminent, the alliance of church and state (even if unofficial) results in an inability to enact certain types of ameliorative legislation. Even in societies with several religions, the alliance of state and religion is seen by the frequent resort to legislation to deal with religion-defined social problems. The Prohibition movement probably represented the high point of religious definitional power in the United States; its resounding failure may have had much to do with the rise of competing definitional powers, which I will discuss momentarily. But religion's labeling power is still very much alive, if severely weakened. Contemporary activities are considerably more circumspect. The tendency today is to downplay the seriousness of social problems where recognition seems likely to call for morally undesirable remedies. In this way, for many years the Catholic church has minimized the severity of world population problems.[23]

In some societies the religious establishment is still an extremely powerful factor in the definition of social problems and in the acceptability of proposed resolutions. Obviously this was even more the case in the past and, once a social phenomenon had been defined as a problem, the label has tended to *persist* as though by inertia. Many of today's labels are accurately described as holdovers from an era of powerful religious movements. Although the role of religion in the definitional process is far from over, as we are reminded by recurrent campaigns against various forms of "indecency," its place in Western societies has become increasingly usurped by two relatively recent perspectives— what we might call the *egalitarian* and *psychiatric perspectives*. These are the expansionist perspectives of the day: despite periodic fluctua-

---

[23]See, for example, Monsignor George A. Kelly, *Overpopulation: A Catholic View* (New York: Paulist Press, 1960). For an overview of the history of Catholic positions on population, see Kevin McQuillan, "Common Themes in Catholic and Marxist Thought on Population and Development," *Population and Development Review* 5 (1979), pp. 689–98.

tions, the long-term historical trend of religious influence is downward. While religious definitions retreat (or at best hold their own), new conceptions of social problems arise to take their place, based either on perceived inequalities in the structuring of rewards and opportunities in society (the egalitarian perspective) or on real or imagined mental difficulties (the psychiatric perspective).[24]

Although to this point I have portrayed organized religion as a force concerned with the preservation of conventional morality, I should state that links between egalitarian social movements and conventional religion have sometimes been very close. The closeness has varied from issue to issue. The earliest egalitarian movements in the modern era, those advocating legal equality and the abolition of a hereditary aristocracy (culminating in the American and French revolutions), were products of the Age of Reason (see Chapter 2) and derived very little impetus from religious foundations.[25] On the other hand, the antislavery movements of the nineteenth century had extremely close ties with organized religion—although there were religious advocates on both sides of the conflict. Then again, the nineteenth-century socialist movements of Europe typically rejected conventional religion as hopelessly supportive of the economic status quo, and were likewise rejected by the established religions of the day.

In the twentieth century many churches developed (or possibly returned to) what has been called a *social gospel*.[26] As Allen put it:

> The social gospel rested on the premise that Christianity was a social religion, concerned . . . with the quality of human relations on this earth. Put in more dramatic terms, it was a call for men to find the meaning of their lives in seeking . . . the Kingdom of God in the very fabric of society.[27]

Many denominations of organized religion today are far more concerned with alleviating injustice and misery on earth than with saving souls

---

[24] Since psychiatric definitions are typically seen as medical and scientific, not moral (except perhaps for sexual psychopath laws), their use actually represents a decline in the moralistic conception of social problems. Discussion of psychiatric definitions is therefore delayed until Chapter 4. The expansion of psychiatric frames of references is perhaps best conveyed in Peter Conrad and Joseph Schneider's *Deviance and Medicalization: From Badness to Sickness* (St. Louis: Mosby, 1980).

[25] The same is true of nineteenth-century movements by the Chartists of England and similar groups on the European continent to extend the vote to the masses. See John Gwynne-Timothy, *Question for Democracy*, vols. 1 and 2 (Toronto: McClelland & Stewart, 1970).

[26] C. H. Hopkins, *The Rise of the Social Gospel in American Protestantism, 1865–1895* (New Haven: Yale University Press, 1967).

[27] A. R. Allen, *The Social Passion: Religion and Social Reform in Canada, 1914–1928* (Toronto: University of Toronto Press, 1971), p. 4.

from the torments of Hell. To be sure, both interests have always been visible in Christianity, but the balance has shifted considerably in this century. From this shift comes the term social gospel.

The ambivalence of linkage between egalitarian movements and religious efforts continues to the present day. The 1960s civil rights movement for blacks in the United States was closely associated with the social gospel component of organized religion. Many of the leaders were ordained clergy, and much of the organization was based in established churches.

The feminist movement, on the other hand, has been completely separate, receiving rather more flak and less support from religious sources. This antipathy stems from fundamentalist interpretations of Scripture—that the man is to assume the leading role in the family—and from the view that some of the specific causes endorsed by or associated with the feminist movement, from legalized prostitution and lesbian rights to contraception and abortion, are contrary to Scripture.

Meanwhile, socialism and the church have moved considerably closer together. Whereas the old socialism condemned religion as an instrument of the status quo—the opiate of the people—and old religion condemned socialism in turn as "Godless communism," the past two decades have witnessed a startling rapprochement, especially in less developed countries with a large Roman Catholic base. In such countries "liberation theology" has taken hold, particularly among the younger clergy, who call for a humane social order (in their conception, socialism) along with a strong Christian faith.

Because egalitarianism in its various manifestations has become a separate force in history (notwithstanding its religious roots) and has in fact become even stronger than organized religion in certain cases, it is best to treat it now in its own section.

EGALITARIAN ENTREPRENEURS

The reasonable man adapts himself to the world; the
unreasonable one persists in trying to adapt the world to himself.
Therefore, all progress depends on the unreasonable man.
                                        George Bernard Shaw

Sociologists have developed an unfortunate tendency to speak of "moral entrepreneurship" with regard to activities they disapprove of, typically those motivated by business interests or by fundamentalist Christianity. They reserve the labels "social reform" or "social movements" for legislative entrepreneurship they espouse, usually humanistic lawmaking.

Although the content of the changes advocated certainly differs, the activities of the advocates are highly similar. Therefore, in this chapter we consider both forms of moralistic legislation as aspects of moral entrepreneurship.

As seen in Chapter 2, a prominent feature of nineteenth- and twentieth-century thought has been the expansion of public consciousness and concern to include the suffering and inequities of ever-wider circles of society—circles for whom earlier generations considered suffering as inescapable. This "democratic revolution" is a significant movement that began around 1760.[28] The American and French Revolutions (roughly 1776 and 1789, respectively) were, as many writers have observed, among the earliest indications of this expansion of compassion, rejecting aristocracies and achieving formal legal equality for all adult white males and limited voting rights. Since that period, the West has experienced movement after movement whose aims have been to expand suffrage (voting rights) and prohibit exploitation. The antislavery movements of Britain and the United States were undoubtedly among the greatest of such developments in the nineteenth century, alongside the emergence of the socialist movement in Europe. In the same period came the expansion of suffrage to men without property. As the twentieth century began, women obtained suffrage; this was accompanied by or followed by the rise of the trade union movement, government-backed security for the aged, the civil rights movement for blacks and American Indians, independence for former colonies of Europe, and, most recently, a rebirth of the feminist movement. In each case, an iniquitous condition formerly taken for granted as part of the natural and inescapable order of things gradually assumed the status of a serious social problem. Again it is logical to ask who the definers of these cultural transformations have been.

Typically, the active members of afflicted groups have served more as "shock troops" than as definers for society as a whole, even though dramatic actions have on occasion provided "propaganda of the deed" to help awaken a sleeping society. It is frequently the inarticulate, inchoate actions of desperate members of a disadvantaged group that first alert the more perceptive of the intellectuals to a sense of their plight.[29] But to see such actions as protest rather than as mindless deviance requires special interpreters: an intellectual vanguard. The first

---

[28] A good source here is R. R. Palmer, *The Age of the Democratic Revolution: A Political History of Europe and America 1760–1800*, vols. I and II (Princeton: Princeton University Press, 1959 and 1964).

[29] Since the black ghetto riots of the 1960s, there has been increased discussion of the latent functions of violence as a form of protest, of which the Luddites and Molly Maguires of the nineteenth century furnish some of the clearest examples. See, for example, Ralph H. Turner, "The Public Perception of Protest," *American Sociological Review* 34 (1969), pp. 815–31.

defining efforts have usually fallen to the unaffiliated intellectual rather than to the downtrodden.[30] Of course the two categories are hardly mutually exclusive, and it is not surprising to find black intellectuals and academic women prominent in the movements of their respective groups and playing key roles in redefining familiar misery. For blacks, American Indians, women, and the working-class in general to become members of the intelligentsia, however, a break in the barriers must first occur within the educational system, allowing access by members of underprivileged segments of society. Eric Hoffer has envisaged social movements divided into stages, in the sense that the types of persons who excel in the first stage ("people of ideas") do not shine in later phases. In those, the "people of words" and then the "people of action" come into prominence. Rarely, says Hoffer, do we find these different roles filled by the same individuals.[31]

OVERVIEW

The definitional aspect of the social problem label is seen most vividly with respect to crime, for while crimes are the activities of social life most severely sanctioned, some people wish to take part in them. The legislators who make the criminal law must therefore decide which part of their constituencies they will listen to: the doers or the would-be preventers.

Several studies have investigated the active sponsorship of legislation and the personal backgrounds of the legislators. That many persons equate criminality with immorality does aid the moral entrepreneur when he or she succeeds in obtaining a new legal prohibition. In terms of enforceability, laws prohibiting "victimless" acts are the most vulnerable to abuse and corruption, and are probably the most questionable outgrowths of the law explosion. The study of moral entrepreneurship would be incomplete without a discussion of modern religious and egalitarian social movements. We did not examine in detail the origins or tactics of such groups, but the discussion served to secure their position as part of the definitional process.[32] Psychiatric conceptions as sources of social problem perspectives and definitions are examined in Chapters 4 and 9.

---

[30]See Barry Krisberg, "The Sociological Imagination Revisited," *Canadian Journal of Criminology and Corrections* 16 (1974), pp. 146–61.

[31]Eric Hoffer, *The True Believer: Thoughts on the Nature of Mass Movements* (New York: Harper and Row, 1951). I have modernized his language slightly.

[32]Probably the best analysis of the origins and "natural histories" of social reform movements is contained in Armand L. Mauss, *Social Problems as Social Movements* (Philadelphia: Lippincott, 1975).

4

DEFINING SOCIAL PROBLEMS: THE VICTIM, THE MASS MEDIA, THE PSYCHIATRIST

The fact that certain circumstances are defined as problems raises several questions related to consensus and perception. The foremost are: Who defines a social problem? Who makes the diagnosis, the people involved? Outsiders? The people in charge, or, if you wish, the power structure? At one time, for instance, wife-battering was not considered a social problem; it was regarded as a rare occurrence. Who finally made the social problem diagnosis? In that case it was primarily feminists and battered women themselves—a crucial feature of the present political situation, for "whoever initially identifies a social problem shapes the initial terms in which it will be debated."[1]

To truly sense the importance of shaping the definitional terms in moral entrepreneurship, we can look at the abortion debate. This debate is essentially a nondebate: each side in its public front resolutely ignores the other's arguments; instead of answering them, each simply keeps reiterating its own position. And no matter what a logician might say about that, it is probably good strategy in this nondebating debate. We thus have two diametrically opposed groups vying to place their preferred labels in the public's consciousness. Observe how carefully the two sides choose their language. On the one side we have "freedom of choice" or "pro-choice." (And who could possibly be against giving a person free choice, especially with regard to her own body?) On the other side we have "right to life." (Who, after all, can oppose preserving

---

[1] James A. Jones, "Federal Efforts to Solve Contemporary Social Problems," in *Handbook on the Study of Social Problems*, ed. Erwin O. Smigel (Chicago: Rand McNally, 1971), p. 561.

life?) The struggle is over that entity in the womb that one side always calls "the fetus" and the other invariably calls "the unborn child." Fetuses sound like one of those bloody things with Latin names inside a person, whereas unborn children prompt an image of poor little helpless people awaiting birth. Anyone who regards these choices of terms as accidental is not getting my point.

The abortion debate is instructive because it is one of the few in North America that has persisted for a long time with no clear-cut winner, yet the entrepreneurs of each side are so hard at work. I do not wish to imply that one should simply be passive and not develop a viewpoint on so important a subject, but if just for the moment the two sides are viewed dispassionately, it is easy to understand moral entrepreneurship at work.

There is usually some disagreement not only on what constitutes a social problem but also concerning the severity or urgency of a social problem and, in terms of policy-making, on its national priority rating. Divergent opinions exist because those concerned will probably see phenomena somewhat differently depending on where they are situated in society and their vested interests and experiences.[2]

LIFE EXPERIENCES AND WORLDVIEW

This matter of perception can be illustrated by the following simple example. After a dry period, farmers will welcome rain since they depend on it for their crops. City dwellers who had intended to spend the weekend in the countryside will be unhappy; their leisure plans are defeated. Motel owners and innkeepers will be disappointed because the expected flow of tourists will not materialize. Children with lenient parents might be happy because they can run in the rain and splash passersby, but other children will be restrained at home and miserable. Therefore, one phenomenon, in this case rain, is perceived differently according to each individual's situation and how each is affected by it. Life circumstances color perceptions of even simple objects; this factor becomes much more complex and differentiated when it involves social situations.

It has been recently maintained, for instance, that heroin addiction came to be defined as a social problem by the population at large

---

[2]I use the term "situated" globally to include sex, age, race, and social class, as well as relevant psychosocial dimensions. A nice discussion of the two "levels" of competition (whether a condition is a problem at all and, if so, its urgency vis-à-vis other problems) is contained in Stephen Hilgartner and Charles L. Bosk, "The Rise and Fall of Social Problems: A Public Arenas Model," *American Journal of Sociology* 94 (1988), pp. 53–78.

only when whites began to be affected by it. According to this perspective, when addiction was mainly restricted to black ghettos it was merely seen as a crime, or as deviance. It did not affect the population at large, and most whites were utterly unconcerned about it—although social scientists and certain reformers had already sounded a warning. But when heroin addiction moved out of the ghettos into the suburbs, into the schools and universities, not to neglect the U.S. Army, a general alarm rang. As numerous white adolescents became addicted, as white police arrested whites like themselves, and as numerous crimes were committed against whites in order to pay for drugs, people came to be affected by this phenomenon in a different way. A vested interest in changing the situation developed. According to this perspective, heroin addiction came to be perceived as a social problem as a result of a shift in the circumstances of those who were in a position to define the situation. A similar process has also taken place with respect to venereal disease.

But it oversimplifies the role of perception to maintain that vested interest is at the bottom of all divergent views on social problems. And to say that one's life experiences influence one's views about events that directly relate to those experiences is no great discovery. What is much more significant is that differences in life experiences, repeated at length, can be equally effective in molding impressions of social problems *even where no personal interest is at stake and one has had no personal contact with a particular problem.*[3] We can see this most clearly in studies of the perceptual differences among persons in different occupations, since work consumes a major portion of an adult's waking experience. Even after differences in education and other variables are controlled, remarkable differences in viewpoint among members of widely divergent occupations have been the rule. Even more striking are studies showing that, across several societies, members of similar occupational groups tend to maintain the same differences from other occupational groups in their respective societies, in spite of considerable variations among the cultures studied. Manual workers, for instance, generally believe that human nature is more rigid than do nonmanual workers of the same culture; they are more interested in job security, place greater stress on obedience in children, advocate greater economic readjustments, join fewer voluntary organizations, and manifest many other prominent similarities vis-à-vis nonmanual occupations.[4] These and

---

[3]This line of research is nicely reviewed in the chapter by James House, "Social Structure and Personality," in Morris Rosenberg and Ralph H. Turner, eds., *Social Psychology: Sociological Perspectives* (New York: Basic Books, 1981), pp. 525–61.

[4]See, for example, Alex Inkeles, "Industrial Man: The Relation of Status to Experience, Perception, and Value," *American Journal of Sociology* 66 (1961), pp. 1–31.

similar findings are constant across cultures that are quite divergent in many respects, leading one to believe that the day-to-day experiences of people are of major importance in shaping their general views of the world (a phenomenon studied under the rubric of the sociology of knowledge). Not surprisingly, this influence carries over into the definition of social problems by various groups in the population; in later chapters I will examine more closely just how their location in society influences the views of intellectuals (Chapter 5) and judges (Chapter 9).

But we have only begun to discuss the question initially raised: "Who diagnoses a condition as a social problem?" I have only said so far that the definition of a social problem depends on the perception of those who take part in the process of defining, and that, in turn, perceptions will be affected by the individuals' general situation in the society, by their situation vis-à-vis the phenomenon in question, and by their vested interests.[5] A corollary to be studied is the distinction between definition of a social problem by the individuals personally affected and definition by people who are relatively untouched by the problem in their personal lives.

DEFINITIONS BY THOSE INVOLVED

People can be affected by a social problem along three general lines of involvement. The first type is *voluntary involvement, with no immediately apparent victim.* Here the persons afflicted by the problem—at least afflicted from an observer's point of view—are also the main agents or play the main voluntary roles in their affliction. Various mental disturbances, drug addiction, alcoholism, and such "victimless crimes" as prostitution fall into this class.[6] (It should be emphasized that under another perspective this same group of individuals can be viewed as victims of particular social conditions. In this interpretation their current affliction is the ultimate result of such conditions.)

The second category again concerns *voluntary involvement,* but covers activities in which the main actors in the problem do not directly suffer from their acts; they usually have *others as victims.* This category contains the predators. However, many criminals—the most ubiquitous actors in this category—eventually suffer because of their acts or the

---

[5] For further discussion on the social origins of modes of thought, see the classic work on the sociology of knowledge, Karl Mannheim's *Ideology and Utopia,* trans. Louis Wirth and Edward Shils (New York: Harvest, 1936).

[6] We are using the concept of victimless crime for prostitution as it is referred to in current literature. However, from other ideological positions, we can consider that prostitution does have a victim in our society: the prostitute.

labels they receive. From the latter vantage point, society itself inflicts suffering in the hope of reducing "aggregate suffering" by punishment of the few. Criminals thus can be both willing agents and victims. Additionally, of course, criminals can be regarded as victims of social conditions that "drove" them to crime.

The third form of involvement consists of the pure victims of others' acts or of society's failings, individuals who *suffer directly but accidentally* from a problem, playing only a derivative or even random role in their plight. Victims of theft, robbery, assault, or homicide come to mind first, but victims of discrimination, unemployment, and harassment, as well as the children of divorce and of various types of psychologically broken homes fall under this category. Witnesses of violent crimes or other undesirable conditions may be included among victims, inasmuch as they are adversely affected by what took place.[7]

It could be advanced that since some crimes that are objectively inoffensive to the bystander and to the actor are defined as social problems by so many individuals, we should have a fourth category of individuals affected by a social problem: those whose values or sense of morality is offended.[8] This is a legitimate viewpoint; however, I have chosen to discuss such "victims" in Chapter 3 under the rubric of moral entrepreneurs. Most individuals whose values are threatened do not become active in moral crusades, but their viewpoints are nevertheless similar.

I should note that individuals may be afflicted by a social problem in more than one way. This is not uncommon and indeed for some problems it is the rule. It is one of the pernicious aspects of heroin addiction, for instance, that individuals regularly progress from one involvement category to the next. In the beginning, they are typically willing agents (possibly also victims of society's failings). As time passes they may first inflict unintentional suffering on their families, and then be driven to property crime to sustain their habit. Ultimately, many addicts become heroin peddlers themselves since this offers one of the more lucrative ways to earn the necessary money. At any point along this progression they may be incarcerated, and suffer various forms of misery at the hands of the law. In this all-too-common "career" progression, an addict's involvement category may change from willing participant to aggressor to victim.

---

[7]In some types of problems the suffering of each victim is minute but suffering is great for the aggregate, for society as a whole. Price fixing, for instance, may cost each customer only a few cents more yet be quite costly for the economy. These and similar white-collar crimes typically do not evoke as much rage in the victim as in the expert who can see the overall damage.

[8]Yet another affected category would be those people professionally involved in dealing with a perceived problem. We will consider these persons in Chapter 5.

Now the importance of this classification of involvement lies in the fact that the impression of whether a condition is a social problem, as well as of its degree of severity, will to a great extent depend on which of the three categories the definer falls into. (Of course, the definer also may be a relatively uninvolved observer, as I discuss elsewhere.) Let us start with the third category. The victim who is unwillingly affected and plays only an accidental role in, say a theft, is likely to reach the conclusion that such a phenomenon is a major problem. He or she is directly involved yet did not wish to be, probably having had no choice in a decision reached by another person.[9] The reactions of victims are varied but generally include feelings of unfairness, anger, hurt, and strong disapproval. These feelings will intensify if victims become aware of and establish contact with others who have gone through the same experience, a process known as "consciousness raising." Of considerable significance in terms of the strength of the reaction is the degree to which the victim felt the adverse condition was intended by those responsible. This is why, for example, violent crime is viewed as a serious problem by everyone, whereas population pressure is viewed as a major social problem only after careful study—even though the latter may in the long run prove a far more serious problem. Also, actions like price fixing, which hurt everyone a little bit, will be seen as less severe and accorded less attention than actions like muggings, which hurt a few people a great deal, even though the aggregate hurt may be much greater for the former.

No discussion of the victim would be complete without a brief look at the burgeoning field of *victimology*. Virtually unheard of twenty-five years ago, the subject at this point in time has generated voluminous literature. Some say it is destined to become a discipline of its own, incorporating parts of sociology, psychology, ethics, and law.[10] Victimology is predicated on the principle that the victim is the forgotten actor in social problems, while perpetrators and the criminal justice system hog the limelight. Examinations start with who suffers victimization, types of victimization, and when and where it occurs. Some studies deal with victim precipitation, emphasizing how some events are triggered, as it were, by the victim.

The major emphasis, however, is on the victim's "second victimization" by the criminal justice system, stressing the offender's sup-

---

[9]The situation is not always so simple; as the growing field of victimology teaches us, there may be on occasion recognizable patterns of victim-precipitated crime. See, on the general subject, *Victimology: A New Focus*, vols. I and II, ed. I. Drapkin and E. Viano (Lexington, Mass.: Lexington Books, 1973).

[10]I will concentrate on the "narrow" conception of victimology, which for the most part considers victims of crime. A far broader interpretation of the field is employed by some. For the latter, see Robert Elias, *The Politics of Victimization* (New York: Oxford University Press, 1986).

posed "paradise of rights" in contrast to the victim's situation. (I must tell the reader that I am not sympathetic to the notion that accused persons have a surplus of rights, much as I empathize with the victim's problems.) At this point the notion is that victims should have rights too. It is clear that in many cases the victim's most active role in the process consists of agreeing to dismiss charges. It is also the sad fate of victims to realize that the criminal justice process is oriented today toward achieving rapid disposition of cases, rather than the adversarial confrontation we hear so much about. When confrontation does occur in a trial, victims are cross-examined so fiercely that many feel it is they who are on trial rather than the defendants.

Most relevant to our concerns in this chapter is the emergence of *victim advocacy*, with its central notion of victim rights. Studies of victims' needs and special problems have been made, and victim assistance programs have been initiated, including victim compensation. Victim advocacy organizations are clearly prominent in defining social problems.[11]

A problematic situation is perceived quite differently by the second category of actors, those who do not suffer immediately from their acts.[12] This is especially well illustrated in the case of organized crime. Some who have been personally victimized may call organized crime a social problem, but the criminal actors themselves do everything to alter this definition and, especially, the consequences of the label—which can involve stiffer penalties, drainage of their illegal market, and loss of power and police cooperation. They frequently use their connections and advantages—legal and illegal—to silence opposition. For them, organized crime is first of all a means of living and a life-style, not a problem, and at times they publicly rationalize certain aspects of their role as providing a "public service." Western culture frequently outlaws activities that many people enjoy doing, and plan to continue to do. Inasmuch as organized crime facilitates these illicit activities, it may on occasion be correct in this "public service" assessment. If the actors have sufficient power and a certain popular legitimacy, a long time may elapse before the consequences of their acts are defined as problematic or, for that matter, are fully brought to the attention of the public.

When the main actors are also the sufferers, as in the first category, their definition of a condition as problematic is typically most ambivalent. This ambivalence is partly created by the situational passivity of certain individuals (e.g., in mental disturbance) and, in other cases, is

---

[11] An excellent overview of the entire field, with voluminous references, is contained in Elias, *Victimization*.

[12] For a classical account of how delinquents rationalize their activities, see G. M. Sykes and D. Matza, "Techniques of Neutralization: A Theory of Delinquency," *American Sociological Review* 22 (1957), pp. 664–70.

because the afflicted enjoy aspects of their problem (e.g., heroin's effects) and, at least for the time being, are sufferers only in the minds of others. The individuals may or may not define their own situation as problematic. Factors that contribute to these individuals' definition of their own situation include the nature of their reference group, awareness of alternatives, and acquaintance with others in the same predicament.

The contention by some that only those persons who are directly afflicted by a situation have the right to label it as a problem is difficult to resolve. For one thing, we would have to specify what is meant by "directly afflicted." For instance, would we include those people whose moral values are threatened by the acts of others (people who disapprove of "free love," for instance)? And if people with serious emotional disturbances never perceive their condition as deleterious, does it mean that mental disorders are not problematic? Does it consequently mean that nothing should be done to help these individuals, except to allow them to follow the threads of what are called their fantasies or withdrawals?

The last-mentioned problem is very complex, generating a wide range of views. At one extreme are those who rigidly codify all behavioral peculiarities as at best neurotic, and who insist on viewing any behavior different from their norms as a symptom of an illness that should be alleviated. At the other extreme are various groups who believe that only individuals can tell what is right and wrong for them and if they do not perceive their "problems" as such, then they are not problems. Within this conception, mental "illness" is considered to be only a myth, conceived by a repressive society that controls individual idiosyncrasies through a cohort of agents of social control (that is, the psychiatric community and brethren).[13] Some advocates of this view also maintain that since it is the society that is mad, the individual's mental state, however it may appear to an observer, is a normal response to unhealthy stimuli. The person's conduct should therefore be left to run its course uninterrupted. Finally, psychological symptoms viewed as pathological by some are seen by others merely as "strategies to achieve autonomy and self-consistency."[14] "Normality" is only a product of repression because it means conformity to an abnormal society.[15]

---

[13] See works referenced in Portland K. Frank, *The Antipsychiatry Bibliography/Resource Guide* (Vancouver: Press Gang Publishers, 1979). Such positions led to the creation of the American Association for the Abolition of Involuntary Mental Hospitalization. A related ideological issue is raised by those who define law enforcement officials as the source of social problems and the "criminals" they arrest as the victims. This is of course an extreme version of the labeling perspective (see Chapter 8).

[14] See David Cooper, *The Death of the Family* (New York: Vintage Books, 1970).

[15] R. D. Laing, *The Politics of Experience* (London: Penguin Books, 1967).

Different types of treatment parallel these polar definitions of mental illness. On one extreme are shock treatments and chemotherapy, usually accompanied by a degree of social isolation. In the middle of the spectrum are various types of psychotherapies, and at the other extreme are very liberal and radical therapies, some of which merely allow psychotic symptoms to be expressed within a protective and supportive environment without chemical or psychiatric interference. However, all these viewpoints still share at least one result: the afflicted individual *is* treated differently, even if the differential treatment consists only in an overnight shelter for an "acting out." It is true that certain theoreticians in the field believe that each of us will sooner or later need to act out "symptoms" and that this is only a natural response to the pressures of an unhealthy environment. But, while it is the unhealthy environment that is the diagnosed ill in such views, a social problem is nevertheless perceived; moreover, it is at least implicitly held that those so touched need assistance, if only special understanding. Therefore, no matter what the philosophical orientation, a problem of some sort is definitely acknowledged.

In the end it proves impossible to restrict the prerogative of defining a problem solely to those directly affected by it. But the notion that they should somehow have *greater* say in its delineation than others who are mere onlookers still seems reasonable.

DEFINITIONS BY THE MASS MEDIA

It is probably obvious that the mass media have become exceedingly important in defining social problems.[16] The reason, of course, is that the public in its definitional role does not respond to reality but to its perception of that reality.[17] The media play a central role in shaping the image of reality to which the public responds: mass communication provides visibility for potential issues.[18] Professional and intellectual definers—discussed at length in Chapter 5—play their definitional

---

[16]My discussion of the media here centers on its definitional role. Mass communications can themselves be considered a social problem in certain contexts. The role of portrayals of violence and crime in the media, media's effect on audience passivity, its intrusion into family relations, and information pollution and overload are some of the issues evoked.

[17]See, for general orientation, Peter L. Berger and Thomas Luckmann, *The Social Construction of Reality* (Garden City, N.Y.: Doubleday, 1966). For greater specificity with respect to mass media, see Daniel J. Boorstin, *Image: A Guide to Pseudo-Events in America* (New York: Atheneum, 1962).

[18]Robert Ross and Graham L. Staines, "The Politics of Analyzing Social Problems," *Social Problems* 20 (1972), p. 22.

roles in great part through the media. The media also fulfill an important role in determining whether a problem is assigned legitimacy as a social issue or is discredited as illegitimate.[19]

It is part of the nature of modern mass communications that a relatively small number of *gate-keepers* at the control centers can determine what we shall see and what we shall read.[20] Many dangers are inherent in this situation, in which what might be called a "delegate approach" to social problems has come into existence. This does not imply that the mass media are all-powerful in invoking a social problem label. Students of communication have long abandoned the simplistic viewpoint that the media audience is passive in favor of considering the audience as interpreters.[21] Rather it is the negative side, that *abstention by the media can frequently* preclude *recognition of a problem, that is so important.* In this respect the importance of the gate-keepers in mass communication can hardly be overemphasized. This potential to bring some issues to the fore and to relegate others to obscurity is known as *agenda-setting.* Who the persons are at the key decision-making posts in television, newspapers, and other media—their personal backgrounds and social position—has come under increasing scrutiny in recent years.[22] The concentration of media ownership into a few hands, such as newspaper chains, cable conglomerates, and communities in which all media (radio, newspaper, etc.) are controlled by a single owner, has been multiplying. With the power this conveys for informal censorship, these trends have repeatedly interested researchers, not to mention congressional investigating committees.[23]

A prime danger inherent in the mass media definition of social problems is that it may invite only the briefest and most superficial pub-

---

[19] *Ibid.* See also Ralph Turner, "The Public Perception of Protest," *American Sociological Review* 34 (1969), pp. 815–31.

[20] For an excellent illustration of the power of gate-keepers, see David Manning White, "The Gate-Keeper: A Study of the Selection of News," in *People, Society, and Mass Communication,* ed. Louis A. Dexter and David Manning White (New York: Free Press, 1968). The study superbly demonstrates the sheer impossibility of reporting all of the news that comes in via the wire services, let alone all news. Selectivity is unavoidable, and the power of the gate-keeper is unmistakable.

[21] This interpretation is most clearly stated in Joseph Klapper's classic, *The Effects of Mass Communication* (Glencoe, Ill.: Free Press, 1959). For recent interpretations giving the media far more power, see the chapter by Kurt and Gladys Lang, in M. Rosenberg and R. H. Turner, eds., *Social Psychology: Sociological Perspectives* (New York: Basic Books, 1981). Certainly it is not impossible for a social problem to rise into prominence with little help from the media. The environmentalist movement, for example, seems to have come to the attention of the daily press very belatedly. See A. Clay Schonefeld et al., "Constructing a Social Problem: The Press and the Environment," *Social Problems* 27 (1979), pp. 38–61.

[22] See, for example, Herbert Gans, *Deciding What's News* (New York: Pantheon Books, 1979).

[23] A valuable work here is Benjamin M. Compaine, ed., *Who Owns the Media? Concentration of Ownership in the Mass Communications Industry* (White Plains, N.Y.: Knowledge Industry Publications, 1982).

lic commitment to solving a problem. Because of the nature of commercialized mass culture, social problems tend to become fads when portrayed by the media. They are "sold" to the public, packaged in attractive, sensationalist wrappings. Newspaper reports of "crime waves," for example, are as old as newspapers themselves, and bear only the vaguest relationship to actual fluctuations in the number of criminal offenses.[24] Because the mass media are money-making ventures, if one topic becomes "obsolete" by no longer attracting as many viewers or readers, it is reasonable to expect a shift to another, more lucrative fad. Even the news reports are affected by the need for novelty. When a problem bursts into public consciousness, it may make the news broadcasts every evening for an entire month, or even longer, as was the case with the hostage crisis in Iran. But rarely is such attention sustained; normally after a few weeks it is no longer news—it is a fact. The mass media neglect it and so do we. It has lost its topicality. In recent memory this has happened to the Palestinian *intifadah* (uprising) in the Gaza Strip and to the starving millions in the Sudan and Ethiopia. One could get the impression that these situations are much improved, or even resolved. We have perhaps become conditioned to having others think for us and define situations for us via the media. When the media shift gear, we tend to erase from our consciousness what no longer appears on the screen. We even may be foolish enough to believe that the problem has vanished, just because we no longer see it. Our conceptions of social problems themselves become fads, temporarily gripping and soon to drift into oblivion—but not erased from reality.[25]

What is it that makes something "newsworthy," at least in the mind of the gate-keeper? We have already touched on the gate-keeper aspect itself, and on the presumed need for topicality or frequent change of topic. One additional feature is the notion of a necessary velocity for an event to become news. Every occurrence needs a time span to unfold itself; the less an event's speed of unfolding matches the usual frequency or speed of events reported by a communications medium, the less likely it will be communicated as news by that medium. News media in

---

[24]For an excellent example of how crime waves are constructed in the media, see Mark Fishman, "Crime Waves as Ideology," *Social Problems* 25 (1978), pp. 531–43. I will discuss this issue again later in the chapter.

[25]One could easily adopt McLuhan's statement that newspaper editors have discovered that "news is what gets printed. If it isn't in print, it isn't news." He might have said, "If it isn't in print, it isn't a social problem." Marshall McLuhan, "The Electronic Age—The Age of Implosion," in *Mass Media in Canada*, by John A. Irvin (Toronto: Ryerson Press, 1962), pp. 179–205. One other effect of this is to bias the impact of news according to its *availability*. The Vietnam War was directly accessible to Western news media, and appeared on television screens daily for years in gory detail, generating unprecedented emotional protest. In contrast, the Iran-Iraq war, which by some accounts had nearly a million casualties, received very little coverage because Western news personnel were forbidden entry. Therefore the war had little impact and generated only scattered protest.

general concentrate on relatively fast-breaking events. The slow, glacial emergence of some problems does not lend these problems to news presentation, and although they may eventually become of overwhelming importance, they are rarely reported.

The population explosion is an excellent case in point. Here we have an event shaping the destiny of nations and affecting the quality of life of every inhabitant on the planet, yet it is not news. At least, it is not "news" as ordinarily considered. It is too slow in its progress. Every day some 250,000 *additional* persons populate the earth—250,000 more than the day before needing food, clothing, shelter, schools, and hospitals. The consequences in the long run are catastrophic, but the operative principle as far as "newsworthiness" is concerned lies in the key words "every day." Since this happens every day, day after day, it is somehow not news. On no single day does the population explosion leap out in some fashion, like the death of a famous movie star. So, too, the gradual despoliation of lakes from acid rain, the gradual erosion of topsoil, and the gradual deforestation of the globe do not generate news on any given day and are "lost." If, however, one hundred persons splash green paint on a monument in protest against deforestation, that will make the news.[26] The long-run effect of such a strange, perverse news situation is clearly to grossly distort public understanding of major forces at work in the world, with commensurate misunderstanding of social problems.

The hypothetical green-paint demonstration just mentioned brings us to a related topic: the "manufacture" of news. The notion of manufacturing can be considered in two related ways. The broader aspects have to do with the growing recognition that life is not a set of discrete public events that can simply be mirrored by newspeople. News is manufactured; it is a product—a product not only of reality-describing activities but also of reality-making activities. Hence a critical sociological task, reflected in a growing list of studies, is to concretely examine newsworkers' transformations of the everyday world into published or broadcast stories.[27] The other meaning of "manufactured" refers to news deliberately created solely in order to convey a particular message. Daniel Boorstin's book, *Image*, deals extensively with media events that have no independent reason for existence other than to attract media atten-

---

[26]For more on this paragraph's topic, see Johan Galtung and Mari Ruge, "Structuring and Selecting News," in *The Manufacture of News*, ed. S. Cohen and J. Young (Beverly Hills: Sage Publications, 1973). For an excellent article on time scales and their general importance, see William C. Clark, "Scale Relationships in the Interactions of Climate Ecosystems and Societies," pp. 337–78 in Kenneth C. Land and Stephen H. Schneider, eds., *Forecasting in the Social and Natural Sciences* (Dordrecht, Neth.: D. Reidel, 1987).

[27]As exemplars of the trend, see Cohen and Young, *Manufacture*; Mark Fishman, *Manufacturing the News* (Austin: University of Texas Press, 1980); Gaye Tuchman, *Making News: A Study in the Construction of Reality* (New York: Free Press, 1978).

tion and get a particular message across. Such "happenings" are engineered or staged. Public demonstrations, hunger strikes, and similar events are sufficiently striking and unusual to be newsworthy; they are the "little people's" equivalent of the press conference of the powerful—also a pure media event.

Related to the idea of manufacturing news is the powerful new conception of *bureaucratic propaganda*. Propaganda was formerly considered a tool of national governments, akin to psychological warfare or possibly to religious proselytization (where the term "propaganda" originated).[28] But recently an extension of the term has been proposed in order to include corporations, industries, and government bureaucracies.[29] Bureaucratic propaganda encompasses vast efforts we have all noticed at one time or another to bring an audience around to the special viewpoint of a particular bureaucracy. It includes such important activities as *institutional advertising*, in which, for instance, oil companies attempt to build trust or show that their profits were justified, rather than just to sell brand X of gasoline. It includes as well all manner of puffery by government agencies on what a great job they did (hundreds of thousands of cases processed) or, conversely, what a terrible task they are facing (rising crime in the streets). In bureaucratic propaganda, the power of major institutions in modern society is harnessed to manipulate or at least shift the attention of the media in the desired direction.

Most social problems are not concerns of the majority of citizens, so the role of important elites and the media in disseminating ideas and "facts" is frequently crucial in influencing public opinion. Inasmuch as the public relies on the media for information, the magnitude of a problem may be grossly misinterpreted. Lack of knowledge and systematic misunderstandings about crime and criminal justice are endemic.[30] I have already noted that fluctuations in media crime coverage over time bear little relationship to fluctuations in the actual number of crimes being committed.[31] A related point is that the crimes mentioned the most in the media are not the crimes that happen most often; in fact one researcher found that "the relative frequency with which crimes were reported bore no relationship to their relative frequency in criminal statistics."[32] So, on what do people rely, the actual rates and fluctuations or

---

[28] See Terence H. Qualter, *Propaganda and Psychological Warfare* (New York: Random House, 1962).

[29] See the innovative work by David L. Altheide and John M. Johnson, *Bureaucratic Propaganda* (Boston: Allyn & Bacon, 1980).

[30] See R. L. Henshel and R. Silverman, eds., *Perception in Criminology* (New York: Columbia University Press, 1975).

[31] F. Janes Davis, "Crime News in Colorado Newspapers," *American Journal of Sociology* 57 (1952), pp. 325–30.

[32] R. Roshier, "The Selection of Crime News by the Press," in S. Cohen and J. Young, eds., *The Manufacture of News: Social Problems, Deviance, and the Mass Media* (Beverly Hills: Sage Publications, 1981), p. 44.

the media rates and fluctuations? Well, in Canada Lynn McDonald has provided overwhelming evidence of the poor fit between fluctuations in fear of crime and actual shifts in volume of crime.[33] And, more directly, a survey carried out in Colorado indicated that perception of the danger from certain crimes was related to the newspaper coverage they received rather than to the crime rates themselves.[34]

Similarly, a study of two U.S. newspapers' coverage of life-threatening events revealed very strong biases: some threats to life were greatly over-reported (e.g., accidents, homicides) and some were greatly under-reported (e.g., disease-related deaths). Further, although the two newspapers were on opposite coasts, their biases were very similar. The authors then looked at people's judgments on the relative frequency of different causes of death and found them to be highly correlated with the biased coverages just described.[35] The mistaken judgments in this paragraph and the one before it stem from the greater availability of certain events in people's memory due to recurrent descriptions in the media.[36]

Media emphasis on certain problems thus blinds us to others still only vaguely perceived, a situation that may have serious consequences. For instance, some black leaders have attacked the emphasis on pollution as a false issue that diverts attention away from the "truly severe crises" in the cities. The treatment of crime has had similar criticism. Burglaries attract far greater press coverage than white-collar or government-sanctioned political crimes, although the latter may cost citizens many times their losses suffered from burglaries and/or may weaken important political freedoms.[37] Popular emphasis on new problems—or more sensational ones—may relegate others already diagnosed to the background, or even to an inadvertent blackout of coverage.[38] Gallup Polls running from 1935 through the late 1970s show certain patterns in public definitions of problems and in the concerns

---

[33]Lynn McDonald, *The Sociology of Law and Order* (Montreal: Book Centre, 1976).

[34]Davis, *Crime News*.

[35]A study by Coobs and Slovic, reported in Paul Slovic et al., "Fact versus Fears: Understanding Perceived Risk," in D. Kahneman, P. Slovic, and A. Tversky, eds., *Judgment under Uncertainty: Heuristics and Biases* (Cambridge: Cambridge University Press, 1982), pp. 463–89.

[36]I am referring to what Kahneman, Slovic, and Tversky in *Judgment* call the "availability heuristic," a key factor in explaining judgmental errors.

[37]See August Bequai, *White Collar Crime: A 20th Century Crisis* (Lexington, Mass.: Lexington Books, 1978); Nelson Blackstock, *COINTELPRO: The FBI's Secret War on Political Freedom* (New York: Random House, 1975); and Julian Roebuck and Stanley C. Weeber, *Political Crime in the United States: Analyzing Crime By and Against Government* (New York: Praeger, 1978).

[38]See Chapter 2 of James C. Hackler, *The Prevention of Youthful Crime: The Great Stumble Forward* (Toronto: Methuen, 1978).

held at different times.[39] As Liazos points out, these responses turn out to be largely dictated by the current fads of the media, which in turn are greatly affected by centers of power.[40]

Finally, it is important to realize that the media influence our views of the world not only through the news they present but also through popular fictional dramas. These dramas inform us, or misinform us, about events, personalities, and historical incidents just as effectively as the material we see in regular news programs. For example, MacDonald has documented the incredible outpouring of fictional depictions of communism during the period of "devout anti-communism" in the 1950s.[41] Whereas the lion's share of research regarding media effects on adults has dealt with the formal news, studies such as MacDonald's of the content of our daily diet of fictional drama can reveal the influences of the media at work here as well.

In a lonely place,
I encountered a sage
Who sat, all still,
Regarding a newspaper

He accosted me:
"Sir, what is this?"

Then I saw that I was greater,
Ay, greater than this sage.

I answered him at once,
"Old, old man, it is
*   the wisdom of the age."*

The sage looked upon me with
*   admiration.*

Stephen Crane

---

[39] See these polls surveyed in Robert H. Lauer, "Defining Social Problems: Public and Professional Perspectives," *Social Problems* 22 (1976), pp. 122–28. A Canadian survey is reported in Reginald W. Bibby, "Consensus in Diversity: An Examination of Canadian Social Problem Perception," *International Journal of Comparative Sociology* 20 (1979), pp. 274–82. For relevant findings on the international scale, see Graeme Newman, *Comparative Deviance: Perception and Law in Six Cultures* (New York: Amer. Elsevier, 1976).

[40] Alexander Liazos, "The Poverty of the Sociology of Deviance: Nuts, Sluts, and Preverts," *Social Problems* 20 (1972), pp. 103–20.

[41] J. Fred MacDonald, *Television and the Red Menace* (New York: Praeger, 1985). For an analysis of ideological dramas in the motion-picture industry, see Terry Christensen, *Reel Politics* (New York: Basil Blackwell, 1987).

DEFINITIONS OF SOCIAL PROBLEMS
BY PSYCHIATRY

Contemporary psychiatry constitutes one of the strongest and most rapidly expanding bases for defining social problems. The twentieth century has witnessed its expansion into entirely new domains formerly thought to be populated by the criminal or the weak-willed—sexual psychopaths (rapists), sociopaths (evil people), alcoholics (drunkards), compulsive overeaters (gluttons), and soldiers with combat fatigue (malingerers and deserters). We need to ask (but not necessarily answer) how much mental illness is real and how much is so defined through a strange alliance of accusers, accused, and professional empire-builders. Along the way we will briefly look at the misuse of psychiatric labels to describe groups whose actions we simply cannot understand. Notwithstanding the expansion successes of psychiatry, the very basis for its authority has come under attack from within, as will be seen in this chapter and in Chapter 9.[42]

It is an old realization that psychiatry needs patients, not only for purposes of employment but in order to socially validate its role. Whenever a group's beliefs are challenged, it can seek "confirmation" (in a psychological sense only) by convincing others of these beliefs and then, in effect, listening to them. This approach, termed "social validation,"[43] can be used in psychiatry because the psychiatrists themselves hold the power of saying how many mentally ill people exist.[44] Thus Sutherland's study in 1950 of the development and diffusion of laws regarding "sexual psychopaths" depicted a tendency of the psychiatric profession to persuade legal authority to redefine existing social problems in psychiatric terms, "from badness to madness."[45] Attempts to "psychiatrize" criminal justice continue, even though the belief that the majority of deviance in society is the product of sick personalities is devoid of scientific support.[46]

[42] See Edwin M. Schur, "Psychiatrists under Attack, the Rebellious Dr. Szasz," *The Atlantic* (June 1966), pp. 72–76. Szasz stood virtually alone at first, but some of his views have since been adopted by a veritable army of advocates.

[43] For an excellent analysis and example of social validation at work, see Leon Festinger, et al., *When Prophecy Fails* (Minneapolis: University of Minnesota Press, 1956).

[44] See Richard Hawkins and Gary Tiedeman, *The Creation of Deviance* (Columbus, Ohio: Merrill, 1975), pp. 152–55.

[45] Edwin H. Sutherland, "The Diffusion of Sexual Psychopath Laws," *American Journal of Sociology* 56 (1950), pp. 142–48.

[46] For a brief overview on this point, see Edmund Vaz, *Aspects of Deviance* (Toronto: Prentice-Hall Canada, 1976), pp. 28–29. For a thorough analysis of the "medicalization" of deviance, see Peter Conrad and Joseph Schneider, *Deviance and Medicalization: From Badness to Sickness* (St. Louis: Mosby, 1980).

Thomas Szasz has introduced a far more radical critique of psychiatric competence by questioning the correctness of the analogy between physical and mental illness.[47] Szasz emphasizes the ability to fake symptoms of mental disorder, the lack of any independent proof, and the transference of the prestige of the medical profession into an arena in which cure rates are low[48] and indeed the very conception of "patients" and "diagnoses" may be *misapplied*.[49] He maintains that he is not antipsychiatry (he is indeed a professional psychoanalyst and a more orthodox Freudian than most), but challenges what he sees as the misuse of psychiatry—for instance, forensic psychiatry's "expert testimony" on the sanity of an accused person.[50] Quite evidently the accused have every reason to fake the cues of mental illness, and the outcome may depend more on faking ability (to escape a harsher environment) than on any psychiatrist's evaluation competence.[51]

The same difficulty is present to a lesser extent outside the courtroom. Szasz correctly notes that advantages often accrue to one who plays a role of being sick; the same advantages apply to mental illness, a deception harder to penetrate.[52] Some psychiatrists have claimed that a person who fakes mental illness *is* mentally ill by virtue of such a strange action, but surely no such complicated explanation is needed to account for the behavior of people who stand to gain much (or think they do) from obtaining verdicts of sickness.

Psychiatric labeling has historically had an important function: to alter the conception of certain deviant behaviors from misconduct to sickness. Inasmuch as the sick are usually treated with greater kindness than miscreants, this amounts to a promotion in terms of public reaction. Two prominent illustrations of this switch are the relabeling of alcoholism as a disease instead of a personal weakness and the

---

[47] Thomas S. Szasz, *The Myth of Mental Illness* (New York: Hoeber-Harper, 1961). See also Thomas Scheff, *Being Mentally Ill* (Chicago: Aldine, 1966); Merlin Taber et al., "Disease Ideology and Mental Health Research," *Social Problems* 26 (1969), pp. 349–57.

[48] See Bernie Zilbergeld, *The Shrinking of America: Myths of Psychological Change* (Boston: Little, Brown, and Co., 1983). See also Joseph J. Cocozza and Henry J. Steadman, "Prediction in Psychiatry: An Example of Misplaced Confidence in Experts," *Social Problems* 23 (1978), pp. 265–76.

[49] For excellent discussions of the failings of the medical model of mental illness, see Scheff, *Being Mentally Ill*, and Geoff Baruch and Andrew Treacher, *Psychiatry Observed* (Boston: Routledge, 1978).

[50] See Sara Fein and Ken S. Miller, "Legal Process and Adjudication in Mental Incompetency Proceedings," *Social Problems* 20 (1972), pp. 57–64.

[51] It is ironically true, however, that persons who are adjudged mentally incompetent to stand trial are sometimes kept in mental institutions for longer than the maximum sentence for which they might have been convicted.

[52] In effect, psychiatrists make decisions on cues "given off" rather than cues "given out," but such cues are not any less amenable to deception than others. Erving Goffman, *The Presentation of Self in Everyday Life* (Garden City, N.Y.: Doubleday Anchor, 1959).

recognition of shell shock as distinguishable from military malingering and desertion. However much the role of the sick carries its own disadvantages (see Chapter 9 on differential treatment), in most cases it is more advantageous than the role of the "weak-willed" that it replaces.[53]

Szasz seems to go one step further than this analysis; he appears to maintain that no mental illness exists at all except that which is organically caused. But there is really no need to take such a radical view in order to recognize the failings of psychiatric diagnosis and the profession's widespread unwillingness to face the reality that symptoms can be faked, accusers can lie, and motivations to do each are often present—with all that this implies.[54]

The importance of the defining potential of psychiatry is quite clear even in the case of persons about whom only an accusation of mental illness has been made; it is more striking when the psychiatric profession itself first brands a person or group as mentally imbalanced. Unofficial psychiatric diagnosis can be applied by laypersons, groups, or the subject of the diagnosis, or indeed any source outside the profession. In fact, this is frequently encountered in the conversation of laypersons as well as professionals; instant diagnosis of the "disorder" of some other person is endemic in sophisticated circles. It has become something of a conversational game to render quick judgment on the "mental problems" of a mutual acquaintance. But while these lay appraisals may be occasionally consequential for the subject being analyzed, it is when the psychiatric professionals themselves appraise candidates for political office, whole sectors of the population, occupational groups, or social movements that the power of psychiatric definition becomes most significant.

The potency of this particular labeling act derives from two primary sources. First, affixing a psychiatric brand to a group or movement may obviate the necessity to answer its arguments. Especially if the group is advocating something very different from current practice, the need for counterargument can be eliminated in a practical sense by explaining its actions as symptoms of an underlying mental difficulty—thus youthful, disruptive war protesters of the 1960s were "Spocked

---

[53]For a general view, see Hawkins and Tiedeman, *Deviance*, p. 250. For a specific topical discussion, see Herbert Fingarette, *Heavy Drinking: The Myth of Alcoholism as a Disease* (Berkeley: University of California Press, 1988).

[54]For spirited and informed *defenses* of the mental illness concept, see David P. Ausubel, "Personality Disorder is Disease," *American Psychologist* 16 (1961), pp. 69–74; Benjamin Pasamanick, "The Development of Physicians for Public Mental Health," *American Journal of Orthopsychiatry* 37 (1967), pp. 469–86; J. K. Wing, *Reasoning about Madness* (New York: Oxford University Press, 1978); and some of the essays in R. B. Edwards, ed., *Psychiatry and Ethics* (Buffalo: Prometheus Books, 1982). Contemporary critics of the medical model are legion; early references are cited in Taber et al., *Disease Ideology*.

when they should have been spanked." In far more sophisticated language, such major figures of modern psychiatric thought as Bruno Bettelheim have explained away leftwing protest by examining the individual backgrounds of the persons involved rather than their arguments. The same approach can be taken with respect to arguments of persons on the political far right.

The second source of power in the psychiatric label is that it is not punitive per se. It disarms resistance by pitying rather than condemning, especially when put into the guise of helpful diagnosis. When this is coupled with the expertise of the professional (and the professional's presumed detachment), the defenses usually available against a forthright attack are relatively ineffectual.

There are clear cases of abuse of the profession's defining and labeling power. In 1964, when psychiatrists were approached by the magazine *Fact* for their opinions of presidential candidate Barry Goldwater's mental condition, more than one hundred freely rendered their very negative "professional opinion" of his sanity without ever having spoken with Goldwater—although, to the credit of the profession, a large number evidently declined to express an opinion or replied that the procedure was incredible. Such branding, with the prestige of psychiatric medicine behind it, has been applied at various times to Hitler, Stalin, the Nazis, the Communists, the police (e.g., "sick authoritarians"), homosexuals, terrorists, ayatollahs, women's liberation supporters, male chauvinists—in fact, to anyone with whom a labeler does not sympathize.

This does not imply that psychiatric categorizing is done with deliberate cynicism; rather, *there is always a tendency to consider positions or actions that we cannot understand as insane,* and it is usually more difficult to consider as rational those positions that we do not agree with than those that we do. In a fine discussion of this form of fuzzy thinking, Elliot Aronson invokes Aronson's First Law: "People who do crazy things are not necessarily crazy."[55] Aronson goes on to point out that it does not advance either our understanding or our defensive effectiveness to apply psychiatric sickness labels to activities such as terrorism in which a sizable number of highly organized and effective persons are involved.

To be sure, some persons *are* mentally disturbed. But the appellations of "crazy," "sick," or "insane" seem to correspond with distressing regularity to the side of the fence opposite that of the labeler. Perhaps the best way to handle groups we cannot understand is to adopt Nietzsche's view in the following epigram.

---

[55] See his book, *The Social Animal*, 3rd ed. (San Francisco: Freeman, 1980), p. 8.

Insanity is the exception in individuals.
In groups, parties, peoples, and times, it is the rule.

F. W. Nietzsche

I can cite this delicious quote here because Nietzsche clearly does not mean insanity in any clinical sense, on pain of applying the term to the majority of humanity. Rather, maliciously, he means that most peoples engage in incomprehensible deviance (from a nonparticipant's standpoint) but few individual people do.

SUMMARY

In this chapter we have broached the central question of social problems: why some conditions become so defined, why others do not, why some are seen as more serious problems than others, and why some conditions exist for very long periods before being labeled problematic. Laying the groundwork for discussions in subsequent chapters, these questions were initially examined from the standpoint of the sociology of knowledge—the influence of one's life experiences and social location on views about the world, including aspects remote from one's own existence.

The discussion covered three possible sources of social problem views. First, the standpoints of persons directly involved were approached, ranging from the victim of the problem to the willing participant, and raising the issues of victimless crime, of the marginal status of much organized crime, and of persons who do not feel they have a psychiatric problem that someone else feels they have.

The singular importance of the mass media in shaping public views and policies toward social problems was emphasized. The numerous distortions that can arise from concentration of media ownership and from gate-keeper editorial control were stressed, as were the distorting requirements of topicality and event "velocity." The agenda-setting potential of the media was illustrated by "crime waves" that had no relationship to changes in crime volume. Finally, the manufacture of news and the import of bureaucratic propaganda was highlighted.

A third source of social problem definition, psychiatry, was addressed. The "psychiatrization" of traditional deviant behavior was examined, in terms of the profession's expansion and in terms of the advantages to the deviant of being considered "sick" rather than weak-willed or evil. The import of lying in response to accusations and of being able to fake symptoms were discussed. The common tendency to regard groups whose actions we cannot understand as mad or sick was seen to be counterproductive to sound explanations. In the next chapter we pursue further our basic concern, focusing on the definitional activities of intellectuals and experts.

5

DEFINING SOCIAL PROBLEMS: THE INTELLECTUAL, THE PROFESSIONAL

Much of the definitional task respecting social problems is performed not by moral entrepreneurs as ordinarily considered, nor by victims, the media, or psychiatry. Much is accomplished by intellectuals, chiefly writers and academics, and by experts on social problems. To take but a single example, the important feminist movement, which today has a very broad base of support, was initiated in the late 1960s almost exclusively by writers and academics.[1] In the pages that follow I consider intellectuals and experts more or less side by side.[2] This is not because of a lack of important differences between the generally knowledgeable person and the "authority," but because, like many other observers, I feel that the links between these two groupings are greater still, and are brought even closer by means of the modern university.

Focusing for a moment on the position of the expert—the professional—the need for specialists in fields of social problems has been increasingly recognized by both the general public and governmental authorities. Accompanying this is acknowledgement of the presumed expertise of the many professionals and semiprofessionals in numerous fields related to social problems. These professionals include criminologists, prison psychologists, social workers, sex therapists, marriage

---

[1] I really should say "regenerated" because of modern feminism's links to the earlier suffragette movement. By the late 1960s, that movement had been more or less dormant for decades.

[2] The debate about the proper definition of "intellectual" is seemingly endless. I will use the interpretation of Alvin Gouldner that intellectuals share a "culture of critical discourse." See pp. 28–29 of his book, *The Future of Intellectuals and the Rise of the New Class* (New York: Continuum, 1979).

counselors, psychiatrists, psychoanalysts, labor/management media-tors, geriatric specialists, suicidologists—the list grows lengthy. In addi-tion, one can detect growing acceptance of formal training programs, which grow in importance at the expense of skills learned on the job. In recent years demand has burgeoned for college-level courses and pro-grams teaching skills related to social problems. Although most of the specialties existed prior to their professionalization, newer fields are composed almost exclusively of professionals in the traditional sense, including such emerging classifications as suicidology and conflict res-olution. I will have more to say about the increasing professionalization of social problem experts in Chapter 11.

The role of the intellectual and the expert has a special cogency in our examination of the defining of social problems. For one thing, there is a long-standing claim that the intellectual is better equipped to diag-nose society's problems (and to prescribe solutions) than anyone else. This has been augmented in recent years by a separate but supportive claim that the intellectual and expert have gained—and are likely to continue to gain—additional power as society changes itself into a form that depends more and more on reliable knowledge. I lay out these claims in the next section and then skeptically examine them in the light of four "cautions." It was hard for me to do this—I am myself a member of the academic fraternity.

THE CLAIMS OF THE INTELLECTUAL AND THE EXPERT

One of the intellectuals' claims is anything but new; it follows the classi-cal notion of "philosopher-king" first articulated more than two thou-sand years ago in Plato's *Republic*. In this perspective, intellectuals (Plato's "philosophers") are best suited to lead society because they know so much more than anyone else, not merely in factual matters but in terms of their sensing of underlying relationships, deep historical and international perspectives, and (perhaps) a wisdom that comes from a lifetime of reading and absorbing ideas. In recent years this claim has been advanced in an oblique fashion by Allan Bloom as part of his well-known examination of the closing of the American mind.[3] Associated with this recurring claim of the intellectual to unique qualifications for the role of philosopher-king is a newer claim, based on social science and

---

[3] Allan Bloom, *The Closing of the American Mind* (New York: Simon and Schuster, 1987). For critical reviews of Bloom, see Harvey J. Graff in *Society* 25 (November-December 1987), pp. 98–101, and Benjamin Barber, "The Philosopher Despot," *Harper's* 276 (Janu-ary 1988), pp. 61–65.

allied disciplines, to what Lilienfeld has called the role of "scientist-king."[4] Some time ago one prominent sociologist depicted this latter claim as follows:

> Modern social scientists . . . no longer believe that men can rid their minds of impediments to lucid thought: *only scientists can*. . . . They assert that there is only one escape from the consequences of irrationality: that is by the application of scientific method. And this method can be used effectively only by the expert few. . . . Instead of attempting to make people more rational, contemporary social scientists often content themselves with asking of them that they place their trust in social science and accept its findings.[5]

The idea of the philosopher-king is ancient, and even the notion of the scientist-king is by now a well-established conceit. But in the last two decades these have been supplemented by a new claim based on the ongoing transformation of the modern world into what some have termed an "information society." In this new situation, on which numerous observers have commented, the production and distribution of knowledge have been systematized and supported as never before; concurrently, the "knowledge industry" assumes a centrality never before witnessed in history. And with this centrality, it is claimed, the scientist and the professional are destined to become more important than ever.

Whereas invention and discovery were formerly undertaken haphazardly, there has been, first, a gradual mating of science and technology and, more recently, the emergence of research and development as an industry in its own right. We are, as has been remarked, the first civilization to systematize the processes of innovation and discovery. (Alfred North Whitehead once noted that the greatest invention of the nineteenth century was the comprehension of the method of invention.) In the developed, industrial countries, research and development activity has attained a size that would have been unbelievable only a few decades ago, with support coming not solely, or even primarily, from universities but also from government as well as business interests. After specific innovations appear, their rapid and smooth introduction into the mainstream of economic and social life has itself become an area with its own expertise. In addition to basic research and development, an enormous coterie of investigators keeps tabs on every facet of our ongoing economic conditions, attitudes, and population characteristics.

---

[4]Robert Lilienfeld, *The Rise of Systems Theory: An Ideological Perspective* (New York: Wiley, 1978), p. 3.

[5]Reinhard Bendix, "The Image of Man in the Social Sciences: The Basic Assumptions of Present-Day Research," *Commentary* 11 (1951), pp. 187–92. Quote is from p. 190.

Throughout the Western world, then, this "knowledge industry" is today one of the largest economic units, and growing even larger.[6]

Numerous scholars have forecast that the production of knowledge will be the most important institution in the emerging society, variously known as the "post-industrial," "post-modern," or "technocratic" society. As stated in one of Daniel Bell's well-known works, the creation and utilization of theoretical knowledge will become the central, axial principle of this society. Decision-making itself will become the subject of an "intellectual technology" run by technocrats.[7] Due to these trends, and the concomitant occupational shifts, some have seen the professional and technical class emerging as the dominant occupational group in post-industrial society, with a commanding role being played by scientists, professionals, and technocrats—the experts I referred to earlier.

One writer, John Kenneth Galbraith, told us in 1967 about the rise of a "new estate" and what should be done with the power it grants. The elitist connotations in his writing are difficult to ignore: the academicians know best, and they now possess power.

> The requirements of technology and planning have greatly increased the need of the industrial enterprise for specialized talent and for its organization. The industrial system must rely, in the main, on external sources for this talent. Unlike capital it is not something that the firm can supply to itself . . . the mere possession of capital is now no guarantee that the requisite talent can be obtained and organized. One should expect, from past experiences, to find a new shift of power in the industrial enterprise, this one from capital to organized intelligence. And one would expect that this shift would be reflected in the deployment of power in the society at large. . . . Most directly nurtured by the industrial system are the educators and scientists in the schools, colleges, universities and research institutions. They stand in relation to the industrial systems much as did the banking and financial community to the earlier stages of industrial development. . . . And the values and attitudes of the society have been appropriately altered to reinforce the change.[8]

---

[6]For an excellent overview of the production, organization, distribution, application, and utilization of technical knowledge in the modern world, see Burkart Holzner and John A. Marx, *Knowledge Application: The Knowledge System in Society* (Boston: Allyn & Bacon, 1979).

[7]Daniel Bell, *The Coming of Post-Industrial Society* (New York: Basic Books, 1973). This theme—that knowledge production will be the major trait of our future society—also has been well developed by Peter F. Drucker in *The Age of Discontinuity* (New York: Harper and Row, 1969).

[8]John Kenneth Galbraith, *The New Industrial State* (Boston: Houghton Mifflin, 1967), pp. 57–58. Copyright © 1967 by John Kenneth Galbraith. Reprinted by permission of Houghton Mifflin Co.

What did Galbraith make of this phenomenon?

> Education . . . has now the greatest solemnity of social purpose. . . .
> With the rise of the technostructure, relations between those as-
> sociated with economic enterprise and the educational and sci-
> entific estate undergo a radical transformation. . . . At this stage,
> the educational and scientific estate is no longer small; on the
> contrary, it is very large. It is no longer dependent on private in-
> come and wealth for its support; most of its sustenance is pro-
> vided by the state. . . . Meanwhile the technostructure has become
> deeply dependent on the educational and scientific estate for its
> supply of trained manpower. . . . The educational and scientific
> estate is . . . growing rapidly in numbers. It still lacks a sense of its
> own identity. It has also sat for many years under the shadow of
> entrepreneurial power. . . . Yet it is possible that the educational
> and scientific estate requires only a strongly creative political
> hand to become a decisive instrument of political power.[9]

Galbraith's 1967 book must be regarded in many respects as a manifesto.
Indeed one journal, in reprinting certain sections, used the subtitle:
"Educators of the World, Unite!"[10]

I have highlighted Galbraith because the elitist program is presented most clearly in his work, but in fairness many other writers of the
period were saying virtually the same thing. Drucker advanced a similar
argument; Walter Lippmann presented an equally beguiling view of the
responsibilities—and the capacities—of the academics; Lipset and
Dobson maintained that intellectuals had become indispensable in both
capitalist and communist societies.[11] David Bazelon summed it up by
saying that "the intellectuals are coming on. They are increasingly
strong, confident, and assertive. They know they are needed—and they
are in fact needed more and more every day."[12]

Much of this sounds a bit embarrassing today. Galbraith and
Drucker writing in the 1960s on the invulnerability of the university in
the contemporary world will not convince academics today who have
watched their paychecks and scholastic budgets shrink all through the
Reagan decade and beyond. Nevertheless, the enhanced importance of
the intellectual and the expert in the emerging "information society,"
although inflated by these now-dated claims, remains an important no-

---

[9]*Ibid.*, pp. 288–89; 294–95.

[10]*Current* (October 1969), p. 19.

[11]Drucker, *Discontinuity*; Walter Lippmann, "The University," *The New Republic* (May 28,
1966), pp. 17–20; Seymour Martin Lipset and Richard B. Dobson, "The Intellectual as
Critic and Rebel: With Special Reference to the United States and the Soviet Union,"
Daedalus 101 (1972), pp. 137–98.

[12]David T. Bazelon, *The Paper Economy* (New York: Vintage Books, 1965), p. 319.

tion. And Allan Bloom has revitalized the claim of the philosopher (intellectual) elite.

The various claims of special enlightenment advanced on behalf of intellectuals and professionals raise a number of issues. First, the analyses of Galbraith and others seem to be saying that increased power for the knowledge industry is virtually inevitable—that, in fact, the industry will unavoidably become the single most powerful sector of society through some sort of structural necessity. But Anthony Giddens points out that this confuses indispensability and power: "if being indispensable necessarily confers power, then in a slave economy the slaves would be dominant."[13] A second issue is whether the evidence in fact shows that increased power is presently flowing to the knowledge sector. To examine this issue in depth here would take us too far off our course. The third issue takes us out of the realm of fact (or theory) in order to examine a normative question: *should* the knowledge sector be accorded a special status in view of its claims? In the remainder of this chapter I look critically at this question in terms of one major aspect: the influences and pressures on intellectuals and professionals that can create distortion in perspectives on social problems. We will examine, consecutively, the effects of common origins and experiences, ambitions and peer pressures, and institutional and expert viewpoints.

SELF-IMPOSED ISOLATION AND LOW EMPATHY OF INTELLECTUALS

In striking contrast to the just-mentioned endorsements of academia's power role, Eric Hoffer, the longshoreman-philosopher, has castigated intellectuals for being out of touch with the people. And indeed this seems to be an unavoidable dilemma: the views people hold are derived not only from a logical analysis of facts but from their own life experiences. If intellectuals are persons who make their way exchanging ideas, then their life experiences will be circumscribed by the world of literature, criticism, and scholarship. As Anderson and Murray put it, "Academics work with ideas, concepts, abstract relationships, and theories about people and things, more than they do with people and things."[14] Most academics have spent their entire adult lives in universities. In

---

[13] Anthony Giddens, *The Class Structure of the Advanced Societies* (London: Hutchinson, 1973), p. 173. See also his comments on pp. 195–96, 256–57, and 262–63.

[14] Charles H. Anderson and John D. Murray, eds., *The Professors* (Cambridge: Schenkman, 1971), p. 185. See also Paul F. Lazarsfeld and W. Thielens, Jr., *The Academic Mind* (Glencoe, Ill.: Free Press, 1958); Edward Shils, *The Intellectuals and the Powers and Other Essays* (Chicago: University of Chicago Press, 1972).

short, their expertise and proficiency with ideas will be great but their common experiences will tend to generate a common worldview, which may or may not be in the best interest of the rest of society.

Correspondence in backgrounds can apply not only to the professional lives and shared experiences of intellectuals but also to their social origins. A self-selection process is at work in most occupations, and intellectualdom is no exception with respect to occupational selection. Persons with certain personalities or values are attracted to such a life; others are repelled by it. As one striking example of this, more than half of the early American sociologists had a ministerial background, and even today an unusually high percentage once considered entering the clergy.[15] (I sometimes seem to concentrate on sociologists, but only because more is known about them than about other academicians.) Bell and Mau suggest that social scientists usually come from similar backgrounds and thus share similar biases.[16] These parallel experiences in both professional and earlier life can scarcely avoid producing certain tendencies in thinking—in particular, I suspect, in thinking about social problems and issues. Many have suggested that academia attracts young persons with liberal-left views because the vast majority of academics hold such views, while equally intelligent young persons with other beliefs move into different occupations.[17]

Another aspect to occupational selection operates here: selection into intellectualdom is based in large part on formal-education attainments, which further narrows the possible recruitment base. Then of course the education requisite for the intellectual life constitutes yet another variety of shared experience all members have in common, thus shaping a more uniform worldview.

What of the possibility of mitigating these tendencies by means of informal contacts? Anderson conducted a study of the friendship patterns of academic intellectuals, with striking results. He found that most academics virtually restricted their friends to other professors.[18] The number of nonacademic friends was small not only in an absolute sense but also in comparison to the situation Anderson found among members of other professions (e.g., lawyers and engineers), who had many more friends outside their own fields. With the further revelation that the aca-

[15]Roscoe C. Hinkle and Gisela J. Hinkle, *The Development of Modern Sociology* (New York: Random House, 1962); Alvin W. Gouldner, *The Coming Crisis of Western Sociology* (New York: Basic Books, 1970), p. 24.

[16]Wendell Bell and James A. Mau, "Images of the Future: Theory and Research Strategies," in *The Sociology of the Future*, ed. W. Bell and J. A. Mau (New York: Russell Sage Foundation, 1971).

[17]The political views of academics are examined in E. C. Ladd and S. M. Lipset, *The Divided Academy: Professors and Politics* (New York: McGraw-Hill, 1979).

[18]Charles H. Anderson, "Marginality and the Academic," in *The Professors*.

demics studied maintained very few ties with their kin and—except for other professors—very few neighborhood ties, the *isolation* of the academicians in terms of interpersonal experiences is striking. In Anderson's words, "Neither clique, kin, neighborhood, nor club acted as a social bridge to surrounding society."[19]

Such self-imposed isolation is not without its benefits in certain cases, but in terms of understanding and empathizing with everyday citizens, and of reordering society for their benefit, the disadvantages are painfully clear. Perhaps relatedly, researches on empathy—although of limited scope—seem to show consistently that social scientists are somewhat *less* competent in judging persons than lay individuals without professional training.[20] After an exhaustive review of such studies, one researcher concluded that "It is astounding that judges and correctional officials continue to view psychiatrists as experts on human behavior when there is considerable experimental evidence and other research which shows laymen superior to psychiatrists . . . in the judgment of people's motives, abilities, personality traits, and action tendencies."[21]

These studies have been concentrated in psychology and psychiatry, but not exclusively so. The research I have described on common backgrounds, common experiences, and self-imposed isolation provide some possible reasons for low empathy.

Another possible consequence of self-selection and self-isolation is a set of social priorities distinct from that of the general populace. Although Lauer did not have this particular issue in mind, his excellent demonstration of the great disparity between sociologists' lists of major social problems and lists generated by forty years of Gallup surveys of the general public is most revealing.[22]

---

[19]*Ibid.*, p. 210. The physical isolation of university towns and the concentration of scholars in cosmopolitan cities may also facilitate a breakdown of contact. See Lipset and Dobson, "The Intellectual," pp. 161–62, 192. And there is now a sufficient number of academics that exclusive mutual contact is feasible. See Edward Shils, *The Calling of Sociology* (Chicago: University of Chicago Press, 1980), especially p. 136.

[20]See, for example, R. Taft, "The Ability to Judge People," *Psychological Bulletin* 52 (1955), pp. 1–23. Taft surveyed some 81 studies of empathy in reaching his conclusion.

[21]M. Hakeem, "A Critique of the Psychiatric Approach to Crime and Corrections," *Law and Contemporary Problems* 23 (1958), pp. 650–82. The quote is from p. 682. Hakeem has made this point recently in *Theoretical Methods in Criminology*, ed. Robert F. Meier (Beverly Hills: Sage Publications, 1985). Taft's analysis has been updated by Theodore Sarbin, R. Taft, and D. E. Bailey, *Clinical Inference and Cognitive Theory* (New York: Holt, 1960), adding ten additional studies but coming to the same conclusion.

[22]R. H. Lauer, "Defining Social Problems: Public and Professional Perspectives," *Social Problems* 24 (1976), pp. 122–30. In this regard Robert Lekachman's account of the disparity between the economic priorities of the public and those of professional economists is also revealing. See his *Economists at Bay: Why the Experts Will Never Solve Your Problems* (New York: McGraw-Hill, 1976).

MOTIVATIONS AND AMBITIONS
OF INTELLECTUALS

Despite their endorsement of values that decry self-serving motivations, intellectuals are frequently seized by ambition, perhaps as frequently as anyone else in their competitive society. The desire of intellectuals for good works notwithstanding, it is perhaps the degree to which they must guard against an open admission of their thirst for fame, power, and wealth that most clearly differentiates them from other professions.[23] It is true that wealth is rarely obtainable, even though intellectuals have long outgrown the cloak of poverty under which they once suffered and with which they protected themselves.[24] But the search for the remaining objectives, fame and power, is quite sufficient to channel writers' expressions, and perhaps their thought, into lines acceptable to the others whom they must impress.

How can pervasive ambition among intellectuals be demonstrated when the norms so strongly militate against its outward manifestation? One way is through indirect evidence. Merton, for example, has studied the ways in which scientists have guarded their intellectual property (ideas and discoveries) against "theft" by other scientists.[25] The lengths and measures he catalogs are extraordinarily clear indicators of the workings of personal ambition, as are the cries of anguish and outrage when an idea is stolen in spite of precautions.[26] Perhaps the best indicator of personal ambition is fraud and deceit in scientific research.[27]

We can also open a window on ambition through the pressure-free writings of persons who have already "made it," and feel an urge to describe their part of the intellectual world as it really appears to them. Thus Podhoretz, in his book appropriately titled *Making It*, describes his early ambivalence toward power and his clear desire for fame, which led him into certain ventures for purely careerist reasons.[28] And in place of the public affectation of surprise and delight when one receives the Nobel Prize, Watson tells honestly of deliberately setting the Prize as his goal, and of engaging in an open race to uncover the structure of DNA to obtain it. Johanson and Edey provide a similarly revealing account of the

---

[23]Podhoretz speaks at length on this norm of concealment, and how it continues to operate long after the virtues it is supposed to protect have vanished. Norman Podhoretz, *Making It* (New York: Random House, 1967).

[24]Anderson and Murray, *The Professors*, pp. 7–8.

[25]Robert K. Merton, "Priorities in Scientific Discovery: A Chapter in the Sociology of Science," *American Sociological Review* 22 (1959), pp. 635–59.

[26]To be sure, our concentration on negative features displays only part of the total picture, for personal ambition often works to the benefit of science.

[27]W. Broad and N. Wade, *Betrayers of the Truth: Fraud and Deceit in Science* (London: Oxford University Press, 1982).

[28]Podhoretz, *Making It*.

personal rivalries, ambitions, and devious calculations in the outwardly stiff scientific race presently underway by paleoanthropologists to discover the earliest traces of man in the valleys of East Africa.[29]

Insofar as ambition and enlightenment are in harmony there is no need for criticism; the negative side of ambition appears whenever assuming a certain position in one's work will damage one's career chances. Here, workers in the humanities and social sciences are far more vulnerable than physical scientists and mathematicians, both because modern society tends to divorce physical laws from ideology,[30] and because the worth of a contribution is more readily ascertainable in the physical and formal sciences.[31]

The traditional way to view the vulnerability of intellectuals has been in terms of pressures from the larger society, for example, the witch hunts of academics by a Senator McCarthy. However, in terms of career progress, the opinion of one's peers has infinitely more control over one's destiny than the opinion of the nonintellectual world—and rightly so. Thus moral cowardice for intellectuals consists of more than failing to attack, expose, or condemn the larger society. These actions may be a matter of routine—even a mandatory routine—in some circles. Trilling has coined the term "adversary culture" for the feeling of obligation in some intellectual circles to be critical of society.[32] Cowardice, it would seem, lies not only in fears of the reaction of a repressive society, but also in a well-grounded fear that attacking beliefs cherished by one's colleagues spells defeat for all ordinary ambitions. Thus intellectuals may commend each other for their bravery in attacking the society at large, when in point of fact it would in some quarters require greater courage *not* to do so.[33] Equally great respect must be accorded to those

---

[29]James D. Watson, The Double Helix (New York: New American Library, 1969); Donald Johanson and Maitland Edey, Lucy: The Beginnings of Humankind (New York: Simon and Schuster, 1981).

[30]It was not always thus. Even today the separation is incomplete, as an investigation of the affairs of Lysenko in the Soviet Union and Velikovsky in America will confirm. See D. Joravsky, "Lysenkoism," Scientific American 207 (November 1962), pp. 41–49; Eric Larrabee, "Scientists in Collision: Was Velikovsky Right?" Harper's 227 (August 1963), pp. 48–55. See also Marian Blissett, Politics in Science (Boston: Little, Brown, 1972).

[31]To demonstrate this, we might consider a situation in which the Nobel Prize was extended to sociology. It seems safe to say that a twenty-four-year-old sociologist with no prior publications simply could not obtain it, but Watson received it in the field of biology for his decoding of the DNA molecule while at that age and status. The youngest laureate in the sciences received his prize at the age of 25; the youngest laureate in the humanities was age 41. The greater ease of evaluation in certain disciplines is confirmed by the youngest doctorate (age 12) and youngest full professor (age 19), both in mathematics.

[32]Lionel Trilling, Beyond Culture (New York: Viking Press, 1965), pp. xii–xiii. Edward Shils, Calling, has greatly elaborated this analysis and offered several reasons for it.

[33]A "paradox" that interested some researchers in the early 1970s was that the groups and individuals supporting radical change were invariably well-off, even privileged, while those who defended the status quo were typically poor, even downtrodden. See The New Class?, ed. B. Bruce-Briggs (New Brunswick, N.J.: Transaction Books, 1979).

intellectuals who have dared, on matters of great importance, to fight their peers even at the risk of ostracism. No political persuasion apparently monopolizes this rare phenomenon—the courageous sociologist C. Wright Mills was further to the political left than his colleagues; Thomas Szasz, the disturber of psychiatry, is apparently to the right of his.[34] It is an understatement to say that the weight of the system militates heavily against this type of independent "counterformity."

Certain subjects seem to be, at any given time, safe and unsafe or "acceptable" and "unacceptable" for academic criticism. Here are two examples of the latter. In the 1950s favorable positions toward socialism were unacceptable in American academic circles, and were absent except for that of C. Wright Mills, who was virtually alone. In the late 1960s and early 1970s, publicly expressing a favorable attitude toward the U.S. position in the Vietnam War was unthinkable in academia, and was absolutely absent. Two similar images, one from a classic work of the 1950s and one from a contemporary work, help us to understand how the intellectual distinguishes these forbidden zones. Riesman used the analogy of a lonely crowd, and within it the further analogy of a delicate personal radar that the "other-directed" person uses to detect areas beyond the pale. More recently, Noelle-Neumann, the originator of the notion of the "spiral of silence," speaks of a "quasi-statistical organ" that enables individuals to measure an increase or decrease in support for a given position.[35] Of course, these writers refer to the general public, but their analyses apply just as well to the intellectual world. In currently "safe" areas, on the other hand, the academic world actually places a premium on original and penetrating criticism.

Intellectuals succeed in publishing if they meet the overt criteria of quality and stay within tacit boundaries of ideology set by their colleagues. Thus already there is a considerable degree of conformity to the norms of the profession. Besides publishing, in order to advance professionally (initial appointments, chairmanships, editorial roles), and even to be accepted in the professional hierarchy, they have again to submit repeatedly to the judgment of their peers. Quite apart from such formal rewards, the judgments of peers provide to intellectuals the simple rewards of acceptance, or the pangs of ostracism. Occupational viewpoints can therefore be stabilized by group censure for participation in

---

[34]For the generally conservative nature of Szasz' thinking on most issues, see Michael S. Goldstein, "The Politics of Thomas Szasz: A Sociological View," *Social Problems* 27 (1980), pp. 570–83. In my judgment, the benefits Szasz has conveyed in the one arena in which he has had any influence entirely overwhelm problems anyone may have with his positions on other subjects.

[35]David Riesman, et al., *The Lonely Crowd* (Garden City, N.Y.: Anchor, 1954); Elizabeth Noelle-Neumann, *The Spiral of Silence: Public Opinion and Our Social Skin* (Chicago: University of Chicago Press, 1984).

disapproved experiences (the military, for example) or for writing disapproved literature.

Long ago, the social psychologist Cooley summarized the situation with an aphorism that might have been written yesterday, except that a contemporary quote would include women.

> *It is strange that we have so few men of genius on our faculties; we are always trying to get them. Of course they must have undergone the regular academic training (say ten years in graduate study and subordinate positions) and be gentlemanly, dependable, pleasant to live with, and not apt to make trouble by urging eccentric ideas.*
>
> **Charles Horton Cooley**

The tension he describes is real: faculties do try to get creative individuals; they simultaneously discourage "wave-makers."

The strains of ambition lead to other negative consequences for the intellectually honest study of social problems. Ambition leads, for instance, to what some have called empire building: the erection of a research empire as a basis for personal power. To a considerable extent social research is dependent on foundation and governmental grant support.[36] Grants for research, especially large awards, are eagerly sought for prestige and power. Because of this, the conclusions reached in a sponsored study can at times be predicted with ease: to better secure the next grant, in the delicate nuances of grantsmanship, results will be in line with the expectations and values of the granting agency's directors. Simon concludes, for instance, that scholars and institutions have an incentive to produce bad news about overpopulation, resources, and environment, and to downplay good news, to get continued funding of their work.[37] Both private and public funding sources tend to avoid topics in which conclusions could inspire public controversy or subject the agency to criticism. Topics that will remain permanently unfunded tend to be under-studied. This is understandable but regrettable; research efforts typically focus on less controversial subjects, irrespective of their theoretical or humane importance.[38]

---

[36]In this connection Gouldner maintains that, historically, the avoidance of radical schemes for social reconstruction was the admission price early sociologists paid for academic respectability. Alvin W. Gouldner, *Future of Intellectuals*, pp. 135–37.

[37]Julian J. Simon, "Resources, Population, Environment: An Oversupply of False Bad News," *Science* 208 (June 27, 1980), pp. 1431–37.

[38]Of course what is controversial for educated persons in one era is no longer so in another, and research on hitherto forbidden topics therefore does occur.

On occasion the research bureau's members are painfully surprised at the unanticipated reception of their endeavors. However, from such experience they learn much—what is absolutely safe, what is questionable, what is risky, what is dangerous, what is fatal. . . . the selection of additional or replacement personnel comes to be predicated not solely on talent or demonstrated skill, but on the individual's capacity to subordinate scientific concerns to institutional needs. . . . Only those outsiders willing to take the vows of conformity, or whose regularity is so transparent as to require no proof, are admitted to the order. The "enthusiast" . . . is subordinated to the bureaucrat.[39]

Then, too, these topics for which funding is provided do get investigated. Monies earmarked for research on particular subjects hardly ever go begging for projects, irrespective of the relative merits of funded and nonfunded subjects. Raymond Mack has called this the "inverse Midas effect" for sociologists—"all that turns to gold, they touch."[40] One important instance in the social sciences was Project Camelot, in which the U.S. Army made in the 1960s a concerted effort through a research institute to harness international social-science expertise to solve a social problem as the U.S. Army saw it: the outbreak of hostile leftist regimes in Latin America.[41] The fact that social scientists flocked in great numbers to this project before it was cancelled illustrates Mack's point. The detrimental consequences posed by lucrative financing imbalances for obtaining a clear picture of social problems should be obvious.

The "inverse Midas effect" [for sociologists]:
All that turns to gold, they touch.

Raymond Mack

In addition to researchers' reluctance to displease granting agencies, a similar decline in integrity stems from the researcher's need to maintain good relations with the individuals or groups being studied, especially if these groups have a high degree of solidarity. Personal contacts highly desirable for future investigations, such as those requiring

---

[39] Wilson Record, "Some Reflections on Bureaucratic Trends in Sociological Research," *American Sociological Review* 25 (1960), pp. 411–14. The quote is from p. 413.

[40] Raymond W. Mack, "Theoretical and Substantive Biases in Sociological Research," in *Interdisciplinary Relationships in the Social Sciences*, ed. M. and C. Sherif (Chicago: Aldine, 1969).

[41] Although the project was well advanced before discovery, the resultant uproar crushed it decisively.

participant observation, might be curtailed or jeopardized by hostile re-actions to forthright, objective reporting. Or ongoing research might be prematurely terminated. One investigative arena in which this is highly relevant to social problems is the observation of police forces. Police have an extraordinarily high degree of internal solidarity vis-à-vis out-siders, and numerous reports have surfaced detailing the difficulties of doing objective reporting of police (including their malpractices) while yet maintaining ties needed for future research.[42] In fact, overcoming this problem while observing any part of the criminal justice system, such as jury deliberations or plea bargaining, has proven extremely difficult.[43]

INSTITUTIONAL PRESSURES

The effects on the intellectual of ambition associated with empire-build-ing and grantsmanship blend gradually and imperceptibly into institu-tional pressures that affect all but the most independent self-employed. In addition to background and ambition, intellectual perspectives are also influenced by pressures from institutions with which most writers and scholars affiliate. Practically speaking, this means primarily univer-sities and research institutes.

From its position as a presumed bastion of intellectual integrity, the university has come under increasingly close scrutiny. In earlier decades, the university resolutely defended academic freedom against direct threats of encroachment that threatened to stifle the free expres-sion of ideas. Even today, no comparable sector of society is so tolerant of strange or dissenting views, and this condition is jealously guarded by academia. But present-day incursions are more insidious in nature, less a head-on clash, with explicit insistence on intellectual conformity, than a "flanking attack" posed by subtle changes in institutional struc-ture. In one examination of this trend, Ralph Miliband listed four grow-ing threats or constraints to the university's capacity for producing independent thinking. First, corporations are increasingly using the universities to obtain consultants, encouraging, for payment, a reason-able view and understanding toward business problems. Second, the university is directly supported to a substantial degree by corporations and wealthy individuals. This discourages views that would upset

---

[42] See R. J. Lundman and J. C. Fox, "Maintaining Research Access in Police Organizations," *Criminology* 16 (1978), pp. 87–97, and the several sources cited there.

[43] See George J. McCall, *Observing the Law: Field Methods in the Study of Crime and the Criminal Justice System* (New York: Collier Macmillan, 1978).

financial promotion and fund raising. Third, the controllers of the university (variously known as governors, regents, trustees) are drawn from persons of upper-class origin or the business elite. The fourth factor is that the business world is increasingly using the university as a training ground for future employees and administrators, including the by now well-established phenomenon of whole faculties for business administration.[44] None of these intrusions is overwhelming, but subtle pressures are increasingly apparent.

Outside the university, the beneficiaries of social or economic research often provide more than grants or consultantships; frequently they act as outright employers as well. Many observers have commented that systems of patronage of science—including both governmental and corporate sponsorship—have steadily expanded in the twentieth century, accompanied by a commensurate decline in academic control.[45] Whereas in earlier periods sociology and psychology were almost wholly academic disciplines, the last few decades have witnessed the rise of applied psychology and sociology, with a small but growing number of these professionals directly employed by governmental or institutional sponsors.[46] These traditionally academic disciplines are thus no longer quite so remote from the condition of the field of economics, in which large numbers of graduates fill both academic and business or government positions.

To some extent the implications of this situation for perspectives on social problems parallels those found with the use of supporting grants mentioned earlier, with the same general difficulties. But in addition the applied workers in the settings of research institutes or "think tanks" have to a great extent lost the freedom to choose their own topics of research, substituting the needs of their clients for what might have interested them on theoretical grounds. The sociologist or psychologist who affiliates with public or private bureaucracies will be expected to deal with problems as the decision-maker/employer sees them, and these problems are likely to concern the preservation or expansion of existing institutional arrangements.

The point is not so much that a number of individual researchers are diverted from their favorite topics but that distortions (via over- and under-emphases) develop in the knowledge of an entire field through the "industrialization" and politicization of its work. Blissett has charged

---

[44]Ralph Miliband, *The State in Capitalist Society* (New York: Quartet Books, 1975), especially pp. 224–26.

[45]See, for example, the discussion in Ron Johnston and Dave Robbins, "The Development of Specialties in Industrialized Science," *The Sociological Review* 25 (New Series, 1977).

[46]As one indicator of this trend, in the American Sociological Association a Section on Sociological Practice was developed in the 1970s.

that this type of scientific technostructure leads to a form of science "not committed to discovery or service to society, but rather to projects or programming aimed at accumulating and developing institutional resources."[47] Similarly, Johnston and Robbins have maintained that major "patrons" not only engender loyalty from their professional personnel but also can in the long run actually *create new specialties* in the discipline to satisfy their presumed needs as they alone define them.[48]

THE SELECTIVE BLINDNESS OF EXPERTS

If the temptations noted above apply to scholars not directly associated with a particular school of thought for the solution of a social problem, how much greater is the difficulty in avoiding bias for those professionals with an established interest in a particular problem! Here the aforementioned ambition is aligned with a feeling of team solidarity; what is good for individual career advancement is also good for a group in whose efforts one believes. Professionalism is not without numerous virtues, but it has often been noted that professions develop vested interests in the maintenance of a status quo. This does not mean that they do not attack social problems, but that they perpetuate existing definitions of problematic areas as well as traditional perspectives and methods of dealing with them. Ultimately they may develop what Veblen called a *trained incapacity* to observe or deal with a situation in nontraditional ways. The helping professions thus at times present a paradoxical picture of institutions with benevolent intentions that, through resistance to innovation, perpetuate the very problems they are involved in removing.[49] Put differently, professionals can be genuinely interested in helping but overcommitted to an established approach to social problems. The usual claim—that the present approach would succeed if only more professionals or more funds were available—may indeed be true. Just where such beliefs fade into cynicism and empire-building for its own sake is sometimes difficult to discern.[50]

One possible outcome of having professional blinders and biases is a one-sided expertise in which much is known about a problem but,

---

[47]Marian Blissett, *Politics in Science*, p. 195.

[48]Johnston and Robbins, "Industrialized Science," p. 90.

[49]With respect to labeling, the paradox may be even greater, as I discuss later in Chapter 8. For a general consideration of the role of the expert in social problem resolution, see Chapter 11 of this book.

[50]Herbert Gans points out that one of the functions of a social problem is to provide employment for persons who are supposed to solve it. Insofar as they are successful, they literally work their way out of a job. See Herbert Gans, "The Positive Functions of Poverty," *American Journal of Sociology* 78 (1972), pp. 275–89.

paradoxically, with poorer insight and judgment. This failure, which can result from an ideological predisposition to ignore components of a problem, might account for the strange results that often occur when predictions by experts are pitted against those by laypersons. Notwithstanding the latter's clear inferiority in related knowledge, study after study finds approximate equivalence in forecasting ability. Thus Kaplan et al., Avison, and McGregor have separately found little or no increase in the ability to predict social events from possession of greater schooling or "expertness." And Armstrong reports the same conclusion across a number of fields, including financial forecasting. Wise, examining some fifteen hundred predictions over fifty years, reported some positive effects from expertise, but only very slight ones. And a more recent review by Chan again concludes that experiments reveal no predictive advantage from education.[51]

A reasonable explanation for these findings, so strange given the expert's overwhelming superiority in these fields in both factual knowledge and theory, would be the existence of conceptual blinders that exclude or conceal some significant part of reality for the professional but not for the layperson. Armstrong also reviewed evidence that education and experience, while not increasing predictive accuracy, do greatly increase *self-confidence* in it.[52] All of this should again tell the discerning reader something about the wisdom of relying wholly on learned perspectives.

IN CONCLUSION: SOME PERSPECTIVE ON THE FAILINGS OF THE LEARNED

We have examined four major "cautions" concerning the entrusting of social problem definitions and interpretations to the intellectual and the expert. These were (1) the common background and self-imposed social isolation of intellectuals, (2) their motivations, ambitions, and obligatory conformity to intellectualdom, (3) the institutional constraints on their universities, and (4) the selective blindness of professional per-

---

[51] W. R. Avison, "On Being Right versus Being Bright," *Pacific Sociological Review* 21 (1978), pp. 67–84; D. McGregor, "The Major Determinants of the Prediction of Social Events," *Journal of Abnormal and Social Psychology* 33 (1938), pp. 179–204; A. Kaplan et al., "The Prediction of Social and Technological Events," *Public Opinion Quarterly* 14 (1950), pp. 93–110; J. Scott Armstrong, *Long Range Forecasting* (New York: Wiley, 1978); G. Wise, "The Accuracy of Technological Forecasts," *Futures* 8 (1976), pp. 411–19; S. Chan, "Expert Judgment under Uncertainty: Some Evidence and Suggestions," *Social Science Quarterly* 63 (1982), pp. 428–44.

[52] Armstrong, *Forecasting*. See also his article, "The Seer-sucker Theory: The Value of Experts in Forecasting," *Technology Review* 83 (1980), pp. 18–24. Also relevant is H. J. Einhorn and R. M. Hogarth, "Confidence in Judgment: Persistence of the Illusion of Validity," *Psychological Review* 85 (1978), pp. 395–416.

spectives. I noted at the beginning that the discussion was difficult for me because I am a member of the academic fraternity and strongly identify with it. So I now will put the failings of my compatriots (and myself, I fear) into a broader perspective.

The negative features of the prior sections do not demonstrate a widespread venality among intellectuals and other professionals. These negative aspects are to be regarded more accurately as an inadvertent result of narrow and stereotyped thinking about social problems among the very experts who set out to improve some unattractive aspects of reality. My criticisms of self-seeking academics and my critique of the vulnerability of intellectuals in general should not be misconstrued. Because of that danger, I should point out that no other collectivity of comparable size brings to bear such a formidable capacity for learning about, and such a depth of understanding on, the problems that beset modern society. Many of the criticisms discussed here for intellectuals would apply with even greater strength to other candidates for the role of definer of social problems. As Walter Lippmann put it:

> I have not forgotten how often the professors have been proved to be wrong, how often the academic judgment has been confounded by some solitary thinker or artist, how often original and innovating men have been rejected by the universities, only to be accepted and celebrated after they are dead. The universal company of scholars is not an infallible court of last resort. Far from it. . . . Nevertheless, in the modern world there exists no court which is less fallible than the company of scholars, when we are in the field of truth and error.[53]

The opposite side of the coin to the problems of elitism is what the elitists of the nineteenth century called the "sovereignty of the unqualified." I do not argue for a return to a day in which intellectuals were ignored! But neither the intellectuals themselves nor society in general can afford to ignore the systematic tendencies we have touched on. The intellectuals—for whom the term itself was derogatory not so long ago—may be in danger of assuming too much for themselves in prescribing for society's ills.

---

[53]Lippmann, "The University," p. 17.

A   T   R   A   N   S   I   T   I   O   N

With this chapter we conclude our examination of just how certain conditions come to be regarded as social problems requiring our attention and active intervention, or, conversely, just how and why some other conditions do not come to be so regarded. In the process, we develop a healthy respect for the great diversity found in history of what has been seen as problematic. We also sense the degree to which social problems are "made" by powerful sectors of the society—the media, the church, the intellectual, the professional—and/or by deeply motivated individuals—the moral entrepreneur, the victim. I have devoted a lot of space in this book to what might at first have seemed a mere definitional matter. In actuality, as I hope you agree, it is much, much more; it is in fact one of the core concerns in the study of social problems.

At this point we shift gears; we start to take the current set of high visibility social problems more or less as given and think about what can be done about them.

P A R T   T W O

6

THE STRATEGIES OF INTERVENTION

THE TERM "INTERVENTION"

Throughout this book I will speak of *intervention* in a social problem as any and all conscious, organized efforts to alleviate that problem. We need a very general term for this purpose, and intervention is my choice.[1] It is worth emphasizing that we shall be examining *conscious, planned* activities. Obviously, social problems can at times be alleviated or even eliminated by unconscious or semiconscious means of social control, such as informal expressions of disapproval or choice of partners or acquaintances. New sociocultural developments also may occur, for reasons entirely extraneous to a given problem, that accidentally help to alleviate it. More questionably, some people have argued that a "natural" or "spontaneous" recovery may develop for some social problems paralleling that sometimes found for physical illnesses.[2] These possibilities are interesting, no doubt, but I will ignore

---

[1] Let me note briefly that some writers restrict the term intervention to apply only to certain reactions to social problems, typically those I will categorize as "amelioration." That convention is not followed here.

[2] For instance, extreme fads or "crazes" have been viewed as having a limited life span. See Rolf Meyersohn and Elihu Katz, "Notes on a Natural History of Fads," *American Journal of Sociology* 62 (1957), pp. 594–601. On the other hand, it may be argued that these seemingly consistent reversions to the norm only appear spontaneous because we do not yet have sufficient knowledge of the causes for the return to the status quo.

them in order to concentrate in the next few chapters on the issues, strategies, and consequences of concerted social action.

The provision "concerted action" also rules out analysis of self-help measures. In a very provocative article, Black has reminded us that a sizeable amount of crime is actually a form of social control in the sense that it is specifically performed in retaliation for the deviant acts of another whom the criminal does not think will be properly punished by the authorities.[3] This is a truly valuable insight, but I feel that we must restrict ourselves here to concerted action by a number of persons. To repeat, we are interested in all of the conscious, organized efforts to alleviate social problems—those sponsored by governments, those that are private but cooperative with government, and those in active opposition to the established government. That is, we are interested in the progress and pitfalls of intervention.

In the sweep of human efforts to control social problems, only a limited number of basic "strategies" have appeared. Although it may not be recognized, each strategy is based on a theory of the problem's cause and on a theory of human nature—on a distinctive "model of humanity." The causes and solutions proposed for specific problems will not be discussed here; instead, this chapter's chief concern will be to lay out the total span of possible strategies in a rough historical development.[4] Toward the end I will try to organize these approaches into a meaningful pattern. This presentation is roughly chronological, but it should be clear that most of the early strategies are still with us today.

Although all of the intervention measures to be discussed have been consciously articulated at one time or another, some of them are not ordinarily presented in the same form as they are described here. To differentiate these, when the proposed reaction has often been articulated as described here, it will be called a *doctrine* (for instance, the doctrine of deterrence). Where, on the other hand, I am collecting scattered proposals into a single category of my own making, the result will be called a *strategy* (as, for instance, the strategy of social reorganization). All doctrines are also strategies, but the reverse is not true; strategy is the more general term.

---

[3]Donald Black, "Crime as Social Control," *American Sociological Review* 48 (1983), pp. 34–45. See also Gary Kleck, "Crime Control through the Private Use of Armed Force," *Social Problems* 35 (1988), pp. 1–21.

[4]This historical plan follows what is generally known as Western civilization; it makes no attempt to follow the development in other parts of the world. Although the sequence is Western, the possibilities are, I think, complete for any culture.

STRATEGIES OF INTERVENTION: EARLIER PATTERNS

Thou shalt give life for life, eye for eye, tooth for tooth, hand for hand, foot for foot, burning for burning, stripe for stripe.

Exodus

The earliest known historical doctrines quite explicitly used a general strategy of *reward and punishment*, most often the latter, in response to social problems.[5] Recorded history begins during an era of "hydraulic civilizations," which display to the archeologist a number of elements in common. Organized around large-scale irrigation agriculture, these were empire states possessing tributary dominions and a hierarchical system of power and authority. All had a rigid class structure with a small elite and a very large number of slaves. Unity tended to rest more heavily on compulsion than consent.[6] Individuals, groups, social classes, or whole captive societies were expected to behave in certain ways and to refrain from behaving in other ways. Persons or groups who did not obey received negative sanctions.[7] The containment of social problems in this era was virtually synonymous with the achievement of social control.

This system had the virtue of simplicity. Like the social structure, the theories of social problems and their remedies were straightforward. Problems were defined by the elite and were seen as produced by the actions of specific individuals. And in a system of heavy-handed domination that had little room for subtlety, the obvious response to undesirable behavior was the negative sanction. Through long periods of history, concepts about limited responsibility, which today would be applied to mental incompetents, the insane, and small children, were

---

[5] It is impossible to ascertain the extent of various doctrines among prehistoric cultures, although punishment can occasionally be discerned in fossil remains. Comparisons with contemporary nonliterate cultures are stimulating, but anthropologists consider them inconclusive for purposes of historical reconstruction. See E. Adamson Hoebel, *The Law of Primitive Man* (Cambridge: Harvard University Press, 1954).

[6] Karl Wittfogel, *Oriental Despotism: A Comparative Study of Total Power* (New Haven: Yale University Press, 1957). See especially chap. 4 and 5.

[7] For two contrasting ideas on why punishment has been so extensively used throughout history, see B. F. Skinner, *Beyond Freedom and Dignity* (New York: Knopf, 1971); Emile Durkheim, "Two Laws of Penal Evolution," in *Durkheim and the Law*, ed. Steven Lukes and Andrew Scull (New York: St. Martin's Press, 1983), pp. 102–32.

often minimal and in many cases nonexistent. Punishments were meted out to such persons, and indeed records exist of trials of children and even animals who had been the cause of injury. As will be seen momentarily, several explicit doctrines fit under the broad umbrella of punishment.[8]

A policy of *retribution* (or revenge) for wrongs or injuries was at one time in wide use as an explicit doctrine. The desire for retaliation, for *lex talionis* ("an eye for an eye"), undoubtedly remains as a concealed motive for some more recent doctrines, but the explicit doctrinal basis has today been largely shifted to other grounds. When developed overtly, retribution involves some conception of a loss of "balance" that can only be restored or "righted" by subjecting the perpetrator to an equivalent unpleasantness. (Punishment in general, as we will see, need not be conceptualized in such terms.) As the state has come to monopolize the legitimate use of force, the rationale behind such retributive institutions as the duel or the blood feud has declined, and those institutions have gradually disappeared.[9] Retribution is enjoying a limited return to favor in contemporary penal philosophy.[10] But in current jurisprudence the legitimacy of vengeance has diminished to a point where it appears, if at all, only as a sub rosa feature of other doctrines.

Two doctrines that have an obvious connection with punishment are *deterrence* and *incapacitation*. Paradoxically, they are based on opposite conceptions of human nature. Deterrence assumes that knowledge of unpleasant consequences for proscribed acts will either prevent the commission of such acts altogether or minimize their frequency. The doctrine is usually divided into general and special deterrence. General deterrence refers to the effects on the population as a whole from the knowledge that someone else has been punished.[11] Special deterrence refers to the effects of sanctions on the specific persons who receive them. Deterrence assumes that if sufficient pressure is brought to bear, people can and will change their behavior. Incapacitation, on the other

---

[8]For a good historical study, see George Rusche and Otto Kirchheimer, *Punishment and Social Structure* (New York: Russell and Russell, 1968, original—1939).

[9]Arthur S. Diamond, *The Evolution of Law and Order* (London: Watts, 1951). The thrust of his work is an attempt to relate legal codes to the type of society in which they were formulated.

[10]For two recent treatments of the doctrine of retribution, see Joseph E. Hickey and Peter L. Scharf, *Toward a Just Correctional System* (San Francisco: Jossey-Bass, 1980); Pietro Marongiu and Graeme Newman, *Vengeance: The Fight Against Injustice* (Totowa, NJ: Rowman & Littlefield, 1987). See also the arguments put forward by van den Haag in Ernest van den Haag and John Conrad, *The Death Penalty: A Debate* (New York: Plenum Press, 1983).

[11]An excellent general treatment is found in Franklin Zimring and Gordon Hawkins, *Deterrence* (Chicago: University of Chicago Press, 1973).

hand, assumes either that certain persons have an incorrigible tendency to behave in certain ways, or that society's responses are ineffectual in altering their behavior. This doctrine therefore sees a reduction in the capacity of such persons to do damage as the only viable solution. Early versions of incapacitation consisted of such intentionally frightful actions as branding the forehead with a letter signifying the act committed, thereby warning others to beware of the branded individual. Other responses were equally cruel: a thief's hand might be severed, a liar's tongue cut out.[12] Death and exile were also forms of incapacitation.

Early sanctions that left a permanent visible mark on the individual were obviously self-confirming in terms of incorrigibility. Such persons could never again take part in normal society because other people would not deal with them; hence they were destined to engage in marginal, proscribed activities in order to live. In certain historical periods whole sectors of cities housed these wretched individuals who banded together in order to survive.[13] The connection between this doctrine and the labeling controversy (taken up in Chapter 8) is most intriguing.

Today, incapacitation takes the form of incarceration and, in some societies, the death penalty. Ordinarily, a felon confined in prison cannot menace the outside populace. Periodically, demands surface for other types of incapacitation—castration of convicted child rapists would be one example. Imprisonment, contrary to popular belief, is a relatively recent approach to incapacitation. Prior to the 1800s, confinement was principally a temporary means to ensure the whereabouts of the offender until the real punishment could be imposed.[14] Confinement as punishment was initially regarded as a progressive and humanitarian reform.

Looking to the future of the incapacitation doctrine, if some people really are incorrigible and cannot learn from punishment or rehabilitation, perhaps it is possible to predict which persons will return to crime. Already, statistical predictions of "future dangerousness" have become a big business for a wide array of crimes as a basis for probation and parole decisions.[15]

Although the doctrines of deterrence and incapacitation are based on diametrically opposed conceptions of the alterability of human nature, in past practice they were not often in conflict because what was

---

[12]So-called poetic justice seems to exert a strong appeal to certain individuals.

[13]See Gideon Sjoberg, *The Preindustrial City* (Glencoe, Ill.: Free Press, 1957).

[14]See Chapter 3, "Mercantilism and the Rise of Imprisonment," of Rusche and Kirchheimer, *Punishment*. But for exceptions, see Sean McConville, *A History of English Prison Administration* (London: Routledge & Kegan Paul, 1981).

[15]See P. W. Greenwood, *Selective Incapacitation* (Santa Monica, Calif.: Rand Corp., 1982).

incapacitating was nearly always also extremely punishing and hence thought to be capable of exerting a deterrent effect. Indeed, paradoxical as it may appear today, imprisonment was at first opposed on the grounds that, while incapacitating, it could not really be expected to *deter* proscribed activities because inmates would find themselves provided with free food, clothing, and shelter. Imprisonment, ironically, marked the first shift toward a rehabilitative philosophy.[16]

Two other early doctrines were *expiation*, for the sins involved in breaking moral rules, and *restitution* by the wrongdoer to those who had suffered from his actions. Like retribution, expiation involved some conception of restoring "balance," but it implied reconciliation of a transgressor with God through atonement, not reconciliation with other persons. (In some pre-Christian cultures the expiatory act cleansed and purged the deviant from his ritual pollution and appeased the gods.) It was a doctrine highly dependent on popular conformity to theological dogmas and the practice of the confessional. Clergy set the penalties involved in expiation. Because of the contemporary lapse in the use of the confession, this doctrine is no longer a viable strategy, although it is still occasionally advocated. Restitution, on the other hand, is still the rule in civil suits (e.g., monetary compensation for damages) and has lingered on in criminal cases in a number of jurisdictions. Currently it is enjoying a limited return to favor in criminal law. These new calls for restitution fall within the purview of victimology, a topic we examined in Chapter 4.[17]

We can now see why an essentially punitive reaction to social problems persisted for so long. Despite their differences, the several doctrines and strategies hung together; explicit punishment, retribution, deterrence, incapacitation, expiation, and restitution—all demanded the calculated infliction of some sort of misery on the offending party. Only the specific form of misery might vary in terms of the doctrine most favored.[18]

---

[16]We shall examine the nineteenth-century movement towards asylums in Chapter 11.

[17]For one of the earlier modern articles on this subject, see Stephen Shafer, "Restitution to Victims of Crime—An Old Correctional Aim Modernized," in *Criminological Controversies*, ed. Richard Knudten (New York: Appleton–Century–Crofts, 1968). See also William MaCauley, "Victim Compensation: Cure or Placebo?" in J. Scherer and G. Sheperd, eds., *Victimization of the Weak* (Springfield, Ill.: Charles C. Thomas, 1982), pp. 136–52.

[18]Harry Elmer Barnes, *The Story of Punishment: A Record of Man's Inhumanity to Man* (Montclair, NJ: Patterson Smith, 1972). The original is dated 1930 but still excellent. Also see Stanley Grupe, ed., *Theories of Punishment* (Bloomington: Indiana University Press, 1971).

In terms of nonpunitive intervention strategies, *denial of opportunity* for wrongdoing has a venerable heritage. City walls and other fortifications to keep out raiders and bandits are found among the most ancient ruins uncovered. Ancient personal seals to prevent forgeries of correspondence have also been unearthed, in the Near East. And simple keys and locks have a very long history. Recently a revival of such protective measures has occurred because of the growth in crime, with the focus now on urban housing and office architecture.[19] Denial of opportunity has been an especially commonplace approach in dealing with minors. Laws forbidding the sale of alcohol or cigarettes to minors or the provision of contraceptive information are measures (increasingly futile) to deny minors the opportunity to acquire "sinful habits" when they "do not know better." At least that was the intended strategy.

A campaign of *moral regeneration* is another ancient nonpunitive strategy that reappears periodically to combat social ills. Biblical accounts of the Old Testament prophets testify to the antiquity of this response and, of course, references appear in the sacred works of other ancient religions as well.[20] The solution to rampant problems is seen either in a return to an earlier, presumably more moral style of life (perhaps extensively exaggerated and idealized), or alternatively, in adoption of a new and radically different moral code.[21] Advocates of the radical shift as the preferred solution tend to emerge during periods of deep social malaise. Cases in point are Jewish messianism in the time of Christ, the growth of Christianity in the late Roman Empire, the Ghost Dance religion among the American Indians of the Great Plains in the late 1800s, and the cargo cults of Melanesia.[22] Such movements are of great interest to sociologists and anthropologists of religion, who have extensively studied what are known as nativistic, chiliastic, revitalist, and messianic movements. In nonreligious cases, such drives have been termed "ideological renewal."[23]

Another nonpunitive doctrine has always been available for those relatively few individuals whose inability to support themselves

---

[19] See, as examples, Oscar Newman, *Defensible Space: Crime Prevention through Urban Design* (New York: Macmillan, 1973); and Robert J. Sampson, "Structural Density and Criminal Victimization," *Criminology* 21 (1983), pp. 276–93.

[20] An excellent treatment is contained in James G. Frazer, *Folklore in the Old Testament* (New York: Tudor, 1923).

[21] Wilson D. Wallis, *Messiahs: Their Role in Civilization* (Washington, D.C.: Amer. Council on Public Affairs, 1943).

[22] See Weston LaBarre, *The Ghost Dance: The Origins of Religion* (New York: Delta Books, 1972); Wallis, *Messiahs*; and Peter Worsley, *The Trumpet Shall Sound* (London: MacGibbon and Kee, 1957).

[23] As an example, see J. Irving, *The Social Credit Movement in Alberta* (Toronto: University of Toronto Press, 1959).

is recognized as a legitimate social problem. Throughout most of human history the greater part of the dependent population has been ignored or, worse, scourged as lazy, shiftless, or weak-willed. In the case of "madness," the person's problem was even seen as the result of divine retribution. But there was always a residual group to whom such forms of derogation could not be applied—the crippled war hero, the blind, the orphaned. Most of these individuals, as with children or the aged, were cared for privately by family and kinfolk, but a *program of relief* was applied to the small remaining sector, the "worthy poor" acknowledged to be a genuine social problem. This problem was to be resolved by the charity of Christian individuals, or perhaps by the parish in which the poor lived. In the Western world the church was the usual agency providing such assistance; until relatively recent times the state assumed few responsibilities, although it might regulate the clergy's humane work.

Healthy adults suddenly overwhelmed through no personal fault— the victims of fire or flood, for example—were also deemed worthy of aid. Here again a formal program of relief sometimes developed, although the most common means of providing assistance was mutual aid between neighbors, practiced especially on the frontier in the New World and in Old World peasant communities.[24] The doctrine of relief has extended unbroken to contemporary times, with a vast expansion in the number of cases of misfortune considered to be genuine social problems and, concomitantly, the elaboration of new relief programs into areas previously untouched.

ALTERNATIVE STRATEGIES: THE BREAK WITH PURE PUNISHMENT

In the modern era of Western culture the first major break with punitive doctrines came in the late 1700s. In England and British North America a new spirit centered around the work of the Quakers and other reform elements.[25] A call was issued for efforts to achieve the moral reformation of offenders. The movement illustrates the terrible disparity between doctrine and practice that is possible in reaction to social problems. "Meditation in solitude is reformative," the movement said, and drove some prisoners insane through complete lack of social stimulation. "Hard work is uplifting," the movement said, and virtually broke the backs of its victims with unprecedented drudgery. The emphasis

---

[24] Peter Kropotkin, *Mutual Aid* (London: 1902).
[25] See Sidney V. James, *A People among Peoples: Quaker Benevolence in Eighteenth Century America* (Cambridge: Harvard University Press, 1963).

was not on physical pain, however, but rather on an attempt to remold the deviant person. The person was required to work, read the Bible, and meditate in solitary confinement or silence. Extreme regimentation, discipline, and daily routinization of activities were expected to reshape the character of the person confined. The Auburn and Pennsylvania Systems of confinement, both of which drew worldwide attention, laid the foundations for modern penal approaches in their contention that rehabilitation was possible—a contention that became a focus of debate for many generations.[26]

The new doctrine of *rehabilitation* called for the "salvage" of wrongdoers. Helped by the development of asylums and institutional centers, programs of rehabilitation were developed around religious and work-centered themes. Parole and probation were added to the repertory of legal responses. Prisons became penitentiaries, then reformatories, finally "rehabilitation centers." In many cases the changes were more linguistic than actual, and it can be questioned whether reform actually took place within the walls. No one doubts, however, that the rehabilitation orientation continually gained in strength.

Several reasons for this shift toward rehabilitation can be isolated.[27] First, an increasing belief in human malleability—in the plasticity of human nature—had emerged. The reformability of individual deviants was emphasized through the recounting of successful examples. Bold pioneers created treatment-based institutions, not always successfully and sometimes at great personal cost. The long-term trend was toward a decline in the belief in incorrigibility.[28] The rehabilitation trend was later strengthened by the emergence of deterministic theories of human nature that maintained individuals were not wholly responsible for their actions. Offensive behavior was now seen as the result of social conditions or childhood experiences beyond the individual's control. The person was seen as a "product" rather than as a free agent. A third force in the direction of rehabilitation was a growing adherence among intellectuals to the relativity of ethical standards. Those who believe in ethical relativity maintain that no moral absolutes exist.[29] The growth of historical and anthropological studies that revealed the diversity of human cultures and standards of ethical conduct, and contact with advanced non-Western cultures with distinctive ethical traditions, stimulated the development of this relativistic point of view.

---

[26]See Chapter 18 of Elmer H. Johnson, *Crime, Correction, and Society*, rev. ed. (Homewood, Ill.: Dorsey Press, 1968). For parallel developments in France, see Michel Foucault, *Discipline and Punish: The Birth of the Prison* (New York: Vintage Books, 1979). The doubts about rehabilitation continue, as I will explain in Chapter 10.

[27]See Wittfogel, *Oriental Despotism*, and Foucault, *Discipline and Punish*.

[28]See Chapter 7 for greater detail.

[29]See Chapter 1 for a more extensive treatment of ethical relativity.

These same forces led not only to the growth of rehabilitation doctrines with respect to wrongdoers but also, for the first time, to forms of intervention that concentrated on changes *not related to individual miscreants.*

Movements now emerged to alter the conditions thought to foster the social problems—to attack the "roots" of the problem, as it was put. These were based on a new set of causal theories that gradually displaced traditional conceptions of free will. With increasing frequency, behavior that led to social problems was seen as traceable to preexisting conditions, and more and more efforts were directed at these "underlying" conditions themselves. This strategy of *amelioration of conditions* is increasingly in evidence today, although it is by no means universally accepted.

The new perspective made its appearance in several ways.[30] It might be cheaper and more effective to safeguard the health of the poor than to treat epidemics, so a new emphasis arose on such measures as public sanitation, mosquito control, and mass inoculation. The supposedly debilitating features of city life brought about a demand for recreation spaces, parks, and rural-like areas for "spiritual renewal."[31] The teaching of hygiene, dietetics, and proper family budgeting was a prominent welfare activity in the early twentieth century. All activities of this sort represented a rudimentary increase in sophistication in the sense that they reacted to underlying factors instead of to specific events. This is not to say that the approaches were always, or even typically, successful.

It is worth emphasizing that what I classify as a single strategy, amelioration of conditions, covers an amazing range of substrategies. Here is an example of the diversity. The regional disparity of socioeconomic conditions is now clearly recognized as a social problem. The heartland of Appalachia in the United States, the Maritime Provinces in Canada, and the northern counties of England are recognized as perennial losers in an economic sense, with hard-core unemployment and other very poor life-chances. What should be done about this? Some discrete approaches to amelioration include: (1) the creation of "transfer payments" via the federal government to the governments of the depressed areas, (2) sponsored migration to other regions, (3) extension of unemployment insurance schemes to cover part-time workers in these areas, and (4) creation of tax incentives to persuade industry to locate

---

[30] Some would call these measures "preventative" rather than "ameliorative." I will discuss this distinction later in the section.
[31] Stephan Thernstrom and Richard Sennett, eds., *Nineteenth Century Cities: Essays in the New Urban History* (New Haven: Yale University Press, 1969).

plants in depressed areas. Clearly, the single strategy of amelioration of conditions encompasses a great many concrete forms of intervention. A second implication, undoubtedly correct, is that my classification of strategies emphasizes the social aspect rather than the economic.

I have concentrated thus far on the individual as offender or deviant because through most of human history the deviant has been the major recognized social problem. General conditions such as war or poverty were regarded either as the inevitable fate of humanity, as desirable for religious reasons, or perhaps as good in themselves. Cases of insanity seemed the result of individual sins or faults, not of social factors.[32] The same was true for most poverty cases. Those social problems not regarded as inevitable were viewed as the product of the behavior of a limited number of persons (as indeed, strictly speaking, they were), and social intervention took the form of outlawing such activity under one or more of the doctrines previously described.

Of course, this is no longer true today. Although some sophisticated theorists still regard such conditions as war, aggression, or racial animosity as invariable components of human society, a large and growing segment of the community now regards them as social problems with possible resolutions.[33] Some of the proposed solutions continue to rely on the outlawing of selected forms of behavior, but a considerable number revolve around amelioration of conditions, and a growing number involve the basic restructuring of society.

This last-mentioned perspective, what we might call the strategy of *social reorganization*, is a relatively new and radically different approach to the solution of social problems. Far from regarding the acts of specific individuals as the source of the problem, its advocates tend to see these acts as symptoms only of a deeper flaw in society. Individuals are seen as victims of the system under which they live, acting out what they are constrained to do by the impositions of a radically defective set of social arrangements.[34]

---

[32]M. Foucault, *Madness and Civilization* (New York: Pantheon Books, 1965). In contrast, see M. Harvey Brenner, *Mental Illness and the Economy* (Cambridge: Harvard University Press, 1973).

[33]As one example of the former, see Pierre Van den Berghe, "Bringing Beasts Back In: Toward a Biosocial Theory of Aggression," *American Sociological Review* 39 (December 1974), pp. 777–88. See older theorists with this viewpoint reviewed in Pitirim Sorokin, *Contemporary Sociological Theories* (New York: Harper, 1928). The old Durkheimian viewpoint that crime is inevitable may actually be gaining in strength. See, for example, Kai Erikson, *Wayward Puritans* (New York: Wiley, 1966).

[34]See as examples Lewis Yablonsky, *Robopaths* (Indianapolis: Bobbs-Merrill, 1972); William Ryan, *Blaming the Victim* (New York: Vintage Books, 1971).

In terms of social reorganization, two great historical foci of discontent can be discerned, each demanding the reordering of a particular aspect of the society. The first to appear was a revolt against *legal inequality*, beginning with attacks on the distinction between commoners and nobility that culminated in the French and American revolutions. Then in succession came revolts against the superiority in law of landholders, the institution of slavery, peonage or economic slavery (as in company towns), colonialism, and, finally, dominance by whites and males.[35] The last struggle continues in the present, while on the horizon loom new conflicts over the legal inequality between adults and children and between humans and animals (the animal rights movement).

A second focus for social restructuring has been *economic inequality*. Its philosophical roots lie in the socialist, and especially Marxian, reactions to the doctrines of classical economics. Discounting early writers of little influence, its period of origin was in the early 1800s, considerably later than the philosophical doctrines that spawned the first revolutions against legal inequality. Many of the early economic struggles have since been resolved: although specific instances of abrogation can still be found, collective organization by workers, old-age security, and a progressive income tax have become so much a part of the contemporary international scene that the bitter, often violent struggles that greeted their emergence have been virtually forgotten. And some of the old demands for social restructuring, such as public ownership of industry, have come to seem less of a panacea to many contemporary reformers.[36] But as income disparities and differential access to services remain acute, new points of contention have arisen, and in the decade of the 1960s these produced a dramatic resurgence of demands for the radical reorganization of the economic sphere.[37] Originally, economic inequality referred to inequality of opportunity; hence the demand for greater mass education. More recently the shift in emphasis has been toward inequality of results or outcomes.[38]

---

[35] This historical sequence fits most closely the progression in North America and Western Europe. These events, however, were the springboards for similar events elsewhere in the world. See S. M. Lipset, *The First New Nation* (New York: Basic Books, 1963).

[36] See "Introduction" in C. G. Benello and D. Roussopoulos, eds., *The Case for Participatory Democracy* (New York: Viking Press, 1971). Also see chapter 23 of Fred Polak, *The Image of the Future* (Amsterdam: Elsevier, 1973, original—1952).

[37] See, for example, Paul A. Baran and Paul H. Sweezy, *Monopoly Capital* (New York: Monthly Review Press, 1966); Irving Zeitlin, ed., *American Society, Incorporated* (Chicago: Markham, 1971). An immensely influential book of the early 1960s, in terms of reinvigorating economic protest, was Michael Harrington's *The Other America: Poverty in the United States* (New York: Macmillan, 1962).

[38] See Julian Le Grand, *The Strategy of Equality: Redistribution and the Social Services* (London: Allen & Unwin, 1982).

Philosophers as divergent as Jean-Paul Sartre and John Dewey have observed how radical, in a historical sense, is the advocacy of a strategy of social reorganization by the intellectual members of the privileged classes. Prior to comparatively recent philosophical innovations, the intellectual elite formed a bulwark of conservatism, a pillar of the status quo unrecognizable in today's liberal or radical intelligentsia.[39] Some of the principal reasons for this transformation are discussed in the next chapter.

To counter the threat of radical ideas, which some have seen as a social problem in itself, a doctrine/strategy of *idea suppression* has often been used. It can be considered either as a doctrine or a strategy since sometimes it has been expressly stated as a way to stop the spread of heretical thought (as in the Soviet Union, with a theory of the press as an instrument of struggle), while at other times this strategic aspect is played down (as in the West, where although only the rich can own the mass media, this is not overtly regarded as idea suppression). The doctrine of idea suppression is an old one, as the Catholic Church's Index of prohibited books demonstrates, but in the twentieth century the approach was expanded. To control ideas now we see control of the press, censorship, systematic rewriting of history, jamming of foreign broadcasts, teacher surveillance, visitor control, and similar totalitarian measures. Of course, from another standpoint such "solutions" are problems in themselves, attacks on freedom of expression. But I must mention them if I am to give a complete survey of all strategies of intervention. The obstruction of access to certain ideas has been seen on more occasions than we like to think as a way to combat, perhaps prevent, social problems.

Some modern viewpoints have arisen that can be called doctrines of *reduced intervention*, that is, arguments for the *removal* of the apparatus of intervention from certain areas in which it has hitherto been active. This general strategy has more than one theoretical (doctrinal) basis. Following the growth of cultural and ethical relativism, a moral

[39] See S. M. Lipset and R. B. Dobson, "The Intellectual as Critic and Rebel: With Special Reference to the United States and the Soviet Union," *Daedalus* 101 (1972), pp. 137–98. Only if religious schism or heresy were to be considered a social problem (for some cultural contexts) could we perhaps find in earlier periods in Western civilization advocacy by the literati of basic restructuring of social arrangements as a counter to a social problem. A true "adversary culture" among the intelligentsia develops only under relatively unique historical conditions. See Lionel Trilling, *Beyond Culture* (New York: Viking Press, 1965), pp. xii–xiii. Eric Hoffer, Edward Shils, and Alvin Gouldner have offered some ideas on what these conditions might be. See E. Hoffer, *The True Believer* (New York: Mentor, 1951), pp. 121–23; E. A. Shils, "Introduction" to Georges Sorel, *Reflections on Violence* (New York: Collier Books, 1961); Alvin W. Gouldner, *The Future of Intellectuals and the Rise of the New Class* (New York: Continuum, 1979).

concern emerged with the law's apparent persecution of deviants who do no one any harm—the "crimes without victims" argument. As older conceptions of homosexuality, adultery, and pornography have altered, it is maintained with increasing frequency that the law has no place in the bedroom, that in general victimless crime should be either legalized or treated much differently than traditionally.[40]

In a sense, the above-mentioned position is not so much a doctrine for dealing with a social problem as a move to redefine a behavior so that it is not regarded as an actionable social problem at all. But another variant of the doctrine of reduced intervention clearly continues to recognize a problematic situation yet still recommends less activity as a means to its reduction. Such a recommendation is made when the prevailing forms of intervention seem to do more harm than good. A prominent example of this doctrine arose in economics in the late 1700s. The doctrine of laissez faire, to be discussed in greater detail in Chapter 7, emerged in reaction to the economic system of mercantilism, which advocated a tightly regulated market.[41] Proponents of laissez faire proposed to advance prosperity beyond the potential of mercantilism by prescribing a hands-off policy by the government toward economic affairs. Modern economies no longer operate according to laissez faire principles—although some governments continue to give it lip service—but the doctrine undoubtedly remains the most prominent historical example of the general strategy of intervention reduction.

For the last two decades a doctrine of intervention reduction has been generated by the labeling theorists (to be discussed in Chapter 8) for treatment of mental illness and juvenile delinquency. According to this perspective, the labeling of someone as delinquent or mentally ill tends to solidify and perpetuate the very condition that the agency involved is attempting to change. Schur's book on "radical nonintervention" made a case quite clearly for leaving adolescents alone whenever possible.[42] From a somewhat different perspective Wilkins came to the same conclusion regarding drug laws.[43] In the case of mental disorder Scheff argued that much of it is a transient phenomenon that,

---

[40]This topic has generated a great deal of discussion in recent decades. See the argument summarized in Edwin M. Schur, Crimes without Victims (Englewood Cliffs, NJ: Prentice-Hall, 1965). In terms of "over-criminalization," see Sanford Kadish, "The Crisis of Over-Criminalization," The Annals 374 (1967), pp. 157–70; and Herbert L. Packer, The Limits of the Criminal Sanction (Stanford: Stanford University Press, 1968).

[41]See E. F. Hecksher and Meyer Shapiro, trans., Mercantilism (London: Allen & Unwin, 1935).

[42]Edwin M. Schur, Radical Non-Intervention: Rethinking the Delinquency Problem (Englewood Cliffs, NJ: Prentice-Hall, 1973).

[43]Leslie T. Wilkins, Social Deviance (Englewood Cliffs, NJ: Prentice-Hall, 1965), pp. 85–94.

however, tends to become stabilized after the imposition of the label.[44] It has been argued that the medical model of mental "illness" encourages psychiatrists to impose the label excessively in marginal cases because in regular medical practice it is better to err on the side of treatment when the physician is in doubt. In all of these cases a policy of reduced intervention (or in some cases, deinstitutionalization) by official governmental agencies was being advocated.

This doctrine of deinstitutionalization—variously known as demedicalization, decarceration, or diversion, with minor changes of meaning—has spread far beyond its original confines to include the elderly, the retarded, and those with chronic physical illness. The doctrine is thus one major thrust of the broader strategy of reduced intervention that, in recent years, has been both intellectually fashionable and widely adopted by governments. That much it has shared with the historical heyday of economic laissez faire. But has it been a success in practice? Suffice it to say it is questionable whether the doctrine actually reduced net intervention at all—although it unquestionably changed its form—and whether it has met its humane objectives.

Yet another major form of reduced intervention has been proposed to deal with our burgeoning nightmare of drug abuse. Again without denying that harm can and often does result from drug use (acknowledging that a social problem exists), the claim is advanced that the present method of coping by means of massive police intervention does more harm than good. Specifically, more crime—including even greater amounts of drug use—results from our present course. Some reluctantly have come to advocate the decriminalization of drugs, along the same line and for the same reason that Prohibition was abandoned some six decades ago. I will discuss the pros and cons of this particular strategy in Chapter 8.

Finally, there is a strategy for dealing with social problems by preventing even the *earliest instances* of a problem from arising. The *preventive strategy* relies on the foreknowledge that if certain proposed social developments are allowed to take place, the outcomes are likely to be deleterious. Hence the developments are never allowed to happen. Now it is true that on a crude level such a strategy is employed continually and has been throughout history. Every time a legislature considers a bill, for instance, it can reject it if problems from its passage can be foreseen.[45] More to the point are developments in society as a whole that can be prohibited in order to prevent new problems. While this

---

[44] Thomas Scheff, *Being Mentally Ill* (Chicago: Aldine, 1966).
[45] See this point made in Adolf Feingold, "Technology Assessment: A Systematic Study of Side-Effects of Technology," *The Canadian Forum* (February 1974), pp. 10–11.

consideration has been incorporated into planning throughout history, I am here referring to recent efforts to evaluate potential problems systematically and with sophisticated methods. Whereas amelioration of conditions and denial of opportunity aim at the minimization of existing problems by preventing further occurrences, the preventive strategy aims at precluding their emergence altogether.

To consider a single example, some years ago the United States banned the overflight of supersonic transport (SST) aircraft above its borders at speeds that break through the sonic barrier. This was accomplished before any commercial use of SST aircraft had commenced, although not before military aircraft had demonstrated the nature of the potential problem posed by daily sonic booms. This step has been correctly evaluated as a major break with a tradition that permitted technological development to occur as it might, only regulating the development *after* its appearance. Proponents of the new SST law maintained that once investment in SST development had been made, the arguments against wasting the hundreds of millions of dollars involved would in reality preclude any truly effective policing.[46] So the prohibition in effect had to be initiated beforehand, as it was.

Subsequent to the success of this attack, legislation established an Office of Technology Assessment in the American government. Before new technologies are introduced, such as recombinant DNA ("genetic engineering"), for example, their likely consequences can, it is hoped, be studied and evaluated in order to explore the advisability of allowing them to take place. To date, this strategy—so radically at odds with traditional Western values—remains relatively untested.[47]

A related development that emerged in the same period is environmental impact analysis. Again the strategy is one of outright prevention of a social (or physical) problem before it can occur. This time the emphasis is not necessarily on new technology but on major new developments of existing technology, such as a large dam project.[48] Everyone can see the benefits of a dam: water conserved for industry or a city, flood control, electricity generation, new recreation sites. But it also will incur

---

[46] See this argument, in general form, cogently presented in David Collingridge, *The Social Control of Technology* (New York: St. Martin's Press, 1980).

[47] For a reasoned advocacy of technology assessment and a history of the movement, see Thomas J. Knight, *Technology's Future*, 2nd ed. enl. (Malabar, Fla: Robert E. Krieger, 1982). An excellent textbook/handbook on the subject is *A Guidebook for Technology Assessment and Impact Analysis*, by Alan L. Porter et al. (New York: North-Holland, 1979).

[48] A good overview is contained in Donald McAllister, *Evaluation in Environmental Planning* (Cambridge: MIT Press, 1980). See also the Canadian Environmental Assessment Research Council's *Evaluating Environment Impact Assessment: An Action Prospectus* (Ottawa: Ministry of Supply and Services, 1988).

possible costs: loss of wildlife refuges, fishery habitat destruction, downstream silting, or increased soil salinity. One of the most significant environmental assessments ever conducted was for the Alaska pipeline project, an assessment that resulted in numerous design changes. Two of the greatest modern environmental disasters, the great Aswân High Dam in Egypt and the Aral Sea land reclamation in the Soviet Union, were both acclaimed as triumphs when first accomplished.

Let me repeat that the strategy of prevention, which aims at preventing a particular problem from ever appearing, should not be confused with intervention policies that aim at minimizing future occurrences of an existing problem—for instance, by amelioration of conditions.

THINKING ABOUT THE STRATEGIES

All intervention doctrines and strategies can be grouped in a primitive classification that distinguishes *essentially preventive* reactions (aimed at precluding additional outbreaks) from *essentially restorative* (or remedial) reactions, aimed at repairing or minimizing damage from a particular occurrence. The strategy of prevention, in the strict sense we have just been considering, is only one of a number of strategies that attempt to limit future occurrences.[49]

In this simple classification the strategies of rehabilitation and social reorganization are capable of fitting both categories.[50]

Essentially Preventive
deterrence
incapacitation
removal of opportunity
amelioration of conditions
prevention
reduced intervention

Essentially Restorative
retribution
restitution
expiation
moral regeneration
relief

rehabilitation
social reorganization

[49] Another terminological convention consists of dividing preventive measures into "primary prevention" (what I call amelioration of conditions) and "secondary prevention," consisting of early diagnosis of individual problem cases and appropriate remedial action (what I call rehabilitation). See Dorothy Anderson and Lenora McClean, eds., *Identifying Suicide Potential* (New York: Behavioral Publications, 1969). There is no universal agreement on terminology.

[50] For other schemes that classify strategies of intervention, see Jessie Bernard, *Social Problems of Midcentury* (New York: Dryden Press, 1957), p. 157; and Bernard Rosenberg et al., eds., *Mass Society in Crisis* (New York: Macmillan, 1964), p. 564. See also Daniel Glaser, *Social Deviance* (Chicago: Markham, 1971), Chapter 5.

I should emphasize at this point that one must distinguish between explicit doctrines and concealed motives, as well as between doctrines and consequences.[51] The possibility of some *covert motivation* behind an expressly stated doctrine is easy to recognize. Revenge, for instance, is only an overt feature in relatively early doctrines, but it almost certainly has been an unmentioned factor in later punitive formulations as well. Sadism may actually be operative in what is ostensibly the honorable (righteous, stern, unbending) administration of punishment.[52] Many of the apparent "control-oriented" features of contemporary penal institutions are actually punitive. This is often recognized by a guard force, who can raise or lower the disruptiveness of their control measures as a means of keeping the inmates in line without appearing to be vindictive. Frequent strip searches, for instance, can actually be a form of mass punishment even while they are justified as necessary for control. Mitford quotes a former psychiatrist at San Quentin as saying

> that psychiatry in the prison consists primarily in therapeutic practices which can have punitive or disciplinary implications: electric shock, insulin shock, fever treatment, hydro therapy, Amytal and Pentothal interviews, spinals and cisternals, and so on . . . that is, everything except psychotherapy . . . Shock treatment was pretty clearly used as punishment: It would take the form of telling the prisoner "unless your behavior changes you're going to get more of this."[53]

On the other hand, feelings of pity for harshly treated deviants are also motives that underlie doctrines with radically different surface justifications. At least some of the effort to substitute rehabilitation for punishment, or to show that certain offenders are not really responsible for their actions, springs as much from concealed motivations of pity as from desire for scientific truth or "greater protection of the public."[54]

Just as there are differences between explicit doctrines and private motivations, disparities can exist between *doctrine and reality*, or

---

[51]See pp. 13–14 and 172 in Sam D. Sieber, *Fatal Remedies* (New York: Plenum Press, 1981).

[52]The concept of sadism today undoubtedly aids in the detection of what may have been guessed on occasion in earlier times but without sufficiently clear understanding. The label most definitely serves what Blumer has called a sensitizing function.

[53]J. Mitford, *Kind and Usual Punishment* (New York: Vintage, Random House, 1974), p. 111. I have combined the psychiatrist's own words and Mitford's paraphrasings.

[54]One prominent early sociologist noted that "in all probability the sentimental philanthropic impulse has done more than the scientific impulse to bring sociology into existence." Albion W. Small, *General Sociology* (Chicago: University of Chicago Press, 1905), p. 36.

between the measures advocated and the actions actually taken. I will reserve until Chapter 10 discussion of whether doctrines and strategies actually alleviate the social problems at which they are directed, but one can see at once that the Quaker practices directed toward rehabilitation were as punitive in their way as the direct physical punishment they superseded. For that matter, real rehabilitation might be psychologically punishing to a person (most conversions are), whereas in debates the rehabilitative orientation is usually *contrasted* with the punitive.[55] Numerous examples show that the disparity between a doctrine and reality is sometimes very great indeed. Thus, our classification of strategies, useful though it is in recognizing the variety of ways humanity has attempted to deal with its social problems, only hints at underlying motives and at the actual results of applying the approaches in practice.

I should also point out that a listing of the basic strategies does not detail the possible variations within each, nor more than hint at the often bewildering number of combinations of strategies that have been proposed for specific problems. By no means does all disagreement occur among advocates of different strategies. Some strategies contain *within* their confines divergent approaches that call forth strong feelings of preference. One example should suffice to show this type of conflict.

Scholars have traditionally held that a child's early upbringing largely determines conduct in adult life. Freudian ideas, by restating this viewpoint in a modern theory, invariably buttressed in contemporary thought the importance of early socialization. Even sociologists, who have developed a concept of "adult socialization," accept the general importance of socialization in childhood. Yet, as Wrong and others have pointed out, the evidence for the supremacy of early socialization in determining later behavior is certainly not sufficient to account for the unthinking endorsement this belief is given in modern sociology.[56]

One's conception of the relative importance (for present-day behavior) of socialization in childhood, as opposed to the day-to-day experiences in the later life of the individual, clearly influences the choices of measures to alleviate certain social problems. For instance, in the 1960s "war on poverty" campaign in the United States, some sociologists favored helping the "unreachable poor" through vastly increased job opportunities—concentrating on adults—while others wanted to break up the intergenerational transmission of what they called a

---

[55] See Herbert L. Packer, *Criminal Sanction.*
[56] Dennis W. Wrong, "The Oversocialized Conception of Man in Modern Sociology," *American Sociological Review* 26 (1961), pp. 183–93. This point is also expressed by the critics of the "culture of poverty" notion.

"culture of poverty"—concentrating on child socialization.[57] Thus the strategy a given theorist chose was partly a result of the relative importance he or she assigned to childhood socialization and to adult experiences in breaking people out of the poverty cycle.[58] Yet notice that both approaches are examples of the *single strategy* of amelioration of conditions. This fact did not prevent the generation of tension, even considerable animosity, between advocates of the two concrete approaches.[59]

In this chapter I have attempted to set forth the various fundamental approaches to the resolution of social problems employed or advocated at different historical periods. Two of the most significant questions are, of course, why particular cultures choose one means over another and why specific historical periods have favored particular strategies. The next chapter deals in various ways with the facets of this problem.

---

[57] A variant of the former approach was the negative income tax (or income maintenance) program, to be discussed in Chapter 10 as an experiment.

[58] See Zahava D. Blum and Peter H. Rossi, "Images of the Poor," in *On Understanding Poverty*, ed. Daniel P. Moynihan (New York: Basic Books, 1969). For an attempt at assessment of the two approaches, see Louis Kriesberg, *Mothers in Poverty* (Chicago: Aldine, 1970).

[59] See, for example, William Ryan, *Blaming the Victim*, and E. B. Leacock, ed., *The Culture of Poverty: A Critique* (New York: Simon and Schuster, 1971). The concept of a culture of poverty originated in Oscar Lewis, *La Vida* (New York: Random House, 1966).

7

HISTORICAL OBJECTIONS TO INTERVENTION

Soon or late, it is ideas, not vested interests, which are dangerous for good or evil.

John Maynard Keynes

As one surveys the history of reactions to social problems, a long-term trend toward expansion of intervention becomes unmistakable. Many reasons have been given for this expansion. In part it stems from the emergence of the social problems concept itself, in part from a reevaluation of the duties of government—its extention into areas formerly touched only by sporadic private philanthropy. Today, when virtually all governments claim in one way or another to be servants of the people, it is difficult to recapture what a radical idea this once seemed—how perverse, even difficult to understand this interpretation was in times when a sovereign state was openly considered the private property of its monarch. So if today a government is "of the people, by the people, and for the people," or calls itself a "people's democracy," the government at least strains toward helping the populace.

It is also true that government services are expanding today partly because of vested interests whose livelihood would otherwise be eliminated or curtailed. These specialists in social problems will be surveyed in a later chapter. In addition, it is probable that such problems as poverty were not attacked earlier because, prior to the industrial revolution, mass impoverishment as we think of it today was truly unavoidable. In this chapter we shall examine a particular set of reasons for the expansion of intervention: *the decline of several fatalistic viewpoints.*

I should briefly note that some historians do not see ideas as very influential forces in history. But many other historians disagree with

111

this view, and so do I.[1] Perhaps it is worth recalling what the greatest economist of the century once said about this, on the last page of his master work:

> ...the ideas of economists and practical philosophers, both when they are right and when they are wrong, are more powerful than is commonly understood. Indeed the world is ruled by little else. Practical men, who believe themselves exempt from any intellectual influences, are usually the slave of some defunct economist. Madmen in authority, who hear voices in the air, are distilling their frenzy from some academic scribbler of a few years back. I am sure that the power of vested interests is vastly exaggerated compared with the gradual encroachment of ideas. Not indeed immediately, but after a certain interval; for in the field of economic and political philosophy they are not many who are influenced by new theories after they are twenty-five or thirty years of age, so that the ideas which civil servants and politicians and even agitators apply to current events are not likely to be the newest. But, soon or late, it is ideas, not vested interests, which are dangerous for good or evil.[2]

I shall concentrate here on those major developments in the history of ideas of greatest relevance to intervention. We shall inspect ideas that see the persistence of social problems as God's will, others that affirm the natural inferiority of certain races and classes and the unalterability of human nature, and finally conceptions of inexorable social "laws" that rule out meaningful change. These ideas have at various times formed potent obstacles to intervention. The importance of the idea of progress also will be stressed in a separate section.

INTERPRETING GOD'S WILL

The oldest disputes on the consequences of intervention have a theological foundation. Religious interpretations of social problems have been declining in importance, but a significant vestige remains and continues to exert substantial influence on some sensitive issues. We can

[1]Excellent arguments for the central role of ideas can be found in R. G. Collingwood's selection in *Theories of History*, ed. Patrick Gardner (New York: Free Press, 1959), pp. 251–62; and Robert Redfield, *The Primitive World and Its Transformations* (Ithaca: Cornell University Press, 1953), especially on pp. 75–83.

[2]John Maynard Keynes, *The General Theory of Employment, Interest, and Money* (New York: Harcourt, Brace, 1936), pp. 383–84.

roughly divide the influence of religious orientations into two components: explicit doctrines and implicit views of the world. We shall look at the doctrinal aspects first.

Some religious groups, basing their position on what they believe to be revealed knowledge from scriptural sources, maintain that certain interventions to resolve social problems are contrary to God's will. These theologically based assertions, which used to be much more common, argue in effect that certain types of changes in the society are sacrilegious, that is, offensive in the sight of God.

The division of social matters into those in which it is legitimate for the rulers to meddle and those in which it is not (the sacred and the secular, God and Caesar) has been a common feature across a great many cultures. Thus, for example, in the High Middle Ages the prevailing division of society into three orders—clergy, nobility, and commoners—was sanctified as the way ordained by Heaven, following the Trinity of Father, Son, and Holy Ghost. Any thought of tampering with this divine scheme of society was condemned as blasphemy. On other matters, deemed secular affairs, it was agreed that mortal men could make social adjustments without committing sacrilege.[3] Since the Renaissance the number of social arrangements considered open for alteration has steadily expanded at the expense of the areas considered sacrosanct and unalterable.[4] But this expansion has been a matter of degree, so it is still quite possible today to find groups who insist that intervention on some issues violates divine commandments and will subject a people to the wrath of God. The sanctity of the family, for instance, of woman's place, and of various forms of marriage and procreation or birth control are discerned in sacred text, and the prohibition of numerous activities is equally seen as not subject to argument. These proscriptions obviously become relevant to our discussion when they conflict with proposed resolutions to social problems or when a pattern endorsed by a religion, such as paternalism, comes to be seen as a social problem in itself.

Turning away from explicit doctrines, let us see how certain implicit world views fostered by religions relate to fatalistic, noninterventionist positions. To anyone socialized in Western culture the following

---

[3]This is not to imply that religious leaders have not themselves made new arrangements of society. Ecclesiastical courts were once as powerful as those of kings, and papal encyclicals were equally powerful. I also do not want to imply here a complete lack of rebelliousness among medieval populations. On the sanctity of the three orders, each with its own God-given function, see Jacques Le Goff, *Medieval Civilization: 400–1500*, trans. Julia Barrow (New York: Basil Blackwell, 1988, original—1964).

[4]Howard Becker has developed the term "sacred society" to refer to cultures characterized by extreme reluctance to change the prevailing arrangements. See comments in Chapter 11 on the increased rationalization of modern society.

ideas will have a familiar ring: Man was put on this earth to suffer; Original Sin must be recompensed; each soul must go through its trial; because of his burden of free will, man must be exposed to temptation. Ideas such as these do not expressly prohibit specific forms of intervention, but they do contain certain fatalistic overtones.[5] As part of the *Geist* or spirit of traditional Christianity, they imply that *suffering is to be expected*. Implicitly they impart an aura of sinfulness in interposing against the God-given condition of man. "Born in throes, 'tis fit that man should live in pains and die in pangs."[6] Even more than the specific prohibitions just mentioned, these once prevalent patterns of Christian suppositions are in decline.

One religious orientation has virtually disappeared in Western culture: the idea of poverty and suffering as glorious in God's eyes. To be sure, this idea survives in language and literature, but the intense feeling of earlier centuries that poverty and suffering are ennobling is conspicuously absent.[7] Again manifestations of this idea sound familiar: Suffering on earth is to be rewarded in Heaven; care not for the body but for the eternal soul; "Lay not up treasures upon this earth, but . . ."; vows of poverty among the clergy; Mother Teresa; poverty as virtuous; mortification of the flesh; worldly goods as a source of evil. Archaic as they seem today, such thoughts were accorded the greatest attention and respect through many centuries of Christian history.[8] In our contemporary culture, on the other hand, it has become virtually impossible to attract new monks and nuns for the most rigorous cloistered orders.

In the age of intense religious commitment, intervention was directed toward saving the individual's spiritual soul, as opposed to dealing with social problems as we think of them today. ("What is a man profited if he shall gain the whole world and lose his own soul?") The established church went to great lengths to save the souls in its keeping. However punitively this commitment was enforced, social reaction was

---

[5] Lowry argues that these religious orientations were reflected in the early stages of social science in what he calls the "natural theory" of social problems. Freudians and social Darwinists argued that social problems were "the natural, inevitable, unavoidable and expected result of *man's evil nature*" (p. 246). They felt that social problems were "an unavoidable part of man's life" (p. 251). See Ritchie P. Lowry, *Social Problems* (Lexington, Mass.: DC Heath & Co., 1974).

[6] Herman Melville, *Moby Dick* (New York: Rinehart, 1959, original—1851), p. 427.

[7] The worldviews just mentioned are splendidly captured in Le Goff's *Medieval Civilization*. Note that a certain ambivalence toward poverty can be detected in the attitudes of earlier times. Poverty was ennobling if self-inflicted and in the service of God. Poverty on the part of serfs, on the other hand, of those born to it, was merely their miserable lot.

[8] In speaking of a singular Christian worldview, I am abstracting certain frequently found components, but this is not to minimize the profound differences between faiths within Christianity.

based ultimately on the belief that the most important pitfall—eternal damnation—was being avoided. In periods of religious dissent the social problems that occupied the attention of concerned persons were those relating to religious schisms and heresies, not, as today, the existence of poverty and iniquitous distribution of income.

The "tranquilizing" aspect of religion is certainly not unique to Christianity. One prominent and frequently cited example is Hinduism and the Indian caste system. The rigid class lines in traditional Hindu culture in theory cannot be crossed. Social mobility from class to class is virtually absent, either during a person's life or between generations.[9] The interesting question is how such a caste system can be maintained with minimal unrest. The answer is contained in the Hindu belief not only in immortality but in eternal existence on Earth—the myth of reincarnation in which the soul moves from one body to another after death. A central belief of reincarnation is that the caste of the body that one's soul next inhabits depends on the faithfulness of one's performance of caste duties (*dharma*) in the present body. Thus this religion has upward-social-mobility-through-reincarnation, and unrest is minimized.

The significance of these religious orientations in the study of social problems is that they form conceptual obstacles to intervention. There is little wonder that for radical critics such as Marx—as well as for other skeptical writers of his day—religion was the "opiate of the people."[10] Intentionally or not, a religious, other-worldly orientation tended to keep underprivileged people from rebelling against their harsh lot while on Earth. It hindered their recognition of what many today consider their true class interests.

Given these manifest or latent positions in religious doctrines, it is tempting to say that the increased secularization of modern society and the decline in intensity of religious belief may explain the corresponding increase in intervention. But matters are not so simple: intervention has increased not only because of the declining strength of religious objection but also because certain religious sectors have themselves embraced it![11] As noted in a previous chapter, many denominations in the twentieth-century church have developed a "social gospel" and are now far more concerned with alleviating misery on Earth than

---

[9] As M. N. Srinivas has shown, the system in actual fact is by no means this tight and probably never was. This does not substantially affect the analysis.

[10] See, as other examples from this period, Friedrich Nietzsche's *Beyond Good and Evil*; Mark Twain's *Letters from the Earth*; and Ludwig Feuerbach's *The Essence of Christianity*.

[11] Even in earlier periods, *reinterpreted* religious doctrines have sometimes served as focal points for peasant uprisings. See Norman Cohn, *The Pursuit of the Millenium*, rev. ed. (Cambridge: Oxford University Press, 1970).

with saving souls from eternal damnation.[12] Some members of the clergy are now, in fact, leaders of activist causes and apostles of intervention—sometimes considerably more so than their own parishioners.[13] Meanwhile, in less developed countries, many of the younger clergy have recently embraced "liberation theology," a more radical variant but with similar implications for fostering intervention.

The principal bases for denying the feasibility of intervention have gradually shifted from religious to secular grounds. As science has gained in public esteem, the supposed unalterability of social problems is based less on divinely inspired literature and more and more on supposedly "scientific" assumptions about the unalterability of "human nature" or the inevitability of a pattern of history. We shall now turn our attention to these more recent secular orientations.

CONCERNING HUMAN EQUALITY

The prevailing view of the nature of humanity held by a society, or perhaps the view held by its dominant members, is of the greatest importance for determining first, the apparent feasibility of intervention and second, the specific forms such intervention will assume.[14] It is time now to look at this relationship. This section will consider specifically the longstanding conflict between advocates of *heredity* and advocates of *environment* (Sir Francis Galton's "nature and nurture") in terms of which factor has the greater importance in shaping human behavior. A culture's position on this issue, as well as its views on human alterability, have profound implications for intervention decisions, as we shall see.

In many historical periods, belief in the inheritance of "character," of ability, and of what we now call personality was absolute, virtually unquestioned. In fact, it is safe to say that throughout history, up to very recent times, whenever the effects of nature versus nurture were weighed, the hereditary or "blood" argument has been strongly favored over that of the environment and socialization. As recently as the turn of the century such views were still predominant. Thus in criminology, for

---

[12]C. H. Hopkins, *The Rise of the Social Gospel in American Protestantism, 1865–1915* (New Haven: Yale University Press, 1967).

[13]Gary T. Marx, "Religion: Opiate or Inspiration of Civil Rights Militancy?" in his book, *Protest and Prejudice* (New York: Harper and Row, 1967), pp. 94–105.

[14]See John Kunkel and Michael Garrick, "Models of Man in Sociological Analysis," *Social Science Quarterly* 50 (June 1969), pp. 136–52.

example, the great Italian theorist Lombroso advanced a hereditarian theory of crime around 1866. The criminal, according to Lombroso, was a genetic "throwback," or atavistic.[15] A few biological advocates survive in criminology even today; around 1900 it was the prevailing view.[16] For an illustration from the late nineteenth century of a biological theory of character, I turn to Robert Dugdale's work, *The Jukes: A Study in Crime, Pauperism, Disease, and Heredity* (New York: 1877). Some of the "tentative conclusions" reached were: "Illegitimacy as such does not invariably entail viciousness or criminality in descendants; crime is correlated with the crossing of a vicious blood with a more vigorous outside strain; pauperism is correlated with the close inbreeding of a vicious and weakened strain" (from the introduction by F. H. Giddings).

The belief in the inheritance of ability and disability encompassed not only individuals (for example, the inherent superiority of royal blood) but extended to include entire races. Certain races, it seemed, were naturally inferior. Everyone agreed that it was too bad, but nothing could be done about it. Intervention to improve the lot of the lower races was not only foolish but pernicious. Not only would such efforts lead directly to the miseries of resistance, revolt, revolution, and reprisals, but all would be for naught because the inferior people *could not* do what the "superior races" did. Blacks, for instance, simply could not survive outside of slavery.

The progression of attitudes toward blacks is most interesting.[17] When black slaves were first brought to the New World, some writers seriously maintained that they were incapable (yes, literally incapable) of learning a European tongue. When it became clear that they could, some felt that blacks should be converted to the Christian faith, while others found this virtually sacrilegious. With blacks speaking English and worshiping Christ, it then seemed blacks could never be taught to read or write. When it became clear that blacks could write, slave states passed laws forbidding the teaching of literacy to blacks. Today a few writers maintain that blacks are poorly suited for scientific or scholarly work.

Similarly, the "savage races" (for instance, North American Indians) simply could not be incorporated into the social mainstream— they were incapable of being "civilized." Thus, cultures that happened to be inferior in powder and shot were dominated and, in some cases,

---

[15] Cesare Lombroso, *L'uomo Deliquente*, exp. ed. (Torino, Italy: Bocca, 1896).

[16] See James Q. Wilson and Richard J. Herrnstein, *Crime and Human Nature* (New York: Simon and Schuster, 1985). For a critique, see the review by Lawrence E. Cohen in *Contemporary Sociology* 6 (1987), pp. 202–5.

[17] A short history of the origins of racism is found in Ashley Montagu, *The Idea of Race* (Lincoln: University of Nebraska Press, 1965).

extinguished at the leisure of the industrialized Western world—not only in North and South America but in Africa, the Pacific Island chains, and the steppes of Central Asia.[18] Colonial exploitation for economic and military objectives was an inevitable by-product of the combination of real military superiority and beliefs in racial superiority.

Two critical points deserve explicit recognition here. First, it should be recognized that in the nineteenth century racism was far more than racial prejudice or vaguely articulated beliefs. Racism was a formal doctrine presented in profuse detail and elegantly elaborated by numerous intellectuals of the day, such as Comte Joseph-Arthur de Gobineau and H. S. Chamberlain, and bolstered by early statisticians Galton and Karl Pearson.[19] Second, it should also be recognized that the concept of race advanced in such times was far more extensive than that held by the experts today on race, the physical anthropologists. Earlier, the concept of race was extended to include any intermarrying group. Thus there was supposedly an Italian race, a French race, and so forth in the most literal sense. There was also a lower-class race—again speaking quite literally. Such groups were considered races not only because their members truly did marry among themselves and did have numerous distinctive eccentricities of behavior, but also because it was thought that these behavior patterns were *inherent*—genetically determined. If Germans were stolid and Italians excitable, for example, it was because of their heredity, not their culture and upbringing. It was recognized that an Albanian brought up from infancy in Britain would speak English, but it was thought that he would still be prone to all of the behavioral features attributed to the Albanians because they were "in his blood."

It is easy to see how such beliefs could enjoy prominence—indeed, they were very difficult to overthrow. Certain peoples did tend to marry only among themselves (more so in former times than today because the sanctions for crossing traditional lines were much more severe); they did tend to manifest unique beliefs and forms of behavior (what today would be called their cultural pattern or "national character"); and, in addition, some *physical* characteristics are clearly, and truly, inherited. How easy to conclude, then, that the detected *behav-*

---

[18]See A. Grenfell Price, *White Settlers and Native Peoples* (Westport, Conn.: Greenwood Press, 1972, original—1950). The most punctilious rationalizations of claims to sovereignty over lands already inhabited were developed by the Spanish with respect to the New World. Either the inhabitants were conceived of as subhuman and not entitled to rights or their social structure was regarded as in "infancy" and in need of a European parental surrogate. See L. C. Green and Olive P. Dickason, *The Law of Nations and the New World* (Edmonton: University of Alberta Press, 1989).

[19]For a survey of racial and hereditarian theories while they were still powerful, see two chapters in Pitirim A. Sorokin, *Contemporary Sociological Theories through the First Quarter of the Twentieth Century* (New York: Harper, 1928).

ioral traits were hereditary. No intermarriage occurred across social class lines, and extremely severe sanctions were given out to members of one class who exhibited behavior considered appropriate to another.[20] Small wonder that it was all seen as linked to heredity. It also appeared there were "natural," biologically determined roles for women (supportive, tender, emotional) and for men (cynical, clearheaded, aggressive).[21] In fact, severe sanctions existed for females assuming male roles, and vice versa.

It might be a mistake to attribute the pervasiveness of such beliefs solely to their obvious usefulness for the dominant groups—although of course they are useful to an aristocracy. The classical counter to racist beliefs is the seemingly obvious point that a Hindu boy brought up from infancy in Ohio by Jewish parents displays far more interest in baseball and his bar mitzvah than in the caste signs used in India. He displays no apparent tendency toward nonviolence and is not noticeably tender toward cows. This is obvious today, but in a time of strict racial separatism and intense concern with "purity" of blood lines, such *natural* experiments had little opportunity to develop—were, in fact, repressed severely. An objective description of results could hardly be made under such conditions.[22] In their absence a racial theory of culture did answer most of the questions posed of it.

Obviously, a belief in inferior peoples, classes, sexes, and individuals had a dramatic effect on efforts to alleviate social problems. Certain forms of amelioration were not so much proscribed as, apparently, considered ridiculous. One did not waste education on the uneducable; hence women long remained without formal schooling. Within the living memory of some, similar arguments were raised in the American South respecting blacks. Certain races were simply "born to servitude and ignorance."[23] So, too, when the Nazis revived ideas of racial superiority, they wasted no efforts on the "sub-human," the *Untermensch*— people such as the Slavs, fit only to be "hewers of wood and drawers of water."[24] Similarly, if someone was a "born criminal," or even a member

---

[20] R. S. Neale, *Class and Ideology in the Nineteenth Century* (London: Routledge & Kegan Paul, 1972).

[21] See Duncan Crow, *The Victorian Woman* (London: Allen & Unwin, 1971).

[22] When a child *was* born of parents from two so-called "races," a form of self-fulfilling prophecy came into effect: the child was tolerated and accorded opportunities at a level somewhere in-between the proper "place" or "station" of each of his parents, as viewed by the dominant culture. At times this self-fulfilling prophecy extended to a whole new class—as with the mestizos (mixed-bloods) in parts of Latin America.

[23] Jack and William Levin, *The Functions of Discrimination and Prejudice*, 2nd ed. (New York: Harper and Row, 1982). The quote is from p. 16.

[24] For racial theories and concentration-camp experiences, see Bruno Bettelheim, *The Informed Heart* (Glencoe, Ill.: Free Press, 1960).

of a "criminal class," it was no use trying to change him.[25] Knowing that such were the beliefs of previous eras—beliefs held until quite recently, in fact—we can understand better the lack of effort toward resolution of what would be considered horrible social problems today.

As if this confusion were not sufficient, in the late 1800s a new ideological supplement to hereditarianism appeared. *Social Darwinists* extrapolated Darwin's evolutionary law of survival of the fittest from its biological origin into the sociocultural arena.[26] If conflict and domination were natural between biological species, and if this was apparently all for the best, perhaps it was so for cultures. If the members of certain cultures were virtually destroyed like vermin, this too was all for the best because the fittest cultures deserved to survive for the long-run development of the human race.[27] These ideas were, as has been remarked by more recent observers, a very odd confusion of evolution with progress (for example, assuming that a wolf is somehow "better" than a brontosaurus), but it had a persuasive scientific ring and it convinced many for several generations.[28] For many writers of the day, social welfarism would result only in the survival of the less fit and hence lower the overall quality of the human race. They preferred instead to advocate *eugenics*, the selective breeding of "better" human stock, as a means of progress. The eugenics movement was very popular in the late nineteenth and early twentieth centuries.[29]

Social Darwinism fit quite nicely with the then-prominent doctrines of classical economics, especially with Adam Smith's vision of the ideal governmental policy as one of minimal interference.[30] The fittest industries and individuals would survive in the conflict of the marketplace, and such noninterference (and nonregulation) of commerce would result in the greatest possible economic good.

In its heyday this doctrine commanded great support and followers did not flinch from its full application. On the basis of this economic doctrine, strictly interpreted, the British government virtually refused to intervene in the terrible Irish potato famine of the 1840s.

---

[25]Johannes Lange, *Crime & Destiny* (New York: Boni, 1930).

[26]One of the best sources here is still Chapter 19 of Howard Becker and Harry Barnes, *Social Thought from Lore to Science*, 3rd ed., vol. 2 (New York: Dover Publications, 1961, original—1938).

[27]This of course assumes that the fittest do survive. Some writers have maintained that in human society this is not the case even for the crudest meaning of "fittest." In war, for instance, the extremely unfit may be exempted.

[28]The classical discussion of the general influence of Social Darwinism is contained in Richard Hofstadter, *Social Darwinism in American Thought* (Philadelphia, 1944). See also Appendix Two of *An American Dilemma*, by Gunnar Myrdal (New York: Harper, 1944). A modern reexamination maintains that the doctrine was not as extreme as has been thought. See Robert C. Bannister, *Social Darwinism* (Philadelphia: Temple University Press, 1979).

[29]See Daniel J. Kevles, *In the Name of Eugenics* (New York: Knopf, 1985).

[30]Classical economics will be discussed later in the chapter.

Incredible as it seems, about a million persons in Ireland eventually succumbed to starvation and related disease.

> Years of partial failure of the Irish potato crop were followed in 1846 by total failure. Because many of the Irish peasants lived almost entirely on a diet of potatoes . . . the result was disastrous. The actions of the British government, torn between the harsh doctrine of Political Economy and whatever humanitarian feelings existed in the breasts of its members, were inadequate to meet the crisis.[31]

Between 1841 and 1851, the population of Ireland declined, by death and emigration abroad, from around 8 million to about 6.5 million.[32] We see here the nadir of nineteenth-century elitism, racism (yes, the Irish were an inferior "race"), and economism.[33] But in spite of such horrors, or perhaps in part because of them, the intellectual climate was gradually shifting.

Was heredity indeed what accounted for the leadership ability of a class, or was it the social training the class received? Were the characteristics of the Italians, as an example, a result of common ("racial") heredity or of common socialization patterns? From an early base among the French (especially the Encyclopedists), the environmentalist viewpoint gradually gained strength in the late nineteenth century as new facts and theories were assimilated. Ethnic patterns, criminal activities, sexual roles, and class mannerisms all came to be viewed as predominantly learned (that is, culturally induced) behavior.[34]

Nevertheless, at the turn of the century, racial-hereditarian viewpoints were still dominant, although weaker than before. One racial authority, Nathaniel S. Shaler, could still say in 1904, "The Negro . . . is, by nature, incapable of creating societies of an order above barbarism, and this . . . feature of his nature, depending as it does upon the lack of certain qualities in his mind, is irremediable."[35]

---

[31] Kenneth Duncan, "Irish Famine Immigration and the Social Structure of the Canadian West," *Canadian Review of Sociology and Anthropology*, Special Edition on Aspects of Canadian Society (1974), p. 142.

[32] R. D. Edwards and W. T. Desmond, eds., *The Great Famine*, 2nd ed. (New York: Russell and Russell, 1975). See also Cecil Woodham-Smith, *The Great Hunger* (New York: Harper & Row, 1963).

[33] The Irish case is the most obvious with respect to the influence of the doctrines discussed, but similar fates overtook the American Indian and Eskimo, with resulting decimation of their populations.

[34] So, too, in the study of mental disorder, explanation shifted away from hereditarianism. For an interesting interpretation of the reason behind the decline in hereditary degeneration theory in psychiatry, see the essay by Martin Stone in Volume 2 of W. F. Bynum et al., *The Anatomy of Madness: Essays in the History of Psychiatry* (London: Tavistock Publications, 1985).

[35] As quoted in Merle Curti, *Human Nature in American Thought: A History* (Madison: University of Wisconsin Press, 1980), p. 272.

As the twentieth century dawned, more sympathetic and realistic treatments of primitive cultures were given by anthropologists, who began to insist on doing their own fieldwork instead of relying on reports of missionaries, explorers, or soldiers.[36] The educated sector slowly recognized that world history included more—much more—than the history of Greece, Rome, the Renaissance, and Western Europe. Contact with sophisticated non-Western forms of thought led gradually from ethnocentric beliefs about the "white man's burden" to a position of cultural relativity.[37] Cultural (and ethical) relativity had roots in much earlier periods, but the writings of anthropologists and antiquarians (students of classical civilizations) did much to popularize the position among intellectuals. The sophisticated study of race by physical anthropologists and others began to tear down the superstructure of hereditarianism and racism. The rise of sociology, with its emphasis on the importance of childhood socialization, undoubtedly played a role by highlighting an alternative explanation for the relation between blood line and behavior.[38]

Although the eugenics movement reached its high tide in the 1920s, resulting in new restrictions on immigration to America, the intellectual turning point away from racial and hereditarian explanations had already occurred. Curti places this critical divide around 1921–22, thanks to a remarkable convergence of key works that appeared in those years.[39] The writers were educator-philosopher John Dewey, social psychologist Charles Horton Cooley, sociologist William F. Ogburn, writer James Harvey Robinson, and biologist Vernon Kellogg. Anthropologist Franz Boas wrote his key work (*The Mind of Primitive Man*) some ten years earlier. The country was still predominantly racist but the intellectuals had turned. The turning of the majority would follow revulsion against the racism of the Nazis.

Throughout most of human history, the hereditarian explanation had dominated over the sociocultural. The situation is reversed today, yet even now we find common verbal expressions that reflect the belief of hereditarian dominance in earlier eras: the "born leader," the "born criminal," "blood will out," or "blood will tell." Modern genetics can document true inheritance of *behavior* only in specific isolated conditions—in some forms of schizophrenia and in rare sex-chromosome ab-

---

[36]Robert H. Lowie, *A History of Ethnological Theory* (New York: Holt, 1937).

[37]See this position discussed in more detail in Chapter 1.

[38]For an excellent summation of criticisms of hereditarian theories, while the battle was still in progress, see Sorokin, *Contemporary Sociological Theories*. For the distinction between ethnic group and race, see Ashley Montagu, *Man's Most Dangerous Myth* (New York: Columbia University Press, 1942).

[39]Merle Curti, *Human Nature*. See especially pp. 274–96.

normality linked with violent crime.[40] That the lessons about heredity took considerable time to be absorbed by the world was made terribly clear by the primitive racial doctrines of the Nazis—still clinging in the 1940s to nineteenth-century beliefs about the genetic superiority of the Nordic "race" and the subhuman character of Jews and Slavs.

THE ALTERABILITY OF HUMAN NATURE

Man is a pliable animal, a being who gets accustomed to everything!

Fyodor Dostoyevski

The question of the *malleability of human nature*, the extent to which perhaps some cultural forms are more "natural" or more congenial to humanity than others, has interested thinkers for thousands of years. In contrast to what historically seems to be the more common belief, the intellectual viewpoint of today endorses a view of human beings as almost infinitely alterable, infinitely moldable by their culture.[41] This vision or "model" of humanity is so taken for granted today that it is rarely made explicit; the best discussions overtly endorsing extreme conceptions of malleability can be found in the anthropological literature of an earlier era, for example, Ruth Benedict's *Patterns of Culture.*[42] The viewpoint is implicit but all-pervasive in sociological and anthropological literature today.[43]

In part, the responsiveness to this view in the modern world (let us say, post-1800) is a function of the increasing rapidity of cultural change. So long as culture changes little over a life span, it is relatively easy to believe in a "natural" way that things should be. When people see vast changes take place in their own lifetime, however, this belief

---

[40] See David Rosenthal, *Genetic Theory and Abnormal Behavior* (New York: McGraw-Hill, 1970); and Roger N. Johnson, *Aggression in Man and Animals* (Philadelphia: Saunders, 1972), especially pp. 87–91.

[41] While I am treating racism-hereditarianism and the question of malleability as two separate issues, it should be noted that throughout the late nineteenth and early twentieth centuries discussion of these issues was intermixed, due in large part to the hyperextension of the idea of race. Thus much of Curti, *Human Nature*, pp. 274–96, is also relevant to an analysis of malleability.

[42] New York: Mentor, 1934.

[43] See Paul Hollander, "Sociology, Selective Determinism, and the Rise of Expectations," *The American Sociologist* 8 (November 1973), pp. 147–53.

becomes increasingly difficult to maintain. Toffler has vividly documented the increasing rapidity of technological and social change.[44]
Then too, the ease with which film and the electronic media can bring
the farthest reaches of the earth into everyday experience must also
heighten awareness of the extraordinary variety of human cultures. Even
if the media typically treat these differences in a superficial fashion, the
impact is still far greater than that experienced by earlier generations.

Although the position of great human plasticity is all-pervasive
in sociology and anthropology today, historically it is an exceptional,
unusual viewpoint, even among the literati. And even today two challenges have arisen. One, sociobiology, arose in the mid-1970s as a new
version of the old idea that behavior is programmed by the genes in
humans, just as it clearly is in certain animal species.[45] The new sociobiology has solved the problem of altruism—how altruistic behavior
could have arisen by natural selection—thus turning what used to be its
greatest failing into one of its stronger suits. Sociobiology tends to support the idea of certain natural forms for culture because it posits a common genetic basis for behavior that, naturally, must apply to all humans
of whatever culture. A second challenge to plasticity comes from recent
findings in linguistics that strongly support the position that we are all
"pre-wired" genetically (the "innateness hypothesis") with respect to
language acquisition.[46] I will tersely summarize the present status of
these theories by saying that the challenge from linguistics is strong in
evidence but extremely limited in intended scope, while the challenge
from sociobiology is very broad in intended scope but extremely limited
in supporting evidence.

Our concern here is only partially with just how malleable humans, and human cultures, really are. Of greater import in this chapter is
the *consequence* for intervention in social problems of people *believing*
in high or low plasticity. On the one hand we wish to be scientifically
correct on the matter; on the other hand we recognize that people's beliefs about their own plasticity—be these correct or incorrect—invariably exert an influence on their intervention decisions. It is important to
recognize that a belief in the malleability of human nature is a congenial
view for persons or groups interested in amelioration of social problems.
If human nature is readily changeable, the obstacles to social reconstruction are far less serious and the conceivable scope is vastly ex-

---

[44] Alvin Toffler, *Future Shock* (New York: Bantam Books, 1970), chaps. 1 and 2.
[45] See, for example, Pierre Van den Berghe, "Bringing Beasts Back In: Toward a Biosocial
Theory of Aggression," *American Sociological Review* 39 (1974), pp. 777–88.
[46] For one indicative article, see Derek Bickerton, "Creole Languages," *Scientific American*
249 (July 1983), pp. 116–22.

panded. One may dream, as did some early sociologists, of forming new religions as part of the reconstruction of society. Conversely, a belief in the existence of a "natural" way for mankind to be—either God-given or based on an interpretation of nature—diminishes confidence in efforts at social and cultural reconstruction. For this reason one may strain either toward or away from this viewpoint, depending on the desire for fundamental change.

Let me give an illustration of this point. In the Soviet Union of the 1930s, authorities desired rapid social transformation and also "proofs" to show that very rapid change was possible. One way to hurry social transformation would be if the social experiences of the parent generation could alter the actual genetic makeup of the human race. The strong desire of Soviet authoritarians that this were so became transformed into the sternly enforced dogma that it *was* so. The doctrinaire belief in the emergence of a "new Soviet man" became so intense that biological science was twisted so as to "demonstrate" great human malleability. The scientifically discredited doctrine of the biological (genetic) inheritance of *socially acquired* characteristics became an officially endorsed dogma, with the full force of the Soviet scientific director, Trofim Lysenko, behind it. Professors who refused to accept the doctrine were dismissed from their posts. *Lysenkoism* seemed to promise that humanity could be reformed (that is, the biology of the human race transformed) at a much faster rate than conventional biological theories predicted, but of course all of this was predicated on the false premise that culture could influence the genes.[47] In the end the doctrine was abandoned after setting Soviet biology back for decades. And the irony was that one does not really need to have this "inheritance of acquired characteristics" in order to have rapid social transformation—all that is required is that humans, in their *existing* genetic makeup, have great plasticity. But this controversy graphically illustrates how the wish may become father to the doctrine with respect to conceptions of human changeability.[48]

---

[47] David Joravsky's article on Lysenko is one of the best available short summaries of this period of Soviet biology. See his "The Lysenko Affair," *Scientific American* 207 (November 1962), pp. 41–49. See also Zhores Medvedev, *The Rise and Fall of T. D. Lysenko* (New York: Columbia University Press, 1969).

[48] Interspersed through the questions of heredity versus environment and human malleability has been the strength of socialization (or education, as it was formerly regarded). Can socialization of the child guarantee the nature of the adult, as the early Jesuits claimed? Psychoanalytic theory and other theories of personality would agree with this idea. But see Denis Wrong's article, "The Oversocialized Conception of Man in Modern Sociology," *American Sociological Review* 26 (1961), pp. 183–93, which notes the importance of situation, culture, and social structure (relative to child training) in the production of adult behavior patterns.

This faith in human plasticity is held by virtually all modern intellectuals.[49] Interestingly, it is at odds with most of the great minds of the past, from Plato to Tolstoy, yet is accepted today virtually without question.[50] To quote the modern Polish intellectual, Milosz:

> All the concepts men live by are a product of the historic formation in which they find themselves. Fluidity and constant change are the characteristics of phenomena. And man is so plastic a being that one can even conceive of the day when a thoroughly self-respecting citizen will crawl about on all fours . . . as a sign of conformity to the order he lives in.[51]

The general faith in the malleability of human nature may be one of the few foci for optimism left in Western thought.[52]

SOCIAL "LAWS" AND SOCIAL REALITY

Another line of thought denies the ability to intervene effectively on certain problematic conditions. This objection maintains that the existence of some scientific "law" of society poses an insurmountable barrier to the solution of a social problem. This obstacle differs from our analysis of human nature since it is now the social structure that is apparently unbending, rather than the "quality" of the individual.

In one sense the examination of social "laws" (or "strong tendencies," as they would probably be called today) is part of the business of the social scientist. This examination intrudes directly on our topic of intervention when the "law" in question predicts that certain efforts to remove a social problem will not succeed. If enough people believe in such a law, then it does not have to be true to have a real, and serious,

---

[49] Infinite plasticity of individuals and cultures does not necessarily mean that human beings are easily pliable in the short run. Amitai Etzioni has argued that persuading individuals is not a very effective way to solve social problems, in comparison with altering the social structure. But the very conceivability of indefinite alterations in the latter reveals his underlying faith in human adjustability. See "Human Beings Are Not Very Easy to Change After All," *Saturday Review* (June 3, 1972), pp. 45–47.

[50] Perhaps the first major writer to claim that human nature is a changeable product of the times was the Neapolitan philosopher Giambattista Vico, in the early 1700s. His remained a minority view until early in this century.

[51] Czeslaw Milosz, *The Captive Mind* (New York: Vintage Books, 1955), pp. 27–28.

[52] See the section on the decline of faith in progress later in this chapter. For an excellent discussion of "the problem of human nature," see the Coda of Herbert Muller's book, *The Children of Frankenstein: A Primer on Modern Technology and Human Values* (Bloomington: Indiana University Press, 1971). This is, in my opinion, a poor title for an exceptional book.

effect. When people believe that something is not possible, they will not try it.

Most of the examples of such obstructing "laws" predate the twentieth century. Let us examine a straightforward example: Ricardo's iron law of wages. Popular during the nineteenth-century heyday of classical economics, the so-called iron law claimed that wages must in the long run remain just above the subsistence level for workers.[53] Here is how Ricardo came to that conclusion. If in the short run wages rose higher than bare subsistence, then more workers would live to, and through, their reproductive ages; larger families would result; and because of better conditions more children would survive. The result? An excessive number of workers (supply) for the jobs to be filled (demand), resulting in a return to lower wages. On the other hand, if wages dropped too low, falling below the subsistence level, more workers would die before producing children, and fewer of the children that were born would survive to working age, thereby producing a scarcity of labor in relation to demand. Wages would rise under these conditions. Hence, wages in the long run would remain at subsistence level. An iron law had been established that all sorts of good intentions for the workers could not overcome. What is more, when examined carefully, the law showed that efforts to improve the workers' lot would not only fail, but also would fail after producing greater misery than would otherwise have taken place.

Ricardo's iron law of wages had the virtue of being explainable in short order—a virtue that was really a vice in terms of repressing needed social reform. Its defect, of course, is that it is not an inexorable economic law at all, merely a relationship that holds true only under certain highly specific conditions. If, for example, the national population and/ or foreign trade was increasing, then an increase in workers' income, resulting in more workers available for work, would not necessarily lower the wages again because more jobs also would be available. The so-called law makes a staggering number of assumptions that are not spelled out—relations of income to family size and to number of surviving children, the absence of worker organizations for collective bargaining, and the absence of minimum wage laws and unemployment payments, just to name a few. The defects of this little scheme are today pitifully obvious, but to earlier industrial England the "law" seemed quite impressive.

The importance of such "laws" stems not from their actual validity but from the fact that as people believed them to be true, reformers

---

[53] See Pierro Sraffa, ed., *Works and Correspondence of David Ricardo* (Cambridge: Cambridge University Press, 1951).

were precluded from taking certain measures.[54] To paraphrase a famous expression, relationships believed to be real were real in their consequences. Belief in an "iron law" will not only affect social intervention, but also the conception of what is a social problem. Whatever people regard as unavoidable or inexorable tends not to be considered a social problem, however unpleasant it may be. (Witness death, which most of us do not want, yet it is not a social problem in and of itself.) Of course the validity of the law is an entirely separate question.

As Piven and Cloward have noted, rarely have self-interest and social theory so neatly coincided as they did in the early nineteenth century.[55] We have already noticed this remarkable congruity with respect to the popular ideas of racial inferiority. These ideas in turn were buttressed by sophisticated theories of the supposedly "prelogical character" of the primitive mind.[56] Another mistaken but popular scientific "law" of the period was that historical sociocultural development had to pass through a specific number of "stages" before reaching the apex of civilization—invariably situated in Western Europe. Not only did such value-laden beliefs deny cultural relativity by presuming that some cultures were better or higher than others, and that this could be infallibly known, but they also proposed a *single invariable sequence* of stages (differing somewhat among theorists) that all cultures had to follow in their "development." This conception of unilinear cultural evolution, whereby all cultures had to progress along a single path, implied that cultures could not skip or leap "stages"; each supposedly had to move through every level in turn before it could approximate the most "advanced" countries. Again, efforts toward social reform were stymied by such theories.[57]

The iron law of wages was but a single segment of a larger body of doctrine known as *laissez-faire economics*. Developed by the classical economists—Adam Smith, Ricardo, Thomas Malthus, John Stuart Mill—

---

[54] As an example, Robert Michels formulated a famous "iron law of oligarchy" which, whatever its intrinsic merits, undoubtedly had side effects in justifying oligarchical trends.

[55] Frances Piven and Richard Cloward, *Regulating the Poor: The Functions of Public Welfare* (New York: Pantheon Books, 1971). Richard Hofstadter has noted that the capitalist Andrew Carnegie became the personal benefactor of Herbert Spencer, the premier theorist of Social Darwinism.

[56] See Lucien Lévi-Bruhl, *Primitive Mentality* (London: Allen & Unwin, 1923). For an attack on this belief, see Bronislaw Malinowski, *Magic, Science, and Religion* (Glencoe, Ill.: Free Press, 1948). For a modern review of the controversy, see William Kay, *Moral Development*, rev. ed. (London: Allen & Unwin, 1970), especially chap. 3.

[57] For the doctrine of unilinear evolution, see Marvin Harris, *The Rise of Anthropological Theory* (New York: Thomas Y. Crowell, 1968). Although this old model is far too restrictive, evidence exists that at least some cultural components do regularly precede others. See Linton Freeman and Robert F. Winch, "Societal Complexity: An Empirical Test of a Typology of Societies," *American Journal of Sociology* 62 (March 1957), pp. 461–66.

the doctrine of laissez faire (French, meaning roughly "let it be") argued that maximum economic good would come from allowing unrestrained competition in the marketplace with an absolute minimum of governmental interference. Only the law of contracts and, of course, laws ensuring the safety of citizens and their property, were considered legitimate functions of government. In his immensely influential book, *The Wealth of Nations*, Adam Smith maintained that out of this unregulated chaos would come the greatest obtainable economic benefit—as though, in his famous phrase, led by an "invisible hand."[58] Followers of the classical economists believed that "that government is best that governs least" and abhorred such "socialistic" proposals of their day as a government-run postal system or public education. They would have been speechless before such unimaginable phenomena as automobile safety regulations or pure food and drug laws.

Not everyone was prosperous in Adam Smith's England, but then not everyone *could* be prosperous; efforts toward that objective had been "scientifically" shown to actually lead to worse conditions. Laws for the relief of the poor, for instance, would encourage indolence. Support for poor families with children would encourage men to marry and have children, which in turn would eventually strain the food supply, leading to greater misery. Placing a ceiling price on food staples such as bread would merely divert farm investment and production into other products for which no ceiling existed. As bread, for example, grew scarce, an illegal black market would develop with unlimited prices, and bread would be even dearer than before. Let it be.

Again my earlier example of the terrible Irish potato famine (the "Great Hunger") is instructive. As mentioned, about a million people in Ireland starved to death or died of disease aided by malnutrition during this four-year period. The British government responded with minimal aid, but as the figure shows it was infinitely too little too late. But what is really impressive, in a ghastly way, and why I bring it up again, is that during the period of this catastrophe *Ireland remained a net exporter of food*. The Irish poor were not part of the money economy, and what food was produced was a cash crop available for export. Classical economics explained why the Irish poor would be even worse off if charity and habits of idleness were encouraged.

Not for nothing was classical economics known as the dismal science. These so-called "laws" only consider what are known as "first-order [direct] effects." The actual possibilities—which indeed include

---

[58]Adam Smith, *An Inquiry into the Nature and Causes of the Wealth of Nations* (New York: P. F. Collier, 1909, originally—1776), p. 351. It should be pointed out that brief summaries unavoidably neglect Smith's subtleties and intellectual range, which can be seen in both *The Wealth of Nations* and his *Theory of Moral Sentiments*.

these outcomes but many others as well—depend also on second- and higher-order effects, and are far more complex than they seem. The significance of laissez faire and related views for our purposes is quite simple: insofar as people believed in these doctrines, efforts to advance economic reform were thwarted.

CHOICE LAWS

In the twentieth century a new form of prohibitive social law has come into existence. In place of the sheer prohibitions found, for example, in the old iron law of wages, we find what might be called *choice laws*, which state that one sometimes cannot increase one good without simultaneously decreasing another, or decrease one evil without strengthening one to which it is linked. Thus it is often maintained in contemporary economics that an economy cannot have full employment without suffering inflation and cannot cure high inflation without increasing unemployment. Unlike iron prohibitions, one can to an extent pick one's evil, but one cannot maximize both desirable goals at once.[59]

We must distinguish here between scientific "laws" (whether correct or incorrect) and political choices, which can look similar. If a nation has a finite amount of revenue to spend and the decision is made to spend it all on project A, this naturally precludes spending the same revenue on project B. Or, if the nation spends two-thirds on A it can only spend one-third on B. We can speak of such decisions as "trade-offs," but they are not inexorable choice laws of society; they are something different.[60]

Here are some more examples of economic choice laws—made more intriguing, perhaps, by the fact that they were written by a future Nobel Prize laureate in the year 1937. Writing of the limits of economics, Oskar Morgenstern said it was possible to show that some desires are mutually inconsistent.

---

[59] As Karl Popper has pointed out, there are numerous parallels to this choice law in the physical sciences and in technology. Thus, for example, engineers will speak of trade-offs between stability and speed in the design of ships where, once again, one cannot maximize both desiderata at the same time.

[60] The inability to expend more than is there depends, I suppose, on a mathematical identity, or perhaps is true by definition. I do not want to imply that such political trade-offs are not matters of legitimate interest. See, for instance, Donald M. McAllister, *Evaluation in Environmental Planning: Assessing Environmental, Social, Economic, and Political Trade-Offs* (Cambridge, Mass.: MIT Press, 1980), or Part I of *Knowledge and Decisions*, by Thomas Sowell (New York: Basic Books, 1980).

If it is our intention to reduce the cost of living, and at the same time we introduce agricultural tariffs; if we want to keep the currency stable and yet do something which increases the money circulation; or if we want to decrease unemployment and at the same time preach that wages should be kept up, we shall not reach our goal. In these and a thousand other cases there is always an either-or: you cannot have your cake and eat it.[61]

Choice laws also appear outside of economics, although not so well formulated. In criminology, for instance, some have said that, while police need to have unmonitored contacts with criminals to develop informants, precisely the kind of contacts needed also permit the development of corrupt dealings. Thus we have an unpleasant trade-off between the effectiveness of crime prevention and the extent of police corruption.[62] In social organization, meanwhile, we encounter what might be called Gorbachev's dilemma: writing some five years before Gorbachev's assumption of power in the USSR, Sieber noted that "participatory planning is necessary to give the members a stake in an organization and to insure a supply of fresh ideas; but strong leadership [centralization of authority] is necessary to enforce standards, cope with crises, and manipulate the environment."[63]

Continuing with the major reforms currently underway in the Soviet Union, all accounts seem to indicate a massive upsurge in "protection" rackets (extortion) since the USSR began to permit small private-service businesses. Of course the theoretical explanation is that for the first time owners have a personal stake in their equipment and shelter and cannot afford to have them damaged. Meanwhile, observers are completely unanimous that the reform has greatly improved the quality of service available. So perhaps we are again witnessing a choice law: entrepreneurial freedom and quality service versus higher levels of extortion crime. Meanwhile, in China, reforms have led to a new mentality of consumerism that simultaneously stimulates productivity and increases theft and black marketeering.[64]

To take a different sort of example, some historians have argued that, although it is common to regard the Middle Ages negatively

---

[61] *The Limits of Economics*, trans. Vera Smith (London: William Hodge, 1937). The quote is from p. 53.

[62] The New York City drug squad in the 1970s, for instance, became at once outstanding and notorious in this way. See Robert Daley, *Prince of the City* (New York: Berkley Publications, 1986). The same upsetting relationship has been found in Britain.

[63] Sam D. Sieber, *Fatal Remedies* (New York: Plenum Press, 1981).

[64] It must be acknowledged that reporting of crime is, as I write, more open in both the Soviet Union and China than in the past. So the possibility exists that these crime increases may reflect, to some unknown degree, greater honesty in reporting.

because of the ignorance, poverty, and physical misery that prevailed, at that time a certain psychic tranquility arose from the orderliness of existence. Psychic tranquility may be at a very low ebb today. One probably cannot have modern "progress" without destroying this, and so again we have a choice of obtainable benefits. As Hollander put it, "sociology [and the other social sciences] if honestly pursued, cannot but conclude with the dispiriting finding that . . . not all highly valued ends are compatible."[65]

I have deliberately put the discussion of choice laws in its own separate section because I have a different feeling about them than I have concerning the socioeconomic "laws" that preceded them historically. Specifically, I happen to think that at least some choice laws may be valid. Whether or not I am right on this, the critical point for this chapter is their effect on intervention. As with their nineteenth-century cousins, the validity of choice-law assertions is one issue; another issue is the effects of such laws on the effort to overcome social problems; and yet a third is the consequences of believing such laws hold even if they do not.[66]

When an evil is said to be inextricably mixed with or caused by the same agents that promote certain beneficial features of society, such an assertion has much the same consequences for intervention as a choice law. The difficulty here, of course, is that to do away with the bad, one must also destroy the good. Indeed we are at times informed that it is naive, or prescientific, to believe that evil always flows from evil.[67] For instance, the same innovative individualism in a culture that leads to scientific advance may be one cause of criminal activity; to diminish the latter, we must resign ourselves to less of the former. This argument can be seen in Daniel Bell's "Crime as an American Way of Life."[68] In sociology this is often expressed as the view that one cannot eliminate certain social problems without simultaneously destroying desirable social features. This last position is so important that I will devote a lot of attention to it in Chapter 8.

---

[65] Hollander, "Selective Determinism," p. 152.

[66] Popper maintains that the discovery of "impossible relations" is one of the most important tasks of the social sciences. See his book, Conjectures and Refutations (New York: Basic Books, 1963). He may be right; I merely point out the consequences for social action of holding such beliefs.

[67] One argument to this effect is provided by Edward Shils. Speaking of "civil politics" (his ideal), he feels for instance that it "requires an understanding of the complexity of virtue, that no virtue stands alone, that every virtuous act costs something in terms of other virtuous acts, that virtues are intertwined with evil . . . " Edward Shils, The Intellectuals and the Powers and Other Essays (Chicago: University of Chicago Press, 1972), p. 62.

[68] Antioch Review 13 (1953), pp. 131–54. The significance of Bell's work is discussed in Becoming Deviant, by David Matza (Englewood Cliffs, NJ: Prentice-Hall, 1969), pp. 73–80. See also Arthur K. Davis, "Social Theory and Social Problems," Philosophy and Phenomenological Research 18 (December 1957), pp. 190–208, especially pp. 200–1.

FAITH IN PROGRESS

I want to turn now to another idea with an impact on intervention: the idea of progress, which refers to a generalized forecast of the future improvement of the condition of humanity as a whole. Although there are always individuals who think their own future will be better, the idea of progress is by no means universal across cultures. Instead, this idea contrasts with an equally common idea of a decline from a "Golden Age" in the past. The latter theme has a great many variations. At times it seems as if all classical mythologies have one. The Fall from Grace is, of course, the familiar biblical version. The early Greeks believed in an initial golden race, succeeded by a race of silver, a race of brass, and finally the present iron race. Even within the last, "as the generations pass, they grow worse; sons are always inferior to their fathers."[69] The idea of progress, of course, points toward the proximate future instead of to the past for an age of glory and happiness.[70]

The sociology of knowledge (that branch of sociology that studies the social basis of ideas) can give us some insight into the factors at work in the development of an idea of progress. In some eras the rate of technological and cultural change was sufficiently slow as to be almost imperceptible. Under such conditions expectations about the future are difficult to predict. Alfred North Whitehead once considered the speed of permanent social change and decided that until the nineteenth century, "the time-span of important change was [in most cases] considerably longer than that of a single human life." But when improvement or decline becomes more noticeable, when marked changes within a single life span can be observed, then social scientists expect optimism or pessimism about the future based on past experiences.[71] When this is linked with a plausible rationale for why progress or decline should occur, it can lead to dramatically intense beliefs. I want to spend a bit of time tracing the intensity of faith in progress over the last few centuries because this faith can have a significant influence on intervention. The relationship is not a simple one, however, as we will see.

---

[69]Edith Hamilton, *Mythology* (New York: Mentor, 1940), p. 69. For a related theme found in our own culture, see Fred Davis, *Yearning for Yesterday: A Sociology of Nostalgia* (New York: Free Press, 1979). For the spread of Golden Age beliefs in the ancient Middle East, see James George Frazer, *Folklore in the Old Testament* (New York: Tudor, 1923). Parenthetically, it is a belief in secular or worldly progress that is our interest here, not a belief in a coming apocalypse.

[70]For the various interpretations of history in terms of human happiness (lineal, cyclical, spiraliform, etc.), see Georges Sorel, *The Illusions of Progress* (Berkeley: University of California Press, 1972, original—1908).

[71]See the excellent discussion in Toffler, *Future Shock*. The first historian to emphasize the accelerating pace of change was Henry Adams, early in the present century.

In the period known to intellectual history as the Enlightenment (roughly 1650–1800), a strong belief in progress arose, based on faith in the power of human reason.[72] The scientific revolution was gathering momentum; the period saw the successes of Copernican and Galilean astronomy, as well as the capstone of early physics—the development of Newtonian mechanics.[73] The writers of the period were in virtual awe of the intellectual accomplishments achieved so recently in the sciences and humanities. It was under the spell of this time that the great philosopher-mathematician Descartes declared, in what seems today an unbelievably naive and optimistic assertion, that all scientific knowledge could be discovered in a single lifetime. Extrapolating into the future, writers foresaw endless improvement. Not only the thinkers but also the ordinary people were beginning to believe in progress; it was becoming a matter of "common sense."

As I noted in an earlier chapter, the Enlightenment has sometimes been termed the "Age of Reason" by historians of social thought—not because the age was so reasonable in the conduct of human affairs, but because of such great faith in the powers of reason.[74] (The unreasoning side of the human psyche was yet to be addressed by Freud and others.) The strength of the idea of progress in this period can be seen in works by such proponents as the Marquis de Condorcet, who, in 1793, wrote *Outline of an Historical Picture of the Progress of the Human Mind.* Characteristically, we find these lines: "nature has assigned no limit to the perfecting of the human faculties, that the perfectibility of man is truly infinite."[75] Sociology itself was born amid optimism and dreams of infinite human progress.[76] Such faith in progress, coupled with a belief in the power of reason, led to great confidence in social experimentation—for example, to the remarkable spirit of innovation that marked the French and American revolutions. Only in such an era could one encounter a Condorcet, sentenced to death during the Terror, yet still optimistic to the end about the French Revolution and human rationality.

In the nineteenth century, faith in the power of reason diminished, but faith in general progress continued unabated. Technological

---

[72]For a discussion of faith in progress during the classical civilizations of antiquity, see the first several chapters of Robert A. Nisbet, *Social Change and History: Aspects of the Western Theory of Development* (Cambridge: Oxford University Press, 1969).

[73]See Thomas Kuhn, *The Copernican Revolution: Planetary Astronomy in the Development of Western Thought* (Cambridge: Harvard University Press, 1957). Although this book is not as famous as his work on the structure of scientific revolutions, it provides very important insights.

[74]See H.G. Nicholson, *The Age of Reason: The 18th Century* (New York: Doubleday, 1961).

[75]As quoted in Becker and Barnes, *Social Thought,* p. 474. See also the discussion in Chapter 13 of their book. The quote encapsulates perfectly the sentiment of the times, which is why I have now used it twice.

[76]See, for this intellectual movement, Frank Manuel, *The Prophets of Paris* (Cambridge: Harvard University Press, 1962).

advances were everywhere at hand. Conquest of several deadly diseases took place. After the Napoleonic era there were long periods without major wars among European powers. Intellectually, utopian writings were prominent and numerous utopian communities were founded.[77] The early nineteenth century also saw the birth of what was called scientific positivism and its proposed extension to the study of human affairs.

But meanwhile, faith in humanity's inherent rationality steadily declined. Starting in the early decades of the nineteenth century among the more conservative, elitist thinkers (for example, Edmund Burke and Joseph de Maistre), the decline spread in the latter half of the century. Fear of the "irrational" masses became prominent among a great proportion of the writers of the time, with repeated references to what were called the "dangerous classes." New scientific theories of irrationality were proposed—Gabriel Tarde's emphasis on suggestibility, Gustave Le Bon's group mind, Freud's unconscious.[78]

In the early decades of the present century the First World War exerted a stunning, dramatic effect on intellectual optimism. Its impact would be difficult to exaggerate.[79] Europeans, it seemed, were savages after all. Reports of atrocities were rampant. The scale of death and misery was absolutely unprecedented, the involvement of innocent non-combatants ubiquitous. Attempts to reestablish a sense of normalcy and tranquility followed the war's end, but they were shattered by a worldwide depression in the 1930s. The Age of Disillusionment had begun. Oswald Spengler's *Decline of the West* was symptomatic of the intellectual malaise of the time.[80]

The First World War also led directly to the triumph of Bolshevism in Russia and to renewed fear of the "masses" elsewhere in the world. But a trend toward uncritical optimism about the Soviet Union also arose. Around 1930 the widespread feeling among the Western intellectuals was that bourgeois civilization was doomed, and some of the best—André Gide, André Malraux, Arthur Koestler, Ignazio Silone, Richard Haldane, and John Strachey, to mention only a few—turned their hopes toward the USSR. They were disappointed to a man. Although

---

[77] The confusing of evolution with progress at this time has already been discussed briefly. For a more extensive treatment, see the first section of Leslie Sklair, *The Sociology of Progress* (London: Routledge & Kegan Paul, 1971).

[78] These intellectual trends are examined at length in Gunter Remmling, *Road to Suspicion: A Study of Modern Mentality and the Sociology of Knowledge* (New York: Appleton-Century-Crofts, 1967). This is another outstanding book with a deceptively poor title, in my opinion. See also Reinhard Bendix, *Social Science and the Distrust of Reason* (Los Angeles: University of California Press, 1951).

[79] See W. W. Wagar, *Good Tidings: The Belief in Progress from Darwin to Marcuse* (Bloomington: Indiana University Press, 1972). Also note Barbara Tuchman's book, *The Guns of August* (New York: Macmillan, 1972), meaning August 1914, the outbreak of the First World War.

[80] Published in 1922, the English translation appeared in 1932 (New York: Knopf).

the love affair with the Soviet Union died in the late 1930s with the purge trials and Stalin's pact with Hitler, serious disenchantment with the West continued amid the intellectual community. The thirties period marks the start in America of a transition from faith in progress within the system, via evolution, to what Lewis Killian called "revolutionary optimism"—faith in progress through *radical transformation*.

The 1930s brought Hitler and his chanting followers. The intellectual world watched the collapse of representative democracy in country after country with morbid fascination. Propaganda reached a new peak of shrillness and sophistication. World War II was the most destructive war in history; the immunity of noncombatants was now virtually nil; the Holocaust annihilated millions of helpless Jews. Belief in humanity's essential *irrationality* was now dominant.

Yet, with the defeat of the Axis powers, a climate of optimism again arose—temporarily. The United Nations, the last great institution founded on the idea of humanity's essential rationality, was slowly but inexorably nullified by the exigencies of the Cold War. After a lengthy period of guarded optimism, corresponding rather closely with the economic rebirth of Europe after the Second World War and with rising standards of living in North America, the intellectual mood again changed in the mid-1960s. This was a period of protest and strong dissent. And yet it carried a measure of hope—a revolutionary optimism that foresaw progress possible through basic structural reorganization.

It is difficult to characterize Western intellectuals today other than to say that now, more than ever before, they sense an urgent need for drastic change and yet despair of either bringing it about or seeing it occur naturally. Having long ago lost their faith in God to bring perfection to the world, they are losing faith in themselves and human action.[81] "Disbelief, doubt, disillusionment, and despair have taken over— or so it would seem from our literature, art, philosophy, theology, even our scholarship and science."[82] The sense of progress is dead among the intelligentsia, and seems, from both objective polling and impressionistic reporting, to be declining with the "man on the street" as well.[83] It may be significant that no utopias are found in contemporary Western writing.[84]

How does faith in progress influence our topic, the feasibility of intervention? As the theorist Polak has shown, forecasts of progress or

---

[81] See Bernard James, *The Death of Progress* (New York: Knopf, 1973).

[82] Robert Nisbet, *History of the Idea of Progress* (New York: Basic Books, 1980), p. 318.

[83] Many European observers have noticed a decline in American optimism. The trend seems even stronger in Britain, with waves of persons wanting to emigrate.

[84] See Chad Walsh, *From Utopia to Nightmare* (New York: Harper & Row, 1962). Utopias still were written of in Soviet literature of the 1960s. See Isaac Asimov, "Introduction," in *Soviet Science Fiction*, ed. Isaac Asimov (New York: Collier, 1962), pp. 7–13.

decline can have complex, seemingly contradictory effects.[85] Popular belief in inevitable progress can lead to a ready acceptance of new innovations as part of the grand pattern of the future. We find such a welcome for new technology occurring in the United States in the early twentieth century. But faith in progress can also lead to complacency. Pessimism about the future can also have contradictory effects. It can lead to despair, lethargy, and alienation, or it can galvanize a population to activity. Polak felt that the effects of optimism and pessimism seemed difficult to trace because we were ignoring a second factor: the *efficacy* of human efforts to change the future, or rather people's belief in their own efficacy, which is also an issue. Efficacy and degree of optimism had to be considered *together*. Pessimism coupled with a belief in the high potency of one's actions can call forth heroic effort, a Battle-of-Britain mentality; pessimism coupled with lack of faith in one's counteractions can lead to passivity.[86] We see again the significance of beliefs about the efficacy of intervention.

In an important way, the mood of the serious writing of a period, its optimism or pessimism combined with its confidence in the efficacy of reform, or its lack of confidence, affects the feasibility of intervention in that period.[87]

SUMMARY

There is no idea so absurd that it has not, somewhere, been seriously advanced by a philosopher.

Karl Marx

The conceptual obstacles to intervention described in this chapter arose in very different historical times. In like manner they are at very different levels of acceptability today. It is clear that many are in decline and some have virtually disappeared. The conviction that suffering is part of God's will, a reflection of Original Sin, plays no real part in social policy.

---

[85] Fred Polak, *The Image of the Future*, trans. Elise Boulding (Amsterdam: Elsevier, 1973, original—1952).

[86] See an excellent analysis of these factors in Wendell Bell and James A. Mau, "Images of the Future: Theory and Research Strategy," in *Theoretical Sociology*, ed. J. McKinney and E. Tiryakian (New York: Appleton-Century-Crofts, 1970). See also Richard L. Henshel, *On the Future of Social Prediction* (Indianapolis: Bobbs-Merrill, 1976), especially parts 3 and 4.

[87] See the importance of this combining of optimism-pessimism beliefs with efficacy beliefs treated at length in Polak, *The Image of the Future*.

Racism is by no means dead; yet when one surveys its pervasiveness in earlier times, it is clearly on the wane. Biological elitism and sexism have become separated from racism; both are on the defensive and in decline.

It is in the contemporary lack of optimism or trust in progress that I find the greatest intellectual obstacles to intervention today. Among intellectuals there exists a growing distrust of bureaucratic solutions. Recognition is increasing of the cyclical nature of reforms, of the evils of careerism and opportunism. Perhaps the only remaining "laws" that seem to mandate the failure of intervention are those that mandate the *humanistic failure of bureaucracies in general*—including those bureaucracies set up for social reform.

That brings me to "choice laws," also called "trade-offs" in the jargon of engineering. These scientific obstacles to intervention are still very much with us and, thanks to the prestige of modern science, they may be more potent than ever—especially when cast in equation form. As pointed out earlier, it is one question whether they are correct; it is another vital question whether the belief itself that they are correct has serious consequences.

And what of the argument that in doing away with some problem we may also automatically destroy some good? Is it true that one cannot eliminate certain social problems without simultaneously destroying desirable social features? Such possibilities bring us close to the idea that efforts to eliminate social problems can have very different, entirely unanticipated consequences.

8

UNANTICIPATED CONSEQUENCES OF INTERVENTION: A CONSERVATIVE AND RADICAL NOTION

The insight that purposeful social action can have unanticipated results, and that these results may be highly deleterious, has an ancient and venerable history. A valuable article in the 1930s, "The Unanticipated Consequences of Purposive Social Action," examined the classical problem in some detail.[1] One major philosopher has called the tracing of unanticipated consequences of human action "the main task of the theoretical social sciences," and in recent years two valuable works on unintended consequences have appeared.[2] Clearly, this possibility is of more than passing concern to anyone interested in the solution of social problems, since a solution—discounting "spontaneous" improvement from chance factors—will ordinarily require some sort of active intervention. If the intervention program is vulnerable to untoward outcomes, it is important to detect these possibilities beforehand.

Instances of unanticipated consequences are legion, as are the studies made of them. Some seem marginal to the study of social problems.

---

[1] Robert K. Merton, "The Unanticipated Consequences of Purposive Social Action," *American Sociological Review* 1 (December 1936), pp. 894–904. Merton lists numerous historical precursors of his article in the modern period.

[2] The quote is from Karl R. Popper, "Prediction and Prophecy in the Social Sciences," in *Theories of History*, Patrick Gardiner, ed. (New York: Free Press, 1959), p. 281. I recommend highly Raymond Boudon, *The Unanticipated Consequences of Social Action* (New York: St. Martin's Press, 1982); and Sam D. Sieber, *Fatal Remedies: The Ironies of Social Intervention* (New York: Plenum Press, 1981). A worthwhile article on the subject is "Reactionary Rhetoric," by Albert O. Hirschman, *Atlantic Monthly* 263 (1989), pp. 63–70. Hirschman only considers certain parts of the subject but has some delightful insights.

For example, we learn from the terrible unforeseen consequences of introducing rabbits into Australia to respect ecological factors, but these consequences have little apparent relevance to social issues. Considerably more relevant are the effects of technological innovations, which have at times produced unexpected social consequences of considerable importance. Some of these innovations have been rather thoroughly studied. Many years ago, for instance, Ogburn made a detailed analysis of the social impact of the airplane.[3] More recently, studies of the introduction and diffusion of the automobile have documented important social consequences. Old patterns of dating and courtship were radically altered; parents lost considerable control over their adolescent offspring; geographic mobility of the population increased enormously; entirely new recreational patterns emerged—these are just a few of the more significant unanticipated alterations brought about by the automobile.[4]

Recently there has been a call to regulate and review emerging technology in terms of its side-effects—insofar as these can be anticipated.[5] With respect to the impact of technology, Western society is characterized by extreme laissez faire attitudes. While we have extensive planning for change at the production level—in order to introduce new products and produce old ones more efficiently—we have virtually no planning for change at the "consequence level." As Servan-Schreiber, the French commentator, noted in *The American Challenge*, we have attained a new plateau of expertise in research and development and the marketing of new innovations. But until recently we have never worried officially about the consequences of our technologizing.[6] One of the most drastic consequences of technology may be the current world population crisis, insofar as it has resulted from the unprecedented success in conquering disease, especially causes of infant mortality, over the past one hundred years.

Finally, some unanticipated consequences, because they are the result of *social* alterations, have a direct and immediate relevance to social problems. Perhaps the ideal example of unanticipated consequences is the American experience with Prohibition, the complete ban-

---

[3]William F. Ogburn, *The Social Effects of Aviation* (Boston: Houghton Mifflin, 1946).

[4]On another major invention, see Ithiel de Sola Pool, ed., *The Social Impact of the Telephone* (Cambridge, Mass.: MIT Press, 1977).

[5]For a brief review, see Adolf Feingold, "Technology Assessment: A Systematic Study of Side-Effects of Technology," *Canadian Forum* (February 1974), pp. 10–11. See also the discussion of the prevention of the American supersonic transport in Chapter 6.

[6]Numerous "sleepers" with potentially serious social consequences have received relatively little attention. For one example, see Richard L. Henshel, "Ability to Alter Skin Color: Some Implications for American Society," *American Journal of Sociology* 76 (January 1971), pp. 734–42.

ning of alcoholic beverages in the 1920s. The "noble experiment" killed numerous drinkers of tainted liquor, reduced tens of millions to the nominal status of lawbreakers, increased corruption and contempt for the law, and—most significantly—created ideal conditions for the growth of organized crime. All of these results were totally unanticipated by the moral entrepreneurs of Prohibition, who simply wanted to do away with "Devil Drink."[7] Eventually the country reluctantly passed an additional amendment to the Constitution with the sole purpose of repealing the earlier amendment that had outlawed alcoholic beverages. Prohibition taught the bitter lesson that depriving half of a nation's population of something it wants results in an increase not in morality but in lawlessness. Come to think of it, perhaps that bitter lesson has *not* been learned yet: we seem to be undergoing the same sequence with illegal drugs.

We have already noted in Chapter 3 the careless, offhand, indeed slipshod way drugs were first outlawed in the United States. It is certain that no one in those hearings had the vaguest conception of the monster the decisions were to eventually unleash on the country. For drugs and the drug enforcement process contain certain decisive characteristics, which I think are worth reviewing in some detail. I have numbered the points for ease of reference. (1) Drugs are pleasurable. They provide a reward the very first time they are used. They therefore may well attract experimentation, especially among the disaffected. (2) But at first drugs ordinarily give no indication of their addictive power. The casual user does not feel threatened immediately. (3) Yet as time passes drugs become intensely addictive, so that persons in their grip feel terrible without them. At this point drugs possess what economists call "inelasticity of demand," meaning that demand will continue irrespective of the price. This, naturally, attracts suppliers. (4) Suppliers are also encouraged because, while addicts will pay extremely high prices for drugs, drugs are very inexpensive to produce and purify (disregarding the costs of avoiding arrest).[8] (5) Given the very high profit margins, this should attract competition among suppliers, which in an open (legal) market would tend to drive prices back down, but in the closed underworld of illegal drug dealings the users may only have contact with one or two trusted suppliers. With such limits on competition, prices drive still higher, attracting more suppliers. (6) Law enforcement crackdowns reduce the number of suppliers, thus ironically increasing the profits of

---

[7]The causes of the movement are more complex than its single aim. See James H. Timberlake, *Prohibition and the Progressive Movement: 1900–1920* (Cambridge: Harvard University Press, 1966).

[8]I am concentrating on the most common drugs in this and some other numbered passages.

those who are left.[9] (7) As time passes, the amount of the drug required for a given "kick" increases; hence the user is driven to demand greater quantities. This increases expenses beyond most users' capacity to provide by legitimate means. Hence the outlawing of drugs produces not only drug offenses themselves but also increases theft, robbery, and other secondary offenses.[10] (8) One of the few ways to obtain enough money to pay for one's habit is to become a pusher; hence users as well as producers become agents for the further spread of the problem. (9) The supplying of drugs eventually becomes so lucrative that drug wars are fought between rival suppliers. This violence constitutes yet another form of crime escalation. (10) Drug profits are so enormous that bribery and payoffs among enforcement officials become possible, and pose a major problem, thus adding even further to crime escalation. (11) As law enforcement catches the "small fry," the latter's new criminal records preclude certain occupations and often diminish chances for legitimate income, once again increasing the volume of predatory crime. (12) A small amount of a drug can produce great pharmacological effects, and small amounts of a drug are easily concealable. Hence more and more taken-for-granted civil liberties are lost as authorities turn to increasingly desperate search procedures. Finally, (13) enforcement doesn't work, and it is clearly seen not to be working, and this breeds despair and disrespect for law enforcement and civil society.

The search for a way out of this nightmare has led some social scientists to propose the legalization of narcotic drugs. With a constant supply of cheap drugs, the unanticipated consequences of anti-drug laws are reduced or eliminated, specifically items *5* through *13*. But legalization carries with it the risk of its own unanticipated consequences. Might it not become more fashionable to take drugs? Might not the new, legal producers attempt to promote their product? Narcotics are generally bad for one's health; if usage increased under legalization, might this have the unanticipated consequence of greatly increasing public health costs?

The present drug-control regime in the United States that is failing so miserably uses essentially a conservative, law-and-order approach. But Sieber points out that "self-defeating social action is politically impartial. The conservative programs of a law-and-order administration . . . are as vulnerable to the angels of self-destruction as the liberal

---

[9]To quote a serious study of the problem, "The profitability of the entire narcotics black market depends on untiring efforts of the law-enforcement agencies to hold the available supply down to the level of effective demand." E. M. Brecher et al., *Licit and Illicit Drugs* (Boston: Little, Brown, 1972).

[10]As one indicator, the *New York Times* of May 22, 1977, cited a three-year Detroit study showing that when the price of heroin rose the rate of property crime increased.

programs of a Great Society or a European socialist state."[11] That is one reason why I have called this chapter "Unanticipated consequences of intervention: A conservative and radical notion." (The other reason, as we will see, is that one of the greatest aids in thinking about the matter has conservative roots, while the roots of one other major aid are radical.) Here is a liberal program with entirely unanticipated consequences:

> Compelling owners of deteriorated buildings in low-income neighborhoods to bring buildings up to code may cause them to abandon the buildings rather than comply, because it does not pay to rehabilitate them . . . It is naive for analysts trying to correct poor housing to suppose that owners will ignore their own economic interests completely, to the extent of causing ownership to result in drastic losses rather than profits. Many would rather give up their ownership first. So about 800 to 900 buildings per year are being abandoned by their owners in New York City alone, and more in other cities.[12]

Analytically, four possible types of unintended consequences must be considered.

1. A reform may turn out *better* than expected because of an unrecognized deleterious feature about the old condition in addition to what was noticed. When the old arrangement is destroyed, both problems are removed.

2. A reform may turn out *better* than expected because of an unnoticed beneficial feature about the reform itself (in addition to taking care of the recognized evil).

3. A reform may turn out *worse* than expected because of an unnoticed or unappreciated good feature about the old arrangement. When it is destroyed to get rid of the problem, the good feature is lost as well.

4. A reform may turn out *worse* than expected because of an unnoticed deleterious feature about the reform itself.[13]

Before proceeding further, we had best pause momentarily to consider the terms "better" and "worse" in the aforementioned categories. These are not terms ordinarily used in sociological analysis. But it is precisely in the realm of intervention, and in the designation of a condition as a social problem in the first place, that value judgments are

---

[11] Sieber, *Fatal Remedies*, p. 8.

[12] Anthony Downs, "Evaluating Efficiency and Equity in Federal Urban Programs," in R. H. Havemann and R. D. Hamrin, eds., *The Political Economy of Federal Policy* (New York: Harper & Row, 1973).

[13] A fifth type of unanticipated consequence—the situation in which a reform has no effect at all—will be surveyed in the context of evaluation research in Chapter 10.

unavoidable. One cannot speak of "problems" without implying a bad condition, nor of intervention (or reform, or solution, or remedy) without implying good. We can speak of better and worse, good and bad, provided we recognize that these terms refer to the values of specific cultures or possibly to powerful elements within them, not to some universally valid standard.[14] The terms "good" and "bad" also must be in reference to a particular audience because usually some degree of value conflict exists within a single culture. Finally, the terms must refer to a particular period in that culture's history, inasmuch as values can be reversed over long spans of time in the same culture. Every age redefines its social problems.[15]

Whether an event is judged good or ill depends on one's place in the social structure as well as proximity to the event. Let us consider a single historical example: the effects of the Black Death on the structure of feudalism. When this epidemic of bubonic plague swept across Europe in the fourteenth century, it killed at least one-third of all the people of the continent in a very short time. That is an average figure; in some areas the proportion killed was much worse.[16] With this incredible disaster came a severe shortage of labor in the following years. As a result, many of the feudal rules that bound the serf to the land of his master were relaxed in order to give some measure of flexibility to the distribution of laborers. To the nobles the entire affair was a disaster— the plague, the labor shortage, and the remedy. To the serfs the remedy did not seem disastrous, but still they undoubtedly regarded the Black Death as infinitely more catastrophic than any slackening of their traditional obligations might have seemed beneficial. Today, however, we recognize that this shift in labor restrictions was one important factor in the ultimate downfall of the tenacious system of feudalism; hence we are tempted to regard the whole affair as good in the balance in spite of the deaths and suffering.

Let us examine the four types of unanticipated consequences. In two cases, numbers *1* and *3*, an unsuspected aspect of the prevailing status quo is the source of planning breakdown. The other two cases have an unappreciated aspect of the intervention itself (the reform).[17] For each source of breakdown the possibility exists that the undetected

---

[14]See Chapter 1 for an extensive discussion of cultural and ethical relativity.

[15]See Herbert Blumer, "Social Problems as Collective Behavior," *Social Problems* 18 (1971), pp. 298–306.

[16]Philip Ziegler, *The Black Death* (New York: Harper & Row, 1971).

[17]Merton ("Unanticipated Consequences," p. 897) reminds us that the problem of determining causality is as applicable to the examination of unanticipated consequences as it is elsewhere in sociology. Specifically, how is it known whether it was the problem condition or the remedy that produced the unexpected effect? The answers (very partial, always tentative) are to be found in works that treat causal inference in detail, but the precaution is a good one to bear in mind throughout the chapter. I will examine this problem briefly in Chapter 10.

feature is "good" or that it is "bad." These values can become transformed, however, for if a reform gets rid of a good feature of the old system, the end result is bad. In summary, we wind up with two outcomes better than expected and two outcomes worse than expected. It is the latter that attract attention, and rightly so, for people plan intervention to improve conditions. If by chance conditions improve more than expected, then there are no repercussions, except perhaps speculation that the measures might have been applied sooner. But if the conditions improve less than expected, this poses practical problems. And it is entirely possible that a reform will not only produce less of a benefit than expected but produce such harmful side-effects that people would be better off without the reform—the acknowledged case with Prohibition and many other cases. No wonder more interest is devoted to the two outcomes that are worse than anticipated: these developments are important to avoid.[18]

MANIFEST AND LATENT FUNCTIONS

One branch of sociological inquiry fits closely with such concerns. *Functionalism* is one of the most basic orientations within sociology. I will make no attempt to cover the manifold questions and issues that have developed around functionalism; the only requirement here is to explore those limited aspects relevant to intervention. Functionalism in social science has a long and multifaceted history. We shall concentrate here on one of the simpler variants, Mertonian or "partial" functionalism.

The key word "function" in functionalism is employed in a utilitarian sense.[19] When it is asked what the function of something is, the answer is given in terms of what the thing *does*—in its consequence.[20] "The function of the heart is to pump the blood." "The function of the public school system is to educate the young in the various forms of accumulated knowledge." Naturally a given sociocultural phenomenon can have more than a single function. Thus a second function of the public school system might be to teach practical skills needed in the surrounding society. Some of the functions may be marginal to the system under consideration—purely accidental and incidental. A heart produces thumping sounds, but it seems strange to say that this is a

---

[18]When studying a specific problem, sociologists must ask themselves what will happen if nothing is done. What will be the social and economic costs if nothing is done? Is there a chance of spontaneous improvement? See the discussion in Chapter 6 of reduced intervention as a strategy.

[19]For the variety of meanings of the perspective, see "Function," in J. Gould and W. Kolb, eds., *A Dictionary of the Social Sciences* (New York: Free Press, 1964), pp. 277–79.

[20]I will avoid the word "purpose" since it seems to imply an awareness that may be absent and will use "consequence" instead.

function of the heart. A school system keeps children off the street, but again it seems odd to call that a function of the school system—or does it?[21] Finally, some systems do unrecognized but important things. A less recognized but significant function of the public school system, for instance, is to indoctrinate children in the dominant values of the culture.

These last functions—products of some system that are unrecognized by the participants—are a special class of particular interest. They are termed *latent functions* (unrecognized), in contrast to the *manifest functions* (recognized) of the system.[22] One example should suffice. The Hopi Indians traditionally performed a sacred dance ritual to bring rain for their crops. People gathered from scattered locations at the time of the rain dance. The manifest function was, of course, to bring rain. The latent, unrecognized function of the dance ceremony was to assemble people together, renew ties, and reestablish group bonds and feelings of solidarity. What is important is that if one took the Hopi at their word and asked them what the dance was for, one could come to the erroneous conclusion that the dance actually served no real purpose (beyond spiritual satisfaction), since it did not really bring rain. One might therefore suppose that the dance could be eliminated with no adverse consequences. But the dance did bring tribespeople together; its latent function was, by all reports, rather important in the life of the tribe—certainly more important than the manifest function. The idea of a latent function underscores one of the chief virtues of the functional approach: its emphasis on the *interrelatedness* of supposedly distinct aspects of society.

In the special language of functionalism, the rain dance is said to be "functional" for social cohesion. In general, one item is functional for another if it promotes or supports, creates or maintains the other. If it weakens, delays, diminishes, or destroys the second item, it is said to be *dysfunctional* for it. Naturally, a single given item can be functional for one thing and dysfunctional for something else. And to say that an item is functional does not mean it is "good," unless what it supports is considered good. Thus a tradition of silence before the authorities is functional for the Mafia, but that does not mean that the code of silence is good, unless the Mafia is good.[23]

---

[21] See, for a recognition of this function, Gwynn Nettler, *Explaining Crime* (New York: McGraw-Hill, 1974), pp. 174–75.

[22] Robert K. Merton, *Social Theory and Social Structure*, rev. ed. (Glencoe, Ill.: Free Press, 1957).

[23] By noting that "functional" and "dysfunctional" refer solely to the effect of one item on another, and by rejecting conventional morality in noting that some supposedly evil things had good latent consequences, the functionalists were wont to speak of their method as being *value free*. This claim eventually precipitated a great deal of trouble for the school of thought, as it became increasingly obvious that biases were indeed showing through. See the discussion on conservatism later in this chapter and Melvin Tumin, "The Functionalist Approach to Social Problems," *Social Problems* 12 (Spring 1965), pp. 379–88.

In the example just given, the breakdown of Hopi tribal solidarity might be a result of abolishing supposedly useless ceremonials. It is little wonder that British anthropologists championing the functionalist perspective early in this century ultimately obtained a strong hearing from the Colonial Office after the latter experienced repeated disaster and hostility within the British Empire.[24] These early functionalists developed their ideas in close association with colonial administration, and they took on a conservative bias as an unavoidable by-product of their brand of functional analysis.

The early functionalists tended, quite correctly, to see numerous hidden uses in existing customs and social arrangements of little apparent utility. But the potential value of these insights was minimized by a failure of conceptualization. Having detected the unnoticed uses of existing arrangements, early functionalists became wedded to the status quo; any proposal for alteration to remove some problematic aspect met with the objection that a very important latent function was served by the prevailing system. If the prevailing conditions were to be altered, this beneficial component also would be lost since the two were inextricably linked. We shall consider the validity of this position momentarily.

Functional analysis has continued to play a largely conservative role by demonstrating either the undesirability or apparent impossibility of proposed alterations. Indeed, Alvin Gouldner has called functionalism the "wise man's conservatism." In order to demonstrate the functionalist approach, we will consider two case studies. One describes some unforeseen vices of a true meritocracy; the other argues the apparent impossibility of a viable classless society.

In 1959 Michael Young published a seminal book called *The Rise of the Meritocracy, 1870–2033.*[25] It is an absorbing "history" book, supposedly written in the year 2034, tracing the development of an equitable employment system in Britain up to that time. Young starts with nineteenth-century Britain (large parts of his book are actual history), a society in which birthright meant considerably more than talent in determining one's final position in society. Tracing Britain's history, he shows how this system slowly gave way to a mixed one in which individual merit assumed an ever larger role, at the expense of class of origin. But even in 1959 the measures of competence were far from perfect—some mediocrities rose and some gifted persons were excluded. Young begins to speculate when, extrapolating from the present, he describes the development of perfect intelligence and competency tests—virtually flawless examinations that reduced the proportion of

---

[24]European colonial administrations and American administrators of Indian affairs experienced repeated disasters and unintended consequences, many stemming from their failure to understand the workings of the cultures they "managed."
[25](New York: Random House.)

errors almost to zero. When these tests were given free rein in selecting persons for the better positions, Britain developed—in Young's future history—into a true meritocracy, a rule by the best.

At first glance this seems ideal, and indeed it is certainly a far better system than one that allocates position by the accident of birth. But Young's truly original contribution comes from his insightful analysis into the drawbacks of such a system. To begin with, the people in lower echelons no longer could excuse their place by reference to the inequities of selection—everyone had been given a truly equal chance, and those who had not "made it" *really were inferior*, at least with respect to the criteria measured. You see, so long as the selection process had obvious flaws, the acceptance of a lower-level position had not been psychologically damaging. Now it was.

Furthermore, a rationale at last existed for differential privilege, since the people at the top really were more competent. Their time really was more valuable and should not be wasted on trivia; hence using servants seemed the logical answer. Since the lower class truly could not understand complex ideas very well, it seemed justifiable not to inform them of many things. Indeed, for their own happiness, it seemed best that they be manipulated. In one pathetic scene Young describes labor–management negotiations being ritually continued but with labor now represented by truly incompetent people.

Perhaps worst of all, Young paints a picture of the first society in which revolution is impossible. (He ends the book with a revolution anyway, but it is rather unconvincing.) In all previous societies, enough inequities in the selection process existed to ensure that talented people (perhaps many of them) were trapped at the bottom. These lowly but talented persons could form the cadre, the backbone and the brain, for a rebellion.[26] But in the meritocracy, we encounter for the first time a repressed class with no potential. The efforts are made, but without insight, strategy, or adequate planning they are doomed to failure— Young's last-page sop to the sentimental reader notwithstanding.[27]

Let us see what is so intriguing about this book. Young has carefully examined a particular social ideal, equality of opportunity, carried it to its logical supreme culmination, and demonstrated how in the absence of other standards of decency it could become a nightmare. The book, which won awards when it first appeared, is a magnificent *tour de force*, but for our purposes it is interesting because it shows unantici-

---

[26]Readers might want to look at a theory of the "circulation of élites" through cycles of revolution. See Vilfredo Pareto, *The Mind and Society* (New York: Harcourt, Brace, 1935, original—Florence, 1916).

[27]For more on the "drainage of talent" hypothesis, see Natalie Rogoff Ramsoy, "On the Flow of Talent in Society," *Acta Sociologica* 9 (1965), pp. 152–74.

pated consequences flowing from the very perfection of certain reforms, and it does so by way of showing us the *latent functions of imperfect selection*. Imperfect selection furnishes people who do not "make it" with an excuse for their final status, restricts the reasons people at the top can give to justify special privileges, and continually provides talented personnel for the roles of labor leader and, if need be, revolutionary general. Does this mean we must forever rest content with an imperfect system? Not necessarily: Young concedes that under certain patterns of values a meritocracy might be acceptable. But his analysis does make the task of creating ideal opportunity structures harder, and that is good because one suspects it is also more realistic.[28]

Perhaps one way out of the dilemma would be a meritocracy in an egalitarian, classless society—one with no differential in the rights and perquisites of different positions in society. Those with talent would be in charge, but would have absolutely no privileges, not even extra prestige. Could this be achieved? In the late 1940s a prolonged debate arose in sociology over the sheer possibility of such a classless, egalitarian society. Two functionalists, Davis and Moore, began the debate with an article that claimed a viable society without stratification was impossible.[29] To summarize the argument briefly: they started by noting that some of the essential occupations in modern society are mentally taxing; some are unpleasant given our cultural standpoint; and some require long periods of preparation. Since people would ordinarily avoid these occupations, which were apparently essential to societal functioning, the question posed by Davis and Moore was how societies obtain the necessary personnel to fill them. If these tasks are to be performed, said Davis and Moore, they must be associated with higher rewards to compensate for the costs incurred. Since even a differential allocation of honor without increased financial gain constitutes a form of stratification, they concluded that a workable society entirely without stratification was an impossibility. Differential rewards were, they said, a functional requisite of every viable society.

In actuality two approaches have been used historically for unpleasant occupations: *coercive service* (for example, the military draft or, in earlier periods, mandatory service in road building), and *differential rewards* of some sort—either prestige, honor, or monetary gain.

---

[28] See this dilemma of Young's work affirmed on p. 64 in Barrington Moore, Jr., *Reflections on the Causes of Human Misery* (Boston: Beacon Press, 1970).

[29] Kingsley Davis and Wilbert E. Moore, "Some Principles of Stratification," *American Sociological Review* 10 (1945), pp. 242–49. It is important to note that their argument did not endorse social classes (meaning enduring strata in which rank is passed on by birth). For a test confirming a small part of their theory, see Mark Abrahamson, "Functionalism and the Functional Theory of Stratification: An Empirical Assessment," *American Journal of Sociology* 78 (March 1973), pp. 1236–46.

Davis and Moore did not consider coercive service—an irony since World War II was still in progress when they were writing. Modern society is slowly purging itself of the coercive route, even in roles where it was used in the past, and some essential tasks simply do not lend themselves to the coercive alternative. It is a practical impossibility, for instance, to force someone to become a nuclear physicist or a heart surgeon. That leaves differential rewards.

The Davis and Moore thesis has provoked extensive controversy.[30] Some of it has been rather irrelevant. Davis and Moore had not tried to justify the prevailing stratification system in America, nor had they justified social classes or denied the virtues of social mobility and equality of opportunity. One important point in criticism, however, was made by Richard Schwartz.[31] According to Schwartz, a stratification-free society was not an impossibility at all—it was merely our values that made such a system virtually unthinkable. We could, for instance, have a system in which people rotated from one occupation to the next, and everyone took turns at the less pleasant tasks. If it were pointed out correctly that such a system would be grossly, terribly inefficient, Schwartz would agree, but that was quite different from saying such a society was impossible. Instead it was our other values, such as the importance of efficiency, that stood in its way, not some functional necessity. For that matter, the requirements of various occupational positions could be modified to render them more equal in terms of their desirability.

This analysis of the feasibility of an egalitarian society illustrates a particular form of functional analysis in which one begins by abstracting certain *functional prerequisites* that every society must have in order to continue.[32] For example, every society must provide some means for the socialization of the young, for producing the necessities of life, such as food and shelter, for peacefully resolving disputes, and so forth. Societies are wonderfully diverse, and it stands to reason that any effort to determine universal necessities (the kind without which a society would collapse) must be very carefully undertaken. Even then, conclusions may be difficult to draw, as we have just seen. Filling occupational positions through differential rewards turned out to be only one way of

---

[30]For an overview of the controversy, see George A. Huaco, "The Functionalists' Theory of Stratification: Two Decades of Controversy," in M. Tumin, ed., *Readings in Social Stratification* (Englewood Cliffs, NJ: Prentice-Hall, 1970), pp. 411–27. More recent contributions are reviewed in John Wilson, *Social Theory* (Englewood Cliffs, NJ: Prentice-Hall, 1983), pp. 68–70. Some interesting points have appeared in Eerik Lagerspetz, "Reflexive Predictions and Strategic Actions," *Social Science Information* 27 (1988), pp. 307–20.

[31]Richard Schwartz, "Functional Alternatives to Inequality," *American Sociological Review* 20 (August 1955), pp. 424–30.

[32]See D. F. Aberle et al., "The Functional Prerequisites of a Society," *Ethics* 60 (1950), pp. 100–113. See also Marion J. Levy, Jr., *The Structure of Society* (Princeton, NJ: Princeton University Press, 1952).

satisfying the functional requirement that persons must fill difficult positions. That at least one other way met this requirement is illustrative of a general principle of functionalism: in most cases, alternative ways—known as *functional alternatives*—can be found to meet specific needs.[33]

Let us recall the discussion of the early functionalists, who tended to favor the status quo because they saw everywhere hidden uses (latent functions) in apparently useless or problematic phenomena. What they failed to realize, or acknowledge, was that *there were usually several ways to accomplish a given function*. If the Hopi abolish their rain dance, it might not destroy tribal unity as long as another, similar mechanism can be substituted. Recognition of substitutes—functional alternatives—has tended to reduce or eliminate the built-in conservatism of early functionalism while retaining its value in anticipating the consequences of intervention.

One other flaw of some early functionalists was their refusal to see that some elements of a culture may have no function at all, manifest or latent. Their emphasis on the interrelatedness of supposedly disparate parts of a culture—itself a largely beneficial insight—precluded any recognition of the persistence of cultural "survivals" that had no remaining functions. Lack of recognition of survivals and functional alternatives leads eventually to making whatever is into a necessity. This prompts me to distinguish two meanings of "conservative." The term could mean advocacy of the status quo, whatever it may be, or it could mean advocacy of specific right-wing positions such as free-enterprise capitalism. Functionalism may indeed have a proclivity for the first meaning but not the second; it is just as likely to be employed, while using a different vocabulary, in maintaining the existing structure of a socialist regime.[34]

Functionalism has been termed conservative for several reasons—some less fair than others. One insightful reason has been set forth by David Matza, with regard to the work of functionalists in the area of deviance or, we might add, social problems.

> What did functionalists actually write about deviant phenomena? Overwhelmingly, they stressed the functions—not dysfunctions—of deviant forms. The dysfunctions were hastily acknowledged in a first paragraph. The actual analysis ignored them, took them for granted . . . [because] the dysfunctions [of deviance]

---

[33]It should be noted here that the sociological search for functional requirements has also been pursued for social systems smaller than whole societies, and for goals other than the mere survival of the system.

[34]On a similar point, see Alvin W. Gouldner, *The Coming Crisis of Western Sociology* (New York: Basic Books, 1970), pp. 331–33.

were manifest. Their reiteration was deemed neither a contribution to knowledge nor a sign of acuity. The important and remembered contributions to functionalist theory always contained an element of surprise—the functions of inequality, of ignorance, of deviance, of crime, of prostitution, of the political boss, of organized gambling . . . To the recitation or publication of manifest functions, the obvious response is yawning acknowledgement. Thus the actual work of most functionalists [when dealing with deviance] focused on the latent contributions of previously maligned phenomena to society. . . . It is precisely on this account that the functionalists have been persistently criticized as conservative.[35]

Matza is certainly correct in asserting that most actual analyses of deviance from the functionalist viewpoint have concentrated on locating unexpected (latent) benefits from supposedly unpleasant activities. Sieber lists numerous works concerned with the positive functions of particular social ills.[36]

What of the claim sometimes advanced that functionalism is conservative in the right-wing sense? Discussions of the positive functions of social inequality, or the dysfunctions of total equality of opportunity, mentioned earlier, might be so considered. But some cases are ambiguous in terms of political orientation. Is a discussion of the positive functions of tobacco smoking conservative?[37] What can be said of the positive functions of lying?[38] Ludwig's book on lying is insightful and informative, but is it liberal (radical) or conservative (reactionary)? It is difficult to say.

Finally, some functional analyses, while confirming Matza's point about concentrating on latent functions, have anything but politically conservative implications. Lewis Coser's famous book, *The Functions of Social Conflict*, lists several features of social conflict—for example, the providing of a measure of power to otherwise powerless groups—that are beneficial from a liberal or radical standpoint.[39]

---

[35] David Matza, *Becoming Deviant* (Englewood Cliffs, NJ: Prentice-Hall, 1969), p. 55. On the surprise aspect of functionalism, see also Murray S. Davis, "That's interesting! . . . ," *Philosophy of the Social Sciences* 1 (1971), pp. 309–44, especially pp. 319–20. See also Merton, *Social Theory*, pp. 68–69.

[36] Sieber, *Fatal Remedies*, especially pp. 55–87, 136–60.

[37] See "Beneficial Effects of Tobacco" in Chapter 13 of *Smoking and Health*, Report of the Advisory Committee to the Surgeon General (Washington, D.C.: U.S. Government Printing Office, 1964).

[38] Arnold M. Ludwig, *The Importance of Lying* (Springfield, Ill.: Charles C. Thomas, 1965). See also Charlotte Olmsted Kursh, "The Benefits of Poor Communication," *Psychoanalytic Review* 58 (1971), pp. 189–208.

[39] Lewis A. Coser, *The Functions of Social Conflict* (New York: Free Press, 1966). See also Coser, "Some Social Functions of Violence," *The Annals* 304 (March 1966), pp. 8–18.

Coser's presidential address to the Society for the Study of Social Problems had the same radical implications.[40] The same is true of Levin and Levin on the functions of discrimination and prejudice.[41] An article by Herbert Gans on the positive functions that poverty provides for the affluent in society also has radical implications.[42] And we will shortly devote a whole section to the *labeling school*, a radical critique of existing criminal justice and mental health establishments that is essentially based on the latent functions of trials and hearings. Herbert Marcuse, at one time a key figure of radical sociology, performed a functional analysis himself (albeit without using the vocabulary of functionalism) in his effort to show that radicals should not grant tolerance to institutions whose values they strongly oppose.[43] Finally, and ironically, evidence mounts that Marx himself frequently adopted functionalist forms of argument.[44]

Functionalism is used typically to explain the persistence or stability of systems (for example, why they sometimes return to their earlier conditions).[45] Of course this ties in with its supposed conservative bias. But functionalism's most essential conception is of the interrelatedness of aspects of society, and under certain circumstances this conception can explain change as well as persistence. Thus if we assume that one cultural component is changed via intervention, the functions of the reform or of the detested condition can explain the emergence of changes in other parts of the society—that is, unanticipated consequences.

One final comment: functionalism, as well as being a theoretical framework, is a *style of thought*. Once one begins functional analysis, it opens a vast new range of insights into social dynamics. But it is only a style of thought, not a foolproof process or method. There is no way to ensure that we have located *all* latent functions, no automatic generating device to guarantee this. The approach depends, in the last analysis,

---

[40]Lewis A. Coser, "Unanticipated Conservative Consequences of Liberal Theorizing," *Social Problems* 16 (Winter 1969), pp. 263–72.

[41]Jack Levin and William C. Levin, *The Functions of Discrimination and Prejudice*, 2nd ed. (New York: Harper & Row, 1982).

[42]Herbert J. Gans, "The Positive Functions of Poverty," *American Journal of Sociology* 78 (September 1972), pp. 275–89.

[43]Herbert Marcuse, "Repressive Tolerance," in *Political Elites in Democracy*, ed. P. Bachrach (New York: Atherton, 1971).

[44]Anthony Giddens, *A Contemporary Critique of Historical Materialism*, vol. 1 (Berkeley: University of California Press, 1981).

[45]See this form of explanation outlined on pp. 84–98 in Arthur Stinchcombe, *Constructing Social Theories* (New York: Harcourt, Brace & World, 1968). For the argument that functionalism has extreme difficulty accounting for revolutionary change in a society, see John Rex, *Key Problems of Sociological Theory* (London: Routledge & Kegan Paul, 1961).

on insight and theory. As Kingsley Davis once pointed out in a rather obscure way, one need not be a functionalist, or even know the term, to use the functional mode of analysis.[46]

Functional analysis is linked to the previous chapter on conceptual obstacles to intervention. The deep conviction, fiercely held, of many writers of the nineteenth century who opposed governmental intervention as dangerous meddling in areas in which little was known, was that we may not realize until too late a positive aspect of the "problem" we are trying to get rid of, or a negative aspect of the "remedy" we apply. Herbert Spencer provided numerous concrete illustrations of suffering caused by misguided legislative decrees.[47] So, too, did a legion of lesser writers. Unforeseen consequences of social action, in short, can be disastrous.

Perhaps the single best response to exclusive concentration on the ills of misguided intervention has been given by a modern-day interventionist, B. F. Skinner. Skinner sees little logic in the arguments of laissez-faire advocates. To be sure, intervention may go astray, but what of it? Do we then place our confidence in blind accident? "It is hard to justify the trust which is placed in accident . . . there is no virtue in accident. *The unplanned also goes wrong.*"[48] Skinner is pointing to what might be called the unanticipated consequences of inaction, of doing nothing. Obviously, once again, such consequences can be either better or worse than expected. The place to look for unanticipated consequences of inaction—especially negative consequences—is in Marxian (and Weberian) analysis.

> *It is hard to justify the trust which is placed in accident . . . There is no virtue in accident. The unplanned also goes wrong.*
>
> **B. F. Skinner**

---

[46]One major subject within functionalism that I have ignored is the tendency to provide explanations of the *existence* of a sociocultural item by reference to the function it provides. This seemingly backwards "teleological" explanation (i.e., explaining the existence of an earlier event by its effect on some later event, or outcome, which supposedly "caused" it) has been the subject of seemingly endless debate. The topic will be ignored here because it is not central to our investigation of unanticipated consequences, but no one can take up functionalism for long without encountering it. See Stinchcombe, *Constructing Social Theories*; and Jonathan H. Turner, *The Structure of Sociological Theory*, 3rd rev. ed. (Homewood, Ill.: Dorsey Press, 1982), chap. 2 and 5. For references to the most sophisticated studies on this issue, see Erik Olin Wright, "Review Essay: Is Marxism Really Functionalist, Class Reductionist, and Teleological?" *American Journal of Sociology* 89 (1983), pp. 452–59.

[47]Herbert Spencer, *Man Versus the State* (London: 1884).

[48]B. F. Skinner, *Beyond Freedom and Dignity* (New York: Knopf, 1971), p. 161. The italics are mine.

INTERNAL CONTRADICTIONS: MARXIAN
AND WEBERIAN CONCEPTIONS

Functionalism is one basic approach to determining unanticipated consequences. Its value for this purpose lies in its ability to sensitize us to the results of *altering* the status quo in some fashion—in terms of this book the results of intervention to resolve a social problem. Another basic mode of analysis in sociology provides a way to anticipate the unexpected consequences of *continuing* with the present system. In this approach, one searches for "strains" in the existing structure of society, for "internal contradictions" among various components of this complex structure. It is from these internal discontinuities, rather than from external forces, that the most basic social changes are seen as taking place. The internal mechanism of change is termed a *dialectical process*, and this form of analysis is called dialectics.[49] The student of internal contradictions looks, for example, to the internal dynamics of the Roman Empire for clues to its decline and fall, not to the barbarians at the gates. Change, in short, is largely generated from within the system and is ubiquitous: change is assumed to be the basic reality, if I may speak loosely. The dialectical approach sees unanticipated consequences stemming from the unfolding or "natural" development of the old system, from continuities, not from purposeful breaks with it. Seeing unintended consequences produced by interventions in this system is the contribution of functional analysis.

The best-known advocates of the dialectical approach are of course the followers of Karl Marx, but as we shall see, the perspective has also been pursued by many others who fall outside of his overall framework.[50] Marx borrowed the idea of the dialectical process from the philosopher Hegel. According to one rendition of Hegelian dialectics, the historical process may be understood in terms of a repeating cycle (or, better, a spiral): a thesis (central idea of the period) begets an antithesis; the two conflict but ultimately mix to create a synthesis, a new central idea that forms the thesis of the next cycle. Marx accepted Hegel's view of historical change as due to an inner unfolding within a given system. But where Hegel had employed the dialectic to explain

---

[49]In this chapter I examine the dialectical approach as a view of historical processes. It also can be a theory of physical processes and/or a theory of knowledge. See, for the latter, Joan Huber Rytina and Charles P. Loomis, "Marxist Dialectic and Pragmatism: Power as Knowledge," *American Sociological Review* 35 (April 1970), pp. 308–18. Needless to say, dialectic is a complex idea. For more information, see Louis Schneider, "Dialectic in Sociology," *American Sociological Review* 36 (1971), pp. 667–78.

[50]Also, Marx employed on some occasions a form of analysis that might be considered a variant of functionalism. See Stinchcombe, *Constructing Social Theories*, pp. 93–98.

the development and emergence of key ideas in history, since he felt that ideas were crucial, Marx was predominantly a materialist, in the sense of regarding ideas as mere "epiphenomena" caused by more basic forces. Although Marx himself often abandoned strict materialism, he was responsible for turning the dialectic on what many of his later followers regarded uncritically as the basic causal mechanism of history: the influence of economic forces. Some of his own writing, and especially the writings of his followers, explicitly takes a position of economic determinism. In these writings Marxists saw economic relations determining not only other aspects of social structure (for example, the nature of family relationships), but also the culture and, ultimately, even the sophisticated ideas of each era, which the wise and educated of the day thought of as independently generated.[51] Economics, in turn, was governed by its own dialectical processes and internal contradictions. Each economic system (feudalism, mercantilism, capitalism) contained within itself the "seeds of its own destruction."

Given the presence of internal contradictions, many Marxists accepted the thesis that each economic system in the history of the world has been successively doomed to ultimate self-destruction and replacement by the next economic order. The new order itself contains internal contradictions, which become more pronounced and apparent as the system matures. The perspective is both deterministic and unilinear, in the sense discussed in the previous chapter. Significantly, it is not external attacks on the established system that lead to its downfall (except, perhaps, when it is already crumbling), nor is it intervention into recognized problems. It is rather the continuation, the "unfolding" or "becoming," of its own internal development that is the system's undoing. The unanticipated consequences stem in fact from the *successes* of the system as it attains a "higher order" of development.

Marx foresaw, for example, the ultimate destruction of capitalism through its very successes, through its essential nature. In one analysis, he forecast that the increasing complexity of capitalism would eventually require the training and education of workers, but this in its turn would give them the tools and potential to revolt against the capitalist system. In a subsequent refinement, Lenin predicted that the capitalist system, requiring control over client states, would arm the working class in order to secure its goals of empire. The workers, thus educated and armed, would then be in a position to overthrow the very order that had provided the means.[52]

---

[51] Marx was a prolific writer, and the early Marx does not always agree with the later Marx. Many times Marx abandoned the theme of economic determinism, and scholars argue over the primacy of this theme in his thought.
[52] I thank Peter Archibald for this example.

In another analysis Marx saw power being concentrated into fewer and fewer hands because the natural order of development of capitalism is toward monopolistic control, or oligopoly. As the process continues, more and more former entrepreneurs are forced out of business through economic crises, squeezed out through the very dynamics of capitalism into the ranks of the lowly proletariat. Economic crises intensify, and after each the residue of bourgeoisie shrinks ever smaller and the proletariat base expands. Thus by its natural tendency to move toward its more "advanced" form (monopoly), capitalism sows the seeds of its ultimate downfall. This was one of the many internal contradictions Marx saw in the capitalist system.[53]

The particular process just described has been subjected to repeated and telling criticism. In fairness, it should be recalled that this particular theory is well over one hundred years old. Analysts have an unfortunate tendency to read only the original Marxian formulations; when these are rejected, the dialectic itself is rejected, and the contributions and alterations of George Polanyi, Joseph Schumpeter, and more recent writers are ignored.[54] In any case, the accuracy of a specific illustration is not so much of interest as the general framework of analysis. The idea of internal contradictions, sometimes rephrased as internal "tensions" or structural "strains," has ultimately become a key conception in the hands of non-Marxian sociologists.[55]

Although many Marxists have done so, there is no compelling reason to assume that ideas exert no causal influence in history, or to refrain from using on them the concept of internal strains. Max Weber considered the spread of ideas to be a key causal force in history, and at one point he became interested in what his widow, Marianne Weber, called "*the tragedy of the idea*." To paraphrase Marx, certain historical ideas may contain within themselves the seeds of their own destruction. For Weber, the relationship seemed stronger still: Marianne Weber concludes that for him, "the idea, in the end, *always and everywhere* works against its original meaning and thus destroys itself."[56]

---

[53] See Karl Marx, *Capital*, vol. 1 (New York: E. P. Dutton & Co., 1930). Marx's theories of the mounting crises of capitalist production, such as the "law" of the falling rate of profit, grow very complex, and I have been able to move only a short distance into them here.

[54] See David Sallach, "What Is Sociological Theory?" *The American Sociologist* 8 (August 1973), pp. 134–39.

[55] See, for example, Wilbert E. Moore, *Social Change* (Englewood Cliffs, NJ: Prentice-Hall, 1963).

[56] Quoted in Louis Schneider, *Sociological Approach to Religion* (New York: Wiley, 1970), p. 104, italics added. On this point, see also Werner Stark, "Max Weber and the Heterogony of Purposes," *Social Research* 34 (Summer 1967), pp. 249–64. Hirschman, "Reactionary Rhetoric," mentions other writers in the late nineteenth century who toyed with this notion.

Weber's study of what he called the Protestant Ethic had convinced him that the complex of religious ideas of early Protestantism was one of the causes for the emergence of capitalism in the economic sphere.[57] According to his interpretation, the set of ideas embodied in some early Protestant doctrines—salvation of the elect, predestination, "stewards of God"—led Protestant believers to have another complex of ideas and behavior with respect to hard work, time budgeting, and self-sacrifice, which in turn produced great accumulations of wealth on both the personal and community level. This drove him to speculate further on whether early Protestantism's very successes led to its ultimate downfall. Far from the former religious glorification of poverty (see Chapter 7), wealth was now welcomed by the early Protestants as a sign that they were among God's chosen. Ultimately, however, the wealth and material well-being they had accumulated exerted a corrosive effect on the puritanical aspects of their religion and way of life. According to Weber, Protestant asceticism brought about its own demise. The very success of the idea led to its ultimate deterioration—hence, the tragedy of the idea. Weber saw not just capitalism but the worst aspects of "victorious capitalism" springing from and ultimately destroying an antithetical religious doctrine. "The early Puritan aimed at salvation; he had no interest in wealth *per se*; the modern capitalist, his direct descendant, has no interest in anything but wealth *per se*; he has forgotten about salvation. The early Puritan revered the Ten Commandments, but the modern capitalist dances around the Golden calf."[58]

Although Weber himself did not do so, Schneider demonstrates how easily this analysis fits dialectical methodology: "Protestant asceticism, featuring industry, thrift, and frugality, works for the 'good,' for the greater glory of God, but then it produces the 'bad,' in the form of temptation to abandon asceticism. The temptation is created by the wealth that asceticism itself brings about. It is a characteristic dialectical element in this that the very emergence of the 'good' . . . contains within itself, as it were, its opposite, the emergence of the 'bad' lapse of asceticism: a phenomenon harbors its own 'contradiction.' "[59]

Here is a modern version of Weber's thesis, called the "penalty of Puritanism," as applied especially to the Catholic order of Cistercians.

The Cistercian ideal demands complete self-abnegation, poverty, simplicity, retirement, purity, and refinement of the spiritual life. But . . . Forbidden to spend on embellishments for their churches and common life, they were often, at least in the twelfth century,

---

[57]Max Weber, *The Protestant Ethic and the Spirit of Capitalism* (New York: Scribner's, 1930).
[58]Stark, "Max Weber," p. 253.
[59]Schneider, *Approach to Religion*, p. 112.

faced with the problem of an unexpendable surplus. Almost of necessity they were driven to spend the surplus which they could not devote to present needs and adornments on the improvement and increase of their estates. They did this not from policy, but from the pressure of opportunity. . . . These puritans of the monastic life incurred the penalty of puritanism; they became rich because they renounced the glory of riches, and powerful because they invested wisely.[60]

Weber's thesis concerning Protestantism and capitalism has been subjected to searching criticism.[61] But it is the extension of the dialectic into the realm of ideas that is of central concern here. Weber also observed the "tragedy" at work in the growing emphasis on reason, because increasing rationalization of society leads to bureaucratization and thence to the stifling of the very impulses reason hopes to promote.[62] Max Horkheimer and Theodor Adorno, in their *Dialectic of [the] Enlightenment*, are quite explicit in applying the concept of self-destructiveness to the ideas of the Enlightenment period. Merton's examination of early science suggests another instance: Puritan desires to appreciate God's works in all their glory and wisdom led to the stimulation of early scientific study of nature, but in the end the very findings of science undermined the doctrinal foundations of religion.[63] Barrington Moore gives yet another illustration through his analysis of the ultimate consequences of the application of direct democracy. From his historical appraisal, he concludes that "direct democracy *generates* revolutionary terror, its own nemesis."[64]

We see in Marx and in the above-mentioned aspect of Weber a concern with unanticipated consequences, with outcomes the opposite of what the principal actors intend or desire. The idea that systems may contain inherent strains or "contradictions" that in the long run cause their demise, although perhaps not so all-embracing as Marxists have assumed, is a terribly important analytic contribution.

Functionalism and dialectics seem to many to be entirely antithetical.[65] They operate under different methodologies, deal with different problems, and, perhaps more importantly, have attracted scholars of

---

[60]R. W. Southern, *Western Society and the Church in the Middle Ages* (Baltimore: Penguin, 1973), p. 261.

[61]See the several challenges surveyed in Schneider, *Approach to Religion*, chap. 6; H. R. Trevor-Roper, *Religion, the Reformation and Social Change* (London: Macmillan, 1972); and Jere Cohen, "Rational Capitalism in Renaissance Italy," *American Journal of Sociology* 85 (1980), pp. 1340–55.

[62]See Stark, "Max Weber," pp. 261–62, and Chapter 11 of this book.

[63]Robert K. Merton, *Science, Technology and Society in Seventeenth Century England* (New York: Howard Fertig, 1970).

[64]Barrington Moore, Jr., *Human Misery*, p. 66, italics added.

[65]See, as one expression of this standard view, Gouldner, *Coming Crisis*.

fundamentally divergent political philosophies. Functionalists have emphasized the degree to which society is held together by consensus on values, while dialecticians have emphasized the conflict and coercion within society. Yet both have much to offer to the serious student of social problems, and both have much to say on the matter of unanticipated consequences.[66]

In the following sections we will look at a specific type of unintended consequence. The labeling of individuals as deviants by agencies designed to change them may actually tend to stabilize and perpetuate their unappreciated misbehavior. This situation can be approached functionally by considering labeling as a latent function of the bureaucratic decision-making process.

LABELING: A "CASE STUDY" OF UNANTICIPATED CONSEQUENCES

Inasmuch as contemporary sociologists tend to be more critical of existing social arrangements than they were in the past, it is perhaps only natural that social-control agencies (police, courts, corrections, mental hospitals, welfare agencies) are now sometimes seen as inadvertently worsening some of the very problems they attempt to control. This emphasis on deleterious consequences produced by formal agencies of control has been accompanied by the development of a reaction theory, or, as it is more commonly termed, a theory of *labeling*. Labeling by official agencies produces an unanticipated consequence that has been subjected to searching inquiry.[67]

In earlier theoretical approaches, the agencies of social control have been seen primarily as reducing the magnitude of social problems or, at worst, as having no effect at all. By contrast, the labeling theorists believe that, inadvertently, public agencies designed to alleviate social problems have become, in a very real sense, a part of the problem themselves through their capacity to impose stigma of various sorts on the persons under their purview. Lemert, one of the earliest labeling theo-

---

[66]For an extensive discussion of functionalism and the dialectic, see Guy Rocher, *A General Introduction to Sociology: A Theoretical Perspective* (Toronto: Macmillan Co. of Canada, 1972). This is in reality more a social theory text than an introduction to sociology for beginners.

[67]For those already familiar with labeling theory, the following passages will appear to concentrate on only one aspect of the theory. I will introduce the second aspect, the labeling of some acts as deviant, later in the chapter.

rists, noted that traditional sociology placed heavy reliance on the idea that deviance leads to social control. But he came to believe that the reverse direction—that social control inadvertently leads to more deviance—was the "potentially richer premise."[68] In the more extreme statements of labeling theory, actions of the agencies of social control are seen as the main, or even the only, source of the very problems they supposedly combat. The affinity of the labeling perspective to the idea of unanticipated consequences already seems clear.

Kai Erikson presents the perspective in this way: "Even the worst miscreant in society conforms most of the time, if only in the sense that he uses the correct silver at dinner, stops obediently at traffic lights, or in a hundred other ways respects the ordinary conventions of his group."[69] Therefore, the definition of deviance requires two levels of analysis: what is a deviant act, and who is a deviant person? "When the community nominates someone to the deviant class, then, it is sifting a few important details out of the stream of behavior [the 'deviant'] has emitted and is in effect declaring that these details reflect the kind of person he 'really' is."[70]

Any agency with official power to impose a label on a person can bring about marked changes in that person's life—not only through altering the person's experiences via prison or hospitalization, but also by changing the person's self-image, the impressions that important others have of the person, and future employment opportunities. The labeling theorists would argue that in many cases an agency takes a marginal individual—one who is not entirely committed to any position—closes off certain paths, and by various devices forces the person to accept its negative designation. By so doing, the person's deviant tendencies may well be heightened instead of reduced. The unintended consequence of the label is that it may perpetuate or accentuate what it is supposed to attack. Subjects may come to see themselves precisely as the agency sees them (for example, "I am a dangerous criminal"), accept the given label (with its own psychological rewards), and become that much more intractable. The emphasis in labeling theory is thus on *secondary deviation*—new deviant behavior produced by society's reaction to an initial deviation, termed the *primary deviation*. Thus the secondary deviation is the unanticipated consequence of the imposition of a label. By examining the preceding sentences we can also see why this is sometimes termed reaction theory.

---

[68]Edwin M. Lemert, *Human Deviance, Social Problems, and Social Control* (Englewood Cliffs, NJ: Prentice-Hall, 1967), p. 5.

[69]Kai T. Erikson, *Wayward Puritans* (New York: Wiley, 1966), p. 6.

[70]*Ibid.*, p. 7.

THE LABELING PROCESS IN GREATER DETAIL

Before proceeding further let me make the point that the notion of "labeling" is used in sociology in two distinct ways. First, it is sometimes used as a particular way to define deviance. Instead of deviance being defined as an act contrary to norms, deviance is defined as an act that is reacted to negatively. Under this definition, if an act is not reacted to in a punitive fashion (and by that means *labeled* as "deviant"), then it is not truly deviant. Second, the term "labeling" sometimes refers to the theory, discussed in the last section, that agencies of social control inadvertently tend to perpetuate the very same disagreeable activities of individuals that they are trying to prevent. In this chapter I will be concentrating exclusively on the second meaning of labeling, but in Chapter 1 we looked at an issue very similar to the first meaning when we debated the objective versus subjective definition of a social problem.[71] Henceforth, when labeling is referred to, the second sense is intended.

Let us examine the process of labeling more closely. The manifest function of the official imposition of a label in criminal trials and insanity hearings is to arrive at a determination (or verdict) of an individual's status so that appropriate actions can be taken. But some other things happen as well. These are the latent functions of trials and hearings, possibly unrecognized by the parties involved but critical in the labeling perspective.

In the beginning, perception on the part of the public or the police that an individual has committed a deviant act leads to labeling the person as "sick" or criminal.[72] Often the objective reality of a situation becomes clear too late to overcome the effects of such labeling. Even if a trial finds an individual innocent, and even if, speaking objectively, this person did not commit the offense, much psychological harm may be done by the arrest, pretrial confinement, and the judicial procedure itself—and the harm may be permanent.

Even before an individual offender is apprehended, indeed even if the person is never apprehended, the effects of *potential* labeling and sanctioning can be detected. Matza has given us an excellent analysis of

---

[71] For a sophisticated treatment of the advantages and drawbacks of the first meaning of labeling, see the chapter by Jack Gibbs in Morris Rosenberg and Ralph H. Turner, eds., *Social Psychology: Sociological Perspectives* (New York: Basic Books, 1981).

[72] Richard Schwartz and Jerome Skolnick, "Two Studies of Legal Stigma," *Social Problems* 10 (1962), pp. 133–42. This is a well-known empirical investigation of the consequences of legal sanctions that simultaneously illuminates the role of public perception of the offender in such consequences. Also, an exchange of opinions between the authors and H. Lawrence Ross is in *Social Problems* (Spring 1963), pp. 390–92, which readers might find important.

this.[73] After performing a forbidden act, the average person is bedeviled, haunted internally. The bedevilment begins to turn the person away from previous outlooks toward greater acceptance of a deviant career. The person also begins to feel transparent in the company of conventional people, afraid of making a slip, so it is easier to consort with fellow deviants among whom one need not fear disclosure. Thus performing a proscribed act already causes changes in personality and affiliation, even without or before arrest.

Suddenly the arm of the state reaches out for some party, guilty or innocent, mentally "ill" or not. Usually everything happens with bewildering swiftness; the person is distracted, distraught, and in a highly suggestible condition. Even before a final determination of the case is reached, the person finds that friends and acquaintances are altering their behavior. The day of the hearing (or trial) arrives. Here, every aspect of bureaucracy is brought to bear to ensure, in the mind of the individual, the significance of the acquisition of a label.[74] Emphasis is placed on the seriousness of the consequences, and therefore the impartiality of the hearing is stressed.[75] There is an aura of sanctity, of the majesty of officialdom, of a sharp cleavage between the innocent and the guilty, the sane and the insane. And then the label is officially imposed. Small wonder that a lasting impression is made in this traumatic situation.

Let us assume first that the labeled person undergoes no period of hospitalization or incarceration. Even without these experiences potent change mechanisms are encountered that can lead to alterations in personality and behavior. Labeling theory relies heavily on George Herbert Mead's classic conception that the self (self-image, for our purposes) arises out of social interaction. As Ichheiser put it:

> The images we hold of other people are not only mirrors which reflect, whether correctly or not, their personalities, but they are also dynamic factors which control the behavior of those people . . . it is often the personality itself which has to adjust to its distorted reflection in the "mirror."[76]

---

[73] David Matza, *Becoming Deviant*. Matza's contributions here are marred by a seeming fascination with new words where old terminology would do perfectly well. Nonetheless his analysis merits the translation required of the reader.

[74] See, for insights, Harold Garfinkel, "Conditions of Successful Degradation Ceremonies," *American Journal of Sociology* 61 (March 1956), pp. 420–24.

[75] But impartiality may be largely mythical. See Chapter 9 on this subject.

[76] Gustav Ichheiser, *Appearances and Realities* (San Francisco: Jossey-Bass, 1970), p. 54. See also James Hackler, "Predictors of Deviant Behaviour: Norms Versus the Perceived Anticipations of Others," *Canadian Review of Sociology and Anthropology* 5 (1968), pp. 92–106.

Individuals who feel that they have been labeled, that society (or at least the offended majority) will henceforth react to them negatively, no matter what their subsequent behavior, may begin to internalize the components of the role that parallels the stereotype and thus move from primary to secondary deviance.[77] Old associates, including most significant others (family, work peers, etc.), alter conceptions of them. Their reference group adjusts and changes its attitude toward them. Usually, of course, they are *welcomed by new associates* as well as rejected by old ones, and this exerts a considerable influence on persons already in a highly anxious state. From new associates they may learn appropriate rationalizations ("neutralizations") of their stigma.

Of course imprisonment or hospitalization intensifies all of these trends. The institution introduces the labeled individual to new peers, all of whom are similarly stigmatized. Different life experiences materialize in the institutional setting. The individual may acquire new, illicit skills to replace legitimate ones.[78] Afterward there are economic consequences: changed employment opportunities, perhaps dismissal from one's previous job, life-style changes mandated by financial conditions. It may be difficult, if not impossible, to obtain loans, bonding, or licenses.

The labeling process with mental illness is at once more profound and more intricate. Since no one has been able to express the viewpoint quite as well as Scheff, I will let him describe it in his own words.[79] First he defines "residual rule-breaking."

The culture . . . provides a vocabulary of terms for categorizing many norm violations: crime, perversion, drunkenness, and bad manners are familiar examples. Each of these terms is derived from the types of norm broken, and ultimately, from the type of behavior involved. After exhausting these categories, however, there is always a residue of the most diverse kinds of violations, for which the culture provides no explicit [term] . . . For the convenience of the society in construing those instances of unname-

---

[77] Mary Owen Cameron, *The Booster and the Snitch* (Glencoe, Ill.: Free Press, 1964), pp. 159–64, takes up the self-perception aspect of labeling, discussing the mechanisms by which shoplifters who do not have an impression of themselves as deviants may begin to acquire such a self-image. Readers intrigued by this analysis might also examine Leroy Gould, "Who Defines Delinquency?" *Social Problems* 16 (Winter 1969), pp. 325–36, on the development of self-perceived delinquency from official labeling.

[78] See an excellent treatment of these issues in Gresham Sykes, *Society of Captives* (Princeton, NJ: Princeton University Press, 1965).

[79] Subsequent quotations are from Thomas J. Scheff, *Being Mentally Ill: A Sociological Theory* (Chicago: Aldine, 1966). Page numbers at the end of each cited section refer to this book. Quoted with permission from Aldine de Gruyter, New York. Copyright © 1984 Thomas J. Scheff.

able rule-breaking . . . these violations may be lumped together into a residual category . . . in our society, mental illness. In this discussion, the diverse kinds of rule-breaking for which our society provides no explicit [term], and which, therefore, sometimes lead to the labeling of the violator as mentally ill, will be considered to be technically *residual rule-breaking*. (p. 34, italics added)

In short, when people do the inexplicable, when they perform norm violations for which no term is available, this may be regarded as a "symptom" of "mental illness." It may be inexplicable only to the observers, not inexplicable in itself, but its weirdness to a number of observers may be sufficient to set a process in motion that ultimately provides its own confirmation and justification. How that may happen is Scheff's next point.

It is customary in psychiatric research to seek a single generic source or at best a small number of sources for mental illness. The redefinition of psychiatric symptoms as residual deviance immediately suggests, however, that there should be an unlimited number of sources of deviance. The first proposition is therefore:

Residual rule-breaking arises from fundamentally diverse sources. (pp. 39–40)

Relative to the rate of treated mental illness, the rate of *unrecorded* residual rule-breaking is extremely high. There is evidence that gross violations of rules are often not noticed or, if noticed, rationalized as eccentricity. Apparently, many persons who are extremely withdrawn, or who "fly off the handle" for extended periods of time, who imagine fantastic events, or who hear voices or see visions, are not labeled as insane either by themselves or others. Their rule-breaking, rather, is unrecognized, ignored, or rationalized. This pattern of inattention and rationalization will be called "denial." (pp. 47–48)

What is the extent of residual rule-breaking that is "denied" by others?

Two elaborate studies of symptom prevalence have appeared, one in Manhattan, the other in Nova Scotia. In the Midtown Manhattan study it is reported that 80 per cent of the [general population studied] currently had at least one psychiatric symptom. Probably more comparable to the earlier studies is their rating of "impaired because of psychiatric illness," which was applied to 23.4 per cent of the population. In the Stirling County [Nova Scotia] studies, the estimate of current prevalence is 57 per cent, with 20 per cent classified as "Psychiatric Disorder with Significant Impairment." (p. 48)

If the percentage of the general population displaying one or more "symptoms" of mental illness is that high (somewhere between 20 and 80 percent of the entire population), how is it handled?

> Most residual rule-breaking is "denied" and is of transitory significance. . . . For this type of rule-breaking, which is amorphous and uncrystallized, Lemert used the term "primary deviation." (p. 51)

What happens in the cases of persons for whom residual deviance is *not* denied?

> If residual rule-breaking is highly prevalent among ostensibly "normal" persons and is usually transitory, as suggested by the last two propositions, what accounts for the small percentage of residual rule-breakers who go on to deviant careers? To put the question another way, under what conditions is residual rule-breaking stabilized? The conventional hypothesis is that the answer lies in the rule-breaker himself. The hypothesis suggested here is that the most important single factor (but not the only factor) in the stabilization of residual rule-breaking is the *societal reaction*. (pp. 53–54, italics added)
>
> It was stated that the usual reaction to residual rule-breaking is denial and that in these cases most rule-breaking is transitory. The societal reaction to rule-breaking is not always denial, however. *In a small proportion of cases the reaction goes the other way, exaggerating and at times distorting the extent and degree of the violation*. This pattern of exaggeration . . . we will call "labeling." (p. 81, italics added)

How might labeling perpetuate the very problem it is supposed to remove?

> Labeled deviants may be rewarded for playing the stereotyped deviant role. Ordinarily, patients who display "insight" are rewarded by psychiatrists and other personnel. That is, patients who manage to find evidence of their "illness" in their past and present behavior, confirming the medical and societal diagnosis, receive benefits. This pattern of behavior is a special case of a more general pattern that has been called the "apostolic function" by Balint, in which the physician and others inadvertently cause the patient to display symptoms of the illness the physician thinks the patient has. (p. 84)
>
> Labeled deviants are punished when they attempt to return to conventional roles. The second process operative is the systematic blockage of entry to non-deviant roles once the label has been

publicly applied. Thus the former mental patient, although he is urged to rehabilitate himself in the community, usually finds himself discriminated against in seeking to return to his old status, and on trying to find a new one in the occupational, marital, social and other spheres. (p. 87)

Finally, we come to what was mentioned before with respect to arrest: the terrible crisis this represents for most people and their distraught state at this time.

> In the crisis occurring when a residual rule-breaker is publicly labeled, the deviant is highly suggestible, and may accept the proffered role of the insane as the only alternative. When gross rule-breaking is publicly recognized and made an issue, the rule-breaker may be profoundly confused, anxious, and ashamed. In this crisis it seems reasonable to assume that the rule-breaker will be suggestible to the cues that he gets from the reactions of others toward him. (p. 88)

The preceding . . . hypotheses form the basis for the final causal hypothesis.

> Among residual rule-breakers, labeling is the single most important cause of [lengthy] careers of residual deviance. (pp. 92–93)

A classical dictum by W. I. Thomas lays the foundation for a discussion of the linkage between labeling, stereotyping, and the self-fulfilling prophecy. Recognizing the possibility of error in people's perceptions, Thomas emphasized that mistaken perceptions can still be important because "situations defined as real are real in their consequences." Although this acknowledges the reality of the effects that can flow from mistaken ideas, it was left to another writer to point out the possibility that these effects might actually include making the originally wrong idea come true.

The concept of a *self-fulfilling prophecy* originated in a famous article by Robert Merton in 1948.[80] He defined it to be a prophecy that, although false at the time it was made, became true as a result of having been pronounced. The simplest example is that of the bank run, where rumors spread about a bank's insolvency, causing depositors to besiege the bank frantically, withdrawing their own deposits. Even if the bank were reasonably sound, it would not ordinarily carry enough funds to

---

[80]Robert K. Merton, "The Self-Fulfilling Prophecy," *Antioch Review* 8 (Summer 1948), pp. 193–210.

meet the demands of all its depositors at the same time. Thus if a false prediction of bank failure is believed by enough people, their own actions can in fact make the prediction come true; it will fail because of their frantic actions. Instances of self-fulfilling prophecies abound in the social world.[81]

The labeling process is a form of self-fulfilling prophecy. The prediction is made that, if allowed to act freely, a particular person will act in a deviant way. To prevent this he or she is forced to undergo certain experiences that may ironically tend to solidify these deviant tendencies. At last the other actors in the drama look in on what they have themselves helped to create, and pronounce it, not surprisingly, in line with their expectations.[82] This is one way in which stereotypes can be made self-confirming. Indeed they also can become self-perpetuating, as can be seen if we explore just a bit more.

The self-fulfilling prophecy is closely linked in its labeling aspect with Walter Lippmann's concept of the *stereotype*.[83] A stereotype, it will be recalled, is a preconceived, standardized, group-shared idea about a supposedly inherent quality of some other group of persons. Mental pictures of Jews as greedy, American Indians as stupid, and Italians as excitable are examples of stereotypes. Stereotypes can become self-confirming in one sense through the direct exercise of power: if an employee, for example, thinks that survival in a job depends on enacting the expected stereotype, he or she will do so and thereby the stereotype is self-confirmed and self-perpetuated as well. (The mechanism is well-documented by case studies of blacks in the South.) But we are more interested in the self-confirmation and perpetuation of a stereotype in the context of labeling. Here, power is employed as well, but the process is more complex. In the next chapter we will follow the process in the labeling of criminals and delinquents.[84]

It is worth noting that the labeling process, with self-fulfilling stereotypes, is not confined to deviance, although that must be our principal interest in this book. We can detect the same processes at work in tracking (or "streaming") in education. It must be recognized that a

---

[81] Richard L. Henshel, "Self-Altering Predictions," in *Handbook of Futures Research*, ed. J. Fowles (Westport, Conn.: Greenwood Press, 1978), pp. 99–123.

[82] Jock Young carefully considers the self-fulfilling aspects of labeling. See his "The Police as Amplifiers of Deviancy . . . " in *Images of Deviance*, ed. Stanley Cohen (Harmondsworth, England: Penguin, 1971), pp. 27–52.

[83] Walter Lippmann, *The Public Philosophy* (Boston: Little, Brown, 1955). In "Public Stereotypes of Deviants" in *Social Problems* 13 (1965), pp. 223–32, J. L. Simmons states that "stereotyping . . . is an inherent aspect of perception and cognition." He analyzes both the correlates of a tendency to stereotype and the consequences of public stereotyping.

[84] A good case also can be made for the self-confirmation of a stereotype in mental-illness labeling. See Scheff, *Being Mentally Ill*, chap. 3.

child placed in a slow track has been labeled just as much as a juvenile labeled a delinquent.[85] The labeling process, in short, has negative potential far beyond the confines of deviant behavior.

PRESENT STATUS AND IMPLICATIONS OF THE LABELING VIEWPOINT

Historically, a 1938 book by Frank Tannenbaum is often cited as the original work in labeling theory. In one section, "The Dramatization of Evil," Tannenbaum explicates concisely the nature of the labeling process and its potentially damaging consequences. The first direct treatment of the strategic distinction between primary and secondary deviation is found in work by Edwin Lemert in 1951. However, it was Howard Becker who popularized the viewpoint in 1963 with a book entitled, appropriately, *Outsiders*.[86] Other early writings include those of Erikson and Kitsuse.[87] Since then, numerous contributors have advanced the perspective, including Aaron Cicourel and Thomas Scheff. In my opinion, the single best overall articulation of the labeling position, with its extensions and implications, is the 1975 work of Hawkins and Tiedeman.[88]

Beginning with Scheff, several attempts have been made to place the labeling perspective into a systematic framework.[89] The labeling perspective has by now been used to analyze such diverse topics as political deviance, mental illness, juvenile rehabilitation, and the police.[90] It has even been coupled with systems analysis.[91]

---

[85] See Sieber, *Fatal Remedies*, p. 141, and the sources cited there.

[86] Frank Tannenbaum, *Crime and the Community* (New York: Columbia University Press, 1938). Edwin M. Lemert, *Social Pathology* (New York: McGraw-Hill, 1951). The book is definitely mistitled. Howard S. Becker, *Outsiders: Studies in the Sociology of Deviance* (New York: Free Press, 1963).

[87] Kai T. Erikson, "Notes on the Sociology of Deviance," *Social Problems* 9 (Spring 1962), pp. 307–14. John I. Kitsuse, "Societal Reaction to Deviant Behavior: Problems of Theory and Method," *Social Problems* 9 (Winter 1962), pp. 247–56.

[88] Richard Hawkins and Gary Tiedeman, *The Creation of Deviance* (Columbus, Ohio: Charles E. Merrill, 1975).

[89] See Thomas Scheff, *Being Mentally Ill*; Edwin M. Schur, "Reactions to Deviance: A Critical Assessment," *American Journal of Sociology* 75 (1969), pp. 309–22; and Schur's *Labeling Deviant Behavior: Its Sociological Implications* (New York: Harper & Row, 1971).

[90] See, in the given sequence, Paul Schervish, "The Labeling Perspective: Its Bias and Potential in the Study of Political Deviance," *The American Sociologist* 8 (May 1973), pp. 47–57; Scheff, *Being Mentally Ill*; Edwin M. Schur, *Radical Nonintervention* (Englewood Cliffs, NJ: Prentice-Hall, 1973); and Jock Young, "Police as Amplifiers."

[91] Leslie T. Wilkins, *Social Deviance* (Englewood Cliffs, NJ: Prentice-Hall, 1965), pp. 85–100.

Theoretical criticisms of labeling have come from many quarters. Gibbs, an early critic, emphasized the vagueness and lack of direction of the perspective. He challenged Becker's apparent intention to distinguish whether a behavior was deviant by reference to the societal reaction to it.[92] Both Gibbs and Schur noted a tendency for extreme advocates of the labeling perspective virtually to deny the existence of primary deviation.[93] Schur also condemned the lack of systematization of the perspective, a failing that Scheff does much to overcome in the area of mental-illness labeling. But Schur also found great value in labeling's sensitizing aspect. Others have felt that the school of thought underestimates the psychological and social factors that caused the initial deviance and ignores those factors that cause some persons to stop the behavior even after being labeled. They feel it has failed to analyze the strength and severity of the reaction necessary to have "successful" labeling (for instance, one who has enough money or power may be able to overcome the effects of the label). Also, theory suggests a possible *deterrent* effect from labeling in addition to the commonly cited reinforcement of deviance.[94] Other sophisticated theoretical critiques have been made by Glaser, Nettler, and Sagarin.[95]

Some of the objections are empirical: does everything really work the way the advocates maintain? For example, when Huffine and Clausen looked at the occupational careers of ex-mental patients over a twenty-year period, they decided that "data provide strong evidence that, in and of itself, being labeled mentally ill does not determine the course of a man's career even though he may be confined for months in a mental hospital. Those men whose symptoms abated have not suffered gross occupational setbacks."[96] Gove examined empirically the role of various agents in mental labeling; he found that experts have by far the greatest say in commitments to mental hospitals and that they reject about two-thirds of public requests.[97] Gove is in fact the name mos' closely associated with critiques of labeling. Beginning in 1970, he and

---

[92]Jack P. Gibbs, "Conceptions of Deviant Behavior: The Old and the New," *Pacific Sociological Review* 9 (1966), pp. 9–14.

[93]Schur, "Reactions to Deviance." See the final chapter of Becker's revised edition (1973) of *Outsiders* for a discussion of this problem.

[94]Bernard Thorsell and Lloyd Klemke, "The Labeling Process: Reinforcement and Deterrent?" *Law and Society Review* 6 (February 1972), pp. 393–403.

[95]Daniel Glaser, *Social Deviance* (Chicago: Markham, 1971); Gwynn Nettler, *Explaining Crime*, pp. 202–12; Edward Sagarin, *Deviants and Deviance* (New York: Praeger, 1975).

[96]Carol Huffine and John Clausen, "Madness and Work: Short- and Long-Term Effects of Mental Illness on Occupational Careers," *Social Forces* 57 (1979), pp. 1049–62. The quote is from p. 1050.

[97]Walter R. Gove, "Societal Reaction as an Explanation of Mental Illness: An Evaluation," *American Sociological Review* 35 (1970), pp. 873–84.

Thomas Scheff carried out a series of debates in the *American Sociological Review*, roughly between 1970 and 1975.[98]

Reports of labeling's success or, conversely, its demise, are always greatly exaggerated, too simplistic, and premature. The approach generates a great many specific hypotheses, some of which are confirmed while others are rejected. And yet still others turn out to have conflicting results, some of which support a labeling view while others do not.[99] Meanwhile, the *central core hypotheses* of the perspective are almost impossible to prove or disprove directly and conclusively, via a critical experiment, for both ethical and practical reasons.

Even the fiercest labeling advocate, furthermore, would concede that labeling does not always occur, that occasionally official intervention produces beneficial results. Conversely, even Tittle concedes that a labeling effect occasionally occurs.[100] The issue is therefore one of degree, which is always much harder to establish. Is the principal effect of official processing (a) to label, stigmatize, and hence channel negatively, (b) to provide help (psychiatric, or other rehabilitative) to those persons designated, or (c) to sanction offenders and hence, by their example, deter others from the act and the same persons from doing it again (the deterrence argument)? Certainly *b* and *c* are the avowed purposes of the governmental agencies of social control, but are they in fact what usually happens or is *a* the more usual result?

Since occasional examples of each effect are not enough (the issue, to repeat, is the question of degree), and since critical experiments

---

[98] A more recent Gove statement is found in his "Labeling and Mental Illness" and "Postscript to Labeling and Crime" in Walter Gove, ed., *The Labeling of Deviance: Evaluating a Perspective*, 2nd ed. (Beverly Hills: Sage Publications, 1980).

[99] Here are a few examples. Some studies show that labeled youths have higher delinquency scores. D. P. Farrington, "The Effects of Public Labelling," *British Journal of Criminology* 17 (1977), pp. 112–26. See p. 114. Others indicate that this may not be the case. G. Fishman, "Can Labelling be Useful?" in *Youth Crime and Juvenile Justice*, ed. P. C. Friday and V. L. Stewart (New York: Praeger, 1977), p. 39. See also, on the relevance of labeling to adolescent self-conceptions, Gary F. Jensen, "Labeling and Identity: Toward a Reconciliation of Divergent Findings," *Criminology* 18 (1980), pp. 121–29. Another conflict is over the relative importance of post-treatment behavior and the stigma of the label. On the one hand, William Cockerham, in his *Sociology of Mental Disorder* (Englewood Cliffs, NJ: Prentice-Hall, 1981), says that "If former mental patients can act relatively normal, they probably can shed their label and live a normal life" (p. 303). See also, for this view, John Clausen, "Stigma and Mental Disorder: Phenomena and Terminology," *Psychiatry* 44 (1981), pp. 287–96. But Bruce G. Link et al., in "The Social Rejection of Former Mental Patients: Understanding Why Labels Matter," *American Journal of Sociology* 92 (1987), pp. 1461–1500, find that "labels play an important role in how former mental patients are perceived" and "labeling theory should not be dismissed as a framework for understanding social factors in mental illness" (p. 1461).

[100] See Charles Tittle in Walter Gove, ed., *The Labeling of Deviance* (New York: Sage Publications, 1975), p. 175.

are ruled out, the debate thunders on, with much research—even much very clever research—but little conclusiveness. In a sense the two sides have been talking past each other, as Petrunik, Feldman, and others have noted.[101]

In the sociology of the activist 1960s, labeling theory came to have many of the qualities of a social movement,[102] and because advocates often made certain *additional* assumptions, it became one of the centers of attention and controversy in studies of social problems.[103] Since it is known that few individuals are actually labeled out of a vast number who break the rules, it has been claimed that the enforcement of moral rules is essentially a *political act*.[104] This claim is not an inherently necessary aspect of labeling theory, but it is sometimes assumed by its supporters. It is also central to the perspective to maintain that the very defining of certain behaviors as a social problem in the first place is a political, or at least ideological, activity rather than one of community consensus—a standpoint I have adopted to a considerable degree in the early chapters of this book. After the definition of a social problem has been made, a decision is reached about the "nature" of a particular person with respect to this problem, and thus a second definition (a label) is affirmed. "The deviant, in short, is made by society in two senses: first, that society makes the rules which he has broken, and secondly, that society 'enforces' them and makes a public declaration announcing that the rules have been broken."[105] One final reason why labeling theory appealed to the radical 1960s was that it was a sociology of the underdog: the agencies of social control were made the cause of a lot of the deviance ordinarily blamed on individuals.[106] Of course it is also true that in the conservative 1980s labeling lost favor in sociology. One might

---

[101] Petrunik states that Gove's 1975 "demolition" of the labeling perspective as not supported by the empirical evidence was a case of first setting up a "sociological strawman" that did not really represent the views of the advocates and then destroying that strawman. See Michael Petrunik, "The Rise and Fall of Labelling Theory: The Construction and Destruction of a Sociological Strawman," *Canadian Journal of Sociology* 5 (1980), pp. 213–35. Feldman at one point states that the apparent differences between Scheff and Gove are nothing more than "the same data [being] interpreted differently." Saul D. Feldman, *Deciphering Deviance* (Boston: Little, Brown, 1978), p. 310.

[102] See Matza, *Becoming Deviant*, pp. 158–59.

[103] For an early exploration of the possible consequences of labeling theory, see James Hackler, "An 'Underdog' Approach to Correctional Research," *Canadian Journal of Criminology and Correction* 9 (1967), pp. 27–36.

[104] See especially the first eighteen pages of Becker, *Outsiders*.

[105] Alvin W. Gouldner, "The Sociologist as Partisan: Sociology and the Welfare State," reprinted in *The Sociology of Sociology*, ed. Larry T. Reynolds and Janice M. Reynolds (New York: McKay, 1970), p. 221.

[106] A review of the various explicit positions taken on whether labeling theory is essentially radical or essentially conservative is found in Monica B. Morris, *An Excursion into Creative Sociology* (New York: Columbia University Press, 1977), pp. 157–59. Without hesitation I can say that the general consensus is that the theory is liberal.

wish that a sophisticated discipline would prove itself a bit more independent of the swings of fashion.[107]

Labeling theory is important for our analysis for two reasons. First, it is a beautiful example of a latent function, and also of an unanticipated consequence. Second, it demonstrates that the concept of unanticipated consequences cannot be placed exclusively in the arsenal of either the progressive or the conservative. In some instances, an awareness of unexpected outcomes assists defenders of the status quo by shutting off superficially plausible reforms. But in the present section an awareness of the unanticipated consequences of official labeling points to the deleterious nature of *existing* social mechanisms, to a pressing need for their reexamination, and possibly toward their alteration.

[107]Recently, a modified labeling theory has revived in the journals, following the lead of Bruce Link. See, as one example, Bruce G. Link et al., "A Modified Labeling Theory Approach to Mental Disorders: An Empirical Assessment," *American Sociological Review* (June 1989), pp. 400–23.

9

STEREOTYPE AND IDEOLOGY AS BASES OF "TREATMENT"

We saw in the first part of this book how ideology permeates the entire subject of social problems, starting with what conditions are selected for inclusion and how they are regarded. But ideology and stereotypes have another outlet as well: the treatment of individuals on the basis of the prevailing viewpoints concerning causes and cures. In this chapter I will deal with the effect of stereotyping and ideology on *involuntary treatment*, that is, some alteration of a person's condition for "improvements" he or she would rather do without. Imposing sanctions for crimes is, even today, the most widely used involuntary treatment, so it is appropriate that sentencing practices have been such a widely studied topic.

SENTENCING FOR CRIME

Historically, sentences imposed for crimes were often either wildly idiosyncratic or quite openly based on matters we would now consider irrelevant—for instance, the offender's status in society. As a result of the writings of legal and juridical philosophers, the situation gradually changed—to a certain extent. Cesare Beccaria, an Italian philosopher–jurist of the eighteenth century, advocated a strictly graduated series of legal sanctions, spelled out clearly in advance, and applied without favor or partiality to everyone convicted of the same offense. Judges were to have no discretion under the system he proposed. Beccaria's writings accomplished many badly needed reforms in the penal practices of the day, but his wisdom on the point noted here eventually came under severe criticism: the complete lack of judicial discretion came to be seen as detrimental to another objective that was coming into high regard. Alteration (rehabilitation) of criminals, to allow them to mend their ways when released, became viewed as a critical objective of the penal process, and, according to the reformers, lack of judicial discretion in sentencing was destructive to this end. Judges should be given a certain leeway in sentencing—the newer theory said—so they could tailor each sentence to the specific needs of the case, in terms of rehabilitation or conversion. Individual differences among the guilty should be recognized. This doctrine of judicial discretion is everywhere triumphant today, so that standard, unalterable sentences are a thing of the past.[1] Judges have been provided with boundaries, typically quite broad, for the sentences permissible for a person convicted of a given offense.

But this alternate way of handling the matter, as well as allowing play for new ideas in penal philosophy, has also brought back the old difficulties of differential treatment. Once again we find persons drawing sentences of varying severity for what are manifestly the same criminal acts. This problem has several aspects. For instance, judges differ in overall severity of sentencing, so a person's sentence depends in part on which judge is drawn.[2] But, above all, what is of concern here is the differential sentencing of offenders on the basis of personal attributes apparently unrelated to either the crime or to rehabilitation.[3] These attributes include the race, sex, age, and social class of the offender.

The one positive aspect about such discrimination is that it is possible to document it. Sociologists have become quite good at this. Essentially, one compares sentence lengths, or proportion of sentences suspended, for persons with differing characteristics who commit the same offense. The sentence and the offense are in each case matters of official record and it is usually possible to ascertain the personal attributes under consideration.[4]

Such analyses have been done. The most widely known "classic" study considered the effects of the offender's race. In a survey in the

---

[1] This judicial flexibility has been further augmented by flexibility through the mechanism of parole. For a sensitive analysis of the pros and cons of discretion in legal matters, see Michael Hill and Glen Bramley, *Analysing Social Policy* (Oxford: Basil Blackwell Publisher, 1986), pp. 163–67.

[2] John Hogarth, *Sentencing as a Human Process* (Toronto: University of Toronto Press, 1971). The disparity has been reduced for federal offenses in the United States by a set of mandatory sentencing "guidelines" prepared by a commission. The guidelines still permit a range, but the range is greatly reduced.

[3] Another problem is how the perceived public outcry against certain offenses is a factor in sanctioning severity, and how this may fluctuate over time. See Hogarth, *Sentencing.*

[4] I am oversimplifying here: one also has to consider variables other than the attribute that may explain a sentencing disparity, such as the proportion of repeat offenders in each category. Furthermore, the real offense is sometimes disguised by reductions of the charge following pretrial bargaining. So the analysis is not easy, but it is definitely feasible. For a sophisticated discussion, see Randall Thomson and Matthew Zingraff, "Detecting Sentencing Disparity: Some Problems and Evidence," *American Sociological Review* 86 (1981), pp. 869–80.

South, blacks were found to be disproportionately sentenced to prison and given longer terms for the same offenses than were whites.[5] The race of the victim also was of marked importance: blacks who victimized whites were clearly treated more harshly than white offenders who victimized whites, but the sentences for blacks who victimized other blacks tended to be more lenient than for white offenders who victimized whites.[6]

Since this early study by Bullock, research on the effects of race has mushroomed into a little "cottage industry." I will only be able to list a few of the increasingly sophisticated researches on this subject. First, research shows that the sentencing disparity continues.[7] Although all of the research agrees on this, there is controversy concerning the extent of the present-day disparity, and over the correct theory to explain it.[8] Finally, the nature of the bias has changed from overt racial discrimination to more subtle forms; investigation of this and other trends in sentencing is an important research task.[9]

Similar analyses have been conducted on other attributes, indicating for instance that young adults (beyond adolescence) are more likely than older persons to receive stiff sentences, working-class persons more so than persons from higher socioeconomic strata, and boys from broken homes more than boys from intact homes. In Florida, where a judge may withhold the label of "convicted" if a guilty person is placed on probation, this favor was given more frequently to persons who were white, well educated, without prior record, younger, and defended by a private attorney.[10] Men are more likely than women to receive a prison sentence for the same offense, and sentences for men also tend to be longer.[11]

---

[5] Henry A. Bullock, "Significance of the Racial Factor in the Length of Prison Sentence," *Journal of Criminal Law, Criminology and Police Science* 52 (1961). See his work elaborated in R. L. McNeely and Carl E. Pope, eds., *Race, Crime and Criminal Justice* (Beverly Hills, Calif.: Sage Publications, 1981).

[6] This influence of the race of the victim also has been found in studies by Marvin Wolfgang and Marc Riedel, "Rape, Race, and the Death Penalty in Georgia," *American Journal of Orthopsychiatry* 45 (1975), pp. 658–68, and by William Bowers and Glen Pierce, "Arbitrariness and Discrimination under Post-Furman Capital Statutes," *Crime and Delinquency* 26 (1980), pp. 535–63.

[7] John Humphrey and Timothy J. Fogarty, "Race and Plea Bargained Outcomes: A Research Note," *Social Forces* 66 (1987), pp. 176–82.

[8] For the controversy over the extent of present disparity, see Kimberly L. Kempf and Roy L. Austin, "Older and More Recent Evidence on Racial Discrimination in Sentencing," *Journal of Quantitative Criminology* 2 (1986), pp. 29–48. For possible causes of the disparity, see George S. Bridges and Robert D. Crutchfield, "Law, Social Standing, and Racial Disparities in Imprisonment," *Social Forces* 66 (1988), pp. 699–724.

[9] Majorie S. Zatz, "The Changing Forms of Racial/Ethnic Biases in Sentencing," *Journal of Research in Crime and Delinquency* 24 (1987), pp. 69–92.

[10] Theodore G. Chiricos et al., "Inequality in the Imposition of a Criminal Label," *Social Problems* 19 (1972), pp. 553–72.

[11] But for minor juvenile offenses it is females who are discriminated against.

The last item, the sentencing difference between women and men, has sparked a minor flurry of studies to further examine results that seem to many to contradict common sense. But the finding of leniency toward females has stood this test, and the best explanation seems to be the paternalistic attitude toward women in serious trouble that lingers from older attitudes toward the sexes in general.[12] The sentencing differential appears to be diminishing, probably as a reaction to the feminist movement.[13]

While the establishment of patterns is important for analysis, interpretation of their meaning is equally essential. The kindest face that can be put on such prejudicial treatment is to speculate that the judges are doing precisely what they are mandated to do—applying sanctions in terms of the perceived "needs" of the offender. Perhaps judges feel that boys from broken homes are more likely to benefit from custody than are boys from homes with both parents. (Such a conclusion would in itself be of questionable integrity unless some supporting evidence were forthcoming.) But, with the possible exception of the aforementioned boys, it seems very doubtful that judges base their practices on the overt grounds that such criteria as race, sex, age, or class are of predictive value in determining the *rehabilitative or preventative worth* of a sentence of a given severity. (For that matter it must be admitted that very little information exists on what judges *do* use as criteria for sentencing.[14])

Therefore, in order to explain differential treatment based on certain attributes, we must fall back onto less admirable explanations, on covertly held ideas about blacks and whites, males and females, executives and laborers. The vast majority of judges are white, upper middle class (or upper class), old, and male.[15] In all but the last they are themselves in the favored category in terms of sentencing. Those holding a self-interest or vested interest theory of class may wish to explain this

---

[12]For a more sophisticated interpretation that attempts to get at the actual reasoning behind decisions, see Kathleen Daly, "Structure and Practice of Familial-Based Justice in a Criminal Court," *Law and Society Review* 21 (1987), pp. 267–90.

[13]Alfred B. Heilbrun, Jr., and Mark R. Heilbrun, "The Treatment of Women within the Criminal Justice System: An Inquiry into the Social Impact of the Women's Rights Movement," *Psychology of Women Quarterly* 10 (1986), pp. 240–51.

[14]See Hogarth, Sentencing, and Edward Green, *Judicial Attitudes in Sentencing* (London: Macmillan, 1961). For a review of existing research on judicial decision-making (and other related topics, such as jury and parole decisions), see Michael J. Saks, "The Social Psychology of Decision-Making in the Criminal Justice System," *Windsor Yearbook of Access to Justice* 6 (1986), pp. 61–92. For an outstanding study of sentencing in one state (Georgia), see Martha A. Myers and Suzette M. Talarico, *The Social Context of Criminal Sentencing* (New York: Springer-Verlag, 1987).

[15]The background characteristics and work experience of federal judges, including the contrast between Reagan appointees and those appointed earlier, can be found in Sheldon Goldman, "Reagan's Second Term Judicial Appointments," *Judicature* 70 (1987), pp. 324–39.

relation on rather obvious grounds. The truth, however, seems to be that judges are themselves largely unaware of these trends and feel that they examine each case on its own merits. Their behavior might be better regarded as exemplifying their stereotypes about the kinds of persons with whom they are dealing.

Certainly judges see before them in the criminal courts many more men than women, workers than executives, younger adults than old, and—in proportion to their ratios in the total population—more blacks and American Indians than whites. And this may in turn lead them to draw certain conclusions about these attributes.[16] When an atypical offender appears before a judge (ideally, an old, white, upper-class lady—already we say "lady"), the tendency is to perceive such a person as basically noncriminal and reformable. When a young, unemployed American Indian or black male appears, however, exactly the opposite is likely to occur. It is not so much that the judge consciously reflects on the person's attributes but that the attributes provide cues that trigger a particular frame of mind. As psychologists might say, the judge is perceptually ready to see certain qualities, good or bad, in the person.[17]

This discussion indicates how important it can be to appoint judges from various sectors of the community. And this does seem to matter: black judges, for instance, do treat the races somewhat differently than white judges.[18] On a related point, the Reagan administration conscientiously sought to appoint judges who corresponded with Reagan's own political philosophy, and this was accomplished to a greater extent and more overtly than under any previous administration. Analysis of decisions reached by Reagan appointees and those judges appointed earlier clearly show sharp differences.[19]

What is true of judges must also occur with juries, although in subtly different ways. Jury members, of course, are not typically upper middle class and old. A juror's perceptual biases may be altogether different from those of the judge, and his or her readiness to appraise the defendant on the basis of specific attributes also may differ. But juries, too, have their preconceptions, for jurisdictions where the juries rather than the judge determine the sentence also display differentials in sen-

---

[16] Biases are already at work in these numerical differences, but I reserve this discussion for later.

[17] An old but excellent source on this is Jerome S. Bruner, "On Perceptual Readiness," in *Current Perspectives in Social Psychology*, ed. E. P. Hollander and Raymond G. Hunt (New York: Oxford University Press, 1964), pp. 42–47.

[18] Susan Welch et al., "Do Black Judges Make a Difference?" *American Journal of Political Science* 32 (1988), pp. 126–36.

[19] C. R. Rowland et al., "Presidential Effects on Criminal Justice Policy in the Lower Federal Courts: The Reagan Judges," *Law and Society Review* 22 (1988), pp. 191–200.

tences based on attributes rather than offenses. For this reason court decisions requiring women and blacks to be eligible for jury duty, in numbers proportionate to their frequency in the population, are so potentially significant.

THE DECISION TO ARREST

We have discussed judicial discretion as a source of preferential treatment, but another covert process in the criminal justice system must be examined here. As has often been noted, it is manifestly impossible for a legislature to set down rules for law enforcement officials that cover the infinity of discrete situations encountered in practice. On many occasions police must use their own judgment in deciding whether or not to make an arrest.[20] This is most typically the case for relatively minor or marginal offenses, in which the statutory language is intentionally vague. In contrast to the relative precision used in defining serious crimes, laws regarding loitering, disturbing the peace, public nuisance, drunk and disorderly conduct, or interference with a peace officer on official duty are necessarily less specific, having to cover a broad range of concrete instances in multidimensional situations. For such offenses, what is termed *police discretion* is quite apparent. The officer must decide whether the person should be ignored, lectured, sent home in a taxi, remanded to parents, or arrested. The person on the spot must be allowed considerable latitude because of the heterogeneity of situations in which a given law may apply.[21]

But this in turn means that when a general tendency of police discretion becomes visible, public dissatisfaction can occur. Two areas in particular have received attention in the last few years: police response in domestic disputes and in complaints of child abuse.[22]

---

[20]Police discretion is also unavoidable in deciding which calls to police headquarters are worth responding to. An excellent illustration from Canada can be seen in "The Discretionary Enforcement of Law," by Brian Grosman, *Chitty's Law Journal* 21 (1973).

[21]It has long been recognized that although marginal offenses consume the bulk of their time, law enforcement personnel typically receive little or no *training* in handling them. A good discussion of this is in the 1967 President's Commission on Law Enforcement and Administration of Justice, *The Challenge of Crime in a Free Society* (Washington, D.C.: U.S. Government Printing Office), especially pp. 91–92, 106–13.

[22]See, on these issues, Sarah F. Berke and D. Loseke, "Handling Family Violence: Situational Determinants of Police Arrest in Domestic Disturbances," *Law and Society Review* 15 (1981), pp. 314–44; and Cecil L. Willis and Richard H. Wells, "The Police and Child Abuse," *Criminology* 26 (1988), pp. 695–715.

In terms of treatment, minor offenses are frequently handled in a discriminatory way. No one doubts that police arrest murderers in a systematic fashion, but what of drunks? The drunk man in his Cadillac in a fashionable section of town is guided to a taxi; the grizzled old man on skid row is arrested and hustled into the drunk tank because it is assumed that he does not have a home. Nor need we depend on casual observation to confirm this trend: observers have accompanied police on their rounds and systematically recorded bias in their decisions to arrest.[23] Many of the same factors come into play with police discretion as with judicial and jury discretion—old, white, female, and middle- or upper-class persons are less likely to be taken into custody. The evidence for discretionary bias against American Indians with respect to minor or marginal offenses is overwhelming.[24]

Let us put some detail into this general picture. In an elegant little study in California, Heussenstamm asked a group of fifteen student volunteers to display prominent Black Panther bumper stickers on their cars at the height of scares about black power. (The Black Panthers were a radical, highly militant black-power organization.) Although none of the students in the group had received a single moving traffic violation in the preceding twelve months, without any conscious change in driving habits they quickly amassed a total of thirty-three traffic citations from police in a seventeen-day period, at which point the study was prematurely halted.[25] This study nicely demonstrates that police discretion can be abused not only on the basis of personal attributes (such as race, age, sex) but also on the basis of *political affiliations*. Additional factors are also at work: the locale of apprehension, the time of day, whether the police think a conviction will "stick" and, most importantly, the *demeanor* of the suspect.[26]

TREATMENT BY POLICE

Another aspect of differential treatment takes place even without arrest: the demeanor of the police—their verbal aggressiveness, gentleness, or

---

[23]The most extensive study is still Wayne R. LaFave's book, *Arrest: The Decision to Take a Suspect into Custody* (Boston: Little, Brown, 1964).

[24]Here is another Canadian study. (After all, I have a Canadian connection.) See the evidence in "Arrests, Dispositions and Recidivism: A Comparison of Indians and Whites," by Rita Bienvenue and A. H. Latif, *Canadian Journal of Criminology and Corrections* 16 (1974), pp. 106–16, as well as the other studies they cite.

[25]F. K. Heussenstamm, "Bumper Stickers and the Cops," in *Contemporary Social Psychology: Representative Readings*, ed. Thomas Blass (Itasca, Ill.: F. E. Peacock Publishers, 1976), pp. 137–40.

[26]LaFave, *Arrest*; Douglas A. Smith and Jody R. Klein, "Police Control of Interpersonal Disputes," *Social Problems* 31 (1984), pp. 468–81.

roughness in handling a person. This treatment depends in large part on the factors and personal attributes already discussed, and especially on the behavior of the subject at the time of confrontation. Is the person arrogant or uncooperative? Police admit privately to the difficulty of the arrest setting and to their own apprehensiveness. At times they must walk into extremely dangerous situations and defuse them solely by their "front."[27] With the feeling that it is vital to obtain quick command of any encounter, they develop a distinctive manner to promote this. An ability to evaluate a situation rapidly is also prized, and this of course requires observance of outwardly visible cues such as race, age, and sex. The front displayed in a given situation is adjusted accordingly.[28]

But while one can be sympathetic with such a difficult task, the picture from the standpoint of suspects is quite different, for if they happen to be displaying the "wrong" cues, they are immediately subjected to aggressive, overbearing, and humiliating hostility, which evokes the most extreme emotions. Blacks often refer to this verbal aggressiveness when speaking of police brutality. The scene frequently degenerates into a status game in which the officer, to attain the security that comes with dominance, places greater and greater requirements on the individual (e.g., demands for identification, a frisk search), while to maintain a feeling of self-worth the suspect performs all required actions with greater and greater disdain and arrogance. Eventually the suspect may feel internally compelled to disobey an order or to verbally insult the officer, which may lead to an arrest arising purely from the confrontation.

Even in the absence of an arrest, it is clear that law officers' stereotypes of the public result in differential treatment, sometimes in an extreme form. Inasmuch as their perceptions of individuals lead to actions on their part that may result in the subjects becoming violent or abusive, it may be said that the police often engage in a self-fulfilling prophecy.[29] In fairness, it must be added that certain members of the public also have

---

[27] This requirement helps explain why police officers back one another to the hilt in investigations of impropriety.

[28] For research on the evaluation of suspects by police, see Irving Piliavin and Scott Briar, "Police Encounters with Juveniles," *American Journal of Sociology* 70 (1964), pp. 206–14; Richard J. Lundman et al., "Police Control of Juveniles: A Replication," *Journal of Research in Crime and Delinquency* 15 (January 1978); and John M. Gandy, "The Exercise of Discretion by the Police as a Decision-Making Process in the Disposition of Juvenile Offenders," *Osgoode Hall Law Journal* 8 (1970), pp. 333–46.

[29] See Kelly G. Shaver, "Interpersonal and Social Consequences of Attribution," in *Contemporary Issues in Social Psychology*, 3rd ed., ed. J. L. Brigham and L. S. Wrightsman (Monterey, Calif.: Brooks/Cole Publishing, 1977), especially pp. 323–25; and John P. Clark, "Isolation of the Police: A Comparison of British and American Situations," *Journal of Criminal Law, Criminology, and Police Science* 56 (1965), pp. 307–19. For an elaboration of such points, and their limitations, in Canada, see Daniel J. Koenig, "Police Perceptions of Public Respect and Extra-Legal Use of Force," *Canadian Journal of Sociology* 1 (1975), pp. 313–24.

preconceptions of the police, which lead *them* to perform actions in the encounter that drive the police to more drastic steps.

Stereotyping of the suspect occurs at every stage in the criminal-justice process—the initial encounter, the decision to arrest, the verdict, and the sentencing.[30] (It is probably at work, too, in parole decisions.) We discussed some of the self-fulfilling effects of such stereotyping when we looked at labeling or reaction theory, so for now it is sufficient to note two points. First is the fact that popular stereotypes, or in some cases, ideologies, result in preferential treatment having nothing to do with the offense and little if anything to do with rehabilitation potential or "individualized" treatment. Second, official statistics on the charac-teristics of offenders (for example, the proportion of convicts who are blacks, men, or juveniles) are distorted by these mechanisms, so that some categories will be over-represented—perhaps markedly so.[31] *Inso-far as such statistics form the basis for selective enforcement, they are to that extent self-fulfilling.* As one example, if blacks are over-represented and police are more or less aware of the statistics, then police will be watching blacks more closely, will be more likely to apprehend a black criminal than a white, and may trigger more illegal reactions from blacks than from whites. As more blacks are brought in, the perception of crim-inality among blacks becomes self-confirming.[32] Much of this cycle has moved beyond the level of speculation. For social class, evidence now shows that police tend to see lower-class youths as more involved in delinquent activity, that police predict more readily that such youths will become repeat offenders, and that police arrest lower-class mem-bers on flimsier evidence.[33]

---

[30] Stereotyping also takes place with respect to the victims of crime; in some jurisdictions officials respond with leniency toward the offender when the victim is a minority group member—the so-called "indulgent pattern" of enforcement—and with greater harsh-ness when the victim is not (the "nonindulgent pattern"). See Bullock, "Racial Factor."

[31] Many mechanisms besides stereotyping lead to the statistical over-representation of cer-tain groups. Financial inequalities lead to differences in the competence of attorneys and the feasibility of appeals. Court procedures may be totally baffling to uneducated defendants. The court language may be unintelligible to those with a poor command of English.

[32] See Aaron V. Cicourel, *The Social Organization of Juvenile Justice* (New York: Wiley, 1968); and Richard L. Henshel, "Effects of Disciplinary Prestige on Predictive Accuracy: Distortions from Feedback," *Futures* 7 (1975), pp. 92–106.

[33] See, among others, M. Haskell and L. Yablonsky, *Juvenile Delinquency* (Chicago: Rand McNally, 1978), especially p. 231; M. Garrett and J. F. Short, Jr., "Social Class and Delin-quency: Predictions and Outcomes of Police-Juvenile Encounters," *Social Problems* 22 (1975), pp. 368–82; and Charles Tittle et al., "The Myth of Social Class and Criminality: An Empirical Assessment of the Empirical Evidence," *American Sociological Review* 43 (1978), pp. 643–56.

SELECTING THE MENTALLY ILL

The term "treatment" in the title of this chapter may apply most closely to the condition known as mental illness; we find here the questions of ideology and perception at least as strong as in the treatment of the accused criminal. The issues involving the definition of mental abnormality and the attachment of medical labels to what may be just problems of living have been covered in an earlier chapter. We are not concerned here with the validity of the medical model, but with the power dimension in the involuntary commitment of individuals. Here once again an ideological component is dominant and the name of Thomas Szasz is preeminent. As before, when he virtually denied the existence of psychopathology, Szasz sometimes allows himself to be carried away in his argument. But the facts he presents regarding the misuse of psychiatry in legal commitment are too strong to be overcome by his failings.[34]

As previously mentioned, Szasz argues that mental illness is, except for behavior produced by brain damage, essentially different from physical illness. In his conception, people defined as "mentally ill" are not sick at all but have problems of living.[35] In contrast to a physical illness in which the afflicted one is almost always among the first to complain, such persons often will not concede their need for any help. At the very least, one must agree with Szasz that a diagnosis of mental ill-health cannot be made with the exactitude one expects in the case of a broken leg or a ruptured appendix.[36] If so, then the decision has much more room for bias—all the more so since the "patient" often does not concur. Yet Szasz has documented the extremely slipshod and hurried ways in which, until recently, people were examined in order to affix a label that will be of the utmost consequence for the rest of their lives.[37] Not only were the described procedures incredibly faulty, with some cases lasting less than five minutes from start to finish, but the legal safeguards designed to catch such errors in labeling in ordinary trials

---

[34]On a related point, see Henry J. Steadman, "The Psychiatrist as a Conservative Agent of Social Control," *Social Problems* 20 (1972), pp. 263–71.

[35]Thomas Szasz, *The Myth of Mental Illness* (New York: Hoeber-Harper, 1961). It is interesting that certain mental hospitals were once renamed "Institutes of Living." See Steve Pratt and Jay Tooley, "Innovations in Mental Hospital Concepts and Practice," in *Major American Social Problems*, by Robert A. Dentler (Chicago: Rand McNally, 1967).

[36]This is also expressed well in E. Erikson, "The Nature of Clinical Evidence," in *Evidence and Inference*, ed. Daniel Lerner (Glencoe, Ill.: Free Press, 1959), pp. 73–95.

[37]See especially Part I of Szasz's *Psychiatric Justice* (New York: Basic Books, 1966), and Luis Kutner, "The Illusion of Due Process in Commitment Proceedings," *Northwestern Law Review* 57 (1962), pp. 383–99.

have been almost totally lacking for decisions involving involuntary commitment to mental institutions.

To understand why this has been the case it is necessary to penetrate the doctrinal foundations of involuntary commitment. Involuntary commitment is said to be for the patient's own good; psychiatry is meant to serve in a helping rather than a punitive role. Hence, this argument goes, a person does not need the legal safeguards in a commitment proceeding as required in a criminal trial—technically it is a case of administrative rather than criminal law unless a crime has been committed. Since no one is against the person—no charge has been made—the person needs no protection; it is not an adversarial system. This has been the official doctrinal basis for such events, supported both by the traditional divisions of the law and by the psychiatric profession's self-conception that it is a healing, helping, certainly nonpunitive endeavor.[38]

As a result of these views, the traditional trappings of criminal justice have been dispensed with, most importantly those safeguarding an accused against erroneous findings. With only minor variations among different jurisdictions, persons generally have no privilege against "self-incrimination"; no right to remain silent; no right to be informed of the claims made against them, nor who made them (and often are not so informed); and no right to summon witnesses on their behalf, nor to compel their testimony. Until recently, they did not have the right to be represented by counsel, and they were frequently not advised of their right to challenge the proceedings or of their later right to seek release. In some jurisdictions they still do not have the right to cross-examine. In many instances, no external psychiatrist may represent their interests or even—in most cases—translate the psychiatric findings into layperson's terms.

This procedure has been justified on the ground that treatment is for the benefit of the patients themselves, as in conventional medicine, but the facts do not always appear to bear this out. In the first place, the essence of involuntary commitment is that the person does not wish to stay. At the very onset, then, we experience a conflict of values that is only rarely found in the medical model.[39] But even under a sort of involuntary humanitarianism, the case for such legal procedures is poor. Most mental institutions are terribly overcrowded, their staffs inadequate, and their deprivations severe.

In recent years legislation has somewhat improved the situation: defense attorneys are now assigned in some jurisdictions; in others, law-

---

[38]See Nicholas Kittrie, *The Right to be Different* (Baltimore: Johns Hopkins University Press, 1971).

[39]Certain religious groups object to vaccination; suicide prevention also exhibits certain ethical similarities.

yers are now assigned to the review board. The disgracefully brief hearings are a thing of the past, and hearings are now overtly adversarial to a far greater extent.[40] Nevertheless, the legal safeguards listed above are still absent, except for the changes I noted. Even though the review process has improved to a degree in the formal sense, from the sociological standpoint inadequacies remain, as highlighted in a now famous research study.

Rosenhan arranged to have a number of willing volunteer graduate students admitted as ordinary patients to twelve different mental hospitals, in order to conduct an experiment on how readily the hospital psychiatric staffs would recognize their sanity. Beyond their initial commitment reason (that they heard voices), the student volunteers were instructed to behave naturally once inside and to answer all questions truthfully. Not only did no psychiatric staff member in any hospital ever recognize their sanity, even once, but also the students experienced great difficulty in getting out, even after the experiment was revealed. This result has been interpreted to show that once a diagnosis is made on a person it sticks; as Rosenhan put it, "the normal are not detectably sane"—especially not inside an institution.[41] When, for instance, some students wrote down their observations inside the institution, hospital staff recorded this as "engages in note-taking behavior."

This reminds me of a delightful little exchange in *Alice's Adventures in Wonderland*.

"We're all mad here. I'm mad. You're mad."
"How do you know I'm mad?" said Alice.
"You must be," said the cat, "or you wouldn't have come here."
Alice didn't think that proved it at all.

Lewis Carroll

Normal activity becomes transmogrified by virtue of being done inside the institution. Yet, even in the newer procedures of the last decade, the psychiatrist's conclusion is still ordinarily taken as definitive. Either other board members defer to expert opinion or, as Decker documents, the person's behavior in the ward or in the interview is often a key issue that boils down to the psychiatrist's word and interpretation against the

---

[40]Not everyone agrees with me that this is a considerable improvement. For a negative evaluation of these and other changes, see Jonas R. Rappeport, "Belegaled: Mental Health and the United States, 1986," *Canadian Journal of Psychiatry* 32 (1987), pp. 719–27.

[41]D. L. Rosenhan, "On Being Sane in Insane Places," *Science* 179 (1973), pp. 250–58. See also Richard Hawkins and Gary Tiedeman, *The Creation of Deviance* (Columbus, Ohio: Merrill, 1975), p. 198.

patient's unsupported word.[42] Not inaccurately, Szasz compares psychiatric hearings to trials in which a life sentence may result. When it is recognized that in the United States close to a quarter of a million persons are involuntarily committed every year, the magnitude of the situation is clear. In most areas, the proportion of involuntary admissions is very high. Moreover, in the United States, it has been found that persons from the lower classes are more likely to be involuntarily committed,[43] and this is particularly true of blacks.[44] The incorrectness of ignoring the inadvertent punitive aspects of such confinement is obvious.[45]

Szasz advances beyond the indisputable charge that important and well-nigh irreversible decisions about people's lives are being made in unconscionably cavalier fashion. He also feels that, while psychiatry is always helpful in theory, in practice it sometimes serves its own interests, at least with respect to involuntary therapy, which Szasz sees as a contradiction in terms. Even in the absence of commitment to an institution, the label "mental illness" is a socially disabling one—however well intended.[46] It is therefore anathema to Szasz to regard whatever the psychiatrist does as being necessarily in the best interest of the patient. It is precisely *because* the mental illness label is not hostile or punitive per se that it is so insidious in its ability to weaken the defenses of the person who is being helped. A person so charged is more vulnerable, more directly accessible to public agencies or individuals who do not always have his or her best interests at heart.[47] This is one of Szasz's chief points in *The Ethics of Psychoanalysis*.[48]

---

[42] Frederic H. Decker, "Psychiatric Management of Legal Defense in Periodic Commitment Hearings," *Social Problems* 34 (1987), pp. 156–71. See also Virginia A. Hiday, "Judicial Decisions in Civil Commitment: Facts, Attitudes, and Psychiatric Recommendations," *Law and Society Review* 17 (1983), pp. 517–30.

[43] W. A. Rushing, "Status Resources, Societal Reactions, and Hospital Admission," *American Sociological Review* 43 (1978), pp. 521–33.

[44] B. A. Baldwin et al., "Status Inconsistency and Psychiatric Diagnoses: A Structural Approach to Labeling Theory," *Journal of Health and Social Behavior* 16 (1975), pp. 257–67.

[45] The argument that a legal decision is nonpunitive because it does not formally involve criminal sanctions is not a new one. The now defunct House Un-American Activities Committee (HUAC) used to justify its persecution of supposed "Communists," "pinkos," and others by the same argument: since it could not fine, imprison, or execute, it had no real sanctioning power and hence the people it spotlighted and called to testify did not require the safeguards of a criminal court. Those who felt the effects of HUAC's blacklisting practices may not have felt so sanguine about its power to punish.

[46] Hawkins and Tiedeman, *Creation of Deviance*. The "Eagleton affair" in the 1972 presidential election, in which Thomas Eagleton—an otherwise excellent candidate for vice-president—was dropped because of an earlier bout of mental disability years before, is a case in point.

[47] Although we have thus far concentrated on involuntary commitment, it is clear that such power extends beyond the walls of the asylum into the lives of persons judged sane enough to manage outside but supposedly not well enough to make an autonomous appraisal of their own mental state.

[48] Thomas S. Szasz, *The Ethics of Psychoanalysis* (New York: Basic Books, 1965).

A realistic view of commitment decisions takes account of the power and conflict involved. By defining people as sick and in need of hospitalization, authorities can get them out of the way and "taken care of," even though they have done nothing illegal and have merely made nuisances of themselves.[49] Such decisions go far beyond psychiatrists' healing role and involve them in nonscientific tasks as *agents of social control*.[50] As Szasz points out, people "put away" other people partly because they do not want them around. The individuals involved in the decision-making process—petitioners (usually relatives), psychiatrists, and court officials—all have certain vested interests in the outcome that they seek to promote. At times these are the easy-to-understand motivations of disenchanted spouses or relatives, but at other times officialdom itself may be the prime mover in the process.

Szasz forcefully condemns the misuse of psychiatry to cover administrative actions. He cites instances in which officials have had bothersome persons committed. Especially iniquitous is the practice of declaring someone incompetent to stand trial. Assessment of fitness to stand trial was originally intended as a protection for accused persons who could not defend themselves. But as it has developed, with prosecutors as well as defense counsel able to request a test, a person thus may be incarcerated in a mental hospital for longer than the corresponding maximum sentence could have been, and without the prosecution needing to prove criminal guilt.[51]

Some of Szasz's arguments appear excessive. In his zeal to divorce psychiatry completely from the legal machinery, he would rule out entirely the insanity plea in criminal trials, even if the accused prefers it. He seems to feel that involuntary hospitalization never does any good to the patient, and he completely overlooks psychiatrists' altruistic motives in favor of self-serving machinations. It is true that many psychiatrists gain from forensic work and that the profession needs patients to validate its occupational role, but these features are considerably exaggerated in Szasz's analysis.[52] In spite of such defects, Szasz has

---

[49]There is something of a parallel between this situation and the enforcement of loitering and vagrancy laws. See Richard Quinney, *The Social Reality of Crime* (Boston: Little, Brown, 1970).

[50]In the past couple of decades, the psychiatric profession has come under attack for acting as an agent of social control with respect to "appropriate" femininity. See, for instance, Phyllis Chesler, "Patient and Patriarch: Women in the Psychotherapeutic Relationship," in *Women in Sexist Society*, ed. Vivian Gornick and Barbara K. Moran (New York: Basic Books, 1971), and her book, *Women and Madness* (New York: Avon, 1972).

[51]See Mark E. Schiffer, "Fitness to Stand Trial," *University of Toronto Faculty of Law Review* 35 (1977), pp. 1–25. The American situation is equivalent to Canada's.

[52]See a more accurate portrayal in Chapter 6 of Hawkins and Tiedeman, *Creation of Deviance*: "Controlling Deviance Is Big Business."

performed a significant service in bringing glaring inequities to the public eye.[53]

SOCIAL CLASS AND TREATMENT OF MENTAL ILLNESS

In the 1950s Hollingshead and Redlich accomplished a landmark study on social class and mental illness.[54] It is by now a very old study, but it continues to attract attention, and its principal findings continue to receive support. In view of the idea that selection and treatment of a social problem tend to proceed along stereotypical lines, these findings are of considerable interest.

For their study of a New England community, Hollingshead and Redlich classified mental patients into one of five social classes, ranging from class V (the lower-lower class) to class I (upper class). They first examined the type of diagnosis for mental illness that members of different social classes received. They found that lower-class individuals were overrepresented among people who were mental patients or were being treated for mental illness. While persons in class V constituted 38 percent of all patients, they constituted only 18 percent of the total nonpatient population. Furthermore, when *types* of disorders were taken into consideration, and globally subdivided into neuroses and psychoses, only about 19 percent of the class V patients had been diagnosed as neurotic, while some 65 percent of class I patients had been so labeled.[55] Neuroses are usually considered milder problems and are less subject to stigma; it is thus interesting to note that so few lower-class patients had received such a diagnosis.[56]

If we ignore the possibility of very large and systematic errors in diagnosis, these disparities are traceable to two possible causes. Either

---

[53]However, there has been no consensus among psychiatrists on this point. See Arlene Kaplan Daniels, "Professional Responses to 'Insider' Critics: Psychiatrists Consider Dr. Szasz," a paper presented at the annual meeting of the Society for the Study of Social Problems, New Orleans, 1972.

[54]August B. Hollingshead and Frederick C. Redlich, *Social Class and Mental Illness* (New York: Wiley, 1958).

[55]*Ibid.*, p. 223. Similar findings have been reported in other studies. See, for instance, Leo Srole et al., *Mental Health in the Metropolis: The Midtown Manhattan Study* (New York: McGraw-Hill, 1962).

[56]In addition to social class, it has been shown that the diagnostic decision is influenced by race and gender. Some hoped that a formal diagnostic system (the *Diagnostic and Statistical Manual*, 3rd ed.) would reduce or eliminate this problem, but recent research shows that it persists. See Marti Loring and Brian Powell, "Gender, Race, and DSM-III: A Study of the Objectivity of Psychiatric Diagnostic Behavior," *Journal of Health and Social Behavior* 29 (1988), pp. 1–22.

the life-styles and experiences of the various social classes were so different that they exerted a strong influence on the type of mental disorder that arose, or, since psychiatric diagnosis depends on observation of the verbal and nonverbal acts of the subjects, the social class backgrounds of different persons showed up in their behavior, and these behavioral differences led to systematic differences in the diagnosis.[57] On the one hand the first hypothesis is supported by certain facts, for, indeed, lower-class persons are subjected to more stressful and insecure life conditions,[58] while at the same time receiving fewer of the rewards that higher-status persons receive.[59] Such a negative imbalance may give rise to more serious emotional problems. Moreover, evidence shows that the socialization pattern of lower-class persons often equips them less adequately to cope with stress than does the socialization of persons of higher status.[60] Bearing on the second hypothesis is recent research that shows an unrecognized link in clinicians' minds between social-class categories and psychiatric diagnostic categories. Indeed diagnostic categories can in some respects be considered the "equivalent" of role stereotypes of the different social classes.[61] Further support for this second hypothesis is the difference in the types of treatment the various social classes receive. (I will describe this momentarily.) At any rate, it is entirely possible for both explanatory hypotheses to be correct.

In the Hollingshead and Redlich study, treatment was divided into three categories for purposes of analysis: psychotherapy (therapy through talking), organic therapy (insulin, electroshock, tranquilizers), and custodial care (which rests on the assumption that little can be done for a mental patient beyond providing a shelter). It should be noted that neurotics usually receive psychotherapy, while psychotics tend to be given custodial care and organic therapy. Since, as we saw, a greater proportion of lower-class patients had received a psychotic classification, proportionately more lower-class patients were subjected to more drastic methods of treatment (e.g., electroshock). But, *even within the same diagnosed condition* there were marked disparities in the extent to

---

[57]The disparity in the proportion of neurotics may also reflect the fact that upper-class neurotics voluntarily appear for treatment proportionally more often than working-class individuals. The latter are more frequently referred by social agencies and the courts (or the police) after their behavior has drawn attention to them.

[58]R. Liem and J. Liem, "Social Class and Mental Illness Reconsidered: The Role of Economic Stress and Social Support," *Journal of Health and Social Behavior* 19 (1978), pp. 139–56.

[59]*Ibid.*; N. Bradburn, *The Structure of Psychological Well-being* (Chicago: Aldine, 1969).

[60]R. C. Kessler and P. D. Cleary, "Social Class and Psychological Distress," *American Journal of Sociology* 45 (1980), pp. 463–78.

[61]Hope Landrine, "On the Politics of Madness: A Preliminary Analysis of the Relationship between Social Roles and Psychopathology," *Genetic, Social, and General Psychology Monographs* 113 (1987), pp. 341–406.

which the three types of therapy were employed on patients from various classes. Neurotic patients from the lower class, for example, received far more custodial care than neurotic patients from other classes. And even when they received psychotherapy, it was the type called directive, whereas neurotic upper-class patients received analytic therapy far more frequently.[62]

Among neurotics who received psychotherapy, lower-class patients were seen by their practitioners for far fewer visits than upper-class patients, and the length of each session was dismally short for lower-class neurotics. And other investigators on the team found that a "patient's class status determines the professional level of the therapist who treats him."[63]

Of course, certain of these treatment differentials are related to the lower income of class V patients, to their inability to secure expensive treatment. However, Hollingshead and Redlich found factors other than income to account for this differential. For instance, in public hospitals where treatment is free for all classes, lower-class neurotics still received more custodial care than neurotics of other classes, and *no* class I neurotic received such a treatment.

Finally, the lengths of time in treatment for each disorder were strikingly different for the several social classes, with psychotics manifesting the greatest social-class differences. In the upper classes, I and II, 50 percent of the patients had been in treatment for less than three years, while in class V, 50 percent of the patients had been in treatment for ten years.[64]

I have so far left out the team's findings on use of electroconvulsive therapy, one of the most controversial treatments, because trends seem to have changed since the old study was conducted. Hollingshead and Redlich found the greatest use of electroshock to be in public hospitals and on members of the lower class. A recent study shows the treatment to have revived in private hospitals, with its main employment now on middle-class patients.[65]

As one looks at the entire spectrum of diagnosis, treatment type, and treatment length, social class was of indisputable significance in the study. These results were also detected in a 1968 follow-up study, which

---

[62]Hollingshead and Redlich, *Social Class*, p. 268.

[63]Jerome K. Myers and Leslie Schaffer, "Social Stratification and Psychiatric Practice," *American Sociological Review* 19 (1954), pp. 307–10.

[64]Hollingshead and Redlich, *Social Class*, p. 298. Part of this discrepancy may be accounted for by the greater proportion of schizophrenics among class V patients, but it is probably due more to the greater use of custodial care as the sole "treatment" of class V individuals—including hospitalized neurotics.

[65]Carol A. B. Warren, "Electroconvulsive Therapy: 'New' Treatment of the 1980s," *Research in Law, Deviance, and Social Control* 8 (1986), pp. 41–55.

again suggested that, quite apart from the illness classification, social factors and the treatment agency operate together to produce significant differences in psychiatric treatment outcome.[66]

Hollingshead and Redlich were not content to set forth these facts as simple data; they searched for the meaning behind them. Why were these regularities found? The authors rejected the idea that these treatment differentials were solely due to biases on the part of psychiatrists and staff. Broadly speaking, successful psychotherapy requires a cooperative attitude on the part of the subject. Investigators found that lower-class patients and their families directed considerable hostility toward the psychiatric profession. In addition, few individuals from classes IV or V could understand interpersonal interaction as a means of therapy. Even after long periods of time, many hoped that after "all the talking" they would get down to "treatment." The hostility toward the psychiatrist and the lack of comprehension of verbal therapy clearly diminished the likelihood of progress for individuals who could have benefited. The investigators also encountered among lower-class families attitudes of rejection toward the member who had been placed under treatment. In most of these cases, psychological support dropped sharply, and the individual's subsequent chances of being cared for at home were very low. Continued hospitalization was seen as preferable in such instances, and undoubtedly this impacted on the statistics that I cited earlier concerning length of treatment.

After all these factors are mentioned, however, it remains clear that they are insufficient to account for the findings on length of treatment, and totally inadequate with regard to type and quality of treatment. Instead, the attitudes of psychiatrists toward patients must undergo examination. Hollingshead and Redlich investigated these attitudes along three major dimensions. They tried to assess whether "(a) those psychiatrists held similar views toward life and society with their patients, (b) they noticed differences in social class between themselves and their patients, and (c) they liked their patients."[67] In general, class I through III patients were liked and class IV and V patients disliked. This is not surprising since most psychiatrists come from class I and II backgrounds. Values and views toward life held by psychiatrists and class IV and V patients were markedly dissimilar, and these differences were definitely recognized by the psychiatrists. In effect the psychiatrist and lower-class patient had little to say to one another, and they experienced grave communication difficulties. The psychiatrists were irritated by

---

[66]Jerome K. Myers and Lee L. Bean, *A Decade Later: A Follow-up of Social Class and Mental Illness* (New York: Wiley, 1968).
[67]Hollingshead and Redlich, *Social Class*, p. 344.

the lower-class patients' inability to think in their terms—partially a result of vast differences in formal education.

With these factors in mind, the treatment differentials become understandable, if not necessarily excusable. Contemporary psychiatry seems most feasible when communication between patient and therapist is relatively smooth. When this is not the case, the temptation is to turn the problem over to organic therapy or to relegate the patient to custodial care. All too often such decisions follow class lines for the reasons already discussed.[68] But such reasoning does not explain why the least skilled and least experienced therapists are assigned lower-class patients: if they are the hardest to reach and yet psychotherapy is attempted, it makes more sense to use the most skillful psychiatrists. The only explanation is that such work is "beneath" the more prestigious therapists, who treat whom they want, and want to treat those with whom they can get along. But the authors present a telling criticism when they point out that "it is not the patient's job to understand the psychiatrist, but it is the psychiatrist's job to understand the patient. . . . The psychiatrist should not overlook the social differences between himself and his patients, but he should understand them, face them squarely, and deal with them in the therapeutic situation."[69] Until this takes place to a significant degree, differential treatment on a class basis will continue, justified by labels that put the onus on the lower-class patient. Again we find cultural and stereotypical factors at work in the treatment of a social problem.

IDEOLOGY AND SELECTION OF "MENTALLY ILL" DEVIANTS

At this point we shift our attention from perceptual and stereotypic effects on involuntary psychiatric treatment to those pertaining clearly to conscious ideology. Admittedly this distinction is sometimes less than clear-cut, but often the degree to which an ideology, as an overt and organized system of thought, intrudes into the selection process is easily recognizable. We begin, as the title indicates, with ideology in the selection of "mentally ill" deviants. Szasz has documented cases of ideologically based selection with considerable care.

---

[68]Most of these interrelationships have been confirmed in a recent study of community mental health outpatients, with a few interesting differences. See Connie E. Bland et al., "Use of Time and Satisfaction with the Psychotherapeutic Relationship," *Sociological Focus* 20 (1987), pp. 33–44.

[69]*Ibid.*, p. 346.

One case that came to public view in the early 1960s was that of General Edwin Walker, a right-winger so extreme that he was forced to retire from the United States Army. When the enforced enrollment of the first black student at the University of Mississippi occurred in 1962, Walker was at the scene as an outspoken supporter of the segregationist rioters. His exact role is in dispute but, while under arrest for various federal charges, he was suddenly whisked away by plane before bail bond could be posted. He was flown from Mississippi to a federal hospital in Springfield, Missouri, to undergo psychiatric examination. Already an affidavit was waiting that affirmed "sensitivity and essentially unpredictable and seemingly bizarre outbursts of the type often observed in paranoid individuals." The affidavit had been made by a government psychiatrist who had never seen Walker but relied on news clippings and his past testimony before a congressional committee. Because of the publicity the case generated and his public prominence, Walker was able to obtain release from the hospital, choose his own psychiatrist, and eventually obtain a ruling of sanity. Lesser known persons caught up in such ideological affairs may not fare so well. It is disturbingly evident that psychiatry was used in this case to get rid of Walker because of his views. Szasz also discusses the insanity case of the celebrated poet Ezra Pound. The views of Pound and Walker were not so far apart, and their cases were in certain respects very similar.[70]

The Soviet Union has had a long history of use of the insane asylum for political purposes, dating back before the 1917 revolution to the incarceration of writers by the Okhraina, the secret police of the tsars. These "sane asylums" were immortalized by Anton Chekhov's novel, *Ward 6*, and more recently publication of Valery Tarsis's novel, *Ward 7*, confirmed the continued refinement of the practice by Soviet authorities.[71] Tarsis, acclaimed outside of the USSR as a brilliant writer, was himself committed to a Soviet institution after publication of an earlier work. His autobiographical novel portrays an institution in which the inmates are quite sane and the hospital staff is more or less aware that it is a branch of the political police. In such a situation we have a highly refined ideological basis of "treatment" of what is evidently taken by authorities to be a social problem—in this case unrepentant, unpatriotic writers.[72]

---

[70]Thomas S. Szasz, *Law, Liberty and Psychiatry* (New York: Macmillan, 1963).

[71]Valery Tarsis, *Ward 7* (New York: Dutton, 1965).

[72]For extensive coverage and documentation of this problem, see Amnesty International's report, *Prisoners of Conscience in the USSR: Their Treatment and Conditions*, 2nd ed. (London: Amnesty International Publications, 1980). See also part two of Eric Stover and Elena O. Nightingale, *The Breaking of Minds and Bodies* (New York: W. H. Freeman, 1985).

How and why does such a system develop? The most straightforward explanation is totally cynical: a psychiatric hospital for political dissenters is more politically acceptable than a prison, because with the hospital doubts may at least linger as to whether such persons are really martyrs or just trouble-making mentally disturbed individuals. In the conventional alternatives of death or prison, the answer is all too clear.[73] This explanation is certainly plausible, but perhaps the truth is more complex, although no less disturbing. The diagnosis employed for these individuals is distinct, embodied in Snezhnevsky's theory of "sluggish schizophrenia," a theory accepted nowhere but the Soviet Union. In Walter Reich's view, if social pressures to find or interpret a certain behavior as mental illness exist, then this increases the chances of it being so diagnosed: "psychiatry's theoretical framework is still so tenuous, its basis for explanation still so narrow, and its capacity for self-justification still so limited and potentially self-serving that almost any action or decision, and diagnosis or treatment, can be rationalized on some ground or other."[74] Reich might have added that the same thing is true in reverse: intense pressure can get an existing mental illness *declassified*. This happened in the West with respect to homosexuality. Homosexuality is a former mental disorder that was removed from the *Diagnostic and Statistical Manual*, Third Edition, following a storm of political criticism.

Here is the latest stage (at time of writing) of Soviet psychiatry. After manifold documentation of the abuses of political psychiatry in the USSR, the World Psychiatric Association was set to expel the Soviet Union from membership when the country suddenly withdrew in 1983. Then several things happened. Worldwide condemnation of the practices gradually intensified; Snezhnevsky, who had dominated Soviet psychiatry for decades, finally died; and *glasnost* (openness) became the new byword of the country's leadership. At the time of writing some promising developments had appeared, including the transfer of responsibility for mental hospitals from the state security ministry to the ministry of health, the release of scores of known dissidents, and the open admission of foreign observers to (some) Soviet institutions.

---

[73] Alan A. Stone, *Law, Psychiatry, and Morality* (Washington, D.C.: Psychiatric Press, 1984).

[74] Walter Reich, "Diagnosing Soviet Dissidents," *Harpers* 257 (1978), pp. 31–37. The quote is from p. 35. This occurs in the West as well: pressure groups forced a new diagnosis called post-traumatic stress disorder into the third edition of the psychiatrists' *Diagnostic and Statistical Manual* (DSM-III). See Wilbur J. Scott, "PTSD in DSM-III: A Study in the Politics of Disease," a paper presented to the Society for the Study of Social Problems, Berkeley, Calif., 1989.

THE IDEOLOGICAL BASIS IN A NON-WESTERN CULTURE

As I have previously pointed out, analysis of social problems is often confined to Western societies. Yet any sophisticated analytical treatment must examine non-Western categories of problems as well. A full adherence to this approach would be so novel vis-à-vis contemporary, parochial discussions that it would demand book-length treatment in itself.[75] We cannot hope to analyze the treatment of social problems of non-Western categories in detail here, but a brief exploration of one particular historical approach is nonetheless instructive in our survey of ideology and treatment. I will take up the efforts in the Peoples Republic of China, particularly in the 1950s, to deal with the survival of "bourgeois tendencies" as these were viewed in China after the abolition of capitalism. This example will prove instructive from the standpoint of ideology and treatment since we can easily see conflicting notions of what the problem and the solutions are. From our Western standpoint the employment of inhumane measures to change people's beliefs constitutes a social problem in itself. From the standpoint of the Chinese cadre in charge of programs, these same measures were solutions. Inasmuch as "bourgeois tendencies," "evil remnants," and "ideological poisons" tend to be ideologically defined, we would expect "treatment" for these matters also to be placed on a doctrinal, ideological basis. I will adhere closely to Lifton's thorough examination of this program in China in his *Thought Reform and the Psychology of Totalism*.[76] Later, we will take note of the psychosocial correspondences between the treatment there and a treatment program for delinquency that has been debated in the United States.

The Communist revolution in China in the years following 1949 was an intensely moralistic affair, and although reeducation proceeded slowly at first, it eventually permeated every aspect of Chinese cultural life. In certain periods it was not sufficient for a person to remain neutral

---

[75] See S. N. Eisenstadt, ed., *Comparative Social Problems* (New York: Free Press, 1964), for a first approximation to this objective. It compares social problems around the world but the categories are those of Western social science. See Vytautas Kavolis, *Comparative Perspective on Social Problems* (Boston: Little, Brown, 1969), for an attempt to find an objective basis for a cross-cultural study of social problems.

[76] Robert Jay Lifton, *Thought Reform and the Psychology of Totalism* (New York: Norton, 1961). Since the "Great Proletarian Cultural Revolution" of 1966, and even perhaps before, Lifton's work has become severely dated in terms of describing practices in China. However, as an example in our survey of the ideological basis of treatment, this difficulty is not especially significant, for I make no effort to be "topical" on what is really a generic aspect of social problems.

or unconcerned about politics: one had to be wholeheartedly committed to the new system and the orthodox ideology, and eventually one had to display one's enthusiasm openly and fervently. Certain categories of persons were especially suspect in the new China, essentially "classes" who had fared relatively well before the revolution, and individuals most critically suspect were systematically subjected to intensive treatment designed to convert them. Such was the experience accorded Westerners in general who remained in China, as well as Chinese intellectuals who had received their education in the West.[77] The former were arrested and underwent what was called "brainwashing" in prisons; the latter were induced and coerced into "volunteering" for reeducation ("thought reform"). But while the outward manifestations differed for these two types, the intent, the doctrinal basis, and the psychosocial mechanisms of their treatment were highly similar.

The medical treatment analogy is well-taken here, for there can be little doubt—either from the nature of the experiences undergone or the official doctrine itself—that authorities were concerned with, in one sense, helping the people selected. They were to be helped to overcome their false ideals and outmoded thoughts and outlooks, and Western influences on their thinking. However painful the treatment, essentially it was done *for* the person. This was, of course, one of the factors that made it doubly hard to resist.

The "old" person was to die and be reborn. This was emphasized both by the official doctrine and by the personal experiences of the participants. By various highly unpleasant means they first lost touch with their former identities and then found it possible to obtain the new ones held out before them. The theme of death and rebirth was dominant, emphasizing a total re-creation of the ego.

It is difficult to be neutral about some of the unpleasant and agonizing experiences described, yet this was no mere case of simple brutality or vengeance on a former oppressor class; it was—as Lifton notes— *totalist therapy*. It was therapy without constraints. It was done for the subject's own good (except for a few occasions with apparently personal motivation), but with *no limitations on what could be done to improve him or her*. As such it was superficially similar to, but basically entirely different from, situations equally extreme, such as the concentration camps of World War II. For, as Lifton notes, unlike concentration camp victims, the subjects of brainwashing or thought reform were never given the opportunity of viewing their own suffering as obviously noble and their oppressors as obviously base and disgusting.

---

[77]Paradoxically, many of the most important Chinese Communists themselves had Western (typically Parisian) educations.

All of these points illustrate that the experiences were in fact intended as the treatment of an individual's problem. It was, to be sure, to the "benefit of the people" to have an important person reeducated, but it was also, in some strange way, seen to benefit that particular individual.[78] Although this aspect had important effects in weakening resistance in the subject (and also, in all probability, in steeling the cadre to its tasks), it is important to us here in other ways. It demonstrates the social problem dimension as well as the existence of a therapeutic intention.[79] And in the selection of the person to be helped, the conception of the nature of the problem to be solved, and the types of personal changes sought, the phenomenon of systematic thought reform (or "brainwashing" or "ideological remolding") exemplifies the ideological basis of "treatment." It also demonstrates once again that one person's solution to a social problem is another person's brand new problem in itself.[80]

A WESTERN DEBATE ON IDEOLOGY AND TREATMENT

An exploration of this phenomenon is incomplete without noting a similar strain toward such total remaking of the personality in delinquency rehabilitation programs in Western society. In at least one case the analogy has been drawn directly between such programs and the total therapy of brainwashing, and the ideological basis has been challenged. In 1962, a letter written to the *American Sociological Review* raised important questions respecting the Provo Experiment in delinquency rehabilitation.[81] It is couched in the rhetoric of the Cold War era, but we can overlook that because the issue raised is still strikingly pertinent.

---

[78] See also Szasz, *Mental Illness*; on p. 208, he examines confessions of witchcraft as "therapeutic." All history teaches us that defining treatment as for the person's own good by no means ensures that the person will appreciate the treatment offered. Even the Spanish Inquisition with its *auto-da-fé* (burning to death) could be justified as therapeutic. The Inquisition was for the good of the subject's immortal soul—better a brief pain now than the everlasting torments in Hell, which the Inquisition foresaw for the eternally damned heretic. Subjects were "questioned" until they confessed and recanted their sins, thus salvaging their souls before execution.

[79] Lifton, *Thought Reform*, p. 15.

[80] For additional insights on thought reform, some supporting and some limiting the points I have made, see Denise Winn, *The Manipulated Mind: Brainwashing, Conditioning and Indoctrination* (London: Octagon Press, 1983).

[81] For a description of the program, see Lamar T. Empey and Jerome Rabow, "The Provo Experiment in Delinquency Rehabilitation," *American Sociological Review* 26 (1961), pp. 679–95.

I suspect that many of us who have read the Empey and Rabow article on "The Provo Experiment in Delinquency Rehabilitation" have been profoundly impressed by it. . . . It is within such a framework that I should like to raise a not unsympathetic question.

In many ways—some of them superficial and some of them not—the techniques used at Pinehills [Provo] are reminiscent of those employed by the Communists in Korea on selected groups of American prisoners of war. One sees the leverage of the group being applied to the individual by way of public confessions, the demand for candor, the infinite patience and inscrutability of authority. There appears the "carrot and stick" technique along with the utilization of role disruption and social anxiety as motivating forces. Beyond that, one is reminded how systematically and thoroughly the integrity of psychological privacy is undermined.

I do not doubt that Empey and Rabow [the organizers of Provo] are fully aware of the parallels between their work and the efforts of the Communists in Korea.

The question which I should like to raise is the obvious one of values. In Korea we were shocked at what seemed to us the cynicism with which American was turned upon American. . . . We perceived something Orwellian and "ghoulish" in the "Rectification Program." I do not wish to suggest that intellectual consistency and ethical gentility require that we dismantle such programs as Empey and Rabow's. Far from it. . . . What I should urge is that we once again return to the classic question of means and ends. . . .

I raise the question and do not propose an answer—an old but honest academic trick. Before we are caught in the position of many nuclear physicists, I should like to urge that we think through with honesty quite what we are doing and what precedents we are establishing. It would be a supreme indictment of the students of society were we not to profit a priori from another social group now often tortured and troubled by its awesome contribution to the modern world.[82]

In their response to this polite but highly critical letter, Empey and Rabow, key organizers of Provo, raised equally important considerations.[83] They first pointed out correctly that many of the psychosocial dynamics that the Provo and "rectification" programs share are also employed in other social practices, many of them quite traditional and

---

[82]Whitney H. Gordon, "Communist Rectification Programs and Delinquency Rehabilitation Programs: A Parallel?", communication, *American Sociological Review* 27 (1962), p. 256.

[83]Lamar T. Empey and Jerome Rabow, "Reply to Whitney H. Gordon," *American Sociological Review* 27 (1962), pp. 256–58.

legitimate. They mentioned the stress of students in universities, of re-cruits in the military. In other words, these processes appear all the time. Even the earlier gang-based socialization of the delinquents (e.g., into toughness roles) is accomplished with considerable stress and strain. But Lifton has elsewhere pointed out that, although we can see certain limited aspects of brainwashing in advertising campaigns, preparatory schools, or congressional investigations, and can therefore see a conti-nuity between total therapy and less extreme programs, this does not satisfactorily resolve the issue. As he put it:

> [Thought reform] has in fact emerged as one of the most powerful efforts at human manipulation ever undertaken. To be sure, such a program is by no means completely new: imposed dogmas, in-quisitions, and mass conversion movements have existed in every country and during every historical epoch. But . . . [thought re-form has] a more organized, comprehensive, and deliberate—a more total—character, as well as a unique blend of energetic and ingenious psychological techniques.[84]

Perhaps the last point is most relevant here: in contrast to earlier histori-cal efforts, we now have some idea of what is happening when we ma-nipulate in this way. With this knowledge, as the phrase goes, comes a heightening of power.

Empey and Rabow were probably on firmer ground with their next point: what are the consequences of *not* changing these persons' lives? They pointed to the probability of years spent in confinement, the cruelty, the hostility, the sense of waste and futility—all of which would be part of the normal expectancies of the subjects of the Provo experi-ment (teenage delinquents) in the absence of effective treatment. To be sure this also implies an ideological stance (i.e., that leading a nondelin-quent life and staying out of prison will make the individual happier), but they were correct in noting that failure to intervene, or to do so ef-fectively, also has its consequences. In all likelihood many of these consequences would be considered undesirable from the subjects' own standpoint.

Finally, the two authors emphasized what they saw as critical differences between their approach and "thought reform." Admitting that Provo used stress and other mechanisms to break a person's unques-tioned ties with old perspectives, they pointed out that Provo then brought out in a realistic way the outcomes the delinquents could rea-sonably expect under different approaches to life, including a delin-quent career, and the defects of each—including the defects of "going

---

[84]Lifton, *Thought Reform*, pp. 4–5.

straight." They saw this as the presentation of several realistic alternatives, a feature that the Communist Chinese programs avoided.

Empey and Rabow might also have mentioned that the analogy may be a bit strained in terms of intensity, as Lifton's case studies graphically illustrate. We see no physiological symptoms of extreme anxiety, nor complete breakdowns or suicides in the Provo experiment. The supreme sanction in Provo was transfer to the regular prison; the supreme sanction noted in Lifton's studies was death. The physical brutality that (only occasionally) entered the thought reform system had no analogue at Provo.[85]

The debate over Provo brings into sharp relief some of the basic dilemmas of "treatment."[86] All involuntary treatment for social problems is permeated by ideology and stereotyping, in contrast to the rational ameliorative and therapeutic justifications provided by the persons in charge. But *failure* to intervene also poses its own problems. Assuming a consensus that a social problem exists, the three essential questions are: what constitutes adequate justification for involuntary treatment; what constitutes appropriate criteria for differential treatment; and what sorts of treatment are ethically permissible?

SUMMARY

In previous chapters we have looked at how both self-conscious, well-articulated ideologies and vague but powerful stereotypes shape the definition of social problems. The present chapter expands this explanation with questions of how individuals are selected for "treatment" on the basis of stereotype and ideology. The term "treatment" is placed in quotation marks because opinions can differ considerably on what constitutes reasonable ways to handle people. I have concentrated on the involuntary treatments that powerful viewpoints can impose on individuals.

In society's reaction to crime, individual discretion within the criminal-justice system can be invoked at several points. Both judicial and police discretion are unavoidable if a desirable flexibility is to be achieved, but this same latitude leaves the door open for abuse. Tendencies of many judges and police to follow stereotypes and unspoken prej-

---

[85] It is perhaps worth noting that neither Provo nor thought reform were as effective as was apparently hoped for, or feared.

[86] For a more recent examination of social control and rehabilitative policies in China, see the Whyte chapter in S. E. Martin et al., eds., *New Directions in the Rehabilitation of Criminal Offenders* (Washington, D.C.: National Academy Press, 1981).

udices in their discretionary decisions is by now extremely well documented. Such miscarriages apparently hinge on both the individual's personal characteristics and political affiliations, with significant consequences. In police conduct and treatment it is clear that the demeanor of suspects (and of others at the scene) is also a major influence. The self-fulfilling nature of stereotypes, through differential enforcement practices, must also be considered.

Discussion next turned to selection and treatments for mental disorder. The extremely slipshod manner in which vitally important commitment decisions have been made has been documented again and again. Procedural safeguards that are accepted without question in courts of law are absent or deficient because of a legal fiction that involuntary commitment is nonpunitive. The power dimension is often ignored in commitment, as is the possibility of covert motivations on the part of relatives or associates. Rosenhan's oft-cited research on the "stickiness" of mental labels once they are applied casts some doubt on the effectiveness of periodic formal reviews of institutionalized persons.

Unconscious stereotyping in psychiatric treatment makes an appearance in several disparities among social classes. Although major social-class differences in diagnosis may be partly a function of real differences brought on by the life experiences of each class, the same cannot be said of class differences in treatment within each diagnostic category, differences in the competence of personnel assigned, or differences in length of hospital stay. Stereotyping affects the situation from more than one direction: patients of different class backgrounds have distinct views about psychiatrists, and the upper-middle-class psychiatrists have vague but influential views about people from classes different from their own. All of these preconceptions influence the treatment provided.

Conscious ideology is also a factor in selection of persons for involuntary commitment. Numerous documented cases have surfaced in Western society, while Soviet misuse of "sane asylums" to get rid of dissidents is well developed and advanced. Also through conscious ideology, the Communist government in China has at various times selected large numbers of people for reeducation or "thought reform." In all such cases, a divergence of views is clear between those who regard the use of such measures as a solution to some social problem (e.g., troublesome people) and those who regard the measures as social problems in their own right.

Moral dilemmas in treatment are highlighted when one notices uncomfortable convergences between delinquency rehabilitation programs in the West (especially the more sophisticated projects) and inhumane, clearly abhorrent "rectification programs" in the East. Are we merely reluctant to acknowledge these similarities because we accept the basis for treatment in the one case (delinquency) and not in the other (bourgeoisie background)? Is our own outlook one that concludes that the state may remold delinquents but not remold adults who disagree with the party in power? Or is the analogy not so close because of some real differences in treatment? This chapter as a whole should raise some serious ethical issues for the perceptive reader.

10

EVALUATION RESEARCH: POLICY AND POLITICS

DESIRABILITY OF SYSTEMATIC EVALUATION

L et us consider a set of very basic questions. What are the effects of a specific instance of intervention? Has it worked? Has it worked as well as planned, or better? For instance, have mental illness, income disparity, and criminality decreased after programs have been applied during the preceding years? Or, if the size of the problem has not diminished, might it otherwise have grown even larger without the program? Is the program worth the economic and social costs of implementation? Does an alternative method work better? Is it preferable to do nothing? Surely the originators of a given program had the alleviation of some social problem in mind when they began. Therefore, at some subsequent time it should be asked whether the program meets the expectations under which it was established. It is reasonable to demand at least tentative answers to such questions, notwithstanding the difficulties involved in answering them. Attempts to provide the answers, to ascertain the effects of planned intervention, are termed *evaluation research*.

The questions above appear to be so basic that it may be shocking to learn that, until recently, they were rarely investigated in any systematic fashion, and even today their pursuit is more the exception than the rule. Yet such is indeed the case; we will examine some of the reasons for this strange state of affairs later in the chapter.

At the outset it should be realized that a primary issue is, what is meant when it is said that the benefits do or do not outweigh the costs? (Before proceeding further, note that "costs" as used in this chapter include negative consequences of a nonmonetary as well as monetary nature.) Ignoring for the moment the difficult question of how this can be investigated, we address the even more primitive question: benefits for whom? costs for whom? Obviously better street lighting is not a gain for the mugger; police dogs that can detect marijuana are a bane for the smoker. But even if we ignore the user of proscribed goods or services, or the offender in a criminal action, we should ask whether *any* intervention has the same costs and gains for everyone. The taxpayers may be outraged at the cost of changes; certain groups will almost certainly benefit more than others; some groups may be inconvenienced by a measure that does them no good at all. One need not adopt an extreme conflict perspective—seeing social conflict at the root of all major change—to recognize that no problem exists, and no remedy, in which costs and gains are the same for everyone. Consider these groups: pesticide manufacturers and ecologists; highway planners and landowners; marijuana cultivators and law enforcement agencies—the list is endless. Therefore, researchers need to specify the relevant group in order to meaningfully evaluate the costs and gains of a new intervention. Any discussion of costs and gains must refer to the values of a particular audience.

The difficulty this problem produces cannot be denied. The usual response is to ignore the issue and tacitly adopt a "consensus model" of society for the duration of the evaluation. That is, the possibility of extreme divergence of values is simply not considered. The difficulty as just presented is perhaps exaggerated in one sense: monetary components sometimes form a major portion of the balance of costs and gains, and monetary measures by nature afford an unusually high degree of comparability (technically known as fungibility). Again, however, this is only a matter of degree, for there are still the obvious discrepancies in viewpoints among population sectors with varying incomes. An impoverished community, for example, may be more interested in the jobs a new plant will provide than in the damage it will do to the local environment. A more prosperous community, given the same options, might choose environmental protection.

Although this conceptual difficulty cannot be ignored, the virtues of performing evaluations are very great indeed. Even if one disregards the struggles that precede intervention, hardships associated with its implementation are inevitable—monetary costs, certain freedoms circumscribed, opportunities relinquished. Naturally one wants to know, in everyday language, if it is all "worth it." Without ignoring the diversity of values, then, it still seems worthwhile to be able to say what a given program is accomplishing.

In spite of the obvious value of the systematic study of intervention, it is at once disturbing and fascinating to know that until very recently this type of study was rarely done, and even more rarely done in a manner that would permit meaningful conclusions to be drawn. In part this failure has been a reflection of a widespread lack of understanding of the essential elements of experimentation, and lack of recognition that the experimental approach could be applied to the appraisal of social reforms. Although this is not a textbook on research methods, their consideration is of such vital importance for the evaluation of social intervention that a limited discussion of research procedures—as they apply to social reform measures—is appropriate.[1]

This chapter takes up the issue of evaluation, beginning with a brief description of research design. The first two sections explicate the ideal approach to evaluation of intervention, for the most part ignoring practical and political difficulties. The next section takes up the expansion of evaluation research in the last two decades and the $100 million income-maintenance experiments of the 1970s. A section on the theoretical weaknesses of evaluation, dealing with conceptual and procedural problems such as inadequate measurement, is included. A section on political-based difficulties follows, taking into account the bureaucratic structure of most forms of intervention, the stakes people have in the outcome, ethical dilemmas of research, and related considerations. Finally, two major instances of the intrusion of politics into evaluation research are examined. Readers *already familiar* with research design may want to turn at once to later sections, starting on p. 212.

EXPERIMENTS AND REFORMS: SOME BASIC ASPECTS OF PROCEDURE

Most sociologists agree that an experiment (in the technically correct sense of the word) is, whenever possible, the best way to evaluate intervention. Classical experimental design was first systematized by John Stuart Mill.[2] He wanted to set forth the "designs" (logical procedures for manipulating events and data) that enable us to ascertain the causal relationship between one variable and another: does variable x produce a change in variable y? (Does, for example, the creation of child guidance centers improve the children's mental health?) Although methodologists have altered Mill's methods, and have realized that answers are

---

[1]The treatment given this complex subject here is necessarily very cursory. On a more advanced level, see Donald T. Campbell, "Factors Relevant to the Validity of Experiments in Social Settings," *Psychological Bulletin* (July 1957), pp. 297–312; Robert A. Scott and Arnold Shore, "Sociology and Policy Analysis," *American Sociologist* 9 (1974), pp. 51–59; and Hubert M. Blalock, Jr., *Causal Inferences in Nonexperimental Research* (Chapel Hill: University of North Carolina Press, 1964). An excellent discussion of experimental design is found in Bernard Phillips, *Social Research: Strategy and Tactics*, 2nd ed. (New York: Macmillan, 1971). For sophisticated designs especially adapted to intervention, see Donald T. Campbell, "Reforms as Experiments," *American Psychologist* 24 (1969), pp. 409–29.
[2]See Mill's book, *A System of Logic*, vol. 1 (New York: Harper, 1891).

always tentative, his basic objective remains. If possible, we also want to learn how much x produces how much change in y, and to know whether a third variable z exists that alters the influence of x on y.[3] For our purposes, the independent variable x is always the *planned intervention*.

We begin with two simple designs, the "after-only" and the "before-after." Understanding the weaknesses of these two designs— which are still employed all too frequently—will be useful in grasping the ideas behind more adequate designs.

If we start with the procedure known as the *"after-only" design*, we make a comparison of the dependent variable y in cases where intervention x has been employed (collectively these cases are called the experimental group) with the status of y in cases where it has not (collectively called the control group). If major differences between the two groups in the prevalence or magnitude of y are noted, it is concluded that such differences were caused by the introduction of the intervention x, since this occurred in only one of the groups.

But, because all of the observations of y take place after x has been introduced—that is, because there were no "before-measures"—the cases in the two groups could have been different at the very start. This is especially possible in social intervention where often the most drastic cases receive attention first. One can "prove" with the after-only design that going to a hospital causes death, since the death rate of people in hospitals is so much higher than the death rate of those outside. But, of course, this argument ignores the fact that the people who became patients (by entering the hospital) were different from the general population *before* hospitalization (x) was "applied." Unless one can be sure that the two groups were comparable before x was applied, the after-only design is not the best approach. Although before-measures are simply not possible in some kinds of inquiry (for example, research on the social effects of disasters, since you cannot tell in advance where the disaster will strike), they should be possible in most cases of planned intervention.

In the *"before-after" design*—another less-than-satisfactory approach—we have measures of y both before and after intervention, but the treatment is applied to all cases. (Or perhaps some control cases exist but no systematic attention is given to them.) In this design the prevalence or magnitude of differences in y before and after the application of x determines whether we believe x exerts an effect on y. (A familiar illustration is the fat-person before-after advertisement.) But a simple before-after difference in y cannot rule out the possibilities of what are

---

[3]This is perhaps the place to note that the attribution of causality is one of the thorniest issues in the philosophy of science. For an excellent advanced treatment, see the chapter on the subject in Jack P. Gibbs, *Sociological Theory Construction* (Hinsdale, Ill.: Dryden Press, 1972).

called history or maturation effects on y, effects that have nothing to do with x. For instance, a psychiatrist might appear to demonstrate an improvement in his or her patients, but a "spontaneous remission" of symptoms might have occurred even without treatment. Mental health may improve as a response to the treatment but might have improved without it.[4] Perhaps it would have improved *more* without it! Who can say from this procedure? With no control group one can "prove" that drinking milk causes death—since all subjects on milk eventually will die. (Before they drank the milk [x], they were alive; afterward, they all eventually died.) Those without milk will die also, but we have no way to establish this without a control group.

Therefore, for an improved test of the effects of x, we need four measurements of the dependent variable y. We *compare the before-after differences in the experimental group with the before-after differences in the control group.* See the right-hand column of the following table. We compare the difference between y_1 and y_2 for the experimental group with the difference between y_3 and y_4 for the control group.

After-only design			Before-after design		Before and after with control group		
	Exper. Group	Control Group		Exper. Group		Exper. Group	Control Group
			Before-measure	y_1	Before-measure	y_1	y_3
Test period	x	—	Test period	x	Test period	x	—
After-measure	y_1	y_2	After-measure	y_2	After-measure	y_2	y_4

It is essential to ensure that the two groups are as strictly comparable as possible in all respects *except* for the presence of the experimental program (the independent variable x) in the experimental group. But since all individuals (and all collectivities) are in fact different, the means of attaining this objective is a most serious issue. Two basic strategies are used: randomization and matching.

Random assignment is a procedure that takes the available persons in the population and allots them on a strictly random basis to either the experimental or control groups. (At times it is not individuals

---

[4] We will later consider a problem of ethics in the creation of control groups that are denied treatment.

who are randomly assigned but larger collectivities such as classrooms, factories, etc. In all cases the logic is the same.) Thus neither the subjects nor the investigator have any say about which group a person is assigned to. The advantage of this procedure is that, if a large enough number of cases are in each group, the extraneous variables (factors other than x) that might influence y will be equally distributed between both groups. Only x, therefore, is present in one group and not the other.

Matching is a process of pairing individuals in the experimental group with others in the control group who possess the same or highly similar characteristics. When random assignment cannot be accomplished, this is another way of controlling for the effects of extraneous variables on y. Since the matched pairs are equivalent on all characteristics except x, which only the party in the experimental group receives as treatment, any consistent differences between the two parties in y must be a result of the administration of x.

Of the two procedures, random assignment is the preferable approach since it automatically takes care of *all* extraneous variables, whereas matching can only take care of explicitly noticed extraneous variables. However, for one reason or another random assignment is simply not possible in certain cases. In these, matching can be of considerable value.[5]

Most evaluation research has been done on projects that were, from the outset, poorly designed. Random assignment, for instance, could have been introduced in a far greater proportion of programs than it actually was. The unfortunate tendency has been to either apply new treatments only to the worst "problem cases" or only to the "best" cases that seem most capable of making effective use of the treatment (for instance, in the granting of scholarships). Although these approaches seem to make sense in the short run, they play havoc with any attempt to do serious evaluation research thereafter, since they did not use random assignment and obviously the experimental and control groups are anything but comparable. This also illustrates the importance of *planning for evaluation research from the onset*, for after certain key decisions have been made in the planning stage, the value of any subsequent evaluation research is more or less fixed. Programs frequently neglect random assignment, or omit the control group altogether, or fail to collect before-measures. In such cases it may still be possible to accomplish some evaluation through sophisticated statistical techniques, but the results will be less conclusive, and in some cases analysis will simply be impossible.

Perhaps a single example of a well-designed experimental program will be helpful. As I mentioned in the last chapter, Empey and

---

[5]It is also true that matching and random assignment are at times used in combination; the reasons for this procedure need not be considered here.

Rabow conducted an elaborate program of delinquency rehabilitation in the early 1960s. Known as the Provo Experiment, it learned from the evaluation pitfalls of earlier delinquency programs and set up a tight experimental procedure.[6] As a delinquent youth came before the judge for sentencing, the judge literally opened a sealed envelope to determine whether the youth would be sent to Provo or to the traditional training-school alternative. (Of course this required the cooperation of the judiciary.) The method provided such excellent randomization that no before-measures were necessary: it could be assumed that over a large number of cases the initial levels of y (let us call it delinquency tendency) were equivalent in both groups. One set of boys then experienced Provo and the other the traditional treatment. Afterwards, the success rates of the two groups were compared on several criteria, with some criteria showing a success for Provo and some merely showing the experimental-group level equivalent to the control-group level.[7]

The Provo experiment can be contrasted to older intervention measures (and, alas, to many new ones as well) that were set up initially in such a way that no meaningful conclusion regarding effectiveness could be reached. Let us continue with delinquency prevention as an example. The Chicago Area Project, one of the oldest American programs, was in existence for more than twenty-five years, but after all that time a review could provide only interesting anecdotal and incidental information on what it had accomplished.[8] As late as 1963 a review found that in all of Europe not a single delinquency program had been subjected to rigorous evaluation.[9] Indeed in a 1972 review Logan was able to find only four evaluative studies of delinquency prevention that met minimal standards in terms of control groups and a sharply defined program.[10]

Using the aforementioned procedures—before and after measurements of y in the experimental and control groups created by random assignment—we can compare the before-and-after difference in the experimental group with the before-and-after difference in the control group. If the before-after differences are not the same in the two groups, it is possible that the disparity is due to the introduction of x into the experimental group. Statistical analysis can then provide the numerical probability that the differences observed between the experimental and control groups were due to chance alone or, as is hoped, due to the

[6]Lamar T. Empey and Jerome Rabow, "The Provo Experiment in Delinquency Rehabilitation," *American Sociological Review* 26 (1961), pp. 679–95.

[7]This synopsis oversimplifies the analysis in several respects. A long succession of boys went through Provo for an extended period of time.

[8]See Solomon Kobrin, "The Chicago Area Project: A 25-Year Assessment," in *Prevention of Delinquency*, ed. John Stratton and Robert Terry (New York: Macmillan, 1968).

[9]Eugene Doleschal and I. Anttia, *Crime and Delinquency Research in Selected European Countries* (Rockville, MD: National Institute of Mental Health, 1971).

[10]Charles Logan, "Evaluation Research in Crime and Delinquency: A Reappraisal," *Journal of Criminal Law, Criminology, and Police Science* 63 (1972), pp. 378–87.

effects of intervention—the independent variable *x*. This design is the simplest that can be employed; in effect, it tells us—within a certain margin of error—*whether the treatment made any difference at all*. At first glance this does not appear particularly useful but, to the contrary, the fact is that many highly touted programs, on later evaluation, were seen to have made virtually no difference at all.

For example, the British psychologist Eysenck wrote a widely known series of articles and a book examining the effects of interpretive (nondirective) psychotherapy. After surveying some nineteen studies, and taking into account the natural (untreated) recovery rate, he concluded that, "with the single exception of psychotherapeutic methods based on learning theory, results of published research . . . suggest that the therapeutic effects of psychotherapy are small or non-existent. . . ."[11] Some of the studies he examined had less than perfect procedures, but one study in particular had considerable significance. The Cambridge Somerville study was an effort to prevent delinquency by administering individual therapy to half of a number of boys, randomly chosen. The conclusions were extensive, but the one of interest here was that "the treatment did not . . . reduce the incidence of [subsequent] adjudged delinquency in the treatment group."[12]

The conclusions of Eysenck and his followers shocked the psychiatric and psychoanalytic communities. I will have more to say later on their validity, but for now it is sufficient to note that the very basic question of whether a program has had any effects whatsoever is not a waste of time at all. It is, in fact, the first question that should be asked.[13]

EXTENSIONS OF THE BASIC DESIGN

Even with success, researchers have to be careful in their evaluation, for it could well be that it is a side effect of the treatment that has reduced the problem, not the treatment per se. For instance, if we wanted to improve the mental health of children and young adults, we might adopt

---

[11]H. J. Eysenck, "The Effects of Psychotherapy," in *Handbook of Abnormal Psychology*, ed. H. J. Eysenck (London: Pitman Medical, 1960). See also Eysenck's *The Effects of Psychotherapy* (New York: Science House, 1969).

[12]N. Teuber and E. Powers, "Evaluating Therapy in a Delinquency Prevention Program," *Proceedings of the Association on Nervous Mental Disorders* 3 (1953), pp. 138–47.

[13]It should be noted that not all evaluation research finds less effectiveness than anticipated. For instance, a monumental nonexperimental study of the effectiveness of U.S. prisons by Daniel Glaser found the recidivist (return to prison) rate far *lower* than most earlier writers had assumed. See his book, *The Effectiveness of a Prison and Parole System* (Indianapolis: Bobbs-Merrill, 1969). The rate of recidivism was still unpleasantly high, however.

a program in which babies and young children were taken out of their homes to a specialized daycare center every day. If evaluation showed a significant difference between children so treated and children in a control group, the difference might not be due to improved childrearing but to other unsuspected factors. Perhaps because the mother was unburdened of her duties several hours daily she was more receptive to the child on its return and in a better frame of mind herself. This could have a favorable effect on the child's mental health. If the family were poor, the child might have obtained better food at the daycare center than at home, and this might have improved its overall health. It also might be that the parents were intrigued and flattered by the experiment and as a consequence involved themselves more with the child.[14] These examples are sufficient to indicate that not only do researchers have to use a control group, but also, whenever feasible, the treatment procedure has to be subdivided into categories or parts, each part being applied to different persons in the experimental group. For instance, a group of children could have been taken to the daycare center but, once there, given only the necessary minimal amount of attention. This could be a partial check concerning the effect of attention and novelty on the children as well as the effect of time off for the mother. Another group could, in addition, be fed at the center. Then a third group could receive the "enriched" program. Hopefully, the second group would fare better than the first, and the third better than the second, as well as better than the controls.

Therefore, our simple initial design, although invaluable for certain problems, is inadequate for many issues in evaluation. Instead of ascertaining whether a given program had any effect at all, we might want to isolate the most significant components of a program or compare the results of two or more competing programs. Perhaps—to return to the discussion of intervention strategies in Chapter 6—we might want to compare the utility of two alternative approaches to the same problem. Or possibly we might want to determine the best mix for a single program, or to find out which component of a given program produced the desired effect.[15] To perform any of these evaluations, a change in the design becomes necessary. Instead of an experimental and a control group, we may now have numerous groups (all preferably formed by a process of random assignment), each of which receives a treatment somewhat different from any of the others. In the two diagrams provided

---

[14]Readers familiar with experimental design will recognize this to be an instance of the Hawthorne effect, or placebo effect as it is known in medicine.

[15]As an example of empirically appraising the value of a basic intervention strategy, see Franklin Zimring and Gordon Hawkins, *Deterrence* (Chicago: University of Chicago Press, 1973).

below, the top diagram is known as the factorial design; the bottom diagram is the randomized-groups design, where only one treatment is provided at various intensities. Since we are in the latter case confident that all treatments produce *some* effect, we need no control group per se. The before and after changes in the dependent variable within each of the groups can be analyzed by statistical techniques to show, again with statements of probability, which treatments and mixes produced *greater* changes in the desired direction.

One excellent example of such research was the "work disincentive" component of the income maintenance experiment, a large-scale project about which I will have more to say later in the chapter. In essence, the negative income tax or guaranteed annual income was a device seen as a supplement to, or replacement of, the current welfare system. Everyone would have a minimal guaranteed income, but to increase the incentive to work, instead of eliminating welfare checks when people found employment, persons who obtained jobs would find their welfare checks reduced by *less* than their gains from their new work. One of the key questions was how *much* less a reduction would motivate people to find work—hence the variations (graduated work incentives) in the experiment. This is an example of a factorial design, in which the treatments A, B, and C correspond to different reductions in welfare payments when recipients secure jobs. The idea was that, before implementing any one income policy, the costs and effects of various options would be experimentally determined.

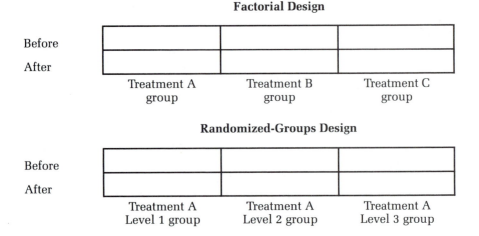

Factorial Design

Before			
After			
	Treatment A group	Treatment B group	Treatment C group

Randomized-Groups Design

Before			
After			
	Treatment A Level 1 group	Treatment A Level 2 group	Treatment A Level 3 group

Experiments of this kind have been all too rare. Typically, solutions to social problems are approached in a pseudo-confident fashion in which, after debate, one and only one program is implemented. Due to the nature of the political process, there is enormous pressure in programs initiated by governments to adopt one measure immediately rather than evaluating several candidate measures in a trial period. This is doubly unfortunate: First, a comparison of alternative programs is largely precluded, and second, even if an evaluation with controls is made of the one program, if it casts doubt on the ongoing project it will encounter entrenched resistance. As Campbell puts it, "if the political and administrative system has committed itself in advance to the correctness and efficacy of its reforms, it cannot tolerate learning of failure."[16]

Some important evaluation questions cannot be resolved through the use of a standard experiment. Although the efficacy of Provo might be ascertainable by a randomly assigned control group, the perennial arguments over the efficacy of the *death penalty* cannot be—for obvious ethical and practical reasons. Other methods of systematic comparison are still possible for such issues, but the conclusions drawn must be regarded with great caution. The issue of capital punishment is instructive in both a historical and a methodological sense.

Numerous ethical and practical arguments about the use of the death penalty do not rely on whether or not it helps deter future crime, but that question has nonetheless assumed a central position in the debate. From time to time social scientists have manifested extreme skepticism about the efficacy of legal punishment of any sort on the pervasiveness of crime, maintaining that deterrent doctrines are outmoded and totally out of place in a modern society.[17] For generations the debate continued at a purely polemical level, with no recourse to the empirical evidence. In the 1950s two separately conceived studies, one by Thorsten Sellin and one by Karl Schuessler, broke from this tradition. Sellin took advantage of the fact that under American law each state has the right to establish its own policies on capital punishment. Some states had abolished it; some retained it. By examining pairs of adjoining states, in which one state in each pair was abolitionist and the other was not, Sellin came to the conclusion that retention of the death penalty did not diminish capital crime. Schuessler examined single jurisdictions at different points in time, considering whether the existence of or lack of executions at any one time made an impact on subsequent rates of capital crime. He concluded they did not. These studies have been criticized on methodological grounds, but their important contribution was simply that they quit arguing over the doctrine and started looking systematically at the data.

Since that time the empirical study of questions of deterrence has expanded enormously. After a period in which only the death penalty

---

[16]Donald T. Campbell, "Reforms as Experiments." The quote is from p. 410.
[17]See, for example, Karl Menninger, *The Crime of Punishment* (New York: Viking Press, 1968). Also interesting is George Bernard Shaw's book, *The Crime of Punishment* (New York: Philosophical Library, 1946).

was investigated, researchers have started to look at whether deterrence might be effective for other types of sanctions, for example, such seemingly simple matters as increasing parking fines.[18] And the methodological sophistication of such studies has increased to the point where early efforts seem very crude indeed.[19] The case of deterrence is instructive on several counts. It is a basic strategy of intervention (as defined in Chapter 6); it serves to illustrate how researchers might evaluate measures without using a controlled experiment; and it shows a historical progression from argument to empirical analysis.

It is worthwhile repeating that *the foregoing discussion of experimental design is extremely limited*. Many of the questions of policy analysis require much more elaborate techniques. As a single example, the researchers in the American income tax experiment wanted to determine whether the amount of income maintenance paid should be varied by age and sex of the recipient as well as by income. Once again they might have created additional groups, by randomization, to study this, but eventually this becomes impracticable if one really wants to look at a large number of variables. Hence, the researchers resorted to other techniques.[20] Readers are referred to the additional references mentioned earlier for a more extensive treatment of these topics.

THE EXPANSION OF EVALUATION RESEARCH

In the 1970s, the basic message of evaluation research suddenly attained the magical status of common sense, and governments at the state and federal level rushed to mandate the evaluation of many programs. Guttentag some years ago cited an estimate that some three hundred new studies with an average budget of about $100,000 had been started each year since the beginning of the 1970s.[21] At the American federal level, evaluation research has been carried out by the Congressional Budget Office, the Congressional Research Service, the General Accounting Office, and the Office of Technology Assessment. Two independent professional societies for evaluation researchers have appeared in the United States. In Europe, a similar expansion can be seen. Starting with the European Poverty Programme (in the years 1975–80), several major cross-

---

[18]See, for example, William Chambliss, "The Deterrent Influence of Punishment," *Crime and Delinquency* 12 (January 1966), pp. 20–75.

[19]An excellent overall summary is found in Zimring and Hawkins, *Deterrence*.

[20]See Robert A. Scott and Arnold Shore, "Policy Analysis."

[21]Marcia Guttentag, ed., *Evaluation Studies: Review Annual*, vol. 2 (Beverly Hills: Sage Publications, 1977), p. 19.

cultural evaluation projects have been initiated. The European Community (EC) Commission in particular has been active, with research underway evaluating poverty programs, improved integration of the handicapped, and the transition from school to work.[22]

With all this expansion, the rush into print of textbooks and handbooks on evaluation research can scarcely be exaggerated. I will footnote here a few of the best references and then move on.[23] In the next few paragraphs we will look at the issues around the income maintenance experiments, a key development in evaluation research.[24] One aspect of these studies has already been explained on p. 210.

The federally sponsored experiments on income maintenance, with costs totaling some $100 million, were the most expensive set of social experiments in history and arguably the largest social-research projects ever undertaken. The justification for such an enormous sum was that the actual programs for which these experiments were the precursors would cost perhaps hundreds of billions of dollars, so the large expenditures were worthwhile to ensure that the programs would not be wasted or counterproductive. Furthermore, the money spent in the experiments actually did some good; they were not merely experimental. The studies were known collectively as the income maintenance, or guaranteed minimum income, or negative income tax experiments, and they ran from 1967 through, roughly speaking, the mid-1970s.

The first study began in 1967 under the sponsorship of the Office of Economic Opportunity. Known as the New Jersey Experiment, it was rigorously designed, incorporating experimental treatments over a period of time to randomly selected parts of the population in several cities in New Jersey and one in Pennsylvania. The total number of families involved was on the order of 1,000. I have already touched on the basic research question that motivated this experiment. Five different support levels, including the zero level for the control group, were combined with three marginal tax rates to try to determine the optimal program. It soon became clear to the investigators that they were involved in all the complexities of running a welfare program (for instance, detecting cheating) as well as running a scientific experiment. Among the complexities was determining just how well the participants understood

---

[22] See Graham Room, *Cross-National Innovation in Social Policy: European Perspectives on the Evaluation of Action Research* (New York: St. Martin's Press, 1986).

[23] Two personal favorites are George W. Fairweather and Louis G. Turnatzky, *Experimental Methods for Social Policy Research* (Elmsford, NY: Pergamon Press, 1977), and Jerry A. Hausman and David A. Wise, eds., *Social Experimentation* (Chicago: University of Chicago Press, 1985).

[24] In the following discussion I rely heavily on the excellent description of these experiments by Robert Ferber and Werner Z. Hirsch, "Social Experimentation and Economic Policy: A Survey," *Journal of Economic Literature* 16 (1978), pp. 1379–1414.

their own program option, since this would affect whether the findings were generalizable.[25] I will mention just a few of the findings of the New Jersey study: Labor force participation declined as expected and was sensitive to both support level and tax rate, but the decline varied considerably by ethnic group. No significant effects of minimum income maintenance were detected on health, fertility, marital dissolution, or school attendance.

The New Jersey Experiment, large though it was, had deliberately been restricted to intact families within a certain income and age range. To fill in the sample gaps as well as to examine additional support options, three follow-up experiments were later initiated by the Department of Health, Education, and Welfare. Several new questions, including the effects of counseling, job training subsidies, and childcare centers, were "piggybacked" on the original economic-type questions. The Rural Experiment was carried out in two different areas; the Gary (Indiana) Experiment focused largely on black, female-headed households; and the Denver and Seattle Experiments were designed to extend the participants' time-horizon by guaranteeing the program for a greater period of time than in the other experiments and also to investigate new support schemes. The last-mentioned experiment was complex enough to warrant additional mention here.

The Seattle and Denver Income Maintenance Experiments (SIME/DIME) involved almost five thousand families and cost more than $70 million. SIME/DIME was considerably more complex than the other experiments, involving some eighty experimental conditions. The summary book of major findings contains chapters on the following outcomes: labor supply of family heads, of youth, job satisfaction, labor supply and childcare arrangements, marital dissolution and remarriage, income and psychological distress, demand for children, welfare payments and family composition, migration, education and training, and utilization of subsidized housing.[26]

Other major projects in this heyday of bold social experimentation included the "supported work" project of the Manpower Demonstration Research Corporation (late 1970s), the Health Insurance Study of the Department of Health, Education, and Welfare (mid-1970s), and the Experimental Housing Allowance Program of the Department of Housing and Urban Development (mid- to late 1970s).[27] It is clear that

---

[25] For the organization and procedures of this experiment, see David Kershaw and Jerilyn Fair, *The New Jersey Income-Maintenance Experiment*, vol. 1 (New York: Academic Press, 1976).

[26] Philip K. Robins et al., *A Guaranteed Annual Income: Evidence from a Social Experiment* (New York: Academic Press, 1980).

[27] For summaries of these researches, see Ferber and Hirsch, "Social Experimentation," and the sources they cite.

the 1970s were a prime time for social experimentation in the innovative sense, and this is not surprising given the radical tenor of those times, especially when compared to the conservativism of the subsequent decade. The 1980s were clearly not the right time for bold new programs, and furthermore, a fiscal crisis was more keenly felt than when these experiments were undertaken. And in fact, conservative fiscal austerity measures terminated the income maintenance experiments before they could be implemented on a larger scale. Of course this does not invalidate the important research that was carried out.[28] Meanwhile, as outlined earlier, evaluation research in its more mundane contemporary form continues to develop.

THEORETICAL WEAKNESSES OF EVALUATION RESEARCH

Having examined some of the basic procedures behind evaluation, we are now obliged to look at some of the weaknesses of this tool.[29] We can roughly divide these weaknesses into two parts, disregarding occasional overlapping. On the one hand are *conceptual and methodological weaknesses* in the methods themselves, and on the other hand are the *political problems* involved in doing the research and in implementing one's findings in the real world. In this section I will cover the conceptual and procedural difficulties.

The foremost conceptual difficulty has already been discussed in the opening section of the chapter. To reiterate: how does one decide which aspects of the treatment are to be considered as costs and which as gains? To what audience does one refer? If a gain for one group is a cost for another, how can one meaningfully evaluate success or failure?[30] Typically, the expedient is to seek some countable, "objective" measure of success for the project (for example, reducing the suicide rate), but obviously this may be a greater gain for some segments of the

---

[28] For a retrospective assessment of the major social experiments described above, see the first four chapters of Hausman and Wise, *Social Experimentation.*

[29] See Howard Freeman and Clarence Sherwood, *Social Research and Social Policy* (Englewood Cliffs, NJ: Prentice-Hall, 1970), for a good treatment of pitfalls and problems in policy research in general and evaluation research in particular. Other book-length treatments include Francis G. Caro, ed., *Readings in Evaluation Research* (New York: Russell Sage Foundation, 1971); Edward J. Mullen et al., *Evaluation of Social Intervention* (San Francisco: Jossey-Bass, 1972); and Edward A. Suchman, *Evaluation Research* (New York: Russell Sage Foundation, 1967).

[30] Another issue is who gains the most, even if a program is clearly beneficial to several parties. In terms of cooperative spending, this issue has become a major point of conflict between federal and state governments.

population than for others.[31] It is the very indicators of success or failure that cause some of the most intractable controversies.

Assuming for the moment that minimal agreement can be reached on the dimension to be evaluated, the next hurdle consists of what together are called *measurement problems*. The abstract dimension selected for evaluation must be translated into practical measurements. This is often far more difficult than it sounds. What is a "cure" in the case of psychotherapy? How does one measure the reduction of intergroup tensions? How is greater worker participation in industry to be examined, speaking concretely? To all such questions tentative answers can and have been offered, but the problem is often not so much that no measurement solution can be proposed but that more than one is available—and all seem reasonable yet yield different conclusions. How, for example, might one measure the success of criminal rehabilitation? Does one look at inmate adjustment while in the prison, reduction in number of prison incidents and increase in volunteerism, length of time after release before new offenses are committed, degree of severity of subsequent offenses? Reasonable arguments can be advanced for all these approaches, yet—and this is the heart of the problem—programs successful on one of these scales are not necessarily successful on another.[32]

Assuming that agreement is reached on both the dimension of success to be evaluated and on the concrete measurement to be made, there are usually great practical difficulties in *translating* this into meaningful data. To continue the example of criminal rehabilitation, if one chooses to examine in-prison adjustment, one must be especially wary of "evaluation apprehension."[33] A prison is a hostile institution; inmates in a climate of deprivation and powerlessness may tend to tell a researcher what they believe he or she wants to hear instead of what they really think, regardless of guarantees of anonymity. If, on the other hand,

---

[31] Possibly this is the time to reemphasize that there may well be some forms of intervention that sizable portions of a population *hope* will fail. This is true to a limited extent with most measures, but it becomes especially acute with repressive doctrines. Unfortunately, they too can be evaluated and "improved."

[32] In spite of this, it is usually seen as desirable to construct measures of social science concepts that use more than one indicator. See this point made in Amitai Etzioni and Edward W. Lehman, "Some Dangers in 'Valid' Social Measurement," *The Annals* 373 (September 1967), pp. 1–15. With regard to the general issue of the choice of measure, often called the "criterion" in evaluation research, some have called attention to a peculiar dilemma: one's theoretical framework can on occasion determine the measurements to be used—for example, in measuring social class or poverty. See Gideon Sjoberg and Roger Nett, *A Methodology for Social Research* (New York: Harper & Row, 1968), for a discussion.

[33] See Robert Rosenthal and Ralph N. Rosnow, eds., *Artifact in Experimental Research* (New York: Academic Press, 1969).

one chooses to examine post-release adjustment, one is hampered by lack of cooperation or, again, by less-than-honest responses. Difficulty in locating former inmates may occur if they have completed their period of parole reporting. Even if one chooses to look at rates of return to prison—a purely objective index known as recidivism—one is troubled by widespread failure to identify former convicts as such, especially if the offender is apprehended in a district far from the site of the previous offense. (Obviously, few repeat offenders will care to volunteer the information that they are ex-convicts.) Finally, the approach that examines the number of prison incidents (riots, escape attempts, sit-downs, etc.) can be attacked on the grounds that it does not really measure rehabilitation at all—technically, this is raising the question of the "validity" of the procedure.[34] It follows from these illustrations that the researcher must be intimately familiar with the situation and its various machinations.

It should be noted that an implicit assumption of all evaluation research is that the future will be like the present, that past outcomes will continue to hold. The facile response is that this assumption is necessary for *any* sort of scientific prediction, in any discipline, social or physical. But while that is true it is also the case that predictions of future performance based on past evaluations are considerably more problematic. This is so because change can occur so readily, both within the program itself—in personnel, in funding, in explicit policy, in level of conscientious effort—and also in the clientele that interface with the program, in their financial situations, their culture, their previous experiences. For these reasons, conclusions drawn about specific programs can only be expected to hold for a matter of years.

As for broader conclusions—about the general efficacy of psychiatry, for example, or whether one form of rehabilitation is generally more effective than another—not only do the above precautions apply but new worries appear as well. Alice Rivlin, a strong advocate of evaluation research, nevertheless has cautioned that when alternatives are being compared, they should be spelled out in complete and formal fashion like one could do with income maintenance alternatives. If, on the other hand, this cannot be accomplished—where alternative treatments are multifaceted, cannot be standardized, and/or interact with

[34] For further discussion of the specific difficulties of evaluating criminal rehabilitation, see Daniel Glaser, "The Assessment of Correctional Effectiveness," in *Law Enforcement Science and Technology*, ed. S. Yefsky (New York: Academic Press, 1967), pp. 181–89; Leslie Wilkins, *Evaluation of Penal Measures* (New York: Random House, 1969); and Stuart Adams, *Evaluative Research in Corrections: A Practical Guide* (Washington, D.C.: National Institute of Law Enforcement and Criminal Justice, 1975).

clientele background—then Rivlin doubts that gross experimental comparison can produce useful preference rules.[35]

Another problem, inherent in many other areas of social research as well as the study of social problems, is the *reactivity* of the persons studied. The simple act of gathering information may affect, in very unexpected ways, the behavior of the individuals or groups being investigated. There are several reasons for this, but essentially the problem is that people who are aware that they are being observed or interviewed sometimes alter their behavior—even if unconsciously.[36] Ways to surmount this problem exist, but the possibility of reactivity considerably increases the difficulty in obtaining meaningful results.[37]

Another conceptual problem exists that must not be ignored. This is the urge to move into *quantitative* measures of success and failure: number of cures, suicide rates, crime rates, recidivism, worker absenteeism, magnitude of income disparities, proportion of national budgets spent on war preparations, and anything else that can be quantified. This is a natural and ordinarily laudable tendency, due for the most part to a desire to obtain the greatest possible objectivity in evaluation. What may become damaging, however, is when this urge is carried to a particular form of excess, a condition the late Pitirim Sorokin labeled "quantophrenia." In the rush to quantify, the tendency is to ignore, to brush aside what cannot be quantified. It is as though evaluators were tacitly accepting the statement of extreme empiricism, "if it cannot be measured, it cannot be known." Since it is impossible to attach a figure to the anguish of a suicide victim's family, to the happiness given up because people are afraid to use the streets at night, and many other important elements, these factors are sometimes completely ignored—or relegated to a footnote in the overall examination. Some things that are impossible to quantify are nonetheless extremely important in evaluating the success or failure of a program.

In addition to emphasizing or neglecting specific aspects of a problem on the basis of their quantifiability, a related tendency is to select the very problem one chooses to investigate on the basis of the availability of some neat, tidy quantitative method to examine it. I do not mean to imply that one should do the opposite. But the importance of a problem is not necessarily related to its amenability to a mathematical

---

[35] Alice M. Rivlin, "Social Experiments: The Promise and the Problem," *Brookings Bulletin* 10 (1973), pp. 6–9.

[36] For details, see Rosenthal and Rosnow, *Artifact in Experimental Research*. Some commonly recognized forms of reactivity include evaluation apprehension, demand characteristics, and Hawthorne or placebo effects.

[37] For possible resolutions, see Rosenthal and Rosnow, *Artifact*; and E. J. Webb et al., *Unobtrusive Measures: Nonreactive Research in the Social Sciences* (Chicago: Rand McNally, 1972).

or statistical solution. Yet this is precisely how, without admitting it, perhaps even without knowing it, some people select the problems they will investigate. But as a renowned statistician once said, explicitly with respect to this tendency:

> *You can always get a precise answer to the wrong question.*
> **John W. Tukey**

The urge to quantify reminds me of another potential problem: what is known in education circles as "teaching to the test." If teachers are evaluated by how well their students do on a standard test, they tend to concentrate their teaching on the particular subjects to be examined. In general, people tend to focus on where they will be subjected to quantitative evaluation, and hence the criterion selected tends to supplant the fundamental goal. Administrators, in turn, select quantifiable criteria because they lend the appearance of objective evaluation.

The problem of excluding nonquantifiable factors becomes especially acute in a form of evaluation known as *cost-benefits analysis* (cost-gains analysis, cost-effectiveness analysis). In this process—a great favorite with technocratic-minded governments in the past decade—one attempts to create a sort of balance sheet for each proposed alternative, listing the various costs of each given program on the one hand and the gains expected on the other. The object, of course, is to maximize what might be figuratively termed "social profit" (gains over losses) by selecting the best program out of the competition. This differs little from ordinary evaluation except that, instead of a single dimension being considered, the candidate programs are evaluated simultaneously in terms of multiple criteria.[38]

It has become clear that in cost-benefits analysis one must be very wary of "hidden" costs in particular programs; eventually the analysis almost becomes an exercise in accounting as one grapples with whether certain items such as training costs should be included. What is more, nonquantifiable items have a way of appearing in a footnote in the introduction and of disappearing thereafter. In principle, a cost-effectiveness analysis is supposed to first quantify what can logically be quantified and then to give a decision-maker the tools for making a decision that *incorporates the intuitive aspects*, but in practice the latter are often simply ignored. Even without such problems, no foolproof calculus

---

[38]This explanation oversimplifies a highly complex process, but it is adequate for the present discussion. For an extended treatment, see Thomas Goldman, ed., *Cost-Effectiveness Analysis: New Approaches in Decision-Making* (New York: Praeger, 1967).

exists to take into account simultaneously gains and losses of differing kinds; ultimately it is an individual decision to determine which items should be more heavily weighted than others. (Only rarely can all items be truly reduced to a common monetary unit of analysis.) Again, in principle, cost-benefits analysis is supposed to place all judgments in plain view and show clearly the logic used throughout. In a sense this is true: analyses of this sort do indeed spell out in detail the analytical procedures they are using. But again, in practice the logic and quantitative procedures are often so difficult to follow for administrators not used to such tools that they tend to uncritically accept the choice of the expert. The latter, in turn, is loathe to emphasize the numerous intuitive judgments at the base of his immaculate, imposing edifice.

In essence, in spite of its great recent popularity, cost-benefits analysis comes down ultimately to a series of political acts—sometimes quite consciously so. That is, it often lends a veneer of objectivity and quantification to a political decision.[39] Only in rather mechanical cases does it really become worthwhile. For instance, one can use the tool to select with reasonable objectivity the best car to be purchased for a police motor pool (even here, some assumptions might be challenged). But to use cost-benefits analysis to determine whether it would be better to replace the existing motor pool at all or to spend the money on improved training is an exercise in futility—or politics. Although promising considerably less than cost-benefits analysis, the basic experimental format of evaluation research—random assignment, experimental and control groups, before and after measurements—poses far fewer questions of validity. Without minimizing the difficulties discussed earlier, it holds out a reasonable promise of meaningful answers to a limited list of questions.

POLITICAL AND ETHICAL CONSIDERATIONS

Before we explore the political weaknesses of evaluation, it should be noted that certain types of experimental programs are simply impossible for a government to establish within a given cultural milieu because of a fear of popular outcry. A governmental proposal has to take into account the probable reaction of media gate-keepers and others with

---

[39]The political acceptability and economic rationale of cost-benefits analysis is taken up in J. Wolfe, *Cost Benefit and Cost Effectiveness* (London: Allen & Unwin, 1973). For a skeptical, sophisticated treatment, see Peter Rossi and Walter Williams, eds., *Evaluating Social Programs: Theory, Practice, and Politics* (New York: Seminar Press, 1972). Now that this technique is on the way out, thanks to extensive criticism, So suggests that the new "buzz word" to replace it will be "strategic planning." See Frank So, "Strategic Planning: Reinventing the Wheel?" *Planning* 50 (1984), pp. 16–21.

influence. For this reason, as Robert Boguslaw has pointed out, it is ordinarily not possible to conduct "live" studies that involve fundamental changes in the social environment. Such changes might offend community sentiment. For although it is feasible to do research and experimentation on social problems in contexts that are socially acceptable at a given time and place, it is usually not possible to obtain support for research that would seriously investigate alternatives to existing institutional arrangements. What the evaluative results of such programs would be can never be known for they are usually strangled in their infancy; neither the program nor its evaluation can be initiated.

Political considerations surround every step in the initiation of social intervention. A lack of fit between the perceived cause of a problem and the means used to combat it may, of course, be due to ideological factors, but it also may be due to administrative inefficiency on the part of the bureaucrats charged with program implementation. Alternatively, lack of fit between cause and attempted solution may be due to ambiguous transmission of instructions through the administrative hierarchy, with lower echelons employing their own interpretations or selectively paying attention only to certain parts of their instructions. Resources (money or personnel) may be insufficient to carry out the program actually needed. In such cases often the political need is to appear to be "doing something," even when it is clear to those directly involved that little benefit will come from the option chosen. Likewise, in governmental bureaucracy unspent funds are supposedly indicative of "slack"; the agency that does not use up all of its resources finds its future budgets reduced. Hence activity itself comes to be a prime concern, and the worth of the activity tends to become secondary.

Failure to offer the best program to counter the perceived cause of a problem may be a result of insufficient popular consensus, support, and cooperation, especially if the public would be inconvenienced by truly effective measures. Powerful interests might have to be challenged were the proper means implemented or, conversely, vested interests might be served by the option chosen (such as the training of new personnel or the satisfaction of a powerful movement). Finally, the administrators themselves may be uncertain of which program to employ, leading them to adopt a useless midpoint policy.

Practical difficulties are compounded by the failure of most agencies to collect evaluation data on their own. This task has usually not been seen as a part of the obligation of organizations that deal with social problems. To be sure, most organizations gather statistical information about some aspects of their work, but data specifically related to whether the activity is meeting its ultimate purpose is rarely collected. Paradoxical as it may seem, organizations are far more likely to seek and systematically collect information that helps in their day-to-day functioning, irrespective of whether this routine functioning ever does any good.

When official statistics do become available, they are at times tainted with such pronounced political overtones that they are virtually worthless as a means of evaluation. To take a single example, consider the compilation of statistics on volume of crime.[40] Clearly it would be highly desirable to compare crime rates in order to determine, for instance, the effects of various policing policies. We could either look at the same place at different times or, preferably, at the results of allocating new policies in a random selection of precincts or districts. Indeed the former approach has been successfully utilized on occasion. But the difficulties introduced by politics are enormous. Total volume of crime, it appears, is a highly sensitive issue. A city or a region could look very bad if it were to appear at the top of a crime index. Tourism, industry, and economic growth could decline. Pressure is often brought to bear by the city officials to "dampen" these statistics. Then, too, police departments themselves look bad if cities have a high proportion of unsolved crimes. Some cities have been notorious for "wiping the blotter clean" at the end of the year.

Criminal statistics can thus become a political football that even reform administrations are loathe to touch: whoever is the first political leader to improve a poor statistical system can later be condemned by the opposition for the "fantastic growth in crime" during his or her period in office. (Despite this, brave or foolhardy administrators do on occasion reform the accounting system, sometimes generating "increases" in crime more than 100 percent in a single year.) More recently it has occurred to official compilers that certain advantages, in terms of increased financial support to combat the crime wave, may accrue from *overestimating* volume of crime. Hence today inaccuracies can be introduced in both directions. Because of these inaccuracies the research situation has seemed so desperate that independent surveys have been conducted in recent years to approach more exactly the actual rate of crime.[41] Such surveys have been so helpful that in some places they have graduated from one-time affairs into systematic, recurring measurements.

---

[40]I am ignoring here certain aspects that render such data even more suspect, such as the large volume of crime never reported to the police. For weaknesses of a supposedly sophisticated crime reporting system, see Marvin Wolfgang, "Uniform Crime Reports: A Critical Appraisal," *University of Pennsylvania Law Review* 3 (1963), pp. 708–38.

[41]For an early model, see James F. Short, Jr., and F. Ivan Nye, "Reported Behavior as a Criterion of Deviant Behavior," *Social Problems* 5 (1957), pp. 207–13. Again I should note that inadequate police reporting is by no means the only reason for inaccuracies in estimating volume of crime.

The example of crime statistics illustrates, without exaggerating, the difficulties of using officially compiled statistics that purport to show how an agency is accomplishing its job. As Altheide and Johnson point out very explicitly in a significant book, official statistics become part of the "bureaucratic propaganda" that organizations develop to justify their existence.[42]

To round out this long list of difficulties, there are times when using a control group is simply inappropriate or, indeed, unethical. If one strongly suspects that a reform measure will be beneficial, to withhold it from a control group merely to have a tidy experiment might be construable as an unnecessary perpetuation of misery. The issue is a difficult one, centering around the degree of people's need of some helpful development and the degree of certainty about the effectiveness of the proposed program.[43] Neither component can be ignored: even with the most serious of diseases, doctors do not administer a new drug to every patient until it has been exhaustively evaluated with experimental and control groups. However, if one is reasonably sure of at least some beneficial effects, it would not do to withhold treatment even for less serious matters.

Controversy continues over the ethics of control groups in medical research. After all, for two distinct reasons caution is necessary in the introduction of a new treatment regime: the treatment might not work, and it might cause serious side effects. The typical progression in medical research on a new treatment is from animal experimentation to terminal human cases (as a last resort), then to controlled experimentation, and finally to general use. Ethical questions arise from both directions, claiming that the trials are either too brief or too extensive. On the one hand we have the tragic thalidomide babies (now young adults) who were born with only small vestiges of their limbs because their mothers took thalidomide during pregnancy. Thalidomide had passed the trials and was being recommended by doctors at the time. Clearly, the trials here were tragically inadequate. On the opposite side we have the contemporary concerns voiced by AIDS treatment volunteers that the trials of new drugs are being deliberately prolonged by unsympathetic or prejudiced administrators to retard the drugs' formal approval. And indeed, for a disease that is virtually 100 percent fatal, it might be reasonably argued that searches for bad side effects could be cut short if treatment volunteers were advised of that fact.

---

[42]David L. Altheide and John M. Johnson, *Bureaucratic Propaganda* (Boston: Allyn & Bacon, 1980).

[43]For a fictional treatment that revolves around this very dilemma, see Sinclair Lewis's classic prize-winning novel, *Arrowsmith*.

Here is an example of a most serious ethical case concerning a control group. In 1932 officials of the U.S. Public Health Service decided to see what the difference in prognosis was for treated and untreated cases of syphilis. A large group of poor black men with syphilis were located in Alabama and were randomly assigned to treatment and control groups. The men in the control group were paid a small sum periodically for their continuing participation in the experiment, but over a period of some forty years they received no medication whatsoever, meanwhile suffering progressive deterioration from the disease.[44] When at last the scandal was uncovered, it was noted that in the earliest days of the study no effective cure existed for syphilis, and the treatment then was considered by many to be almost as bad as the disease. But penicillin had been discovered less than ten years into the experiment and yet the control group was maintained for another thirty years without treatment. A court award of $37,500 to each survivor appeared to many observers to be far too little, too late.

This senseless cruelty contrasts with the occasional use of a false "ethics" issue as a facade for those anxious to avoid evaluation. For years the ethical issue formed a part of the rationale behind the refusal of the psychoanalytic profession to submit to controlled experimentation: ethically it could not refuse to treat a part of the population that badly needed its help merely in order for others to ascertain the natural untreated recovery rate. Of course this argument assumes that one *knows* that psychoanalysis is indeed beneficial—the very question that needed to be studied. George Fairweather relates one such incident.

> The experimenter came under severe criticism from practitioners [service personnel] who were advocates of either group or individual psychotherapy. From their point of view, people in the fourth group were being denied one of the best treatments. It must be noted here that the adoption of this position rests upon the assumption that the merits of the three psychotherapy conditions had already been established. As far as experimental verification was concerned, however, it was equally tenable that the no-psychotherapy fourth condition might bring about the same or even more desirable results than any of the three psychotherapy programs. The research eventually did proceed, but only with great misgivings on the part of these service personnel.[45]

---

[44]See Bernard Barber et al., *Research on Human Subjects: Problems of Social Control in Medical Experimentation* (New York: Russell Sage Foundation, 1973).

[45]George Fairweather, *Methods for Experimental Social Innovation* (New York: Wiley, 1967), p. 31.

In the end, the experimental results showed that the no-psycho-therapy fourth group fared just as well after eighteen months of community living as those receiving one or the other form of psychotherapy.

When an evaluation is made, it runs considerable risk of being ignored—not because of its technical defects but because of a number of practical and/or political reasons. To begin with, a considerable time lag between program implementation and evaluation may be politically indefensible. New programs usually emerge as the direct result of social crises. The *lead time* required before results may be known through systematic evaluation research is always considered excessive by administrators and political figures, and in some cases it may in truth be too slow to cope with a rapidly evolving situation.[46]

Popular demand may override findings that run contrary to common-sense appraisals. The politicians and bureaucratic elite may themselves be only vaguely familiar with evaluation research; like the general public, they may not accept conclusions that conflict with their own intuition. This seems to have occurred, for example, with research showing no deterrent effects from capital punishment. Then, too, politically or ideologically distasteful findings can simply be suppressed, with the study never released to the public or surrounded with copyright restrictions and printed obscurely. For this reason the sponsorship of research is very important with regard to honesty—the social organization of the research effort is a critical issue. It should not be assumed that the overriding of findings is always due to suppression of results acknowledged to be valid. Sometimes it is due to a simple inability to re-examine long-held beliefs.[47] Whatever the reason, conscientiously prepared evaluations are sometimes destined to "gather dust" rather than be usefully employed.

Instead of appraisal results being suppressed, they may on other occasions be demanded with such persistence, and accepted with such alacrity, that programs are prematurely evaluated. Potentially worthwhile efforts thus may be rejected as unproductive before the project

---

[46] A short but excellent overview of the political dilemmas of social policy research is in Walter Buckley, *Sociology and Modern Systems Theory* (Englewood Cliffs, NJ: Prentice-Hall, 1967), pp. 172–76.

[47] Systematic research shows that most people, including scientists, have a strong bias toward searching for confirming evidence rather than disconfirming evidence. Similarly, the theory of diagnostic inference indicates that people find it difficult to change from their initial causal explanations because the strength of such explanations is not greatly reduced by the introduction of alternative explanations. See A. Koriat, S. Lichtenstein, and B. Fischoff, "Reasons for Confidence," *Journal of Experimental Psychology: Human Learning and Memory* 6 (1980), pp. 107–18; and H. J. Einhorn and R. M. Hogarth, *A Theory of Diagnostic Inference: Judging Causality* (Chicago: University of Chicago Graduate School of Business, Center for Decision Research, 1984).

staff has had time to make necessary adjustments. It has been suggested that evaluation research can at times result in the loss of the more progressive administrative staffs since they are more likely to sponsor an evaluation of their own programs. The late Erving Goffman wrote of "latent secrets," meaning facts incompatible with the impression fostered by an agency and that have not yet been collected and organized into a usable form.[48] In the bureaucratic morass, volunteering to have one's latent secrets analyzed amounts to exposing oneself to a form of criticism that the traditionalist avoids. Among traditional programs, Hackler points out, evaluative research will encounter not only antipathy but downright hostility. "To say that the status of evaluator is 'ambiguous' is to put it nicely. Evaluators are damned unpopular people in the eyes of those who are being evaluated."[49]

TWO EXAMPLES OF POLITICS AND EVALUATION

I will conclude our examination of evaluation research by looking at two contemporary fields in which the avowedly neutral process of evaluation has become a highly charged political matter. One field is criminal/delinquent rehabilitation and the other is psychiatric treatment.

In the mid-1970s, just as American society was turning decidedly more conservative, Martinson wrote a pessimistic review of delinquency/criminal rehabilitation research in which the key idea was that *nothing works*.[50] This expression—nothing works—was to become a byword of the resurgent right wing's attack on all correctional rehabilitation programs, coinciding nicely with the growing fear of a fiscal (government overspending) crunch. The "rehabilitative ideal" was said to be untenable. Ultimately, the orientation that nothing in the rehabilitation agenda worked spilled over into such extraneous topics as mandatory sentencing, abolition of parole, waiving of juveniles to adult

---

[48]Erving Goffman, *The Presentation of Self in Everyday Life* (Garden City, NY: Doubleday, 1959), p. 144.

[49]James Hackler, *Why Delinquency Prevention Programs Should NOT be Evaluated* (Edmonton: University of Alberta, 1973), p. 56. For documentation of the combative nature of policy research, see several of the contributions in R. Lance Shotland and Melvin M. Mark, eds., *Social Science and Social Policy* (Beverly Hills: Sage Publications, 1985). It is noteworthy that none of the authors in this collection seem dismayed by this feature of their work.

[50]The most sophisticated statement of the position is to be found in Douglas Lipton, Robert Martinson, and Judith Wilkes, *Effectiveness of Correctional Treatment: A Survey of Treatment Evaluation Studies* (New York: Praeger, 1975).

prisons, and incapacitation as the chief goal of confinement. In the end, Martinson repudiated the overblown implications of his own statement, a recantation just before his death that has yet to fully catch up with the fame of the original position.

How and why did Martinson arrive at his pessimism? In part the answer lies in a history of overinflated claims for new rehabilitation schemes that did not live up to honestly held expectations. One by one, the experimental programs at Highfields, Provo, Silverlake, and Atlantic Street provided little or no clear evidence of delinquency reduction. And, paradoxically, the very faith that the advocates had in their programs led them to permit comprehensive evaluation research that demonstrated their failings. The simple fact is, said Martinson, that the expected differences between experimental and control conditions either failed to materialize or were so minimal that the intensive programs required to produce them were inherently wasteful. More generally, most researches show that variations in treatment or caseload or treatment personnel have very little effect on the recidivism outcome.

In part, the failings of evaluated programs in rehabilitation can be viewed in the wider context of the failings of social programs in general. As one commentator has put it, "social programs have rarely proved sufficient to cope with major social ills."[51] It may be in fact the fate of evaluation research to come up with predominantly negative results. On a more immediately relevant basis, the "nothing works" position is probably a great oversimplification in the area of rehabilitation itself. As Greenwood and Zimring note:

> The study says that indeed many programs have failed, but all have not, and the conclusion that "nothing works" comes from lumping all programs using a common intervention strategy (say, vocational training) together, finding little or no improvement in recidivism rates overall, and then concluding that that particular form of intervention is worthless.[52]

It is fair to say that proponents of rehabilitation have regrouped and are counterattacking. A 1986 conference called "Reaffirming Rehabilitation" was subtitled "Confronting the Nothing Works Myth." Its featured speakers included Douglas Lipton, the senior author of the most sophisticated Martinson work, who is now defending the rehabilitation

---

[51]Carol Weiss, quoted in Joseph W. Eaton, "Review Essay: The Mushrooming of Applied Sociology," *Contemporary Sociology* 9 (1980), pp. 768–71. The quote is from p. 770.
[52]Peter Greenwood and Franklin Zimring, in Peter W. Greenwood, ed., *Intervention Strategies for Chronic Juvenile Offenders* (New York: Greenwood Press, 1986).

effort.[53] Martinson's expression seems destined to be co-opted: a 1989 conference on drug abuse treatment and prevention research was entitled "What Works."

Finally, Hackler has asked whether we are investigating the right questions concerning rehabilitation programs. Ought we to evaluate existing programs in delinquency as they stand now or should we do "softer" research aimed at improving our understanding of just what we are doing so we can improve it?[54] And—a final point—perhaps we might be better advised to be pleased with less: to take an analogy outside of social science, no one expects doctors to cure all diseases; often we are content if they prolong life, or relieve pain.

Let us turn now to a second contemporary field in which evaluation research has become highly politicized. As mentioned earlier, Hans Eysenck reviewed research on the effectiveness of psychiatry and concluded that psychiatric intervention made no difference to outcome. (In actuality, he did see one variant, behavioral therapy, as effective and technically he merely "failed to reject the null hypothesis" on the others, but I refer to the sense of his conclusions as they reached the educated public.) Needless to say, such conclusions, reiterated on several occasions by Eysenck himself and picked up by several other writers such as Rachman and Gross, had a galvanizing effect on the psychiatric community. Eysenck had called for better research on psychiatric outcomes—up to that time hardly any evaluations had used control groups. Casting the ethical objection aside, psychiatry began to conduct more methodologically adequate studies, slowly at first but ultimately reaching a crescendo of literally hundreds of separate researches.[55] Ironically, Eysenck was proven incorrect in the end by the very outpouring of quality researches that he had called for and indeed stimulated. (Perhaps that is the ultimate compliment, although it is doubtful that he would fully agree.)

The most comprehensive review of the by now voluminous set of separate researches is that of Smith, Glass, and Miller.[56] Their condemnations of Eysenck, Rachman, and other critics of psychiatric efficacy are severe, to say the least. Although Eysenck left himself open to several

---

[53] See also the carefully considered defense of rehabilitation in Clemens Bartollas, *Correctional Treatment: Theory and Practice* (Englewood Cliffs, NJ: Prentice-Hall, 1985).

[54] James C. Hackler, *The Prevention of Youthful Crime: The Great Stumble Forward* (Toronto: Methuen, 1978). See also on this point Donald T. Campbell's "Reforms as Experiments."

[55] See these reviewed in Mary Lee Smith, Gene V. Glass, and Thomas I. Miller, *The Benefits of Psychotherapy* (Baltimore: Johns Hopkins University Press, 1980). In addition to the Eysenck challenge, research was also clearly stimulated by the prospect of mental health cutbacks from governments.

[56] *Ibid.*

serious methodological criticisms, he nevertheless pioneered in an extremely important way.[57] The magisterial review of Smith, Glass, and Miller leaves little doubt that psychiatry can indeed make a positive contribution to patient well-being, and this conclusion applies across the board to a great many different psychiatric procedures. Confidence in these conclusions is further strengthened by noting that the positive effects were stronger in the most tightly controlled researches—in direct opposition to the conclusion on that point by Eysenck and Rachman on much smaller subsets of studies.[58]

It is important to note exactly what is being demonstrated in all of the researches above. They collectively make it clear that psychiatric intervention *can* make an improvement in many of its patients. That is important, valuable knowledge. But this is not the same as saying that such intervention *typically* has a beneficial effect in the multitude of private and state-supported facilities. Recall the Fairweather study cited earlier: in a concrete context no difference in outcome was detected between treated patients and controls. Even while reaching their overall conclusion of beneficial effect, Smith, Glass, and Miller note that a substantial minority of the studies they reviewed found no differences between experimental and control groups. And the Eysenck-stimulated researches were conducted, in all likelihood, on some of the better programs with, furthermore, the full awareness of the staff that their efficacy was being evaluated. Thus a sharp distinction exists between knowing that *psychiatry* can help and knowing that a particular concrete psychiatric *program* is helping.[59]

The politicization of psychiatric evaluation is not quite the same as that found in delinquency rehabilitation. In the latter, the intrusion of politics in the strict governmental meaning of the term has been all too clear. In the case of psychiatry, although government cutbacks are very real and on occasion have cited Eysenck et al. for justification, the principal political struggle has been within the profession (and at its margins), among the believers, skeptics, and nonbelievers. But in both cases we can see how the avowedly neutral process of evaluation has become part of a highly charged political struggle.

---

[57] For a tribute to Eysenck's stimulant role, see Chapter 7 of Bernie Zilbergeld, *The Shrinking of America: Myths of Psychological Change* (Boston: Little, Brown, 1983).

[58] Smith, Glass, and Miller also dispute both Eysenck's and Rachman's conclusion that psychiatry can be harmful to some individuals. For clear evidence of harm from a psychiatric fad, see H. B. Peck, ed., "Encounter and T-Groups," *International Journal of Group Psychotherapy* 20 (July 1970).

[59] I ought to briefly mention the "eight myths of psychiatry" synthesized by Bernie Zilbergeld (a practicing psychotherapist) in his provocative work, *The Shrinking of America*. These touch on several less quantifiable but probably no less important issues in psychiatric efficacy.

SUMMARY

The preceding sections of this chapter should more than suffice to show the grave difficulties involved in conducting evaluation research. It is by no means a simple or even straightforward process. Indeed, the types of problems enumerated here are of such magnitude that some observers have concluded that the results of evaluation research are meaningless and that such research should therefore be abandoned.[60] Yet it should be realized that projects rarely encounter more than a small fraction of the *potential* political difficulties described here, and means to overcome the technical problems have been found and continue to be suggested.[61] I have been able to review only the most basic evaluation techniques in this chapter. In the final analysis, unless we are to return to an era in which sheer argumentative power carried the day, in which "common-sense logic" dictated the programs to be employed and anecdotal examples (or "testimonials") constituted the only feedback on the success of a program, evaluation research—difficult as it is to carry out in practice—is a necessity.

---

[60] See Hackler, *Great Stumble Forward*. For a strong defense of evaluation, see Chapter 1 of Leslie T. Wilkins, *Social Deviance* (Englewood Cliffs, NJ: Prentice-Hall, 1965).

[61] See, as examples, the techniques proposed in Campbell, "Reforms as Experiments," and Fairweather, *Experimental Social Innovation*.

11

EXPERTISE: BLESSING AND CURSE

I have saved for the last chapter what may be the most important issue: where are we going in terms of coping with social problems? Are current trends hopeful or discouraging? Are we becoming more or less effective today in coping with problem conditions, and why?

A full treatment of this question would require a historical survey of the gradual development of new tools for combating social ills. We might consider the emergence of formal codes of law, self-conscious lawmaking, taxation, and state service, the first gathering of social statistics. If we chose more recent developments, we might examine professional planning or the creation of economic and social indicators. It is important to recognize that modern modes of coping with social problems are the result of numerous social inventions. Many of these innovations seem so commonplace today that it is difficult to conceive of their having a definitive period of origin in the same manner as a physical invention, yet their advent is a matter of historical record.

I will concentrate on one particular development with marked implications for the future of social intervention: the triumph of the expert and the specialized group. The chapter will consider the growth of *technique* and *specialization*, the advantages this provides in terms of competence for combating social problems, and its drawbacks in terms of ethical blindness and impersonality. A tension between expertise and humanity exists—between bureaucracy and efficiency on the one hand and compassion and democracy on the other. It is time to examine that tension in the arena of social problems.

In the following section I lay the groundwork by examining the meaning of the social condition known as technicism, the search for and blind employment of expert techniques in all areas of life. The next section traces the historical emergence of experts and specialized social-problem agencies up to the present day. The tendencies within technicism conducive to ethical blindness are explored in detail. Finally, we look at some of the advantages of specialization and see clearly the dilemma before us: how can we obtain the blessings of efficient expertise and yet escape its terrible costs?

Before we begin I should warn the reader that the effects of technicism are complex. We will have to move, for instance, from the large-scale level of the technocratic assault on democracy to the small-scale, interpersonal level to look at the lack of compassion of the impersonal expert. But this cannot be helped; the effects are entangled and multidimensional. A lot of things are linked together, and in this chapter in particular it is difficult to draw hard and fast boundaries. But the subject is important enough to make the effort worthwhile.

TECHNICISM IN MODERN SOCIETY

A favorite theme of critics of modern society is the extent to which technology has come to dominate life. Some perceptive observers have penetrated beyond this commonplace insight to attack what they see as a far broader problem, the problem of technicism. We will want to discuss the rise of technicism in the treatment of social problems, but first it is essential to understand precisely what technicism is.

By now numerous books and countless articles have appeared on the problems associated with the ascendancy of technology in modern society.[1] It is true, as the writers of such works say, that modern technology has rendered the contemporary world more remote from the life of eighteenth-century Europe than the latter was from the life of ancient Rome.[2] Since the Industrial Revolution, the vision of humanity being warped by the machines it supposedly controls is a recurring theme. One thinks of Charlie Chaplin pathetically ruled by machines in the movie *Modern Times*, of the nineteenth-century Luddites smashing the machinery that had taken away their jobs, or of the modern phobias about computers. Assaults on technology started with the revulsion of the Romantic writers at the excesses of the early Industrial Revolution.

---

[1]For example, Jean Meynaud, *Technocracy* (New York: Free Press, 1969); or Hans Morgenthau, *Scientific Man Versus Power Politics* (Chicago: Phoenix Books, 1965). Lewis Mumford, *Technics and Civilization* (New York: Harcourt, Brace, 1934), was an early precursor, as was, in its way, Norbert Weiner's book, *The Human Use of Human Beings: Cybernetics and Society* (New York: Avon Books, 1967, original—1950).

[2]Herbert J. Muller, *The Children of Frankenstein: A Primer on Modern Technology and Scientific Values* (Bloomington: Indiana University Press, 1971). This chapter has been profoundly influenced by Muller's insights, sometimes in ways not suitable for citation. The intellectual debt is considerable.

Their protests were directed more against the historical by-products— human suffering in factory towns, loss of contact with nature, uprooting of families—than against the triumph of machine civilization itself. "Technologism" commonly refers either to the glorification of technology or to the social condition in which technology is ascendant.

Analyses of technicism are considerably broader and more profound than the standard critique of technologism. I will concentrate on one such analysis, that of the French writer Jacques Ellul. As noted in Merton's introduction to the English translation, the title of Ellul's principal book on the subject has been mistranslated.[3] The book is really a critique not merely of technology but of *the encroachment of "technique" or expertise into all aspects of life*. To be sure, we find technicism in technology, but we also find it today in such widely diverse areas as politics (how to sell the political candidate), the "art" of sex (the legion of "how to do it better" books), personal manipulation (starting with Dale Carnegie's old book, *How to Win Friends and Influence People*), and negotiation ("psychological strategies for gaining negotiating advantages," as a series of recent management seminars were called).[4]

Technicism, *the transformation of all aspects of life into a set of techniques*, is an amorphous, difficult concept. Yet it is a profoundly important insight.[5] Ellul calls technicism "the real religion of our times." Similarly, for Giddens, it is "not just the application of technical methods to the solution of defined problems but a pervading ethos, a worldview which subsumes aesthetics, religion, and customary thought to the rationalistic mode."[6] The foundations for advancing expertise across all fields of endeavor and the spread of technicism can be detected in the decline of the realm of the "sacred and the sacrosanct." As Max Weber pointed out long ago, we live in a world that has become, in a special sense of the word, "dis-enchanted." Every social convention and arrangement can be subjected today to examination and challenge: patriotism, religion, paternalism, the family, and so forth. In place of the sanctity of the traditional comes increasing *rationalization* of all sectors

---

[3] Jacques Ellul, *The Technological Society*, introduction by Robert K. Merton (New York: Vintage Books, 1967, original—1954). Ellul also has a more recent work that has not attracted the same amount of attention: *The Technological System* (New York: Continuum, 1980).

[4] It should be noted that some writers use the term somewhat differently. Manfred Stanley, in his book, *The Technological Conscience* (New York: Free Press, 1978), restricts "technicism" to the *inappropriate* use of scientific and technological concepts, especially in the social sciences.

[5] Ellul's usage of the term is important but risks being carried too far. Is an opera singer's technique "technicism" in a meaningful sense? For an attempt to sort out the definition, see Victor Ferkiss, *Technological Man: The Myth and the Reality* (New York: Mentor, 1969), pp. 37–38.

[6] Anthony Giddens, *The Class Structure of the Advanced Societies* (London: Hutchinson, 1973), pp. 257–58.

of society, a long-term trend to which many writers, especially Max Weber, have called attention. And linked with the extension of rationalization and technicism to all quarters is the growth of what Weber called the rational bureaucracy.[7] Bureaucracy is a modern social invention having few parallels in earlier cultures, yet today an increasingly standardized organizational structure can be found in contexts as diverse as organized religion, the military, big business, big unions, and the university.[8] And, according to Weber, bureaucracy is ubiquitous in all modern societies, capitalist and socialist.

Bureaucracy seems to be both a prominent outcome of increased rationalization as well as one of its sources. The existence of our representative democracy cannot be taken as any assurance against incursion of bureaucratic control. For that matter, the decisions of a legislative body are today carried out by bureaucracies, a point long ago noted by Weber. Even at the turn of the century, when Weber wrote, it was becoming clear that "the day-to-day exercise of authority was in the hands of the bureaucracy, and even success in the struggle for votes and in parliamentary debate and decision-making would come to naught unless it was translated into effective control over administrative implementation."[9]

In democratic theory as it has evolved, the relation between the democratically elected representatives and the senior bureaucrats is supposed to be a division of labor on the basis of policy versus administration. Policies are supposed to be set by the elected representatives who then leave the implementation or administration of the policies to the career bureaucrats. But in practice the career expert has a great influence on policy. The transient cabinet secretary or minister is often no match for the permanent senior bureaucrat—an expert by dint of years (decades) of experience in the tacit understandings and details of his or her chosen area. As Beetham notes:

> Administrators, especially at their higher levels, typically act as advisors to politicians on policy. And since they usually have the advantage over a minister of greater experience and expertise in the policy area, at least collectively, their advice can be crucial in

---

[7] For Weber's ideas on bureaucracy, see Reinhard Bendix, *Max Weber: An Intellectual Portrait* (Garden City, NY: Doubleday, 1962). Many of the topics to be discussed here, including the professionalization, bureaucratization, and secularization of society, are excellently treated in Guy Rocher, *A General Introduction to Sociology: A Theoretical Perspective* (Toronto: Macmillan of Canada, 1972). See the section on "Technological Society."

[8] See William H. Whyte, Jr., *The Organization Man* (Garden City, NY: Doubleday, 1956). For an excellent discussion of proto-bureaucracies in earlier societies, see William Delaney, "The Development and Decline of Patrimonial and Bureaucratic Administrations," *Administrative Science Quarterly* 7 (March 1963), pp. 458–501.

[9] Bendix, *Max Weber*, p. 433.

determining the content of that policy. After all, what *should* be done is dependent upon what *can*, and, if it can, upon what effects it will have, especially on other policies. Assessing such possibilities and consequences constitutes the distinctive expertise of officials, and is one of the sources of their influence.[10]

Nor is such advice merely idiosyncratic and therefore no great threat to democratic control. On the contrary, bureaucrats are frequently unanimous in the advice they render.

[B]ureaucracies possess well-developed cultures of their own. . . . These cultures embody elaborated codes governing the way administration is conducted, as well as larger assumptions about the world, which set their own limits to the range of policies considered possible or acceptable. . . . [The bureaucratic cultures] serve to define the parameters of what can be legitimately thought or seriously entertained.[11]

Nor can socialism be counted on to answer the bureaucratic challenge; according to Weber, socialism merely extends and multiplies the existing bureaucracy to such an extent that it penetrates into every nook and cranny of society, resulting in a "dictatorship of the bureaucrats," not of the proletariat. Some modern socialist thinkers strongly agree. Oppenheimer, for instance, distinguishes "elite socialism" from "socialism-from-below" and notes that "a simplistic either-or view of the future [either capitalism or socialism] blinded socialists to the dangers of bureaucracy as an independent force which could [become] a third alternative." The growth of bureaucracy was for Weber one of the most ubiquitous and unpleasant developments in modern society; indeed it was "the most crucial phenomenon of the modern Western state."[12]

Ellul, of course, is adamantly opposed to technicism, and an affinity is apparent between Ellul's work and Franz Kafka's fictional masterpiece, *The Trial*, with its emphasis on the nightmarish qualities of an uncaring, unfeeling bureaucracy. It is simplistic to treat the bureaucratic phenomenon as an unmitigated evil, but important to recognize the trend toward technicism in its various manifestations.

---

[10]David Beetham, *Bureaucracy* (Minneapolis: University of Minnesota Press, 1987). The quote is from p. 48.

[11]*Ibid.*, pp. 51–52. See also the excellent treatment in Ronald M. Glassman et al., *Bureaucracy against Democracy and Socialism* (Westport, Conn.: Greenwood Press, 1987).

[12]Martin Oppenheimer, "The Limitations of Socialism," in *The Case for Participatory Democracy*, ed. C. G. Benello and D. Roussopoulos (New York: Viking Press, 1971); Max Weber, "The Essentials of Bureaucratic Organization," in *Reader in Bureaucracy*, ed. Robert K. Merton et al. (Glencoe, Ill.: Free Press, 1952), p. 24.

Not only the physical machinery used in work but also the very organizing of the work has become a matter of technicism—symbolized in the twentieth century by the efficiency expert with time-and-motion studies and by the rationalization of industrial work. The early decades of the century were especially congenial to this so-called "scientific management" approach. Although later decades have softened its rough corners with "human relations" in the factory, this merely blurs the outlines of the triumph of technicism in the organizing of work: production schedules, assembly lines, time clocks. All these, difficult as it may be to believe, are social inventions of the present century. The factory itself is a social invention only a few centuries old.

So great is the triumph of technicism that the search for new technologies, and the rapid introduction of these innovations into the mainstream of economic and social life, have themselves become matters of expertise. Whereas inventions were formerly created haphazardly, first a gradual (sometimes reluctant) mating of science and technology has occurred and, more recently, research and development has emerged as an industry in its own right. We are, as has been remarked, the first civilization to *systematize* the processes of innovation and discovery. Alfred North Whitehead once noted that the greatest invention of the nineteenth century was the comprehension of the method of invention. In the United States research and development has long been a multibillion dollar activity, with support coming from government as well as from business interests, while throughout the Western world the "knowledge industry" is today one of the largest economic units. Numerous scholars—notably Daniel Bell and John Kenneth Galbraith—have forecast that the production of knowledge will be the most important institution in the "post-industrial" or "technocratic" society. Technicism is thus introduced at the very creation of new technology; *we are now expert at creating new areas of expertise.*

As a result of these trends, and the concomitant occupational shifts, the professional and technical class has been seen as the dominant occupational group in the "post-industrial society." According to many writers (prominently, Bell, Galbraith, and S. M. Lipset), the creation and utilization of theoretical knowledge will become the central, axial principle of society, with decision-making itself the subject of an "intellectual technology" run by technocrats.[13] Many writers also have forecast that in the society of the future a predominant role will be played by scientists, professionals, technicians, and technocrats.

One particular feature of the technocratic development is nicely expressed in a book review by Terence Ball:

---

[13] See the discussion in Chapter 5.

More and more the expert is *in* authority because he or she *is* an authority—in medicine, management, science, accounting, law, education, or any one of a dozen domains. Our social practices and institutions increasingly exemplify and embody an ideal that is less democratic than technocratic.[14]

In his latest book, Ellul characterizes the technological "system" as "autonomous," an end in itself. Technology now exists as an organized whole because machines are vertically integrated; technology is unified into a system of interdependent parts. According to Ellul, every sphere of human effort is becoming technicized; all aspects of human existence are thus engulfed and deeply modified.[15]

Our purpose in the remainder of this chapter is to examine the triumph of technicism in one particular domain: in the treatment of social problems. We want to see how it happened and to consider the ethical and practical consequences of this ascendancy. We first consider the growth of technicism from a historical perspective. While reading the following section, it is helpful to recall the historical material examined in Chapter 2 on the emergence of social problem ideas. Here, however, we are more interested in the changes that took place in organization and training than in the transformation of ideas.

THE HISTORICAL GROWTH OF TECHNICISM IN INTERVENTION

Prior to the nineteenth century no institutional facilities were devoted to the care of social problems. Criminals were only held in jails until they could be fined, whipped, or executed. The mentally ill were cared for in undifferentiated almshouses. The poor were either warned out of town or, if "worthy," given outdoor relief. All of this began to change in the early 1800s with, as David Rothman calls it, the "discovery of the asylum." The asylum was regarded at the time as a great innovation.[16] Given the difficulties subsequently experienced with large centralized facilities, it is painful to recall the enthusiasm that once greeted them. Today, of course, we know by sad experience the severe disadvantages of placing all criminals into a single facility where they can reinforce each

---

[14]Terence Ball, book review of Thomas L. Haskell's *The Authority of Experts*, in *Contemporary Sociology* 13 (1984), pp. 743–44. The quote is from p. 743, italics added.
[15]Ellul, *The Technological System*.
[16]See David Rothman, *The Discovery of the Asylum* (Boston: Little, Brown, 1971).

other's attitudes and learn new techniques of crime.[17] We know also the disadvantages of the centralized mental institution: the patient's isolation, cut off from family and friends, in itself retards improvement.[18] The isolation of a large central facility, remote from public view, also increased the ease of mistreatment.

But such reflections were far in the future from the heady reform atmosphere surrounding the emergence of the asylum. In centralized facilities treatment would be possible, humane intentions made workable at last. To be sure, the period's idea of "humane" differed radically from our own, incorporating ideas of robot-like orderliness that we would find abhorrent. But the central point was that instead of detaining-centers for the infliction of physical pain, prisons would be places where habits of industry and religious belief could be incubated. In retrospect, although the degree of enthusiasm was naive, asylums did make treatment *possible*—however much it was subsequently neglected in practice. Taken in sum, then, the asylum was a major development in the transformation of intervention.

Although the earliest asylums were undifferentiated, with young orphans, the insane, criminals, and paupers all mixed together, this gradually gave way to more specialized institutions. Facilities that we take for granted today—mental hospitals (formerly insane asylums), penitentiaries, orphanages, and so forth—gradually emerged. This differentiation of facilities reached its culmination in the Progressive Era around the turn of the twentieth century.

> Progressives aimed to understand and cure crime, delinquency, and insanity through a case by case approach. From their perspective, the [early 1800s] commitment to institutions had been wrong, both for assuming that all deviants were of a single type, the victims of social disorder, and for believing that they could all be rehabilitated with a single program, the well ordered routine of the asylum.[19]

The differentiated asylum, or specialized institution, developed in conjunction with *specialized treatment personnel*.

---

[17]The earliest prisons tried to avoid this problem through segregation of prisoners or by rules of silence, but these attempts disintegrated in practice.

[18]The trend today in mental health care is toward community-centered facilities. Interestingly, the earliest asylums in the United States followed similar patterns. See Norman Dain, *Concepts of Insanity in the United States, 1759–1865* (New Brunswick, NJ: Rutgers University Press, 1964), p. xiii.

[19]David J. Rothman, *Conscience and Convenience: The Asylum and Its Alternatives in Progressive America* (Boston: Little, Brown, 1980). The quote is from p. 5.

In the realm of personnel, the gradual growth of a body of experts in particular types of social problems followed the emergence in the nineteenth century of the social-problem concept and the asylum. In the early stages of the asylum there was very little specialization and virtually no training of personnel.[20] The keeper at the insane asylum was largely interchangeable with the prison guard or, for that matter, the caretaker of an orphanage. And many of the public-sector specialties taken for granted today, such as police or firefighters, were nonexistent.[21] When police forces first came into existence around 1830, their composition and organization was highly similar to that of the military—a relationship hardly surprising since it was through the inadequacies of the military's traditional intervention in civil disturbances that the police originally came into being. As Bordua puts it, "the establishment of the modern uniformed police constituted a recognition that coercive social control could not remain in the hands of nonspecialists."[22] Gradually, a special body of technique evolved for civilian police that decisively distinguished them from their military forebears.[23] (Indeed the police detective was among the earliest true specialists in social problems.) Other specialized roles gradually emerged in a process of differentiation that continues unabated to the present day. Meanwhile, the now-familiar specialized agencies of the state—police, fire, prison, orphanage, public health, insane asylum, homes for the blind, war veteran—were replacing church-based organizations or largely undifferentiated, primitive state arrangements.[24]

As discussed at greater length in Chapter 2, the growth of science led to a search for scientific solutions to social problems. And much of the earliest work in sociology, particularly in the United States, was devoted to exploring new ameliorative approaches. At first the social sciences were, by necessity, staffed by men trained originally in other fields. Indeed this was the case with all of the early great minds in

---

[20]One historian, noting that the insane were as a rule locked up with criminals in prisons, has maintained that no real hospitals existed for the treatment of the mentally ill up to the end of the eighteenth century—only places where they were kept. See George Rosen, *Madness in Society* (New York: Harper & Row, 1968), p. 151.

[21]An early effort to provide such services in eighteenth-century Prussia was largely abortive. See Reinhold Dorwart, *The Prussian Welfare State Before 1740* (Cambridge, Mass.: Harvard University Press, 1971).

[22]David J. Bordua, ed., *The Police* (New York: Wiley, 1967), p. vii.

[23]For the history of the early police, see T. A. Critchley, *A History of Police in England and Wales, 1900–1966* (London: Constable, 1967); and Clive Emsley, *Policing and Its Context, 1750–1870* (New York: Schocken, 1984). For an excellent analysis of the novelty of the idea of police, see Allan Silver, "The Demand for Order in Civil Society: A Review of Some Theories in the History of Urban Crime, Police, and Riot," in Bordua, *The Police*, pp. 1–24.

[24]Hospitals, courts, and jails were considerably earlier developments.

the classical era of sociology: Weber, Marx, Durkheim, Pareto, all were trained in other fields and then "migrated." Gradually the situation changed, and various milestones highlight the transition. The first social science associations, bridging the transition from the amateur to the professional, appeared in several countries in the 1860s. Around the same time, the first university courses in social problems appeared in the United States. The first chair in sociology appeared a few years later at Yale. And around the turn of the century the first department of sociology was formed at the University of Chicago.

The social worker, as a distinct occupation, appeared on the scene in the 1880s.[25] Around this time the idea developed that charity by itself was not enough if it was not translated into the actual *good* of the deprived and unfortunate, and that such benefits did not automatically follow from mere benevolent intent. To ensure the translation of good intentions into beneficial results required expertise and special capabilities—hence the need for special training in social work. Consider this statement by Rabbi Abba Silver in 1928:

> The last few decades have introduced a purposefulness and an intelligence which have made [charity] more helpful than heretofore. The sporadic giving of doles became, in the hands of trained and capable administrators, an organized system of service, of study, of investigation and supervision, so that the recipient of aid was not pauperized, and the public not victimized. Charity has become more scientific. This does not mean that it has lost spontaneity, or that it has become cold, tardy and impersonal. Rather, it has become more expert.[26]

Observe the confidence! We shall look at the drawbacks of such expertise momentarily.

Although very simple statistical measures had been in use for a long time, statistical analysis as a true discipline, capable of handling complex relationships or testing probabilistic hypotheses, is a relatively recent development. The emergence of statistics as a separate field of

---

[25] Some excellent materials are now available on the emergence and transformation of social work. See Roy Lubove, *The Professional Altruist: The Emergence of Social Work as a Career 1880–1930* (Cambridge, Mass.: Harvard University Press, 1971); Don S. Kirschner, *The Paradox of Professionalism: Reform and Public Service in Urban America, 1900–1940* (Westport, Conn.: Greenwood Press, 1986); and John H. Ehrenreich, *The Altruistic Imagination: A History of Social Work and Social Policy in the United States* (Ithaca: Cornell University Press, 1985).

[26] Abba Hillel Silver, "The Widening Horizon of Social Service," *Proceedings of the First Annual Meetings*, Canadian Council on Social Work (1928), pp. 21–24. The quote is from p. 21.

endeavor took place in the mid- to late nineteenth century.[27] Statistical analysis, for all its obvious benefits, presents a formidable barrier to the uninitiated and reveals the terrible oversimplification of many non-statistical analyses. Although the marriage of sociology and social statistics only took place in the 1920s, the long-run implications for the triumph of technicism in the treatment of social problems would be profound.

In Chapter 2 I reviewed the slow conversion among the educated of beliefs about insanity—from divine retribution (or divine will) to organic brain damage. This conversion led to the establishment in the United States of some carefully planned, medically oriented regimes, with medical superintendents as directors.[28] Technical training specifically for the care of the insane began in the late nineteenth century.[29]

The last decades of the nineteenth century witnessed the emergence of what historians today call the child-saving movement.[30] Juvenile delinquency was invented—that is, invented as something distinct from adult crime, with which it had formerly been grouped. One aspect of this movement generated increased specialization in a number of institutions. Around the turn of the century, juvenile delinquents, who had formerly been housed with adult offenders, were now provided separate facilities that, in a naive way, were focused specifically on delinquency. In addition to these reformatories (or Borstals, in Britain), the movement also produced the institution known as juvenile court. The emergence of the social problems expert was unmistakable by the early twentieth century.

THE TRIUMPH OF TECHNICISM IN INTERVENTION

The developments described above have been augmented in recent decades with some important additional trends. To begin with, as I first noted in Chapter 5, both the public and government officials

---

[27]See Theodore M. Porter, *The Rise of Statistical Thinking, 1820–1900* (Princeton: Princeton University Press, 1986).

[28]However, many so-called medical practitioners of the 1800s were charlatans; most did not possess medical degrees, nor was the possession of a medical degree a guarantee of sophistication, especially in psychiatric affairs. See Dain, *Concepts of Insanity*, p. 25.

[29]See Gerald N. Grob, *Mental Illness and American Society, 1875–1940* (Princeton: Princeton University Press, 1983). The book's title can be misleading: it is primarily an excellent examination of the emergence of and professionalization of psychiatry in this period.

[30]Anthony Platt, *The Child Savers: The Invention of Delinquency* (Chicago: University of Chicago Press, 1969).

increasingly feel a need for specialists in various fields of social problems and increasingly recognize the expertise of professionals and semiprofessionals in several fields: criminologists, prison psychologists, social workers, sex counselors, marriage counselors, psychiatrists, psychoanalysts, labor/management mediators, suicidologists—the list could be greatly extended. To contend with the ethical dilemmas we now have professional ethicists. The commensurate acceptance of formal training programs is in contrast to and at the expense of skills learned on the job. In recent years the demand for college-level courses and programs in skills relating to social problems has burgeoned.

In each of the emerging specialties there is a steady drive for the trappings of "professionalism," as this is variously defined by the different practitioners. Associations are formed; gradations of rank appear and proliferate. Increasingly vocal demands for certification by the state emerge, ostensibly to weed out incompetents but often in practice to eliminate practitioners without formal training. A steady growth occurs in credentials and also in "credentialism."[31] And demands arise for accreditation of institutions that teach the requisite skills. In these respects, as in others, specialization in social problems parallels the development of "professions" in other areas.[32] Although most of the specialties existed prior to their "professionalization," newer fields are composed almost exclusively of professionals as traditionally conceived (for example, suicidology, or conflict resolution). New fields have nonprofessionals only where there is unusually lucrative financial inducement (for example, marriage counseling).[33]

Two of the most frequent recommendations today for combating social problems involve the training of additional personnel and the expansion of existing research. Both of these proposals are most directly supportive of the *careers* of the professional and the technician, although they also may aid the target population with the problem. It is true that virtually every sector of social services could use more personnel; the creation of new skills and the development of new professionals should in most cases be considered a positive accomplishment. And who could argue that additional research on a social problem is not needed? But it is a question of priorities. In some cases problems have been "studied to death" and training programs can barely replace resig-

[31] See Randall Collins, *The Credential Society* (New York: Academic Press, 1979).

[32] See Harold Wilensky, "The Professionalization of Everyone?" *American Journal of Sociology* 70 (September 1964), pp. 137–58.

[33] For contrasting views on the virtues or problems posed by the growth of professions, see the first two essays in Thomas L. Haskell, ed., *The Authority of Experts* (Bloomington: Indiana University Press, 1984).

nations due to lack of support. The two recommendations have been cited separately, but it should be recognized that they overlap considerably: one of the principal ways to train aspiring professionals is to involve them in funded research. After the training and research handouts are completed, all too often very little is left to "trickle down" to the target population—the poor, the handicapped, the unemployed.

Too frequently grants designed to help people with problems end up more as a means to support graduate students than as aid for the persons the students study. This should scarcely evoke surprise when it is remembered that the technicians and the experts are articulate members of the middle and upper-middle classes, while most of the target populations are working class—even, in many cases, the "unreachables" at the bottom of the working class. Most pressure groups, it will be recalled, are composed of the middle class or higher. Ironically, when students complete their training they are often priced out of the market.

> The longer the time spent in the training of a specialist, the higher the price of his service. It follows that the higher the price, the farther removed it is from the reach of the poor.[34]

The triumph of the expert goes hand in hand with educational "upgrading," but there is very little reflection and even less real research on whether formal training really improves one's capacity to deal with social problems. This strange situation poses serious questions about how helpful some of the training actually is. Research on empathy, for instance, seems to show that social scientists are somewhat less competent in judging persons than lay individuals without professional training.[35] In recent years it has been repeatedly noted that many job requirements are "overqualified" in terms of excessive demand for formal educational attainments. Meanwhile, however, the trends toward specialization, formal training, and certification continue; the process appears inexorable. A mutually stimulating relationship between the development of the modern university and the growth of the professions has evolved; in part the increased legitimacy of both universities and professions in the modern world can be traced to this symbiotic relationship.[36]

In addition to the fact that training is sometimes of questionable value, and unquestionably diverts funds, growing evidence shows that

---

[34]William C. Richan and Allan R. Mendelsohn, *Social Work: The Unloved Profession* (New York: New Viewpoints, 1973), p. 8.
[35]This is documented in Chapter 5.
[36]See the essay by Thomas Bender in Haskell, *Authority of Experts.*

for many types of problems it is better to use someone with background and experience similar to those being helped, even at the cost of supposedly essential expertise. Workers who come from the "problem" neighborhood itself, or who have been through similar experiences, understand the "street scene" much better than an outsider. Although this is a venerable concept in such organizations as Alcoholics Anonymous, it is resisted by many in the social-work and penal bureaucracies—rejecting, for instance, the use of ex-convicts in prisons. In part, such nonexpert workers may experience hostility from professionals because they do not come from the same social background; in part they are resisted because they do not possess the proper credentials. Regardless of demonstrated effectiveness, this concept is regarded as a threatening step backwards because nonexperts work, and even succeed, without the usual training.[37] Also they may work, and even succeed, for much less money.

A number of studies of the historical course of professionalization have indicated that

professionalism did not emerge, in the nineteenth and early twentieth centuries, in response to clearly defined social needs. Instead, the new professions themselves invented many of the needs they claimed to satisfy. They played on public fears of disorder and disease, adopted a deliberately mystifying jargon, ridiculed popular traditions of self help as backward and unscientific, misleadingly legitimated themselves in terms of the mantle of science, and generally created or intensified demands for their own services. The most important case for the utility of the helping-healing-human service professions rested, not on their technical or scientific superiority and efficacy, but on their ability to control clients. . . . These critiques emphasize the professional invention of the very need that professional groups claim to satisfy, as well as the creation or intensification of popular demand for their own services.[38]

These claims are still controversial, but no one doubts they are right at least for certain historical instances.[39]

---

[37] See Lubove, *The Professional Altruist.* In social work in particular a threat is perceived in the very idea that a person without expertise can be an effective altruist.

[38] Burkhart Holzner and John H. Marx, *Knowledge Application: The Knowledge System in Society* (Boston: Allyn & Bacon, 1979). The quotes are from pp. 351 and 352.

[39] For this perspective advanced in the human-service professions in particular, see Thomas L. Haskell, *The Emergence of Professional Social Science* (Chicago: University of Illinois Press, 1977).

TECHNICISM IN THE MARSHALLING OF PUBLIC SUPPORT

To this point we have concentrated on technicism among the practitioners themselves. But technicism is relevant for intervention in another major way. Expertise has also triumphed in the *"people-handling" groups* that relate to social problems by (a) convincing people that a particular problem does or does not exist, and by (b) convincing them to follow a particular course of action to counter it. The social definition of social problems has been treated in the beginning chapters of this book. It was demonstrated by repeated example that a major process is involved in transforming an objective problem condition into one that is in the forefront of the public's consciousness. The means to accomplish this are familiar—advertising, special pleading lobbies, propaganda, demonstrations. Behind the concrete techniques—even behind supposedly spontaneous manifestations of sentiment—exists an extensive armory of manipulative methods. *Technicism has come to the marshalling of public support.* Extensive literature on mass persuasion exists.[40] In this particular area no one can doubt that the findings of social science research have diffused to the practitioners of persuasion—to the propagandists, the public relations people, the advertisers, and to leaders of social movements. As Martinson has put it, "We live in an age in which 'people-changing' has become a skill, a profession. . . . That is what is new. It should not be confused with the pledge, the moral campaign, or frenzied efforts to promote virtue historically engaged in by concerned amateurs."[41]

Demand for a product or service is created by plan—through advertising campaigns and promotional "blitzes." Advertising is an entire industry consisting of experts in the manipulation of public buying habits.[42] (Herbert Muller has called them specialists in psychological technology.) In the United States, with by far the world's largest advertising business, it is at last count a $100 billion a year activity. As Galbraith has pointed out, demand is manufactured along with the products themselves, and in many cases advertising creates new wants and "needs" at the service of the highest bidder.[43] But more than new

---

[40] See, as an illustrative example, Terence H. Qualter, *Opinion Control in the Democracies* (New York: St. Martin's Press, 1985). A dated but still excellent source is Arthur Cohen, *Attitude Change and Social Influence* (New York: Basic Books, 1964).

[41] Robert Martinson, "The Age of Treatment," in *Crisis in American Institutions*, ed. Jerome Skolnick and Elliott Currie (Boston: Little, Brown, 1970). For a famous exposé that is still insightful, see Vance Packard, *The Hidden Persuaders* (New York: McKay, 1957).

[42] See Benjamin Singer, *Advertising and Society* (Toronto: Addison–Wesley, 1986).

[43] John Kenneth Galbraith, *The New Industrial State* (New York: Houghton-Mifflin, 1967). For a critical review of the concept of the "managed" consumer, see Irving Kristol, "Professor Galbraith's 'New Industrial State,'" *Fortune* (July 1967), pp. 90–91 and 194–95.

products and services are advertised. As government penetrates ever further into the marketplace to regulate (or subsidize) businesses, advertising is increasingly used to put across a particular industry's *policy* to the public. The vast expenditures of the firearms industry, in "public service" advertisements through the National Rifle Association (NRA) that promote their positions on gun control, are an excellent case in point.

Technicism in manipulating public support does not apply only to advertising. Social science findings on the dynamics of social influence are also being applied to public relations drives and to political campaigns.[44] And a significant book has extended the traditional view of propaganda as confined to ideological conflict to include the notion of bureaucratic conflict: "bureaucratic propaganda" is the term for how organizations use records, reports, and statistics to justify themselves.[45] We can now speak without exaggeration of "the engineering of consent," meaning technicism in the realm of public policy in a democracy.

Technicism has also extended to the marshalling of support by *opposition movements* of the left and right. In contrast to the formless, inchoate protests and social movements of the past, the techniques of dissent have become increasingly systematized.[46] I will write here mainly of the special techniques of marshalling support used by the left wing, because the right wing can often make use of the conventional advertising and public relations apparatus of the corporate elite and are thus in method not very different from mainstream persuasion. But before looking at the left I will say a little about new developments in persuasion from the right. One aspect of the reinvigoration of the right wing in the 1980s was the emergence of computer-based fund-raising techniques, which the radical right has improved to a new peak of efficiency, especially in its ability to target particular blocs of people for specific issues. Another development of the right wing has been the rise of televangelism from a very small beginning into a giant structure of great financial clout and mass persuasive power. Finally, the right has begun, with misgivings, to adopt some of the techniques of the left, particularly civil disobedience around abortion clinics.

From Hobsbawm's primitive rebels to the modern social protest organization of the left is quite a contrast, growing ever more remote. Zald and Ash (in Helfgot) see social movements becoming more bureaucratized. This process transforms the movement from a loose collec-

---

[44]Two excellent illustrations are Joe McGinnis, *The Selling of the President, 1968* (New York: Trident Press, 1969) and Harold Mendelsohn and Irving Crespi, *Polls, Television and the New Politics* (Scranton, Pa.: Chandler, 1970).

[45]David L. Altheide and John M. Johnson, *Bureaucratic Propaganda* (Boston: Allyn & Bacon, 1980).

[46]See Eric Hobsbawm, *Primitive Rebels: Studies in Archaic Forms of Social Movements* (New York: Norton, 1965); and George Rudé, *The Crowd in History, 1730–1848* (New York: Wiley, 1964).

tion of individuals with similar beliefs and grievances to a highly developed organizational vehicle with differentiated roles for movement
participants.[47] Social movements are no longer primarily forms of collective behavior but are comprised of social-movement organizations
(sometimes referred to as SMOs), which can be equated with other
complex organizations. And it therefore follows that today's social-
movement organizations embody the institutional dynamics of ongoing
complex organizations. Indeed, McCarthy and Zald use the term "social
movement industry" to refer to the collection of all SMOs that share a
similar set of preferences for social change—for example, civil rights.[48]

Today, technicism from the left can be observed in many ways;
I am providing several brief "snapshots" in the remainder of this
paragraph. Books have been written on how to organize, how to sustain "spontaneous" mass mobilization. Saul Alinsky has prepared handbooks on the proper procedures for organizing protest.[49] Literature such
as *The Organizer's Handbook* is readily available.[50] The organizers of
mass demonstrations often undergo role-playing sessions before assuming their leadership functions. The content of public service "counter-
advertising" (for example, anti-smoking spots on television) has been
based on the same motivational analysis as the commercial advertising
with which it contends. Jay Schulman and his associates have perfected
a computerized method of jury selection for defense attorneys, applicable only for radical defendants, in which the background characteristics
of the most favorable jurors of previous trials are isolated to aid in the
selection of new jurors. Their success rate in terms of acquittals has been
virtually perfect.[51] John Sink has written a technical book on how the
defense at political trials should operate in order to win.[52] Inside

---

[47] J. H. Helfgot, ed., *Professional Reforming* (Boston: D. C. Heath, 1981).

[48] *Ibid.* John D. McCarthy and Mayer N. Zald, "Resource Mobilization and Social Movements: A Partial Theory," *American Journal of Sociology* 82 (1977), pp. 1212–41.

[49] See Alinsky's books, *Reveille for Radicals* (New York: Random House, 1969); and *Rules
for Radicals: A Pragmatic Primer for Realistic Radicals* (New York: Vintage Books, 1972).
Some typical rules from the latter include: "A good tactic is one that your people enjoy,"
"The threat is usually more terrifying than the thing itself," "Pick the target, freeze it,
personalize it . . ." (pp. 128, 129, 130).

[50] Martin Oppenheimer and George Lakey, *A Manual for Direct Action: Strategy and Tactics for Civil Rights and All Other Nonviolent Protest Movements* (Chicago: Quadrangle,
1964); The O. M. Collective, *The Organizer's Manual* (New York: Bantam Books, 1971);
David Reed, *Education for Building a People's Movement* (Boston: South-End Press,
1981).

[51] See Jay Schulman et al., "Recipe for a Jury," *Psychology Today* (May 1973), pp. 37–44
and 77–84. Also see V. P. Hans and Neil Vidmar, "Jury Selection," in N. Ken and R. M.
Bray, eds., *The Psychology of the Courtroom* (New York: Academic Press, 1982); and
Lawrence Wrightsman, *Psychology and the Legal System* (Monterey, Calif.: Brooks/
Cole, 1987), especially p. 236.

[52] John M. Sink, *Political Criminal Trials: How to Defend Them* (New York: Clark Board-
man, 1974). The latest word is that jury consultants are no longer confined to supporters
of the left. They have banded together to form the American Society of Trial Consultants.

SMOs, trained professional canvassers, who earn their living solely by soliciting, are given quotas of signatures, money, votes, and so forth. I can summarize these developments, and many others, by the well-established phrase "the professionalization of reform."

When we shift our attention to the extreme left, we note that the sophistication of the cadre of underground revolutionary movements has long been recognized. In this realm, the laudatory notion is that of a "vanguard party"; the negative, that of an "organizational weapon."[53] In the extreme case, as Gouldner notes, "Revolution itself becomes a technology, to be pursued with 'instrumental rationality.'"[54] In summary, technicism is dominant today in both establishment and antiestablishment handling of social problems.[55]

THE ETHICAL BLINDNESS OF TECHNICISM

Ellul takes note of a general emphasis in technicism on goal attainment rather than ethics, of a narrowing of the specialist's focus to the point that broader standards of principle are ignored in the quest for achievement of narrow objectives. Capability tends to define what is "good"— "can" implies "should" not only in technology but in all spheres touched by technicism.[56] A symptom is the oft-noted emphasis on *pragmatism* in bureaucracies: if something works to further organizational objectives, the feeling that it should be used regardless of its other consequences grows. Weber felt that pragmatism was one of the central characteristics of bureaucracy.

In many cases an organization's pragmatism is manifested principally to ensure its *self-perpetuation* and self-aggrandizement.[57] What this may do to an agency's capacity to deal with social problems was

---

[53] See Philip Selznick, *The Organizational Weapon* (New York: McGraw-Hill, 1952).

[54] Alvin W. Gouldner, *The Future of Intellectuals and the Rise of the New Class* (New York: Continuum, 1979), p. 4.

[55] Wherever labor unions fall along this continuum—and some would argue they have become a part of the establishment—the complexity of labor–management negotiations and tactics makes it clear that expertise has also triumphed in the realm of labor relations.

[56] See H. Ozbekhan, "The Triumph of Technology: 'Can' Implies 'Ought,'" in *An Introduction to Technological Forecasting*, ed. Joseph P. Martino (London: Gordon and Breach, 1972).

[57] These objectives seem to hold true even in organizations ostensibly motivated by the pursuit of profits. Large corporations do seek profits, to be sure, but even more do they choose organizational perpetuation and self-aggrandizement. Galbraith, *New Industrial State*, talks of organizational continuity and predictability of operations as the main objectives of the modern corporation. For an interpretation of social-work agencies in these terms, see Richan and Mendelsohn, *Social Work*.

noted in the political section of the last chapter. A classic case of self-perpetuation occurred, for example, when a fund-raising organization called the National Foundation (the "March of Dimes") was about to go out of business because a cure had been found for polio. Rather than proclaim success and fade away, its directors suddenly found new diseases with which the foundation could be identified. So, too, when American aerospace companies found their budgets dwindling, they shifted to earthbound projects, with varying success, and defense "think tanks" such as the Rand Corporation shifted to thinking about domestic problems. Organizations, it is said, have "negative entropy"—they do not die easily.

The problem with pragmatism is that it leads to organizations pursuing goals by any means, irrespective of the larger goals of society as a whole or of the needs of individuals. What comes to pass, then, is a social condition in which the dominant tendency is to

> treat [each person] as an object to be calculated and controlled, exemplified in the almost overwhelming tendencies in the Western world to make human beings into anonymous units to fit like robots into the vast industrial and political collectivisms of our day.[58]

A kindred problem is that of *ritualism*, a condition whereby persons lose sight altogether of the ultimate ends and purposes of their actions—even the goals of the organization—yet continue ritually to observe the "proper" means without understanding why they exist.[59] We have all encountered ritualists—the nurse who wakes patients so they can take their sleeping pills, the fictional sergeant in *From Here to Eternity* who refuses to unlock the armory during the attack on Pearl Harbor because he has not received the proper authorization. The means tend to become ends in themselves, perhaps the only ends that the actor respects, a process known variously as the displacement of goals or the autonomy of means.

Although pragmatism may be an important attribute of the bureaucracy, in actual operation the erection of rules and standard operating procedures is highly conducive to the creation of ritualism. The apparent paradox of a bureaucratic system oriented around pragmatic efficiency becoming entrapped in ritualistic adherence to formula can

---

[58]Rollo May, *Love and Will* (New York: W. W. Norton & Co., 1969). See also the discussion of Roszak's "objective consciousness" later in this chapter.

[59]Robert K. Merton, *Social Theory and Social Structure*, rev. ed. (Glencoe, Ill.: Free Press, 1957).

be explained by the central fact that one pragmatic way a bureaucracy can increase efficiency in most cases is to set up standardized rules and require adherence to them by its functionaries. But the rules ultimately come to be treated as absolutes instead of useful tools, and when new situations emerge for which they do not work, the rules tend to be followed anyway. Thus, as Merton puts it, "the very elements which conduce toward efficiency in general produce inefficiency in specific instances."[60] The process also has been analyzed, in psychological terms, as the "functional autonomy of motives."

The modern bureaucracy erects a shield of secrecy around its activities that gives it a measure of power over its clientele and an unanticipated degree of autonomy from supposedly overseeing agencies. The importance of secrecy for the bureaucracy was recognized long ago by Weber.[61] (See also the discussion of latent secrets in the previous chapter.) Speaking of specialists and consumers of their services (for example, doctor–patient, lawyer–client), Moore and Tumin stress the importance of secrecy and of ignorance on the client's part in maintaining the authority and legitimacy of the specialist.[62] As a famous writer once put it:

All professions are a conspiracy against the laity.
George Bernard Shaw

Since the bureaucratic experts suffer from their own unique form of shortsightedness, these patterns of secrecy become ethically questionable. Although an expert can often perceive aspects of a situation that escape a layperson, some very important mechanisms operate to maintain a degree of ignorance and blindness by the expert—although the expert's ignorance is much more selective than a layperson's.[63] In order for the reader to appreciate the expert's ignorance, a few lines are devoted here to current thinking on distortions of reality; some of the social dynamics of reality distortion in modern society have by now be-

---

[60]*Ibid.*, chapter on "Bureaucratic Structure and Personality." Philip Selznik has dubbed this the "organizational paradox."

[61]Hans H. Gerth and C. Wright Mills, eds., *From Max Weber: Essays in Sociology* (New York: Oxford University Press, 1958), p. 233.

[62]Wilbert E. Moore and Melvin Tumin, "Some Social Functions of Ignorance," *American Sociological Review* (1949), pp. 787–95.

[63]I also noted this in Chapter 5 from a slightly different standpoint. Parts of the following passage are taken from Richard L. Henshel and Robert A. Silverman, eds., *Perception in Criminology* (New York: Columbia University Press, 1975).

come well documented. First, *occupational selection*, whereby persons with specific personalities or values are attracted or repelled by particular occupations, plays a major role in producing different orientations toward identical facts by those in various fields of expertise. Then, too, occupational selection is also based on diverse *educational attainments* that further discriminate the experts of different fields. And the educational requisites themselves constitute a mode of *shared experiences* that again differentiates occupational groups from one another, while at the same time heightening the similarity of views within each group. Evidence from a wide variety of sources confirms that once similar persons are attracted to certain niches, "consensual affirmation" of norms and *consensual validation* of the attitudes they share intensifies their eccentricity of thought, as do the common experiences that those with highly similar jobs tend to acquire. The occupational viewpoints that emerge are then stabilized by *group censure* for participation in disapproved experiences or in reading disapproved literature, and further stabilized by *psychological* mechanisms: selective exposure to new ideas, selective perception, and selective retention.[64] These and other obstacles to the spread and acceptance of innovative thoughts or methods are well covered in Rogers and Shoemaker.[65] Experts, in short, come to share and maintain a particular set of blinders that shut off certain aspects of reality, a problem reinforced in a way by their very competence and arrogance about their expertise. Ultimately, they may develop what Thorstein Veblen called a *"trained incapacity"* to observe or deal with situations except in the traditional ways to which they are accustomed.

Accompanying the general advance of bureaucratization and rationalization has been what some observers see as a basic change in the *typical personality* in modern society. Admittedly, such alterations are difficult to isolate (and still more difficult to prove), but analysts in the 1950s seemed to agree that a fundamental long-term shift had occurred. Riesman and his co-workers wrote of the "lonely crowd," of a long-term change in personal character from what they called "inner-directed" people to "other-directed" people. Whereas inner-directed persons take their positions on the basis of values received early in life (Riesman used the gyroscope as his analogue for this), other-directed persons do so on the basis of their immediate surrounding associates (a sensitive radar

---

[64] See the literature on these strong tendencies reviewed in Joseph T. Klapper, *The Effects of Mass Communication* (New York: Free Press, 1960), pp. 19–25 and 64–65; and Bernard Berelson and Gary F. Steiner, *Human Behavior: An Inventory of Scientific Findings* (New York: Harcourt, Brace & World, 1964), pp. 529–33.

[65] Everett Rogers and F. Shoemaker, *Communication of Innovations* (New York: Free Press, 1971).

was the analogue here).[66] The contention was that the proportion of inner-directed persons has declined steadily, from a strong majority at the turn of the century to a small minority at the time of writing. Similarly, Whyte wrote in the same period of the replacement of a Protestant Ethic pattern of conscientious individualism with a conformist pattern (what he called the social ethic). In the place of the independent entrepreneur he saw the rise of the "organization man," a man (person) whose chief loyalties are to the organization of which he is a part, and who is found, in virtually interchangeable settings, in big business, big labor, organized religion, the university, and the military.[67] The significance of such a shift toward "other-directedness" and the "organization man" lies in the inability of such persons to combat the majority opinion of their peers on matters of ethical principle.

The long-term historical rationalization of society has fostered the growth of an *objective consciousness*, a mode of thought that allows one to avoid thinking about the likely consequences of one's actions by reverting to impartial, scientific language. For one example Theodore Roszak quotes from a British medical journal the description of an experiment in which a rabbit is given Lewisite gas in its eye, which proceeds to rot away over a period of several weeks. The language is virtually of engineering, describing a mechanical process as if no beast was involved at all. "Note how the terminology and the reportorial style distance us from the reality of the matter," Roszak says, and he is entirely accurate.[68] Only a portion of the description can be included here, which is probably all for the best!

> Very severe lesions ending in loss of the eye: . . . in two eyes of the 12 in the series of very severe lesions the destructive action of the Lewisite produced necrosis [decay] of the cornea before the blood vessels had extended into it. Both lesions were produced by a large droplet. In one case the rabbit was anaesthetized, in the other it was not anaesthetized and was allowed to close the eye at once, thus spreading the Lewisite all over the conjunctival sac [eyeball]. The sequence of events in this eye begins with instantaneous spasm of the lids followed by lacrimation in 20 seconds (at first clear tears and in one minute 20 seconds milky Harderian secretion). In six minutes the third lid is becoming oedematous [swollen] and in 10 minutes the lids themselves start to swell. The

---

[66]David Riesman et al., *The Lonely Crowd* (New Haven: Yale University Press, 1950).

[67]W. H. Whyte, *The Organization Man*. See especially pp. 4–22.

[68]Theodore Roszak, *The Making of a Counterculture* (Garden City, NY: Anchor Books, 1969), p. 276. Copyright © 1965, 1969 by Theodore Roszak. Used by permission of Doubleday, a division of Bantam, Doubleday, Dell Publishing Group, Inc. The appendix, "Objectivity Unlimited," pp. 269–89, is the most valuable part of the work.

eye is kept closed with occasional blinks. In 20 minutes the oedema [swelling] is so great that the eye can hardly be kept closed as the lids are lifted off the globe. In three hours it is not possible to see the cornea and there are conjunctival petechiae [minute hemorrhages]. Lacrimation continues.

In 24 hours the oedema is beginning to subside and the eye is discharging muco-pus. There is a violent iritis [inflammation] and the cornea is oedematous all over in the superficial third . . . On the third day there is much discharge and the lids are still swollen. On the fourth day the lids are stuck together with discharge. There is severe iritis. The corneae are not very swollen . . . On the eighth day there is hypopyon [pus], the lids are brawny and contracting down on the globe so that the eye cannot be fully opened . . . In 10 days the cornea is still avascular, very opaque and covered with pus. On the 14th day the center of the cornea appears to liquefy and melt away, leaving a descemetocoele [a membrane over the cornea], which remains intact till the 28th day, when it ruptures leaving only the remains of an eye in a mass of pus.[69]

Roszak provides equally striking "objective" analyses of an experiment on a feeble-minded woman, an investigation of the effects of nuclear bombardment, and an analysis of the emotions of prisoners awaiting execution.[70]

Similarly, Abraham Maslow recites his own experiences with objective, "scientistic" consciousness in medical school:

The first operation I ever saw was an almost representative example of the effort to desacralize, i.e. to remove the sense of awe, privacy, fear, and shyness before the sacred and of humility before the tremendous. A woman's breast was to be amputated with an electrical scalpel that cut by burning through. As a delicious aroma of grilling steak filled the air, the surgeon made carelessly "cool" and casual remarks about the pattern of his cutting, paying no attention to the freshmen rushing out in distress, and finally tossing this object through the air onto the counter where it landed with a plop. It had changed from a sacred object to a discarded lump of fat . . . This was all handled in a purely technological fashion—emotionless, calm, even with a slight tinge of swagger.

---

[69]Ida Mann et al., "An Experiment and Clinical Study of the Reaction of the Anterior Segment of the Eye to Chemical Injury, with Special Reference to Chemical Warfare Agents," *British Journal of Ophthalmology*, Supplement XIII (1948), pp. 146–47, as quoted in Roszak, pp. 276–77.

[70]Merton calls this "sociological euphemism" when conducted by sociologists. See his article, "Insiders and Outsiders: A Chapter in the Sociology of Knowledge," *American Journal of Sociology* 78 (July 1972), pp. 9–47, especially pp. 38–39.

The atmosphere was about the same when I was introduced—or rather not introduced—to the dead man I was to dissect. I had to find out for myself what his name was and that he had been a lumberman and was killed in a fight. And I had to learn to treat him as everyone else did, not as a dead person but without ceremony, as a "cadaver." . . .

The new medics themselves tried to make their deep feelings manageable and controllable by suppressing their fears, their compassion, their tender feelings, their awe before stark life and death, their tears as they all identified with the frightened patients. Since they were young men, they did it in adolescent ways, e.g. getting photographed while seated on a cadaver and eating a sandwich. . . .

This counterphobic toughness, casualness, unemotionality and profaning (covering over their opposites) was apparently thought to be necessary, since tender emotions might interfere with the objectivity and fearlessness of the physician. I myself have often wondered if this desacralizing and desanctifying was really necessary. It is at least possible that a more priestly and less engineerlike attitude might improve medical training.[71]

Maslow concluded that such "insensitivity training" may be necessary for surgeons, but it is very questionable for the average doctor and totally counterproductive for the psychotherapist.

Of course it is possible to reveal even more horrible examples of objectification if one is willing to accept the *actor's view* that the actor is helping alleviate a social problem. The Nazis officially regarded the continued existence of Jews as a pressing social problem and their extermination as its "final solution." So pressing did they regard this "problem" that they diverted a very large amount of resources to it in the midst of a total war. Europe, especially Germany, had to become *Judenrein*—literally "clean of Jews." Raul Hilberg has described not only the technological/organizational feat of destroying six million people, but he also has given us a sense of how, by translating genocide into terms of transportation problems, organizational structure problems, and similar routine activities, German bureaucrats were able to cope psychologically with their tasks.[72] Especially through a translation process in

---

[71] Abraham Maslow, *The Psychology of Science* (New York: Harper & Row, 1966), pp. 139–40. Copyright © by Abraham Maslow. U.S. rights only. Of course one can go too far in attacking the real defects of scientism. For a reasoned *defense* of objective consciousness, see the postscript to Frank Cunningham, *Objectivity in Social Science* (Toronto: University of Toronto Press, 1973).

[72] Raul Hilberg, *The Destruction of the European Jews*, rev. and def. ed. (New York: Holmes & Meier Publishers, 1985). See also Robert Jay Lifton, *The Nazi Doctors: Killing and the Psychology of Genocide* (New York: Basic Books, 1986).

which death became "cleansing" (and similar euphemisms existed for every stage), the "objective consciousness" of the bureaucracy in charge of the program obscured its horrible reality.[73] Again Max Weber:

> The more the bureaucracy is "dehumanized," the more completely it succeeds in eliminating from official business love, hatred, and all purely personal, irrational, and emotional elements which escape calculation. This is the specific nature of bureaucracy and it is appraised as its special virtue.[74]

But of course in the handling of a social problem these human qualities may be of the greatest value. Again and again we see this all-encompassing emphasis on the organization's goals, and a blindness, heightened by an objective style of thought and language, toward any ethical standards outside of them.

It would be comforting to be able to exclude the practitioners of social science from this survey of ethical myopia, but in truth they too have been attacked more than once as the "servants of power."[75] Already mentioned are the uses of social-influence findings in public relations, advertising, and propaganda. We have a superfluity of studies of the poor (the better to manipulate them, say the cynics), yet few studies of the rich and powerful.[76] Of course it is easier to study the poor: they cannot erect the barriers that the upper class can afford. A few "elite studies" are only now emerging, and it becomes clear that reasons behind their rarity go beyond the sheer technical difficulties of such studies and into subtle matters of ideology. It seems that we have a social problem of poverty but not one of wealth; the very choice of which end of the spectrum is to be designated the "problem" seems instructive.

Other evidence of a tendency of social science to sell to the highest bidder is unhappily not difficult to find. Military psychology and sociology for a long time concentrated on how best to bring the wayward soldier into line, or how to increase troop morale, with little, if any, attention paid to the involuntary servitude aspects of conscription or to military inequities. Project Camelot was an ill-fated effort by the United States Army to look at the "preconditions of internal conflict," to predict

---

[73] But ironically the very force and impact of Hilberg's account is intensified by the objectivity and dispassionate style in which he describes the phenomenon. The impact comes from reading page after page of horrors, described dispassionately and—thereby—believably.

[74] Gerth and Mills, *Essays in Sociology*, p. 236.

[75] See Loren Baritz, *The Servants of Power* (New York: Wiley, 1965). The book deals exclusively with the social sciences.

[76] Alvin Gouldner presents strong criticism of sociological work for the "welfare state" with respect to providing legitimacy for controlling the poor. See his book, *The Coming Crisis of Western Sociology* (New York: Basic Books, 1970).

the likelihood of left-wing revolution in Latin America. After it was pub-
licized, an intense outcry arose and the project was ultimately cancelled.[77] The Mayo school of industrial sociology felt that the principal
source of labor difficulties involved a breakdown of contact between
management and the worker—a failure to communicate. It therefore
sponsored the training of management personnel in human-relations
approaches to employees. The possibility of an *inherent* conflict of interest between labor and management was scarcely considered, and the
human relations approach has been bitterly criticized as a manipulative
tool for management to use. At one time or another, industrial sociology,
personality measurement, and motivational psychology have been sin-
gled out as the servants of power.[78] As Muller says, "If the new elite is
not actually corrupted by its eminence, at least it is not inclined to be
highly critical of the powers that employ it. And its professional devo-
tion to method or technique raises the usual questions about its ruling
values, or the measure of its wisdom."[79]

Nor may the far left be declared free of the ethical blindness of
technicism. The left wing has developed its own theories of how to deal
with social problems. Typically these call for a basic restructuring of the
social arrangements of society. But although the old emphasis on radical
criticism of contemporary society remains intact, another focus of the
"old left" has diminished. Only rarely do we now get an outline of what
the new order will look like; instead the emphasis has shifted increasingly to the technique of revolution itself. Techniques and tactics of
disruption become more and more polished and sophisticated, but no
longer are any coherent alternative programs set forth for the end.[80] In
addition, a new factor has come into play: the romantic *mystique* of
revolution, of revolution as a cleansing end in itself, of revolution itself
as the blueprint.[81] Such orientations were implicit in some of the writings of Che Guevara; they were made quite explicit in Régis Debray's
internationally popular *Revolution within the Revolution?* Frantz Fanon

---

[77] See the chapter on Project Camelot in Gideon Sjoberg, ed., *Ethics, Politics and Social Research* (Morristown, NJ: General Learning, 1967).

[78] See especially Loren Baritz, *Servants of Power*; and Martin L. Gross, *The Brain Watchers* (New York: Random House, 1962).

[79] Muller, *Children of Frankenstein*, p. 354.

[80] To be sure, in a way the new route is ideologically safer, since one of the principal ways to attack the old left was to criticize its proposed programs. It is sometimes argued with false humility that not enough is known to provide a "blueprint" at this point in time. But to encourage revolution without a program invites the worst excesses of a pragmatic, ad hoc tyranny once a conflict is underway.

[81] Some have termed this position "revolutionism." See Kenneth Boulding, *A Primer on Social Dynamics: History as Dialectics and Development* (New York: Free Press, 1970); and Abdul Said and Daniel Collier, *Revolutionism* (Boston: Allyn & Bacon, 1971).

in particular placed great emphasis on the necessity and virtue of violence. Following Georges Sorel's early eulogizing of the virtues of violence in principle, Fanon developed an idea of the cathartic effect of violence in a revolution.[82] But as McRae maintained, "To favor revolution and oppose power is a temporary stance at best, for one is driven to ask: Revolution for what?"[83]

Thus the recent decades have witnessed a retreat from the explicit postrevolutionary programs of old-line socialism toward a vague romanticizing of the revolution itself, at the extreme of which we find Debray and Abbie Hoffman's 1970 example, *Revolution for the Hell of It*.[84] Again, as with conservative positions, an almost obscene triumph of technique (and left-ritualism) is seen and, in spite of the excellent critiques of the status quo, an uncomfortable measure of ethical blindness occurs.[85] Such ethically blind positions were more prevalent and popular in the radical sixties and seventies, but their complete demise in the conservative eighties is probably too much to hope for. They almost certainly will be heard again in the next radical resurgence.

IN THE END: THE ADVANTAGES OF COMPETENCE

I have, of course, been unfair. I have been unfair, first, in concentrating exclusively on the ethical blindness of technicism. Not all agencies are full of ritualists and time-servers.[86] Nor does all reform apparently end in futility. Not all of social science has served the powerful. Not all of its "human relations" courses for industry were without effect except as

---

[82] Régis Debray, *Révolution dans la Révolution?* (Paris: Maspero, 1967), trans. as *Revolution in the Revolution?* (New York: Grove Press, 1967); Frantz Fanon, *The Wretched of the Earth* (New York: Grove Press, 1963).

[83] Duncan McRae, Jr., "A Dilemma of Sociology: Science versus Policy," *The American Sociologist* 6 (June 1971), pp. 2–7. Even those highly sympathetic to the call for revolution can take revolutionism to task. Thus, A. Norman Klein notes that it is one thing to direct and mobilize a people for the trials of guerrilla warfare; it is a different matter to rhapsodize on the virtues of violence. See his article, "On Revolutionary Violence," *Studies on the Left* 6 (1966), pp. 83–89.

[84] Abbie Hoffman, *Revolution for the Hell of It* (New York: Pocket Books, 1970).

[85] Always the realist, Saul Alinsky faced squarely such issues as the use of harsh means to justify good ends. See his chapter on "Of Means and Ends" in *Rules for Radicals*. He presents a rationale for justifying virtually any means in terms of the ends to be gained, and notes that "the tenth rule . . . is that you do what you can with what you have and clothe it with moral garments," p. 36.

[86] Analysis shows that many of the apparently ritualist qualities of such agencies as social welfare are actually due to the legally mandated welfare structure in which social workers have to operate. See Nina Toren, *Social Work: The Case of a Semi-Profession* (Beverly Hills, Calif.: Sage Publications, 1972).

manipulative fraud.[87] For that matter, not all corporate public-relations practices have resulted in deception of the public.[88] Certainly many radical groups have not become mesmerized by the revolutionary process: serious thought is devoted to developing alternative social structures.[89] The defects we have examined are *tendencies*; they are ethical traps for the persons and groups involved with defining or handling social problems, but they are traps that can be surmounted. Furthermore, bureaucracy is not always antidemocratic; Beetham lists the particular conditions in which it becomes so.[90] The analysis was not intended to evoke a sense of defeatism. It is distinctly unfair, too, to attribute all ills to technicism as though separate causes could not be found for some of the disorders mentioned. As Muller notes, it is too easy to blame everything on technology.[91] Indeed a danger exists of substituting an unreasoning hatred for science and technology (the "new devils," as they have been called) for our earlier uncritical worship of scientism and "progress."[92] But I had a reason for emphasizing the defects of technicism: its advantages are so open and obvious, and so often glibly stated, that it is especially worthwhile to point out that the drift to expertise, the fascination with technique, is no panacea. As discussed, technicism carries with its advantages severe tendencies toward distortion and ethical blindness.

What are some of the advantages of expertise? Certainly the availability of expert knowledge does make a difference in many cases, and technical agencies possess the facilities and resources to effect positive intervention. Bureaucracy is accepted because it seems so efficient, and it probably is in fact more efficient than alternatives.[93] When their efforts are not misdirected, intervention agencies maintain in the public eye a legitimacy that increases their effectiveness. And, in terms of inau-

---

[87] Muller points out that the human-relations approach assured at least a measure of dignity to the worker, however superficial, and constituted a vast improvement over the "brutal impersonality" of the last century.

[88] Robert Heilbroner notes that "if public relations has cheapened the face value of good conduct, at the same time it has enormously increased the prevalence of good conduct." "Public Relations: The Invisible Sell," in *Voice of the People*, ed. R. M. Christenson and R. O. McWilliams (New York: McGraw-Hill, 1962), pp. 473–86. The quote is from p. 486. This may indeed be true, but only by way of contrast with the robber-baron mentality of the late 1800s.

[89] See, for example, C. George Benello and Dimitrios Roussopoulos, eds., *The Case for Participatory Democracy* (New York: Viking Press, 1971).

[90] Beetham, *Bureaucracy*, ch. 3.

[91] Muller, *Children of Frankenstein*, p. 412.

[92] Stanley, *Technological Conscience*, is representative of writers who condemn antimodernism as well as technicism and who attempt to chart a middle course between them.

[93] See, on the conditions for compliance with bureaucracy, Gerth and Mills, *Essays in Sociology*, pp. 214–16. Merton, in *Social Theory*, lists the presumed virtues of bureaucracy as precision, speed, expert control, continuity, discretion, and optimal returns on input.

gurating needed reform, expertise in the care and feeding of social movements is clearly required when so many of the vested interests can
command their own experts in public relations and infinitely greater
resources of wealth and power.[94] If protest has become professionalized,
so has the management or containment of protest. Revolution is sometimes justified, always difficult, and impossible without technique. This
is part of what Barrington Moore has called the "iron law of revolutionary politics." Even the emphasis on pragmatism and goal attainment is
beneficial under the right circumstances, where the goals sought are ethical, humane, and meaningful. It is even more difficult to imagine evaluation research being conducted by dilettantes than by bureaucracies.

Dissent on whether other-directed personalities are as undesirable as was thought also has been increasing. Muller notes that "the
goals of other-directed men who seek security and happiness are not
necessarily more . . . inhuman than the goals of wealth, power, or fame
sought by inner-directed men, who could easily be ruthless or . . . aggressive."[95] Riesman later reconsidered his position on other-directedness,
and in a sequel to *The Lonely Crowd* he noted that "groupism" possesses many virtues, especially the capacity to adjust to a rapidly changing society.[96] And in such a society, in which the breakdown of family
and other traditional socialization institutions has been pronounced, it
may be that the fleeting primary group offers the only viable source of
support for many.[97]

Even the bureaucrat can be somewhat different from what critics
have maintained. In a very enlightened study, Kohn found empirical
evidence that supported the conclusion that:

> There is a small but consistent tendency for men who work in
> bureaucratic organizations to be more intellectually flexible,
> more open to new experience, and more self-directed in their
> values than are men who work in nonbureaucratic organizations.[98]

These findings are amazing in view of the standard stereotype of the
bureaucrat, but perhaps people remember best the most odious, offi-
cious bureaucrats. Then, too, perhaps the bureaucracy is staffed by relatively humane individuals who are nonetheless constrained by their

---

[94] According to Ehrenreich, in *Altruistic Imagination*, the "central lesson" of the entire
history of social reform in America is that "without [organized] social movements there
is no social reform." (p. 224)
[95] Muller, *Children of Frankenstein*, p. 346.
[96] David Riesman, *Individualism Reconsidered* (Glencoe, Ill.: Free Press, 1954).
[97] See John P. Hewitt, *Self and Society*, 4th ed. (Boston: Allyn & Bacon, 1988).
[98] Melvin L. Kohn, "Bureaucratic Man: A Portrait and an Interpretation," *American Sociological Review* 36 (June 1971), pp. 461–74.

work requirements to fulfill the stereotype of the bureaucrat. In any event the effects of bureaucratization are considerably more complex than they appear on the surface.[99]

Perhaps some of the sins attributed to increasing technicism would be with us without it, as a function of the times. We might consider what might have been seen had the problem of increasing technicism been examined from a vantage point early in the present century. One could not help but note, when regarding the professional altruists and reformers of that day, the strong connection between middle-class reformism and the containment of the "dangerous classes," a great fear of revolt from below, contempt for immigrants—all this along with the frequent equating of Anglo-Saxon morality with virtue, or even with scientifically-based standards.[100] One might at that time have thus equated advancing technicism with racially tinged "containment" policy, and even created a plausible theory linking the two. But that would have been shortsighted. So, too, it might be argued that some of the attributes we associate with technicism today are actually merely transient features of the present era.

Finally, I cannot resist noting that at least one major social theorist of the early part of this century recognized and then glorified technicism. I refer to the rebel economist Thorsten Veblen, the same who gave us the seminal notion of "conspicuous consumption." Veblen organized all his books around a single master idea, or rather distinction.[101] In capitalism, "business enterprise" continually interfered with the "machine process." "Business enterprise" referred to the legalistic pursuit of financial gain in a world of currency, contracts, rules of inheritance, and judicial precedent. The "machine process" was a regrettably clumsy term for what we can call technicism—the technology of factory production, standard measurements, the coordination of workers and production, indeed "wherever manual dexterity, the rule of thumb, and fortuitous conjunctures . . . have been supplanted by a reasoned procedure on the basis of a systematic knowledge of the force employed . . . even in the absence of mechanical contrivances."[102]

For Veblen, technicism was virtuous, the stuff of the sensible people who worked the machines and ran the factories, an aid to human survival conducive to an instinct of workmanship. In contrast, business

---

[99] Also, Warren Bennis, Morris Janowitz, Rensis Likert, Talcott Parsons, and others have examined indications that we are moving toward a post-bureaucratic model with greater sharing of decisions. See these writings reviewed in Delaney, "Patrimonial and Bureaucratic Administrations."

[100] See Kirschner, *Paradox of Professionalism.*

[101] Robert Lekachman, *Economists at Bay: Why the Experts Will Never Solve Your Problems* (New York: McGraw-Hill, 1976), p. 240.

[102] Thorsten Veblen, *Theory of Business Enterprise* (New York: Scribner's, 1906), p. 6, as quoted in Lekachman, *Economists at Bay,* p. 241.

enterprise contributed nothing and continually got in the way of the people who knew what they were doing. Business enterprisers stayed as clear as possible from the actual workings of the factories and learned as little as possible about what was actually happening. Instead, they became immersed in paper and paper transactions. These did no good and produced very great damage. (No wonder Veblen is known as a rebel economist.) This description gives merely the smallest taste of how much Veblen lionized the engineer, the scientist, the expert, and indeed technicism in general.[103] Right or wrong, he is a startling contrast to all of the later critics of the trend.

And what of the future of technicism? The shift toward technically proficient but impersonal agencies in dealing with social problems seems inevitable in a modern, complex, highly differentiated society. Older forms of helping—the church, the family, mutual aid among neighbors—cannot work as well as in previous eras. Increased geographical mobility and the transience of interpersonal relationships have slowly broken down the feasibility of mutual aid, as the old theories of social disorganization long maintained. The extended family is weakening; the established church no longer gathers enough money or patrons to fill the need for help with social problems. To be sure, the help from these institutions remains useful, but the long-term trend is toward the state's assumption of more and more control over the traditional forms of intervention and its complete ascendancy with respect to many newly conceived forms of intervention.

In bringing up the future of technicism I have raised a serious question but cannot possibly explore all the conceivable answers. Instead we will look briefly at two thought-provoking possibilities of very different scope and magnitude. First, perhaps technicism will continue to advance but some of its effects will be moderated by concurrent changes in society. Haug once speculated that rising levels of education and sophistication in the American population would result in the general weakening of the professional's knowledge monopoly, and also would diminish public faith in professional good will. These in combination could result in the erosion of professional autonomy. Of course this conclusion, as well as others that see a decline in the professions, or even their "proletarianization," clashes with the trend described earlier.[104] Second, perhaps technicism is peaking in the present day.

---

[103] Of course when one considers that "business enterprise" is itself largely in the grip of encroaching technicism it is clear that Veblen did not favor technicism in all of its possible forms. Nevertheless, he remains a stark contrast to later writers on the subject.

[104] Marie R. Haug, "The Deprofessionalization of Everyone?" *Sociological Focus* 8 (1975), pp. 197–213. For a recent work that rejects both professional decline and the sort of professional ascendancy seen by Ellul and Foucault, see Eliot Freidson, *Professional Powers* (Chicago: University of Chicago Press, 1986).

Sorokin's classic work on social and cultural dynamics provides a challenge to the Weberian vision of ever-increasing rationalization in society. According to Sorokin, cultural phenomena such as rationalization move in great cycles hundreds of years in duration, oscillating among what he termed sensate, ideational, and idealistic forms.[105] Before his death Sorokin predicted that the sensate mentality had nearly reached its peak and would shortly begin the long changeover to the ideational. The largely unanticipated birth or resurgence of antiscience and antitechnology ideas, New Age mysticism, astrology, occult explanations of humankind's past, satan worship, Jesus cults, and belief in Eastern gurus in the last twenty years might be taken for initial confirmation. Sorokin's very-long-range vision commands careful attention.

This chapter has concentrated on the drawbacks of expertise because they are less obvious, but the commonsense idea that expertise is valuable is not without merit. Although compassion and altruism are always desirable, an impersonal expert is (usually) of greater benefit to social problems than an impersonal novice or dilettante. What would be best, of course, would be the *compassionate expert*, but training and cynical attitudes among the professional groups themselves seem to drive out the novice's compassionate impulses with discouraging regularity.

Jack Douglas at one point nicely framed a key dilemma of the future:

> Ironically, ordinary people will see the solution of their objective problems coincide with their greater estrangement from the decision-making process.... [T]echnocracy will overtake democracy. Truth will achieve power, but will it be content?[106]

Can we have the best of both worlds? Can we address social problems with true expertise, a willingness to examine all alternatives, evaluation research, and organizational efficiency—without impersonal coldness, cynicism, elitism, ritualism, and even perhaps selling to the highest bidder? Can we have both compassion and competence? These are the great challenging questions to those who would reconstruct society or society's assault on social problems—not to do away with expertise but to humanize it, make it harmonious with human dignity.

---

[105]Pitirim Sorokin, *Social and Cultural Dynamics* (Totowa, NJ: Bedminster Press, 1962, original—1941).

[106]Jack D. Douglas, ed., *The Relevance of Sociology* (New York: Appleton-Century-Crofts, 1970), p. 183.

12

THE FINAL ANALYSIS

In the final analysis, the study of social problems involves some inescapable "facts of life." The very notion of a social problem has, as we have seen, a developmental history in Western thought. In certain periods social problems have been variously attributed to individual sinfulness, to malevolent spirits, or in later periods, to an inferior heredity. The idea that iniquitous conditions are the responsibility of society as a whole, or that such conditions are not inherent, unchangeable aspects of life was struggling for acceptance less than a hundred years ago. Even today the idea that all deleterious conditions are resolvable through some form of concerted social action is little more than an article of faith. (Indeed, as the labeling school of sociology would have it, the very attempts at amelioration are one of the sources of renewal for certain problems.)

The social problems notion emerged in a historical period that combined blatantly obvious suffering with recognizably novel conditions of urbanization and industrialization to which the suffering could be tied. But the cultural traditions of the period were equally essential for the notion's emergence: an unbounded optimistic faith in progress and in the power of human reason, together leading to the idea of a social science that could rectify the social problems of the world like natural science was resolving physical problems. Not all social problems have emerged into public consciousness at the same time; the push for legal equality and the egalitarian drives for abolition of slavery, social-welfare legislation, women's rights, civil rights, and anticolonialism are all more or less linked to specific periods in the last two hundred years.

Not only does the modern idea of social problems itself have historical roots, but also specific social problems have each followed their own unique developmental patterns of thinking—as we saw by tracing the evolution of ideas about our two case studies, mental illness and poverty. That historical approach could be easily turned on a host of other commonly accepted social problems, each illuminating a sometimes strange course of development of ideas. Nor need we feel smug, believing perhaps that the rethinking process evident in the history of mental illness and poverty has ended; the sometimes startling new challenges to the conventional wisdom about present-day psychiatric treatment should warn us that the rethinking will continue.

Just what is a social problem? We explored the difficulties encountered with this concept. Certainly one definitional aspect is that a significant number of individuals must be adversely affected by a phenomenon, or believe that they are. And, for a social problem, we added the qualification that in its origin and treatment such a phenomenon must be related to social factors. But this at once leads to complications, since all major problems have their social dimension: the goals of equal protection for all members of society, lack of stigma for blameless victims and, at the heart of the matter, mobilization of the society to deal with the problem. Thus even physical diseases can have social problem aspects. But the most serious question to debate is Blumer's conception of a social problem as the result of a definitional activity rather than an objective state of affairs. If people are starving and, hypothetically, do not regard this as a problem, is it one nonetheless? If only victims regard a certain phenomenon as a social problem, is it, or does it take recognition by the society at large? If only nonvictims regard the phenomenon as a problem, should they be allowed to impose this definition on willing "victims"? We then encounter such illogical oddities as victimless crimes. With such questions we enter, unwillingly, the sticky morass of cultural and ethical relativism in which no easy answers exist.

The question of what constitutes a social problem comes most clearly into focus in criminal law, for after rejecting simplistic notions of crime as sin or wickedness we find competing virtues for both legalistic and social conceptions of crime. The old divisions of crimes *mala in se* (evil by nature) versus *mala prohibita* (offensive by law) prove useful too, for it is clear that most criminal law today is the latter, while we still tend to think of crime as the former. The century's law explosion has occurred by defining more and more acts as *mala prohibita* crimes, while the number of acts defined as *mala in se* has remained more or less stable. We can consider whether victimless crime is the one division or the other. Certainly it is the closeness of victimless activities to *mala prohibita* that make laws against them so hard to enforce—and so lucrative to organized crime.

A strange feature of the law is that prohibited actions become immoral (even sinful) to many people simply by virtue of being illegal: we can in fact "legislate morality," in a peculiar sense, because what we legislate *becomes* morality. On the other hand, this is true only if the vast mass of citizenry cooperate. When a critical threshold of people continue to disobey a law, especially a victimless activity, then the law itself comes into disrepute, organized crime may be greatly encouraged, ordinary citizens incur criminal records and, ultimately, as with Prohibition, the law must be repealed to avert social disaster. A central debate today asks what would be the effect on society of *decriminalizing* victimless crimes and/or other crimes *mala prohibita*.

Returning to our basic question, a current view holds that a social problem can only be defined in terms of what the members of society feel. This has been called the public awareness conception (or the subjective conception) of social problems. But obviously this assumes a degree of conceptual unity that the people in a society only rarely possess. In a way, it makes more sense to think of "social problem making" as a process of conflict in which people's definitions clash. In many cases the act of defining pits some individuals or groups against others. The process can be seen most clearly in the creation of criminal law, in which some moral entrepreneurs attempt to invoke the severe machinery of the law against another group that regards its actions as justifiable. Eventually one conception about a condition succeeds and most members of the population feel compelled to at least pay lip service to the now-established consensus. If the winners are a defining group, a new social problem appears (such as male chauvinism); if the victors are what we might call "removers," a social problem is erased—not because the condition has changed but because most people no longer view it as a problem (e.g., the sale of intoxicating beverages). On the other hand, the victorious group may represent the status quo—neither introducing nor removing anything from the prevailing list of social problems.

Obviously, how one reacts to a given condition depends on how one experiences it: whether one is victimized by it, stands to gain from it at others' expense, or gains personally with no one else involved. Reactions also depend on how severely one is victimized: activities in which a few are terribly hurt attract greater public outrage than white-collar crimes in which millions may be hurt a little bit—even though the aggregate damage may be far greater for the latter. Whether anything is ever done about the condition depends not only on how an abstract majority may feel but also more directly on the moods of powerful decision-makers and on the gate-keepers of mass communication. Although the power of the mass media can be easily exaggerated, its capacity in "agenda setting" is of the greatest importance. Coverage in the media can be manipulated directly by gate-keepers and through concentration of ownership, less directly by skillful bureaucratic propaganda and institutional advertising. Indirectly, it is also influenced by the requirements of event velocity or rhythm and by "topicality," both of which inadvertently magnify the importance of some events and relegate others (possibly of greater significance) to obscurity.

Not only may those directly affected by a condition act to redefine it, other recognizable sectors of society also commonly intervene in this process. Moral entrepreneurs, the people who seek new legislation and new definitions on moral grounds, are frequently a powerful factor. In earlier periods their basis was exclusively religion (variously interpreted), and even today religious entrepreneurs are a continuing source of some new legislation and definitions. Religion and the state at one time virtually combined to produce social-problem perspectives, and law, for society. Growing secularization has dramatically increased the definitional role of other sectors, so that today psychiatrically-based definitions and an ever-expanding circle of egalitarianism, aided by the social-gospel sector of organized religion, provide the focal points for modern moral entrepreneurs.

Key figures in the definitional process—both as definers and removers of social problems—are intellectuals and professionals, the social problem experts. Their role is definitely expanding, some would say decisively. As I hope was made clear in Chapter 5, no group can safely be granted the exclusive definitional prerogative, no matter how great its expertise or general learning. As a group the intelligentsia possesses self-interests, distinctive life experiences, and self-imposed social isolation, which may set it at odds with the desires of the rest of society, not to mention the group's trained incapacities that blind it to alternative perspectives. Its training may in many cases be used to provide a poor substitute for often deficient empathy with others. The ambitions of intellectuals and desires for "empire building" militate against free expression of views that contradict peer opinions. This is not to say that the insights and understandings of such individuals may not be far superior to those of the ordinary citizen, merely that they cannot be universally depended on.

Throughout this book I have tried in numerous sections to emphasize the impact of life experiences on outlook. Whether it is judges (and juries), legislators making laws for us all, victims with direct experience, or intellectuals far removed but with (it is hoped) broader vision, their experiences affect their ideas even when they are convinced of their ideas' sheer logical development and complete independence. This "sociology of knowledge" component in the creation and acceptance of ideas and outlooks is one reason why consensus throughout a community is so hard to obtain. A single society today is so complex and so differentiated that commonly shared experiences—experiences undergone by all, or even a majority—are really very few in number. That is why, on the one hand, the few experiences universally shared by a society (the Great Depression, for example, or the Second World War) have exerted such striking effects on thinking, but why, on the other hand, in most instances today consensus on social problem matters is virtually impossible to obtain.

Once a social problem definition has been made, it is common to select certain individuals for involuntary treatment in an attempt to resolve or diminish the problem. Such treatment may be informal, as with police street-intervention, or highly formalized and structured, as for mental illness or criminal activity. It may have rigid procedural safeguards to prevent abuse or it may have virtually no safeguards at all. Again we have a definitional component (a label) and a conflict over its applicability, but now it is specific individuals rather than groups, organizations, or larger collectivities who are involved in some sort of adversary process, whether reasonable or grossly unfair. As we have seen, both the process of selection of particular individuals and the nature of their subsequent treatment are dependent not only on personal attributes or past behaviors legitimately connected with the problem but also on extraneous, irrelevant personal attributes, on political affiliations, or on the basis of group stereotypes. The hard evidence showing such intrusions into supposedly fair, objective decisions about a person's fate has become overwhelming. In addition to unconscious stereotypes, on numerous occasions well-formulated ideologies also can be seen at work in the selecting of particular individuals for treatment. And the mere fact that a treatment is undertaken for the subject's own good, however defined, is no guarantee of decency in a situation allowing totalist therapy.

If we can ever agree on what the social problems are, we can try to work out strategies to get rid of them—or at least to reduce them to manageable levels. We can perhaps implement laws based on one or another punitive doctrine, as so many of the early interventionists did. The differences among expiation, restitution, retribution, deterrence, and incapacitation are by no means trivial; indeed deterrence and incapacitation rest on diametrically opposite assumptions. But they all have in common a notion of individual responsibility and, of course, are likely to include a great deal of deliberate unpleasantness. Speaking of deliberate unpleasantness reminds me of covert motivations versus overt doctrines: people can be awfully mean while pretending that their behavior is only for control purposes or even for "therapy."

It does not do to think of all early strategies as punitive: very early instances exist for the moral regeneration campaign, for denial of opportunity, and for programs of relief. But in spite of this the early modern era was in truth a watershed of sorts—a real and important shift away from punishment as the major strategic method. And gradually we have developed the full panoply of strategies we see at work today, from rehabilitation to amelioration of conditions to the preventive approach in technological assessment. Probably the most unique strategy from a historical vantage point is social reorganization, but the doctrines included within the strategy of reduced intervention also would have astonished people of earlier centuries.

It helps to recall that my intention was to provide a complete listing of strategies, the complete picture of all preventive and restorative modes of intervention. At least one strategy, idea suppression, is morally repugnant in any form, and to me constitutes a social problem in itself. I listed it for the sake of completeness. It also helps to recall that several concrete approaches may be found within a single strategy—and some very concrete fights can take place within a single strategy.

Let us say we have agreed that some condition is a social problem, and furthermore we have picked some strategy, or combination of strategies, to combat it. We might end up doing better than we expected, about as well, less well than expected, bring about no change at all, or make matters worse. Stated so bluntly this seems obvious, but it is very hard for people to accept in practice. In other words, we might bring about unanticipated consequences (good or bad, given our values) or we might bring about nothing at all (probably bad, given the effort and resources expended). Ideally we hope to foresee unanticipated consequences, that is, to anticipate the strange twistings and turnings of events, or at least when they appear we need to be able to recognize them and cope with them. And we need to check whether our *anticipated* consequences are in fact happening.

The conceptual apparatus of functionalism, especially the key manifest-latent distinction, helps anticipate unintended effects of intervention. Functionalism reminds us of the interconnectedness of things. If we change one component of a society it can have repercussions on down a whole chain of other components—just consider the chain from those seemingly innocuous decisions made long ago to outlaw drugs in the United States. Does dwelling on functionalism make us "conservative" in a status-quo sense? And we recall that functional analysis is not foolproof—how do we know if it is correct?

If we decide to stick with present arrangements we have no guarantee of safety from unanticipated consequences: the Marxian dialectic delights in contemplating the automatic, immanent "unfolding" of a social system, in particular its self-destructive development as it "matures." And non-Marxist variants of this perspective demonstrate the same "tragic" potential for self-destruction in the life of major ideas. I think this set of notions is a bit hard for Americans to see at first; if so it repays rereading.

Labeling is a beautiful example of many things—an unanticipated consequence of intervention, a self-fulfilling prophecy, a latent function. It clearly exists, but just how significant is it? No critical exper-

iment can provide the answer, but that has not stopped the learned po-
lemics. Labeling is therefore also a good example of the intrusion of
politics into supposedly objective debate: it can hardly be accidental
that the theory soared during the radical era and barely floats (to change
metaphors) in a conservative time.

The possibility that an intervention will accomplish nothing at
all is itself an unanticipated consequence of no small importance. Some
of the most promising social programs have in fact been zeroes, and this
certainly would have been true of many of the more conventional interventions—had they ever been evaluated. I provided a few very simple
methods of evaluation because they help in understanding how evaluating research works in general, but no one should be fooled into thinking
that this did more than scratch the surface. Serious theoretical difficulties exist—in measurement, in stability, in reactivity. Inevitably researchers have an urge to quantify and, if some aspect simply cannot be
quantified, they tend to ignore it in the evaluation.

That politics continually intrudes into evaluation research can be
seen most graphically by the premature discontinuation of the enormous income-maintenance experiments. And indeed the more one reflects on it, the more alien objective, scientific program evaluation seems
from the standpoint of the rough and tumble of politics. In saying this I
refer not alone to politics "writ large" but also to the micropolitics of
organizations, the organizations that inevitably will be affected by the
findings of an evaluation. The successful evaluator must be a politi-
cian—even a diplomat—as well as an able researcher.

Intervention proposals are evaluated not only by objective means
and after they are in operation, but also beforehand: before any proposed
implementation is approved it is evaluated in terms of beliefs about
whether its proposals are justifiable. People generally do not intervene
when they think it is wrong or evil to do so or when they think interven-
ing will do no good. Out of these simple tendencies comes the significance of theoretical objections to intervention. Fatalistic doctrines come
in many forms, but for our purposes can be divided into the secular and
the sacred or theological—although this is a risky simplification. The
sacred can affect intervention in three distinct ways: as explicit doctrine
that prohibits alteration of some current practice, as a general belief in
an afterlife conditional on acceptance of one's earthly fate, or conversely, as a social-gospel/liberation theology that espouses reform and
change. In any event, the long-term historical trend is away from the
sacred, toward secular and toward scientific rationalizations.

Secular objections to intervention shade only gradually into the
scientific. Ideas of superior peoples, races, sexes, and blood lines (families) far antedate any attempt to examine such differences scientifically.
When the scientific ethos developed, insights into biological differences

were at first thwarted, not only by long established ideas, but also by the sheer impossibility of natural "experiments," given the severe sanctions for intermarriage and for behavior "inappropriate" for one's age, sex, class, or race.

Whenever we analyze the secular rationalizations for nonintervention we have to remember to distinguish between the truth of the position, the general effect on behavior of believing the position even if it is incorrect, and the specific effect of the position, and the ensuing behavior on the possibility of intervention. Nowhere is this more evident than in the question of the alterability of human nature. The position of high malleability is very congenial to those who would push for social reorganization or other types of major reform. And, of course, the opposite position is congenial for those in opposition to change.

Science mixes most directly with fatalism when it explicitly posits laws of society or economics that prohibit the success of certain forms of intervention. Prohibitive laws of economics were especially popular in the nineteenth century, but remnants appear even today— particularly their modern variant, the choice law or "trade off." Once again we have to disentangle the correctness of the law in itself and its sometimes profound effects on the practical possibility of intervention.

Beliefs about progress are sort of fascinating: there has been such total acceptance and breathless faith in progress in some historical eras, and such a belief has been so weak, virtually to the point of nonexistence, in others. And the consequences of the strength or weakness of this belief for intervention are not so straightforward: before we can make sense of its influence we have to mix in the prevailing belief about the efficacy of social action.

Now that many of the traditional fatalistic objections have been largely discredited and others are in decline, the scope of intervention in social problems has greatly expanded in the last half-century or so. We should not be surprised, in view of the long-term trend toward scientific preeminence and the increasing rationalization of society as a whole, to find the social problems expert increasingly ascendant. Technicism advances across the society and penetrates a broad range of intervention strategies. But what a sharp two-edged sword, a mixed blessing this is.

Since I expect that readers will have just finished the chapter on technicism, I probably do not need to review it here. So I will conclude on a somewhat different note by asking: what is the nature of this book, taken as a whole? Superficially it is about "social problems theory," but precious few theories are given here in the rigorous scientific sense. Rather, in the final analysis, what this book is about is wisdom in the treatment of social problems.

Not, I hasten to add, my own wisdom; I included a few ideas of my own in the book, and I rather like them, but the wisdom I am speaking of is the product of a great many minds, over a great many centuries, much of it very painfully learned. Most of it is still in the form of wise questions. I have had the pleasure of being the reporter and interpreter of this wisdom in the preceding chapters. If one looks again at this summary chapter in this light one can see clearly that if this book has value it is here, not in the numerous examples and facts set out.

Can wisdom be acquired by a book, or by any means other than living and gaining experience? I think the answer is "yes, to a degree." And what is the alternative? To directly experience every source of insight or remain ignorant of it? A famous expression, I think by George Santayana, is to the effect that those who do not learn from history are doomed to repeat it. That is equally applicable, I feel, to thinking about social problems.

NAME INDEX

Aberle, D. F., 150n
Abrahamson, Mark, 149n
Adams, Henry, 133n
Adams, Stuart, 219n
Adorno, Theodor, 159
Alinsky, Saul, 249, 259n
Allen, A. R., 45
Altheide, David, 12n, 61n, 225, 248n
Altman, Dennis, 6n
Anderson, Charles H., 75–76, 78n
Anderson, Dorothy, 107n
Anttia, I., 209n
Archibald, Peter, 156n
Argyle, Michael, 41n
Armstrong, J. Scott, 86
Aronson, Elliot, 67
Austin, Roy L., 176n
Ausubel, David P., 66n
Avison, W. R., 86

Bailey, D. E., 77n
Baldwin, B. A., 186n
Ball, Terence, 238, 239n
Bannister, Robert C., 33n, 120n
Baran, Paul A., 102n
Barber, Benjamin, 71n
Barber, Bernard, 226n
Baritz, Loren, 257n, 258n
Barnes, Harry Elmer, 31n, 33n, 96n, 120n
Barrow, Julia, 113n
Bartollas, Clemens, 230n
Baruch, Geoff, 65n
Bazelon, David, 74
Bean, Lee L., 191n
Beccaria, Cesare, 174

Becker, Howard, 31n, 33n, 40, 113n, 120n, 134n, 169, 170, 172n
Beetham, David, 236, 237n, 260
Bell, Daniel, 16n, 73, 132, 238
Bell, Wendell, 11n, 35n, 76, 137n
Ben-Yehuda, Nachman, 40n
Bender, Thomas, 245
Bendix, Reinhard, 72n, 135n, 236n
Benedict, Ruth, 123
Benello, C. G., 102n, 237n, 260n
Bennis, Warren, 262n
Bequai, August, 62n
Berelson, Bernard, 253n
Berger, Peter L., 57n
Berke, Sarah F., 179n
Bernard, Jesse, 28n, 29n, 35n, 107n
Bettelheim, Bruno, 67, 119n
Bibby, Reginald W., 63n
Bickerton, Derek, 124n
Bienvenue, Rita, 180n
Black, Donald, 37n, 92, 92n
Blackstock, Nelson, 62n
Blalock, Hubert M., Jr., 205n
Bland, Connie E., 192n
Blass, Thomas, 180n
Blissett, Marian, 79n, 85n
Bloom, Allan, 71, 75
Blum, Alan F., 8
Blum, Zahava D., 110n
Blumer, Herbert, 8, 18, 108n, 144n
Boas, Franz, 122
Boguslaw, Robert, 223
Boorstin, Daniel J., 57n
Bordua, David J., 241
Bosk, Charles L., 50n
Bossard, James H. S., 3

SUBJECT INDEX

Abortion, 43, 46, 48–50; and civil disobedience, 248
Addiction, 50–51, 53–54, 56. *See also* Narcotics legislation
Adversary culture, 79–80, 103
Advertising: and bureaucracy, 247–48; and "counter-advertising," 249; institutional, 61, 268; and marshaling public support, 247–48; and the mass media, 61; and technicism/ specialization, 247–48
Age of Disillusionment, 135
Age of Reason, 31, 45, 134
Agenda setting, 58
AIDS: as a social problem, 6; and the ethics of treatment, 225
Alcoholics Anonymous, 246
Alcoholism, 18, 52, 267. *See also* Addiction: Prohibition movement
Alienation, as pessimism and despair, 137
Almshouses, 25
Alterability. *See* Malleability of human nature
Amelioration of conditions, 100–101, 109–10
American Association of Social Sciences, 32
American Psychiatric Association, 23n
American Revolution, 45, 134
Anti-Semitism. *See* Racism
Aristocracy. *See* Hereditarianism
Asylums, 22–23, 96n; facilities, 240–41; historical development of, 239–43; for the insane, 239–40, 240n, 241–43, 241n; and mental hospitals, 241;

and the Soviet "sane" institution, 193–94. *See also* Mental hospitals; Orphanages; Penitentiaries
Atonement, 96

Beggars/Begging, 24–25. *See also* Poverty
Bible, Judeo-Christian, 112–16, 133; and the idea of progress, 133; with reference to moral regeneration, 97; as revealed knowledge, 111–12. *See also* Catholic church; Christianity; Divine Will; Religion
Birth control. *See* Contraception; Population problem
Brainwashing, 196–200
British North America, 98–99
Bureaucracy: callousness of, 252, 256–57; humanistic failure of, 254, 256–57; and the labeling process, 163; and personality change in, 253–54; pragmatic character of, 248–49, 250; and propaganda, 248, 268; as a rational organization structure, 235–37; rise of, 252; and the role of experts in, 252–54. *See also* Bureaucrats; Rationalization; Technicism
Bureaucratic propaganda, 61
Bureaucrats, 236–37, 261–62. *See also* Bureaucracy; Personality, modal

Cambridge Somerville study, 210
Cancer, as a social problem, 5, 6, 18
Cannibalism, 37, 38
Capital punishment, 213–14